Attention-Deficit/ Hyperactivity Disorder

What Professionals Need to Know

Donna Geffner, PhD, CCC-SLP/A
With Forewords by Andrew Adesman, MD,
and Judy Montgomery, PhD

Thinking Publications • Eau Claire, Wisconsin

10   09   08   07   06   05   8   7   6   5   4   3   2   1

Library of Congress Cataloging-in-Publication Data

Geffner, Donna

   Attention-deficit/hyperactivity disorder : what professionals need to know / Donna Geffner.

     p. cm.

   Includes bibliographical references and index.

   ISBN 1-932054-34-0 (pbk.)

    1. Attention-deficit hyperactivity disorder. I. Title.

RJ506.H9G44 2005
616.85'89—dc22

                                2004066294

Printed in the United States of America

Cover design by Debbie Olson

Trademarks: All brand names and product names used in this book are the trade names, service marks, trademarks, or registered trademarks of their respective owners.

**THINKING
PUBLICATIONS®**
A Division of McKinley Companies, Inc.

424 Galloway Street · Eau Claire, WI 54703
715.832.2488 · Fax 715.832.9082
Email: custserv@ThinkingPublications.com

COMMUNICATION SOLUTIONS THAT CHANGE LIVES®

To my patients whom I have served,
to my family,
and to an Earth Angel,
Nancy McKinley
(April 29, 1952–January 8, 2005),
who inspired me to do this book.

Contents

Forewords

Let me see if Philip can, Be a little gentleman;
Let me see if he is able, To sit still for once at table:
Thus Papa bade Phil behave; And Mamma looked very grave.
But fidgety Phil, He won't sit still;
He wriggles, And giggles, And then, I declare,
Swings backwards and forwards, And tilts up his chair.

Heinrich Hoffman, a German physician, wrote this fictional nursery rhyme about "Fidgety Phil" in the mid-1800s. In the early 1900s, Dr. George Still provided the first formal description of "restless" children in the medical literature. Since that time, from the days of Fidgety Phil to the modern-day "Dennis the Menace," there have been extraordinary advances in our understanding of attention-deficit/hyperactivity disorder—its causes, prevalence, clinical course, associated features, and treatment. Nonetheless, controversy continues to surround AD/HD—with experts divided on many aspects of its clinical diagnosis and management.

Some may think that there is "information overload" regarding AD/HD. The broadcast and print media are constantly presenting the findings of the latest research study to the public, and the Internet is replete with websites offering information and advice—some of which is confusing, contradictory, or just plain controversial—to interested readers. The abundance of information about AD/HD is likewise evident when one surveys the number of books written about this disorder. With more than 100 titles available at bookstores, readers may ask if there really is a need for yet another book. Does this book provide its readers with something that other books do not? Is there really something unique and special about this book? The answers to these three questions, quite simply, are "yes," "yes," and again, "yes."

Attention Deficit/Hyperactivity Disorder: What Professionals Need to Know provides readers with an up-to-date, broad overview of AD/HD and the disorders commonly associated with it. Not only is the text nicely organized and written in an extremely clear style, but readers are provided with helpful definitions of unfamiliar terms in the margins of each page as well as in a glossary at the end of the book. Moreover, therapists, educators, counselors, and health-care personnel will find the list of resources in Chapter 14 extremely helpful, since professionals often need to direct families to credible and reliable resources for additional, accurate information. Lastly, and perhaps most exceptional about this book, is its companion CD-ROM, where readers can choose to learn more about select topics and print helpful forms, tip sheets, hand-outs, and other clinically valuable materials.

Children with AD/HD often benefit from a multidisciplinary approach to diagnosis and treatment, especially when other conditions are suspected or associated with it. Professionals from a multitude of different professional backgrounds need a thorough understanding of AD/HD, not just from their own disciplinary perspective, but also from that of their colleagues. *Attention Deficit/Hyperactivity Disorder: What Professionals Need to Know* strives and succeeds in providing therapists, educators, counselors, and health-care personnel with a detailed understanding of AD/HD from multiple vantage points. Dr. Geffner's authoritative insights, clear writing style, practical perspective, and touches of humor all work together to make this book both an interesting read and a valuable resource. Congratulations to Dr. Geffner for achieving this accomplishment, and to you, the reader, for recognizing the tremendous value of this book and its accompanying CD-ROM. Let the learning begin!

—Andrew Adesman, MD
Chief, Developmental and Behavioral Pediatrics
Schneider Children's Hospital

What is attention-deficit/hyperactivity disorder? For children, the question is critical—is it just the "fast life" or is it a disability? This book makes a strong statement for the disability side of this quandary, and then at the end, reminds us that there are some very satisfying parts of living with this condition. Dr. Geffner knows children and adults with attention-deficit/hyperactivity disorder (AD/HD)—and she knows them well. She appreciates their drive, their spirit, and their exuberance. She also knows if you are in third grade and not an accomplished reader yet, this same exuberance will get you in deep trouble in school. These children have to do much more than identify their wandering attention each day; they must be able to wrestle it to the ground and force themselves to focus on the next item of information in the classroom. It isn't easy. It takes self-discipline. It takes energy and courage to concentrate when far more interesting things are vying for their attention. The personal stories in this book attest to that courage.

A few years ago I was tossing out old journals. Thumbing through one, I came upon a full-page ad for the drug Ritalin. I stopped to read it because today it is a fairly conventional medication for AD/HD. This ad, circa 1962, announced that housewives who were exhausted and bored should take this drug to perk them up and bring new zest to their lives. The photograph of an exhausted woman vacuuming her home and obviously needing some sparkle in her life was a far cry from today's view of Ritalin's use. It seems it didn't take the pharmaceutical industry long to realize that the market was not "tired housewives" but rather highly active children.

This book is sensitive to this societal development and many others that surround highly active children. When is it amusing and how does it become pathological? Donna Geffner acknowledges that it is a fast-paced world. As a New Yorker, she experiences that daily. She concludes that AD/HD can present as a neurobiological condition that makes it difficult for children to control their behavior, self-regulate, attend, and focus. This makes learning very difficult. It also makes social contacts a challenge. Who wants a friend in constant motion, who is oblivious to your needs? Numerous professionals have a role to play in diagnosis and intervention, including speech-language pathologists and audiologists. Donna Geffner offers a wide range of assessment and intervention tools, and a rich glossary and resource section for parents and professionals. She concludes that there is a combination of ways to manage this disorder, and that adulthood itself may bring many satisfying outlets for the excess energy that the *DSM–IV* manual finds so negatively charged in childhood.

The information on AD/HD in this book has been collected from many sources and brings professionals, families, and friends together to examine what it means when a child has a diagnosis of AD/HD. Interventions stretch from diet to relationship building, from coping strategies to daily plan books. The right combination of interventions is recognized as a key to student success. This book lifts the cover off years of guesswork about what is related to AD/HD behaviors and strongly suggests that every aspect of life will be altered by it. And sometimes the role of parents, teachers, and students is simply to embrace it.

—Judy K. Montgomery, PhD, CCC-SLP
Professor, Special Education and Literacy
Chapman University
Former President of ASHA
President of the Division of Communication
Disorders and Deafness

Preface

This book was written to provide a comprehensive collection of information regarding the population of children and adults with attention-deficit/hyperactivity disorders (AD/HD). It is written for the professional (speech-language pathologist, audiologist, psychologist, social worker, special educator, family physician, occupational therapist, physical therapist) who comes in contact with a child who has or could have AD/HD. Family members could find answers to their many questions as well. It has been my contention that the knowledge about this disorder has been available in many psychological, medical, and counseling texts, but not within one source. What I have learned, I learned through colleagues and experience. I am ever grateful to my colleague and friend, Dr. William Koch, child psychiatrist, who 20 years ago called me up and said, "Donna, I am seeing so many children with attention problems (formerly known as minimal brain dysfunction) and I know they have listening difficulties. They have language problems. I think this AD/HD thing is a processing disorder. Would you have a look at them and tell me what is going on with their auditory processing?"

It was from that day—and from the moment I met Richard, my first client, who was diagnosed with an attention-deficit/hyperactivity disorder—that I knew my discipline of speech-language pathology and audiology had a role to play in helping individuals who have this disorder. There were clearly auditory processing issues. There were language issues, not in the traditional sense, with limited vocabulary, but with word retrieval and with formulating thoughts and getting to the point. It was so clear to me that there were unique problems attributed to this population. Many years, and thousands of patients later, this has crystallized in my thinking. I thank William for his insight and for all that he has taught me from the medical point of view, including the effects of medication. I have read, attended conferences, and consulted with developmental pediatricians, neurologists, and psychologists—which have all framed my thinking, resulting in this book. I believe this information is crucial to professionals in my field and in related disciplines since so many children pass through our doors that have attentional problems. Not all children with attentional problems have AD/HD, but surely children presenting with auditory processing problems and language problems are at risk for a comorbid condition, and as such should be evaluated and treated.

I also have come to realize that many of the children I have seen with auditory and language processing disorders and attentional deficits also have learning disabilities and are dyslexic. So many of them present with a multitude of problems that it behooves the clinician to be thorough in the diagnostic process to ensure that these children receive the services and intervention they so desperately need. We need to work collaboratively as a team.

I wish each of you readers could hear from the families who, at the conclusion of an evaluation, say, "Well I finally have a better understanding of my child's problem and needs." You could meet some of these individuals on *Attention-Deficit/Hyperactivity Disorder DVD: The Journeys—The People and Their Stories*, also available from Thinking Publications (Geffner, 2005). They speak to us.

It has been an experience putting this book together. I wanted to present research findings and personal experience, then bridge the research base with clinical applications. I hope this book demonstrates that with the knowledge base and the research findings we have come to accept, we can be better clinicians and more effectively apply what we know. I also have hopes that after reading this book, it will be clear that the audiologist and the speech-language pathologist have inextricable relationships with other professionals involved in serving those with AD/HD. Particularly when working with this population, the language and auditory issues require the input of several disciplines. I hope that by reading this book, the professional will be inspired to work effectively, the researcher will be motivated to seek new findings, and we—as team members—can serve this population well to improve their lives.

I have learned a great deal from each and every one of the patients I have tested, treated, and counseled. I have come to know the families, the teachers, the psychologists, the special educators, and the relatives of these individuals. It has been a privilege to learn from them, since each and every one is different. I continue to learn and grow from each new patient. I hope I have inspired the reader to approach this subject with the desire to improve all we do for those with attention-deficit/hyperactivity disorders.

This book includes a CD-ROM of additional printable information (such as checklists, tables, lists of ideas, etc.). When information is available on the CD, a Study More icon appears in the margin. Simply place the CD-ROM in the CD drive of your computer and open. Click on the title of the Study More you wish to view and/or print. All files are portable document format (PDFs), printable with Adobe Reader 5.0 or higher. Printing from your computer is convenient and efficient.

Acknowledgments

This book is dedicated to the many patients whom I have served over the past 30 years, even when the term AD/HD was not yet known or fashionable. I have learned from each and every one. I have grown in my understanding and depth of knowledge. I thank Dr. William Koch, child psychiatrist, for his tutelage. I thank Richard, my first patient, for introducing me to the "thing" called attention-deficit/hyperactivity disorder. I thank Richard's mother who had incredible faith in me as a clinician and taught me about the trials and tribulations of being a parent of a child with AD/HD. She never gave up hope for her son, or that so many other parents carrying the heartbreaks and struggles of parenting a child with AD/HD might find the help they needed.

I am grateful to my students who helped me in the long process of researching the disorder. I appreciate those who conducted comorbidity studies and those that provided background literature.

I am indebted to the late Nancy McKinley who helped me transform my knowledge and experience into print. She, like she did for so many others, made it possible. My dream of writing a book about AD/HD came to fruition because of her. I will remember her always.

I owe a great deal of gratitude to my precious, incredible, and indispensible Agnieszka Dynda, my graduate assistant, who by her nature and brilliance has been the ever-steady force in this work. Without her help, I could not have produced a work of this dimension. Agnieszka is a doctoral student in school psychology. I couldn't convince her to switch majors. It is psychology's gain. She has a brilliant career ahead and many more books to her credit.

I want to thank my reviewers: Janet Harrison, Rebecca Steining, Christine Radziewicz, and Jay Lucker for their insight, helpful suggestions, and support.

I am gratefully indebted to Dr. Andrew Adesman who not only provided a poignant foreword for the book, but astutely read the book and offered valuable insight and medical knowledge, as he is so adept at doing. He is truly not only an admirable expert in the field but a caring clinician. I appreciate Dr. Judy Montgomery, a woman of many talents and expertise, who graciously agreed to provide a foreword for the book. Her valuable contribution to the field of speech-language pathology and literacy have influenced my thinking as well as so many others.

Finally, I thank my family, who has encouraged and supported me throughout my career. And I thank my husband, Sandy, who many a night had to take dinner alone, see a movie alone, and wait for me to show up.

Identifying and Understanding Attention-Deficit/ Hyperactivity Disorder

Chapter 1

Although some children may be more active than others, there is a group of children who exhibit behaviors that are more hyperactive, distractible, and inattentive than usual. These children may spin in constant motion, make noise, refuse to wait their turn, crash into everything, get into trouble, jut out into the street without looking, or fail to attend to or finish what they are doing. Such behaviors are so present or severe that they interfere with their ability to live normal and productive lives. Such children pay a price socially for these behaviors. That is, they have trouble getting along with siblings and other children at school, at home, or in social situations. Those who have trouble paying attention have trouble learning at school. Those who are impulsive may put themselves in physical danger. Left untreated, more severe forms can lead to serious lifelong problems such as failing grades, lawbreaking, failed relationships, incarceration, and an inability to keep a job—all leading to impoverished lives.

What Is AD/HD?

Attention-deficit/hyperactivity disorder (AD/HD) is a condition of the brain that makes it difficult for an individual to control his or her behavior, to self-regulate, to attend, and to focus. AD/HD is recognized as the most prevalent mental health disorder of childhood, affecting about 3 to 5 percent of school-age children worldwide (Children and Adults with Attention-Deficit/Hyperactivity Disorder (CHADD), 2005). AD/HD is a **neurobiological** disorder.

Neurobiological Encompassing neuroanatomy, physiology, neurochemistry, and neuropharmacology (Chermak & Musiek, 1997).

1

Attention-Deficit/Hyperactivity Disorder

The American Academy of Pediatrics (AAP, 2000) released recommendations for the assessment of school-age children with attention-deficit/hyperactivity disorder. AAP research in various community and practice settings shows that between 4 and 12 percent of all school-age children in the United States may have AD/HD, making it the most common childhood neurobiological disorder. Children with AD/HD may experience functional problems such as school difficulties, academic underachievement, troublesome relationships with family members and peers, and behavioral problems.

About 60 percent of children with AD/HD will continue to experience the disorder throughout their life. In adults, AD/HD accounts for 2 to 4 percent of the population (AAP, 2000). More than eight million adults in the United States have been diagnosed with the condition (United States Census Summary File, 2000). Adults with AD/HD often experience career difficulty (e.g., lose jobs due to poor work performance, have inattention and organizational problems, or show difficulty with interpersonal relationships). Adults with AD/HD can be easily distracted; have difficulty sustaining attention and concentrating; or are often impulsive and impatient, with frequent mood swings and short tempers. They have difficulty organizing and planning ahead. They may feel restless internally and have difficulty controlling impulses. Other consequences may include depression, conduct disorder, failed relationships, and substance abuse. Once they find their area of strength, they may thrive professionally. Early identification and treatment increase the likelihood of positive long-term outcomes.

To identify AD/HD, clinical practice AAP guidelines were developed by a panel of medical, mental health, and educational experts, including the Agency for Healthcare Research and Quality, who provided background information for the new policy. The guidelines were designed for primary care physicians diagnosing AD/HD in children ages 6 to 12.

The AAP guidelines suggest that AD/HD identification could be initiated by primary care physicians for children who show signs of school difficulties; academic underachievement; troublesome relationships with teachers, family members, and peers; and other behavioral problems. The diagnosis can be made by a psychologist, psychiatrist, or pediatrician. To confirm the diagnosis, the behaviors must occur in more than one setting; be more severe than in other children the same age; start before the age of 7; continue for 6 months; and interfere with the child's ability to function in school, home, or social situations. The AAP Clinical Practice Guidelines for AD/HD are summarized in Study More 1.1 on the CD-ROM and displayed as a thumbnail view in Figure 1.1.

Figure 1.1

American Academy of Pediatrics
Clinical Practice Guidelines for AD/HD

The clinical practice guidelines recommended by the American Academy of Pediatrics (AAP) were published in 2000. The guidelines were developed by a committee (selected by the Committee on Quality Improvement of the American Academy of Pediatrics) composed of pediatricians and experts in the fields of neurology, psychology, child psychiatry, child development, and education. These guidelines are not intended for children with complicating conditions, such as mental retardation, pervasive developmental disorder, moderate to severe sensory deficits in vision and hearing, or for children subjected to abuse. They were intended to provide guidance in the assessment and diagnosis of school-aged children between the ages of 6 to 12 with attention-deficit/hyperactivity disorder.

There are two sets of guidelines intended for use by primary care professionals. The first set provides guidance in diagnosis and the second set is intended to provide treatment recommendations.

The following are recommendations for diagnosis of AD/HD. The diagnosis guidelines are not intended to replace clinical judgment and are not considered the only appropriate approach to evaluation.

Recommendation 1
In a child who presents with inattention, hyperactivity, impulsivity, academic underachievement, or behavior problems, between the ages of 6 to 12 years old, evaluation for AD/HD should be initiated by a primary care clinician.

It is understood that children with the inattentive subtype of AD/HD, where hyperactivity and impulsivity symptoms are absent or minimal, may not be recognized by teachers, but may be underachievers in school.

Recommendation 2
The diagnosis of AD/HD requires that a child meet the Diagnostic and Statistical Manual of Mental Disorders (4th ed.; DSM-IV; American Psychiatric Association, 1994) criteria.

These criteria are more substantial than other available diagnostic criteria in the literature. The *DSM-IV* criteria define three subtypes of AD/HD:

- AD/HD primarily of the inattentive subtype (ADHD/I, one meets at least 6 of 9 inattentive behaviors)

- AD/HD primarily of the hyperactive-impulsive subtype (AD/HD/HI, one meets at least 6 of 9 hyperactive-impulsive behaviors)

school-based evaluation, if available.

Recommendation 4A
Use of rating scales is a clinical option when diagnosing children for AD/HD.

Attention-Deficit/Hyperactivity Disorder

DSM–IV
Diagnostic and Statistical Manual of Mental Disorders (4th ed.; text revision), The American Psychiatric Association's guide to diagnostic terms and codes.

ICD–9
The International Statistical Classification of Diseases and Related Health Problems (10th revision), the latest in a series that was formalized in 1893 as the Bertillon Classification or International List of Causes of Death. While the title has been amended to make clearer the content and purpose and to reflect the progressive extension of the scope of the classification beyond diseases and injuries, the familiar abbreviation "ICD" has been retained.

Questions to parents regarding school and behavioral issues may help alert physicians. Often the classroom teacher is the first to recognize problems. Parents' alertness to the child's poor performance at school often prompts a referral for a diagnosis. AD/HD can coexist with other disorders such as oppositional defiant or conduct disorders, mood disorders/depression, anxiety disorders, learning disabilities, and auditory processing disorders.

In addition to the AAP guidelines, the American Psychiatric Association (APA) also has guidelines for identification of AD/HD. They are presented in the ***Diagnostic and Statistical Manual-IV*** (APA, 2000). The APA defines AD/HD under two separate dimensions; inattention and hyperactivity-impulsivity (see these specific subtypes in Sidebar 1.1 on pages 5–6). This is more frequently used because it is associated with codes. Codes for each type are presented as **International Classification of Disease (ICD–9)** numbers. For instance ICD 314.00 is designated for the Inattention subtype, 314.01 is designated for the Hyperactive subtype or the Combined subtype. In cases where the person is not otherwise specified, 314.9 is used. This code diagnosis must be accompanied by a coding note stating that the individuals who currently display symptoms no longer meet full criteria, or are "In Partial Remission." Examples may include individuals who meet the criteria for AD/HD Hyperactivity or Inattentive subtypes, but whose age at onset is 7 years or after; or individuals with significant impairment whose symptoms do not meet the full criteria for the disorders but have a behavioral pattern marked by sluggishness, daydreaming, and hyperactivity.

Although children with AD/HD often exhibit hyperactive and impulsive behavior that may be disruptive, this behavior would not by itself violate age-appropriate societal norms and therefore would not meet the criteria for other impairments (e.g., conduct disorder, oppositional defiant disorders). The language characteristics of the three subtypes of AD/HD can be found in Study More 1.2 on the CD-ROM. Figure 1.2, pages 7–8, provides a thumbnail view of the Study More.

There is evidence that children with AD/HD have an increased incidence of serious trauma, likely a consequence of the disorder. Dr. Daniel Coury's (2001) study at Children's Hospital in Columbus, Ohio, found that an increased risk of trauma was attributed to this population. The child's increased level of activity, such as riding a bike more often than being a passive passenger in a car, for example, would cause the child to be at increased risk for serious injury.

American Psychiatric Association
Diagnosis Criteria for AD/HD

Sidebar 1.1

Maladaptive
The imperfect action or process of adapting, fitting, or suiting one thing to another.

A. Either 1 or 2:

1. Six (or more) of the following symptoms of inattention have persisted for at least 6 months to a degree that is **maladaptive** and inconsistent with developmental level:

   Inattention

   a. Often fails to give close attention to details or makes careless mistakes in schoolwork, work, or other activities

   b. Often has difficulty sustaining attention in tasks or play activities

   c. Often does not seem to listen when spoken to directly

   d. Often does not follow through on instructions and fails to finish schoolwork, chores, or duties in the workplace (not due to oppositional behavior or failure to understand instructions)

   e. Often has difficulty organizing tasks and activities

   f. Often avoids, dislikes, or is reluctant to engage in tasks that require sustained mental effort (such as schoolwork or homework)

   g. Often loses things necessary for tasks or activities (e.g., toys, school assignments, pencils, books, or tools)

   h. Is often easily distracted by extraneous stimuli

   i. Is often forgetful in daily activities

2. Six (or more) of the following symptoms of hyperactivity-impulsivity have persisted for at least 6 months to a degree that is maladaptive and inconsistent with developmental level:

   Hyperactivity

   a. Often fidgets with hands or feet or squirms in seat

   b. Often leaves seat in classroom or in other situations in which remaining seated is expected

   c. Often runs about or climbs excessively in situations in which it is inappropriate (in adolescents or adults, may be limited to subjective feelings of restlessness)

   d. Often has difficulty playing or engaging in leisure activities quietly

Continued on next page

5

Sidebar 1.1—Continued

e. Is often "on the go" or often acts as if "driven by a motor"

f. Often talks excessively

Impulsivity

g. Often blurts out answers before questions have been completed

h. Often has difficulty awaiting turn

i. Often interrupts or intrudes on others (e.g., butts into conversation or games)

B. Some hyperactive-impulsive or inattentive symptoms that caused impairment were present before age 7 years.

C. Some impairment from the symptoms is present in two or more settings (e.g., at school [or work] and at home).

D. There must be clear evidence of clinically significant impairment in social, academic, or occupational functioning.

E. The symptoms do not occur exclusively during the course of a pervasive developmental disorder, schizophrenia, or another psychotic disorder and are not better accounted for by another mental disorder (e.g., mood, anxiety, dissociative, or personality disorder).

AD/HD Subtypes Using ICD–9 Criteria

AD/HD, predominantly inattentive type (ICD–9 314.00)

Meets inattention criteria (section A1) for the past 6 months, but Criterion A2 is not met for the past 6 months.

AD/HD, predominantly hyperactive-impulsive type (ICD–9 314.01)

Meets hyperactive-impulsive criteria (section A2) for the past 6 months, but criterion A1 is not met for the past 6 months.

AD/HD, combined type (ICD–9 314.01)

Meets criteria for section A1 and section A2 for the past 6 months.

AD/HD not otherwise specified (ICD–9 314.9)

Prominent symptoms of inattention or hyperactivity-impulsivity that do not meet the criteria for AD/HD in partial **remission** (ICD–9 314.01)

From the *Diagnostic and Statistical Manual of Mental Disorders (4th ed., text revision;* pp. 83–85), by the American Psychiatric Association, 2000, Arlington, VA: Author. © 2000 by the American Psychiatric Association. Reprinted with permission.

Remission
Diminution of force or effect; lowering or decrease of a condition or quality.

Figure 1.2

Language Characteristics of AD/HD Subtypes

Predominantly Hyperactive/Impulsive Subtype

- Often blurts out answers to questions before the questions have been completed.
- Often blurts out a response that has nothing to do with the subject being discussed.
- Often does not seem to be listening, but when questioned does know the answer.
- Often talks excessively.
- Often interrupts or intrudes on others.
- Has poor turn-taking skills.
- Has difficulty describing things in an organized, coherent manner.
- Has difficulty with social entry.
- Has increased experience with unpleasant verbal exchanges.
- Doesn't perceive or act appropriately upon interlocutor's nonverbal cues.

Predominantly Inattentive Subtype

- Has expressive difficulty with auditory processing.
- Is easily distracted by extraneous stimuli.
- Has difficulty sustaining attention over time.
- Lacks foresight and planning.
- Often does not seem to be listening.
- Has difficulty following through on instructions from others.
- Uses non sequiturs during discourse.
- Frequently manifests false starts and verbal mazes because he/she may change his/her mind while structuring a response.
- Has difficulty describing things in an organized coherent manner.
- Has difficulty with social entry and ongoing interaction.
- Experiences problems with verbal reciprocity; tends to be less responsive.
- Uses an excessive number of fillers and pauses because verbal expression occurs with minimal planning.
- Uses inappropriate register.
- Doesn't perceive and act appropriately upon interlocutor's verbal cues.

Continued on next page

Figure 1.2—*Continued*

Predominantly Combined Subtypes
(Hyperactive/Impulsive and Inattentive)

- Often blurts out answers to questions before the questions have been completed.
- Has difficulty following through on instructions from others.
- Often does not seem to be listening.
- Often talks excessively.
- Often interrupts or intrudes on others.
- Uses non sequiturs during discourse.
- Has poor turn-taking skills.
- Frequently manifests false starts and verbal mazes because he/she may change his/her mind while structuring a response.
- Has difficulty describing things in an organized, coherent manner.
- Does not tell stories or use narrative skills effectively due to disorganization and impulsivity of thought; has general difficulty with expressive language organization.
- Uses an excessive number of fillers and pauses because verbal expression occurs with minimal preplanning.
- Has difficulty with social entry (limited knowledge of how to successfully initiate or join ongoing interactions).
- Experiences problems with verbal reciprocity; tends to be less talkative and responsive when others initiate interactions.
- Has increased experience with unpleasant verbal exchanges.
- Uses inappropriate register; for example, one may use the same interactive style with both adults and peers.
- Doesn't perceive and act appropriately upon interlocutor's nonverbal cues.
- Does not use comprehension-monitoring strategies; for example, he/she does not request a repetition of information when he/she experiences a comprehension breakdown.
- Experiences difficulties with auditory processing.

Source: Ramer (2001)

The Possible Causes of AD/HD

AD/HD is one of the most comprehensively researched disorders in medicine. Goldman, Genel, Bezman, and Priscilla (1998) indicated that data on its overall validity are more compelling than for most mental disorders and medical conditions. However, the causes of AD/HD remain largely speculative.

According to Barkley, DuPaul, & McMurry (1990), AD/HD is a failure in the development of the brain circuitry responsible for inhibiting and controlling oneself. Other researchers (Sowell et al., 2003) claim to have found that a portion of the brains of children with AD/HD is smaller than in typically developing children, which may be linked to genetic factors. Tannock (1998) concluded that AD/HD is caused by brain dysfunction of probable genetic origin. Research suggests that AD/HD runs in families approximately 50 percent of the time (Ziegler Dendy, 2000). On the other hand, Joseph (2000), of the California School of Professional Psychology, weighed the evidence in favor of a genetic base or **predisposition** through his research based on twin studies of both identical and fraternal twins raised in the same environment and/or by adoptive parents. His study did not find support for a genetic base cause.

Predisposition
A tendency, suscepti-bility or inclination toward.

A team led by Elizabeth Sowell from the University of California at Los Angeles, using high-resolution magnetic resonance imaging and surface-based computational image-analyzing techniques to map brain size and gray matter, found abnormal brain structure in the frontal cortices of the brains of AD/HD children. The reduced regional brain size was localized to inferior portions of dorsal prefrontal cortices on both sides of the brain. Brain size was also reduced in anterior temporal cortices on both sides of the brain, with prominent increases in gray matter seen in the posterior, temporal, and inferior parietal cortices of AD/HD children. These abnormalities occur in regions that are known to subserve impulse control (Sowell et al., 2003).

At least two genes have been reliably documented as associated with the disorder. According to Peter Jensen (2001a), current director for the Center for the Advancement of Children's Mental Health at Columbia University (formerly with National Institute of Mental Health), the identification of genes associated with AD/HD is based on "candidate genes" (the process of studying people to find out how often various forms of specific genes appear). As soon as researchers can show that treatments like

Attention-Deficit/Hyperactivity Disorder

Psychostimulants
Pharmacological substances with potent actions of affect and motor activity, they affect how the brain controls impulses and regulates behavior and attention by influencing the availability of certain chemicals, called neurotransmitters, in the brain.

Genome
All the genetic information possessed by any organism (for example, the human genome, the elephant genome, the mouse genome, the yeast genome, and the genome of a bacterium). Humans and many other higher animals actually have two genomes—a chromosomal genome and a mitochondrial genome—that together make up their genome.

psychostimulants affect specific brain regions and specific receptors, and as soon as they can identify the genes that code for these receptors, they will know if people with AD/HD are more likely to have different forms of candidate genes than persons without AD/HD. Candidate-gene research compares children with and without AD/HD, as well as multiple family members, to see if specific forms of genes show up more often in affected children than they would by chance.

Jensen (2001a) noted that researchers have studied a number of candidate genes and found that a specific form of the dopamine-transporter gene (DAT1) is associated with AD/HD. Another candidate gene being looked at is the dopamine 4 (DRD4) gene. Genes of the dopamine system are considered candidates for involvement in causing the disorder. The genes that have been investigated are the ones encoding the five receptors in the brain, D1–D5, through which dopamine acts. Misener et al. (2004) of the Toronto Western Research Institute, University Health Network, found a relationship with the DRD1 gene and inattentive symptoms of AD/HD, but not with the hyperactive/impulsive symptoms. This research supports a genetic risk. The work of scientists now is to figure out how the genes work together during development and how they interact with nongenetic factors when AD/HD occurs.

It appears that researchers are narrowing in on another of the many genes that play a role in AD/HD. In genetic studies, researchers have found the general location of a gene that could account for as much as 30 percent of the genetic cause of attention-deficit/hyperactivity disorder. This gene is located in a region of the human **genome** that has also been implicated in autism, suggesting an overlap of both conditions. Smalley et al. (2002) looked at genetic couples samples of 27 biological siblings with AD/HD and narrowed down the area where the gene could be located to 100–150 genes on chromosome 16. Smalley likens finding a specific gene to finding a contact lens in Disneyland. The mapping of the human genome in recent years has, however, been possible with the blood samples of 203 families. Variations in the same genes may work together in complete and surprising ways to influence people's susceptibility to conditions such as AD/HD and autism. According to Dr. Smalley, learning the genetics of AD/HD, which is also influenced by environment, could lead to early diagnosis of the condition and intervention or prevention. Whole genome scan studies are now underway to identify links between specific chromosomal markers and AD/HD traits, but results are not yet available (Jensen, 2001a).

On the other hand, there are also environmental factors contributing to AD/HD, but little solid evidence indicating which specific factors are responsible. Such theories propose that some children's problems with impulse control come as a result of our increasingly "rapid-fire culture," **escape behavior, sensory addictions,** and/or prevalent **streams of stimulation.** Identical twins from the same home share the same environment, as well as the same gene pool, making conclusive research difficult.

Other contributing environmental factors are exposure to toxins such as lead, alcohol, nicotine, or mercury thimerosal-containing vaccines. Vaccines with high levels of thimerosal—containing ethyl mercury to prevent bacterial contamination and known to be **neurotoxic**—have been linked to autism, AD/HD, and speech delay in children. Thimerosal was used in vaccines against hepatitis, haemophilus influenza, and combined to ward against tetanus and diphtheria. It has since been removed from vaccines.

Food additives, as well as sugar and food allergens are considered possible factors contributing to AD/HD, but there is controversy regarding their unproven role. Only a few cases can be attributed to these environmental factors solely, but the combinations of trauma, toxin, and brain insult, coupled with presence of certain patterns of susceptibility genes may produce a full-blown AD/HD syndrome.

There are also nongenetic factors, in addition to environmental ones, that contribute to the onset of AD/HD. Such factors include risks in mothers of children with AD/HD who had complications during pregnancy,

Escape behavior
Operant conditioning based on the idea that a behavior is more likely to be repeated if it results in the cessation of a negative event.

Sensory addictions
A phenomenon linking the behaviors seen in individuals with AD/HD to the frequent sensory stimulation from TV programs, movies, computers, and other technological advances that may affect biological or neurological development, especially at a time when the brain is just forming connections and synapses, that may result in, but is not limited to, AD/HD.

Stream of stimulation
Constant exposure to external stimuli.

Neurotoxic
Poisonous or destructive to nerve tissue.

such as toxemia, lengthy delivery, or excessive weight loss or gain. Poor quality pre- and post-natal care may increase the likelihood of children developing AD/HD. Closed-head injuries, such as a bang on the forehead from a car windshield, can yield subtle injuries to the brain.

How and why AD/HD exists can be further explored through the newer techniques of structural and functional imaging of the brain. Using magnetic resonance imaging (MRI) to study brain structure, the prefrontal cortex, basal ganglia, and cerebellum in children with AD/HD can be scrutinized. Such studies (Sowell et al., 2003) report that children with this disorder have specific brain structures that are about 5 to 10 percent smaller that those of unaffected children. The prefrontal cortex and basal ganglia—where medications such as psychostimulants do their work—are rich in dopamine receptors. **Executive function** and motor planning—both often compromised in those with AD/HD—also take place in this area. The cerebellum can also be compromised (Jensen, 2004). In addition, single proton emission tomography (SPECT) brain imaging is used to study blood flow in regions of the brains of children with AD/HD. Many SPECT studies show lower-than-normal blood flow in the regions important to executive function. Functional MRI (fMRI) is another tool used to find blood-flow reduction in specific regions of the brains of AD/HD children and adults. One recent finding showed that Ritalin increased the blood flow to these regions (Shafritz, Marchione, Gore, & Shaywitz, 2004). Positron emission tomography (PET) has recently been used to search for metabolic changes in people with AD/HD. These neuroimaging tools are promising as methods to unlock the neurobiological basis of AD/HD.

Executive function Component of metacognition; set of general control processes that coordinate knowledge and metacognitive knowledge, transforming such knowledge into behavioral strategies, which ensure that an individual's behavior is adaptive, consistent with some goal, and beneficial to the individual; the act of executing a plan (Chermak & Musiek, 1997).

The Demographics of AD/HD

Boys Versus Girls

While it has long been thought boys with AD/HD outnumber girls with it by approximately 3:1, Quinn (2002) showed that the actual numbers may be nearly equal. Girls with attention-deficit/hyperactivity disorder face greater impairment in areas of social development, including self-esteem, social relationships, and family relationships, than do boys with the disorder. Such findings imply that gender has an impact on diagnosis and treatment.

In a survey documenting perceptions surrounding gender differences among parents of adolescents with AD/HD (ages 12–17), their teachers, and the general public, conducted by Harris Interactive on behalf of Novartis Pharmaceuticals Corp. (developers of Ritalin), girls were reported as having more difficulty than boys in such areas as making friends, getting along with their parents, getting things done, and focusing on school work. They were also less likely to feel good about themselves or feel happy (Novartis Pharmaceuticals Corporation, 2002).

The study found girls with AD/HD were more likely to be treated for depression before being diagnosed with AD/HD, as were boys with it. In fact, as many as 75 percent of girls with this condition may go undiagnosed, particularly if the girls have the inattentive subtype characterized by forget-fulness, **timidity**, difficulty listening, anxiety, and high distractibility—which may be accurately diagnosed only 50 percent of the time. Often, girls are misdiagnosed with depression because they internalize their symptoms. Parents of girls (74 percent) strongly agreed that untreated AD/HD has serious long-term effects on self-esteem, as compared to 63 percent of boys' parents.

Timidity
Hesitating or state of being hesitant, awkwardness or lack of self-confidence in the presence of others.

The survey also found that girls' parents are more likely to seek medical assistance for their child's symptoms than boys' parents, which may be attributed to the misconception that hyperactive males are "boys being boys." More boys' parents were reluctant to treat with medication (59 percent) than girls' parents (39 percent). Of interest was the fact that almost all parents reported that their children were helped with medication (94 percent for boys, 96 percent for girls).

Perception regarding AD/HD differs depending on gender. Among girls with AD/HD, 85 percent of their teachers thought girls more likely to go undiagnosed, 92 percent thought girls don't act out, and 42 percent said it is more difficult to observe behaviors in girls, and such behaviors are often more evident at an older age. The public's perception is somewhat different. Among the general public, 57 percent thought girls more likely than boys to go undiagnosed because they don't act out, and 64 percent attributed this to girls being more likely to suffer silently.

Huessy (1990) found that girls with AD/HD had severe problems with the onset of puberty. Apparently, increased hormonal fluctuations during certain times of the month can worsen the symptoms. New findings regarding women and hormones revealed that women with AD/HD, who are frequently subjected to fluctuating hormone levels, had further complications in worsening attention and focus that contribute to co-existing mood and behavioral disorders (Nadeau & Quinn, 2002b; Quinn, 2002). The brain is a target organ for estrogen and estrogen's neuronal effects have functional consequences. Estrogen stimulates certain populations of dopamine and serotonin receptors in the brain. The cyclical production of estrogen may increase symptoms of AD/HD by down-regulating dopamine activity or contributing to mood disorders as decreasing estrogen levels exert their effects on serration (Quinn, 2002).

Adults

AD/HD is an adult disability as well. In the past, clinicians believed that children outgrew AD/HD before adolescence, when hyperactivity was seen as the major symptom. The major symptoms in adulthood are primarily inattention and impulsivity, not hyperactivity. Impulsivity and inattention may continue into adulthood, while hyperactivity can decrease with age. In fact, a significantly higher proportion of adults present with inattentive symptoms rather than hyperactive-impulsive symptoms. AD/HD behaviors have been shown to persist into adulthood in 10 to 60 percent of cases with documented childhood onset (Manuzza, Klein, Bessler, Malloy, & LaPadula, 1993).

Introversion
Personality style where the individual has the tendency to focus energy inward resulting in decreased social interaction.

Extroversion
Personality style where the individual prefers outward focus and group activity as opposed to inward focus and individual activity.

A study by Robin, Tzelepis, and Bedway (1998) categorized 233 adults with AD/HD (any subtype) based on Theodore Millon's index of personality styles (MIPS). Results yielded three personality clusters associated with AD/HD: (1) half were characterized by pessimism, negativity, passivity, self-centeredness, **introversion,** and disorganization; (2) slightly less than half were characterized by optimism, assertiveness, **extroversion,** nurturance of others, and less disorganization; and (3) 5 percent were motivated by a balance between seeking pleasure and avoiding pain, ruggedness, and self-centeredness. Thus, not one personality pattern appeared, but rather a few; which helps to explain why some AD/HD adults are more successful than others. The most common subtype of AD/HD in adults is the combined type, with 60 percent presenting with the combined subtype, 40 percent with the inattentive subtype, and a small percentage with the impulsive-hyperactive subtype. There were no differences seen between adult males and females in overall percentages, but more adult females had the inattentive subtype of AD/HD. A National Institute of Mental Health (NIMH) study found 20 percent of adults were identified as clinically depressed and 15 to 25 percent as substance abusers (NIMH, 2000).

Perimenopausal women are susceptible to an amplification of symptoms. Symptoms arising during these years include memory loss, mood changes, and hot flashes—all related to lack of estrogen. This period is also associated with depression, even in women with no previous history of depression. These women report feeling more tired, irritable, worried, and less energetic. Dealing with depression and cognitive deficits associated with perimenopause and menopause in addition to AD/HD may cause women with AD/HD to become less functional as they enter this stage in their lives (Quinn, 2002).

Many adults with AD/HD do not typically recognize that they have the disorder until it is brought to their attention, although they have struggled with symptoms all their lives. Often, these adults develop ways to compensate. Medications available to children appear to benefit up to 75 percent of adults with AD/HD. Research continues to show that AD/HD is under-recognized and under-treated in adults.

Perimenopausal
Relating to, being in, or occurring in perimenopause (i.e., the time during which a woman no longer or intermittently menstruates).

Summary

This chapter provided information on the definition, identification, possible causes, and findings associated with the prevalence of AD/HD in children and adults. The genetic and environmental factors associated or linked as possible etiologic indicators were explored. For more information, see these websites:

- Children and Adults with Attention-Deficit/Hyperactivity Disorder
  www.chadd.org

- Attention Deficit Disorder Association
  www.add.org

- Molecular Psychiatry
  www.ovid.com (Type "Molecular Psychiatry" into the site search box, and click #1 result, Molecular Psychiatry).

- National Resource Center on AD/HD
  www.help4adhd.org, 800-233-4050

Chapter 2

Comorbid Conditions and Concomitant Problems

AD/HD is one of the most common chronic childhood disorders managed by primary care physicians. It is frequently associated with other **comorbid** conditions, such as learning disabilities, **psychiatric disorders,** or other developmental disabilities. Mental health and behavioral disorders such as anxiety, depression, oppositional defiant disorder, post-traumatic stress disorder, and bipolar disorder may have overlapping features of AD/HD that may be mistaken for this condition. These developmental or medical disorders may mimic AD/HD, making the accuracy of diagnosis and treatment difficult at times.

Despite the immense body of research regarding AD/HD, the diagnosis still generates controversy. Guidelines by organizations such as the American Academy of Pediatrics (see Study More 1.1 on the CD-ROM) and the American Academy of Child and Adolescent Psychiatry have been developed to standardize diagnostic protocols. However, the disorder may still be overdiagnosed or misdiagnosed.

In a study by Kube, Peterson, and Palmer (2002), separate or comorbid *DSM–IV* diagnoses (see guideline in Sidebar 1.1 on pages 5–6) were present in 50 percent of the group with a chief symptom of AD/HD. Of this group, 70 percent were diagnosed as having behavioral problems, and 50 percent had learning problems. Such diagnoses included disruptive behavior disorder—not otherwise specified, oppositional defiant disorder, depressive disorder, anxiety disorder, post-traumatic stress disorder, and bipolar disorder. There were 12 out of 189 children ages 2 to 15 referred for evaluation of AD/HD with pervasive developmental disorder or autism. Six of these 12 children had more than one *DSM–IV* diagnosis. There was

Comorbid
The presence of coexisting or additional diseases with reference to an initial diagnosis or with reference to the index condition that is the subject of study. Comorbidity may affect the ability of affected individuals to function and also their survival; it may be used as a prognostic indicator for outcome.

Psychiatric disorders
Medical disorders concerned primarily with mental illness.

17

Attention-Deficit/Hyperactivity Disorder

no significant difference among the age groups regarding the final diagnoses, comorbid diagnoses, and other *DSM–IV* diagnoses. More females (40 percent) were diagnosed with mental retardation than males (21 percent). Gender was not a contributing factor in the diagnosis of AD/HD, in specific learning disabilities, in developmental language disorders, or in each age group. This study confirmed that developmental language disorders, mental retardation, learning disabilities, and other *DSM–IV* disorders are common both as sole primary diagnoses and as conditions comorbid with AD/HD.

Psychiatric disorders are much more common in children whose chief symptom is a behavior problem. Such comorbid disorders in children include mental health and behavioral disorders, which are more common in subjects younger than 5 years of age (Kube et al., 2002).

Oppositional defiant disorder (ODD), conduct disorder, mood disorders, and developmental disorders are often comorbid with AD/HD. In adults, AD/HD coexists with depressive disorders, anxiety, substance abuse, and antisocial disorders. Children with Tourette's syndrome, obsessive-compulsive disorder, post-traumatic stress disorder, and sexual abuse history are often misdiagnosed because AD/HD symptoms are similar to these disorders. Patients with AD/HD should be reevaluated at adolescence or adulthood for common AD/HD **sequelae** which include major depression, bipolar disorder, anxiety disorders, substance abuse disorders, and antisocial disorders.

As many as 40 to 60 percent of children with AD/HD have at least one other major disorder. The most common **concomitant** disorders are these:

- Disruptive behavior disorders
- Mood disorders
- Anxiety disorders
- Tics and Tourette's syndrome
- Learning disabilities
- Memory disorders
- Sleep disorders
- Substance abuse
- Allergies
- Autism

Oppositional defiant disorder
A type of disruptive behavior disorder characterized by a pattern of recurrent, disobedient behavior toward those in authority (APA, 2000).

Sequelae
Conditions or events which follow, as a consequence of, a disease or injury.

Concomitant
Accompanying, joined with another.

- Asperger's syndrome
- Fragile X syndrome

These concomitant disorders are described in the sections that follow.

Disruptive Behavior Disorders

Oppositional Defiant Disorder

According to CHADD (2001), about 40 percent of individuals with AD/HD have ODD. Unfortunately, children diagnosed as having a disruptive disorder may have behavioral problems that later become consistent with AD/HD, but at the time of the evaluation sufficient criteria are not available or are not present enough, or the duration, severity, social impact, or limited number of settings mitigated against making the diagnosis. Individuals with oppositional-defiant disorder lose their temper easily, annoy others on purpose, are **defiant** and hostile toward authority figures, refuse to follow rules; they are angry, resentful, spiteful, and vindictive. The *DSM–IV* states that the essential feature of ODD is a recurrent pattern of negativistic, defiant, disobedient, and hostile behavior toward authority figures that persists for at least six months and is characterized by the frequent occurrence of at least four of the following behaviors:

Defiant
The act or an instance of challenging, disposition to resist or contradict, willingness to contend or fight.

- Losing temper
- Arguing with adults
- Actively defying or refusing to comply with the request or rules of adults
- Deliberately doing things that will annoy other people
- Blaming others for his or her own mistakes or misbehavior
- Being touchy or easily annoyed by others
- Being angry and resentful
- Being spiteful or vindictive

To qualify for ODD, the behaviors must occur more frequently than is typically observed in individuals of comparable age and developmental level and must lead to significant impairment in social, academic, or occupational functioning. Negativistic and defiant behaviors are expressed by persistent stubbornness, resistance to directions, and unwillingness to compromise, give in, or negotiate with adults or peers. Defiance may also include deliberate or persistent testing of limits, usually by ignoring orders, arguing, and failing to accept blame for misdeeds. Hostility can be directed at adults or peers and is shown by deliberately annoying others or through aggression. Manifestations of the disorder are almost invariably present in the home setting, but may not be evident at school or in the community. Symptoms of the disorder are typically more evident in interactions with adults or peers whom the individual knows well, and thus may not be apparent during clinical examination. Usually individuals with this disorder do not regard themselves as oppositional or defiant, but justify their behavior as a response to unreasonable demands or circumstances.

Conduct Disorder

Conduct Disorder (CD) is also common among those with AD/HD, occurring in 25 percent of children, 45 to 50 percent of adolescents, and 20 to 25 percent of adults (CHADD, 2001). According to the *DSM–IV*, the essential feature of conduct disorder is a repetitive and persistent pattern of behavior in which either the basic rights of others or major age-appropriate societal norms or rules are violated. These behaviors fall into four main groupings:

- Aggressive conduct that causes or threatens physical harm to other people or animals
- Nonaggressive conduct that causes property loss or damage
- Deceitfulness or theft
- Serious violations of rules

Clinically significant
Scores falling above or below one standard deviation from the mean score.

Three (or more) characteristic behaviors must have been present during the past 12 months, with at least one behavior present in the past 6 months and the disturbance in behavior causes **clinically significant** impairment in social, academic, or occupational functioning. The behavior pattern is usually present in a variety of settings such as home, school, or the community. Children or adolescents with this disorder often initiate aggressive behavior and react aggressively to others. They may display bullying, threatening, or intimidating behavior; initiate frequent physical fights; use a weapon that can cause serious physical harm; be physically cruel to people or animals; steal while confronting a victim; or force someone into sexual activity. Deliberate destruction of others' property is a characteristic feature of this disorder and may include deliberate fire-setting with the intention of causing serious damage or deliberately destroying other people's property in other ways.

Deceitfulness or theft is common and may include breaking into someone else's house, building, or car; frequently lying or breaking promises to obtain goods or favors or to avoid debts or obligations; or stealing items of nontrivial value without confronting the victim. Children with this disorder often have a pattern, beginning before age 13, of staying out late at night despite parental prohibitions. There may be a pattern of running away from home overnight.

CD is associated with efforts to break rules without getting caught. Such children may skip school or break curfews. CD is often described as delinquency and children who have AD/HD and conduct disorder may have lives that are more difficult than those of children with AD/HD alone. Students with both AD/HD and CD, *but not other AD/HD children*, are at greater risk for social and emotional failure. Studies now suggest that AD/HD and CD may be a particular subtype of AD/HD, since multiple family members often have both of these disorders.

Jensen (2001a, 2001b) discovered that these types of comorbid conditions occur more in children with primarily hyperactive/impulsive and combination subtypes of AD/HD. In boys, the rate of comorbid conduct disorders is about 25 percent and in girls it is about 8 percent.

AD/HD and CD students treated with **stimulant** medicines are not only more attentive, but less antisocial and aggressive. Medication combinations, such as a psychostimulant with an **antidepressant**, appear to be very effective for these patients.

Mood Disorders

Both sad, depressive moods and persisting elevated or irritable moods (mania) occur with AD/HD more than would be expected by chance. The *DSM–IV* describes mood disorders as divided into depressive disorders (unipolar depression), the bipolar disorders, and two disorders based on **etiology**—mood disorder due to a general medical condition and substance-induced mood disorder. The depressive disorders (i.e., major depressive disorder, **dysthymic disorder,** and depressive disorder not otherwise specified) are

Stimulant
An agent or remedy that produces stimulation.

Antidepressant
An agent that stimulates the mood of a depressed patient, including tricyclic antidepressants and monoamine oxidase inhibitors.

Etiology
The study of factors of causation, or those associated with the causation, of disease or abnormal body states.

Dysthymic disorder
A chronic type of depression that occurs on most days and lasts for a period of two or more years. In children and adolescents, mood can be irritable and duration must be at least one year. Also, the person has to display at least two of the following symptoms during the two year period: poor appetite or overeating, insomnia or hypersomnia, low energy or fatigue, low self-esteem, poor concentration or difficulty making decisions, or feelings of hopelessness.

Attention-Deficit/Hyperactivity Disorder

distinguished from the bipolar disorders by the fact that there is no history of ever having had a manic, mixed, or **hypomanic episode.** The bipolar disorders (i.e., bipolar I disorder, bipolar II disorder, cyclothymic disorder, and bipolar disorder not otherwise specified) involve the presence (or history) of manic episode, mixed episodes, or hypomanic episodes, usually accompanied by the presence (or history) of major depressive episodes. Major depressive disorder is characterized by one or more major depressive episodes (i.e., at least two weeks of depressed mood or loss of interest accompanied by at least four additional symptoms of depression).

Some individuals emphasize somatic complaints (e.g., bodily aches and pains), rather than reporting feelings of sadness. Many individuals report or exhibit increased irritability (e.g., persistent anger, a tendency to respond to events with angry outbursts or blaming others, or an exaggerated sense of frustration over minor matters). In children and adolescents, an irritable or cranky mood may develop rather than a sad or dejected mood. This pattern should be differentiated from a "spoiled child" pattern of irritability when frustrated.

Psychomotor changes include agitation (e.g., the inability to sit still, pacing, hand-wringing or pulling or rubbing of the skin, clothing, or other objects), or retardation (e.g., slowed speech, thinking, and body movements; increased pauses before answering; speech that is decreased in volume, inflection, amount, or variety of content, or muteness). The **psychomotor agitation** or **psychomotor retardation** must be severe enough to be observable by others and not represent merely the subjective feeling of the individual.

Decreased energy, tiredness, and fatigue are common. A person may report sustained fatigue without physical exertion. Even the smallest tasks seem to require substantial effort. The efficiency with which tasks are accomplished may be reduced. For example, an individual may complain that washing and dressing in the morning are exhausting and take twice as long as usual. The sense of worthlessness or guilt associated with a major depressive episode may include unrealistic negative evaluations of one's worth or guilty preoccupations or ruminations over minor past failings.

Distractibility and **low frustration tolerance** can occur in both AD/HD and major depressive episode. If the criteria are met for both, AD/HD may be diagnosed in addition to the mood disorder. However, the professional must be cautious not to overdiagnose a major depressive episode in children with AD/HD whose disturbance in mood is characterized by irritability rather than by sadness or loss of interest (American Psychiatric Association, 1994).

Depression

Studies suggest that between 10 to 30 percent of children with AD/HD, and 47 percent of adults with AD/HD, also have depression (CHADD, 2001). Typically, AD/HD occurs first and depression occurs later. Genetic factors may contribute. Environmentally, as children with AD/HD get older, they may feel left out. About one in four may become clinically depressed. While all children have bad days where they feel down, depressed children may be down or irritable on most days. Children with AD/HD and depression may also withdraw from others, stop doing things they once enjoyed, have trouble sleeping or sleep the day away, lose their appetite, criticize themselves excessively, and talk about dying. (Sidebar 2.1 lists common

---

Sidebar 2.1   **Signs of Depression**

- Change in appetite, where there is either a significant weight loss or weight gain
- Disrupted sleep patterns, including frequently awakening, early morning awakenings, inability to fall asleep, or sleeping too much
- Anhedonia, or loss of feelings of pleasure and enjoyment in activities of previous interest
- Continuous fatigue and loss of energy
- Irritable mood
- Persistent feelings of worthlessness and inappropriate guilt
- Indecisiveness and difficulty concentrating
- Recurring thoughts of death or suicide, wishing to die, or attempting suicide
- Physical symptoms, such as headaches or stomachaches and psychomotor agitation
- Frequent crying episodes
- Difficulty maintaining social relationships, wanting to be socially isolated
- Sensitivity to rejection and failure

Source: Netherton, Holmes, and Walker (1999)

---

signs of depression.) Fortunately, AD/HD by itself is not associated with increased risk of suicidal behavior. AD/HD and depression may share a common underlying genetic link.

Treatment of children with AD/HD and depression involves minimizing environmental trauma and applying different medical regimens. Stimulants (such as Ritalin) can be combined safely with antidepressants such as flouxetine (Prozac). In addition, bupropion (Wellbutrin) and venlafaxine (Effexor) have been found effective in some individuals. Some antidepressants (Paxil) have been linked to an increase in suicide rates and higher rates of self-harm and agitation (CHADD, 2001).

Mania/Bipolar Disorder

Up to 20 percent of individuals with AD/HD also manifest bipolar disorder—abnormally elevated mood contrasted by episodes of clinical depression. *DSM–IV* describes it as a clinical course that has one or more manic episodes (an abnormal and persistently elevated expansive, or irritable mood). This period of mania must last for one week and be accompanied by three additional symptoms which include inflated self-esteem; decreased need for sleep; incessant, loud, rapid, unclear speech, or mixed episodes. The essential feature of bipolar I disorder is a clinical course that is characterized by the occurrence of one or more manic episodes followed by a depressive mood. In addition, the episodes are not better accounted for by schizoaffective disorder and are not superimposed on **schizophrenia**, **schizophreniform disorder, delusional disorder,** or psychotic disorder not otherwise specified. Bipolar I disorder is a recurrent disorder—more than 90 percent of individuals who have a single manic episode go on to have future episodes. Roughly 60 to 70 percent of manic episodes occur immediately before or after a major depressive episode.

Approximately 10 to 15 percent of adolescents with recurrent major depressive episodes will go on to develop bipolar I disorder. Mixed episodes appear to be more likely in adolescents and young adults than in older adults. Recent epidemiological studies (American Psychiatric Association, 1994) in the United States indicate that bipolar I disorder is approximately equally common in men and women. Gender appears to be related to the order of appearance of manic and major depressive episodes. The first episode in males is more likely to be a manic episode.

Schizophrenia
A functional psychosis characterized by apathy, withdrawal from reality, excessive fantasy, and also, in some cases, delusions and hallucinations. There are several different diagnostic types.

Schizophreniform disorder
Diagnosis for people who have all the symptoms of schizophrenia, except that the disorder lasts more than two weeks but less than six months.

Delusional disorder
A paranoid disorder where the delusions are characteristically systematized and not bizarre; other characteristics of the active phase or schizophrenia are absent or only fleetingly present; personality functioning remains relatively intact outside the area of the delusional theme, and overall impairment remains less than in schizophrenia.

The first episode in females is more likely to be a major depressive episode. Women with bipolar I disorder have an increased risk of developing subsequent episodes in the immediate postpartum period. Adults with mania may have long (days or weeks) episodes of being ridiculously happy, and even believe they have special powers or can receive messages. They may go days without sleeping and engage in tasks that ultimately get them into trouble—go on shopping sprees which get them into debt, become hypersexual, or contact people at all hours of the night.

Children with bipolar disorder experience rapid change of mood several times a day. They are greatly irritable and explosive. They may also experience periods of mania where they act silly, giddy, and goofy, and their behaviors are intensely hyperactive. The combination of AD/HD and bipolar disorder, with episodes of mania, often leads to severe difficulty with functioning.

It is extremely important to recognize that a child may have an onset of bipolar disorder, since overlooking it may exacerbate the condition if stimulant medication is prescribed. A more appropriate treatment would be prescription of **mood stabilizers** such as Lithium, valprate (Depakote), or carbamazepine (Tegretol). It might also be helpful to temporarily add an atypical **antipsychotic** to control rage and subdue mania. These do not improve the AD/HD symptoms, therefore stimulants or antidepressants are often added.

Mood stabilizers
A psychiatric medication used in the treatment of bipolar disorder to suppress swings between mania and depression.

Antipsychotic
Tranquilizer used to treat psychotic conditions when a calming effect is desired.

Anxiety Disorders

Anxiety disorders are the most common of psychiatric disorders in childhood, and their comorbidity with AD/HD is far above chance. Up to 30 percent of children and 25 to 40 percent of adults with AD/HD will also have an anxiety disorder (CHADD, 2001). Anxiety disorders are often not apparent. As with depression, the child's internal feelings may not stand out to parents or teachers. Patients with anxiety disorders often worry excessively about a number of things (school, work, etc.), and may feel edgy, stressed out or tired, tense, and have trouble getting restful sleep. Patients report brief episodes of severe anxiety (panic attacks), which intensify for a period of approximately 10 minutes with complaints of pounding heart, sweating, shaking, and choking. Children with AD/HD and

Attention-Deficit/Hyperactivity Disorder

anxiety appear to be at a lower risk for conduct disorders. These children have more social difficulties, but appear to have no difference in school performance. They appear slowed down or inefficient. Genetic research thus far suggests that AD/HD and anxiety are separate disorders inherited independently of each other.

Dysphoria
A psychological state that causes feelings of anxiety, restlessness, and depression.

On the other hand, many children with AD/HD have no foresight and lack the appropriate amount of anticipatory anxiety for events (such as studying for a test). When the test is over and they are grounded for a poor grade, they may express **dysphoria** or nervousness. It is critical when the interviewer is taking a history from the parent to distinguish between true performance anxiety and unhappiness about the consequences of misbehavior. To recognize anxiety disorder, the symptoms should have sufficient frequency to impair functioning. Older children and adolescents may use the word *nervous* to describe their AD/HD symptoms. When asked to give an example of their nervousness, adolescents with AD/HD will describe a symptom more akin to motor restlessness or impatience. One child may complain of "being too nervous," as evidenced by an inability to stop talking in class or impulsively laughing at inappropriate times. Anxiety has a more painful quality; it is an internal experience as opposed to a reaction to immediate environmental stimuli.

Inhibitory control
To regulate one's need to suppress or restrain (behavior, an impulse, or a desire) consciously or unconsciously.

It appears that **inhibitory control** and sensitivity in the detection of emotion are found to be specific to children with AD/HD and comorbid anxiety. Children with anxiety selectively encode emotionally threatening information, and they have greater difficulty in perceiving emotional targets. These children are more impaired on tasks of working memory, but they do not show deficiencies on tasks of reaction time (Clark, Prior, & Kinsella, 2000).

Treatment of AD/HD and anxiety requires attention to precipitating stressors. Relaxation techniques and alternative ways to think through stressful situations may be helpful. Alternative medication regimens may be necessary. Tricyclic antidepressants (e.g., desipramine (Norpramin), nortriptyline (Pamelor), imipramine (Tofranil), benzodiazepines lorazepam (Ativan), clonazapam (Klonopin), alprazolam (Xanax), etc.) and more recently buspirone (Buspar) may benefit these patients.

Tics and Tourette's Syndrome

Tics are characterized as sudden, rapid, recurrent, nonrhythmic movements or vocalizations, excessive eye blinking or throat clearing. Tourette's is a much rarer, more severe tic disorder. Patients may make noises (e.g., barking a word or sound or sniffing) and movements (e.g., repetitive flinching or eye blinking, grimacing, or shrugging.) It is believed that 1 to 3 percent of school children have Tourette's syndrome, one quarter of these children are in special education classes. Only about 7 percent of those with AD/HD have tics or Tourette's syndrome, but 21 to 90 percent of children with Tourette's syndrome have comorbid AD/HD (CHADD, 2001). These transient tics usually go away gradually as the child reaches adulthood.

The *DSM–IV* describes the essential features of Tourette's syndrome as multiple motor tics and one or more vocal tics. These may appear simultaneously or at different periods during the illness. The tics occur many times a day, recurrently throughout a period of more than one year. During this period, there is never a tic-free period of more than three consecutive months. The disturbance causes marked distress or significant impairment in social, occupational, or other important areas of functioning. The tics are not due to the direct physiological effects of a substance or a general medical condition.

The anatomical location, number, frequency, complexity, and severity of the tics change over time. The tics typically involve the head, and frequently, other parts of the body, such as the torso and upper and lower limbs. The vocal tics include various words or sounds such a clicks, grunts, yelps, barks, sniffs, snorts, and coughs. Complex motor tics involving touching, squatting, deep-knee bends, retracing steps, and twirling when walking may be present. In the bouts of a single tic, which is most frequently eye blinking, there can be less frequent tics involving another part of the face or the body. Initially, symptoms can also include tongue protrusions, squatting, sniffing, hopping, skipping, throat clearing, stuttering, and uttering sounds or words.

The treatment of children with chronic tic disorders and AD/HD with stimulant medication is problematic, as the stimulant medications may exacerbate underlying tics. While these medicines no longer appear to cause tics, they may unmask or exaggerate tics (CHADD, 2001). Other medicines such as nortriptyline (Pamelor or Aventyl), clonidine (Catapres), or guanfacine (Tenex) may be used to decrease tics while treating AD/HD.

Pharmacological treatment is effective for children with chronic tic disorders, including Tourette's syndrome, concurrent with AD/HD. As many as 9 in 10 children with tic disorders also have AD/HD. Previously, the use of medications most commonly prescribed to treat children with AD/HD had been discouraged for those who also had tic disorders, either because their benefits had not been established clinically or had been associated with a worsening of tics. According to research (Kurlan, 2002), methylphenidate (MPH) and clonidine, especially when used together, are effective in treating these children, with minimal side effects. Methylphenidate, a stimulant also known as Ritalin, has long been the mainstay of treatment for AD/HD; clonidine is the most commonly pre-scribed alternative. The Medical Center in Rochester, NY reports that the most effective treatment for AD/HD is the combination of clonidine and MPH (Kurlan). Improvements related to MPH were observed in the areas of on-task behavior and attentiveness, while improvements related to cloni-dine included reduced occurrence of crying, frustration, restlessness, excitability, and impulsiveness. There were four groups of 136 participants: MPH alone; clonidine alone; MPH and clonidine; and **placebo.** The respons-es of participants were measured using 10 rating scales, including teacher and parent observation and task and functioning testing, at baseline and every 4 weeks of the 16 week study. The results showed that not only did tics not worsen during treatment with MPH, but that the severity of tics actu-ally decreased in all treatment groups, while the benefits of the combined drug therapies were significant in treating AD/HD (Kurlan, 2002).

Placebo
A treatment condi-tion used to control for the placebo effect where the treatment has no real effect on its own. An inactive substance which may look like medi-cine but contains no medicine, a "sugar pill."

Learning Disabilities

Children with AD/HD have a greater frequency of learning disability (LD) than children without AD/HD. In 1981, the National Joint Committee on Learning Disabilities (NJCLD) presented the following definition of learning disabilities:

> *Learning disabilities* is a generic term that refers to a het-erogeneous group of disorders manifested by significant dif-ficulties in the acquisition and use of listening, speaking, reading, writing, reasoning, or mathematical abilities. These

disorders are intrinsic to the individual and presumed to be due to central nervous system dysfunction. Even though a learning disability may occur concomitantly with other hand-icapping conditions (e.g., sensory impairment, mental retar-dation, social and emotional disturbance) or environmental influences (e.g., cultural differences, insufficient/inappropri-ate instruction, psychogenic factors), it is not the direct result of those conditions or influences. (Hammill, Leigh, McNutt, & Larsen, 1981, p. 336)

Most states operationalized this definition according to the guidelines originally developed when Public Law 94–142 was adopted in 1975:

A severe discrepancy between achievement and intellectual ability in one or more of the areas: (1) oral expression; (2) listening comprehension; (3) written expression; (4) basic reading skills; (5) reading comprehension; (6) mathematics calculation; or (7) mathematics reasoning. The child may not be identified as having a specific learning disability if the dis-crepancy between ability and achievement is primarily the result of: (1) a visual, hearing, or motor handicap; (2) mental retardation; (3) emotional disturbance; or (4) environmental, cultural, or economic disadvantage. (C.F.R. 34 § 300.541)

In accordance with this definition, the majority of the states required an IQ test for the identification of a child with a learning disability, and over two-thirds required some form of discrepancy (Frankenberger & Fronzaglio, 1991). Research has since strongly questioned the validity of classifying learning disabilities based on discrepancies of IQ and achieve-ment (Fletcher et al., 1998). The discrepancy is no longer necessary to diagnose LD, according to the Individuals with Disabilities Education Improvement Act of 2004 (IDEA 2004). However, discrepancy can be a consideration for identification. The use of IQ discrepancy for the identifi-cation of children as learning disabled determined groups of children with academic skill deficiencies—one group that was discrepant and one that was not discrepant, relative to their IQ scores.

Up to 50 percent of children with AD/HD have a coexisting learning dis-ability. Estimates of the prevalence of LD vary per academic area: 15 to 50 percent for reading, 24 to 60 percent for math, and 24 to 60 percent for spelling. Mayes, Calhoun, and Crowell (2000) also indicate that written expression is another factor which affects academic performance in children with AD/HD. Children with both AD/HD and LD may have a specific problem, such as reading or calculating, but they are not less intelligent than their peers.

Overall, according to Barkley (1998), 25 to 50 percent of children with AD/HD have LD. This concurs with earlier research where learning disability estimates ranged from 26 to 41 percent (Holborow & Berry, 1986) to as high as 80 percent (Safer & Allen, 1976). For reading disabilities—the most common form of learning disability—estimates are around 15 percent of children with AD/HD have a reading disability (Shaywitz, Fletcher, & Shaywitz, 1994). In children with language disorders, AD/HD is the most frequently identified emotional disorder, with as much as 45 percent prevalence (Cohen, Vallance, Barwick, & Horodozky, 1997). Ackerman, Dykman, and Gardner (1990) found that children with both AD/HD and a reading disability performed poorly on tasks of phonological processing. Reading disability was characterized by language processing problems in phonological processing. Children with both language impairments and AD/HD had more severe memory deficits as well (Cohen et al.).

A major limitation of previous research investigating the prevalence of LD in children with AD/HD is that the studies did not assess children for LD in written expression. Children with LD frequently have difficulty with writing. More current studies are looking at written expression, particularly through the use of comprehensive achievement test batteries.

Mayes et al. (2000) investigated the comorbidity of learning disabilities with AD/HD by using current and comprehensive IQ and achievement tests. All children in the study were administered the Wechsler Intelligence Scale for Children–3rd Edition (WISC–III; Wechsler, 1991), and the Wechsler Individual Achievement Test–2nd Edition (WIAT–II; Wechsler, 2001). The WIAT–II was chosen because scores are derived from the same normative sample as the WISC–III. Therefore, scores on the WISC–III and WIAT–II are directly comparable, which is not possible using other measures of academic achievement. All major academic areas were assessed, including basic reading, reading comprehension, math, spelling, and written expression. The WIAT–II Written Expression subtest, a comprehensive analysis of compositional writing skills, was used to evaluate the child's composition. It was scored for ideas and development, organization, vocabulary, sentence structure, grammar, capitalization, and punctuation.

The magnitude of learning problems between children in four diagnostic subgroups (AD/HD and LD, AD/HD without LD, LD without AD/HD, and no AD/HD or LD) were analyzed.

Results showed that referred children with AD/HD had a significantly greater frequency of LD than children without AD/HD. LD frequencies in reading, math, and spelling in children were consistent with prior research, with prevalence of LD close to one third in each group. However, the overall prevalence for LD doubled (70 percent) when written expression was included in the assessment. Given the presence of writing disorders, children with writing deficits can benefit from the use of word processors and spell checkers, oral or dictated performance, production prompts, and additional time for written assignments.

Compounding a learning disorder is the possibility of anxiety, hyperactivity, or aggressivity. These children appear withdrawn, disinterested in reading, and have difficulty paying attention to what they are reading. The learning disorder impacts school performance, and both family and peer relations.

Adolescents and adults with AD/HD often exhibit subtle but high-level forms of language learning disabilities or dyslexia. Comorbidity of AD/HD and dyslexia is present in all populations, but is especially common among school children. In many ways, dyslexia parallels AD/HD as the child is disinterested in reading, has difficulty paying attention to what he/she is reading, and becomes withdrawn. When conducting evaluations for children with suspected language problems, the speech-language pathologist should determine whether the problem involves attention, language, or the combination of two.

Persons with dyslexia may appear to have AD/HD because of their disinterest in reading and their difficulties paying attention to what they are reading. The child may appear withdrawn but is actually attempting to process verbal information. When dyslexia is suspected, the evaluation should include an assessment of reading, an IQ test, and a neuropsychological evaluation. Using a broad assessment battery will help to determine the presence of comorbidity.

Children with AD/HD and reading deficiencies perform significantly worse in the areas of attention, vocabulary, degraded word recognition, and memory for letter sequences. These children also show impairments on measures of neuropsychological function (Seidman, Biederman, Monuteaux, Doyle, & Faraone, 2001). Riccio and Jemison (1998) concluded that AD/HD and reading may be a heritable occurrence—45 percent of the deficit in reading was due to genetic factors that also influence the hyperactivity in AD/HD.

Causes of dyslexia have been attributed to genetic factors. Dyslexia and AD/HD both involve genetic components. Genes that cause dyslexia may be the same ones that cause AD/HD (Iskowitz, 1998; Light, Pennington, Gilger, & DeFries, 1995; Riccio & Jemison, 1998). In a study involving children with a comorbid diagnosis, genes that cause both disorders were identified (Iskowitz). These genes may affect areas of the brain that influence reading, concentration, attention, and behavioral/impulse control. Besides the frontal lobes (part of the brain responsible for impulse control and attention), other areas are also affected. Dyslexia has been associated with involvement in the left perisylvian region (for right-handers) and the superior temporal gyrus. In individuals with both disorders there appears to be diffuse involvement, including areas of corpus collosum, right hemisphere, temporal lobe, and occipital lobe. These genes affect areas of the brain that affect reading, concentration, attention, and behavioral/impulse control.

Memory Disorders

Children with AD/HD also have concomitant memory problems—attributed to the inattention associated with AD/HD, rather than to a separate problem. Conversely, deficits stemming from a learning disability affect short-term memory skills used for spelling, sounding out words, and other reading-related tasks. In AD/HD children, it is sometimes difficult to determine whether certain learning difficulties are caused by inattention, memory disorder, or both. Physicians often correctly diagnose the attention problem, but overlook the memory issues.

Memory testing determines whether a child has difficulty learning because of poor listening skills attributed to AD/HD, or because of difficulty remembering things, which is attributable to a learning disability. This paradigm may explain why children with AD/HD who receive medication may have improved attention but still display memory problems. In cases where medication is not helpful, children with AD/HD must receive specialized memory training. One such way to assess a child's visual and verbal memory is to administer a color span test (see Johnson, Altmaier, & Richman, 1999), which requires a person to retain color names in increasingly lengthy sequences. It requires both pointing and oral responses. Children with AD/HD, whether they had a learning disability or not, had significantly more memory deficits than others with undifferentiated attention deficit disorder (Johnson, Altmaier, & Richman, 1999).

For children with AD/HD who also exhibit LD problems, medication can be helpful in alleviating some of the symptoms which prevent them from focusing and attending. It is also important, however, to address the environmental factors in school and at home that may be contributing to the issues.

In school, a child should be seated in the front of the class and close to the teacher, far away from windows and doors. They should be given notes in advance of the lesson, so they can pre-learn the material. They would greatly benefit from word processors and spell checks, repetition of directions, and additional time for written assignments.

At home, a person who serves as a coach could provide a focused, structured environment. This could improve focus necessary in organizing and doing homework, and study skills. Parents, siblings, or hired tutors could serve as a coach in this manner.

Sleep Disorders

Children with AD/HD are more active while they sleep, as well as when they are awake, than children without AD/HD. Sleep disturbances are comorbid with AD/HD in about 80 percent of children and adults (Hart, 2001). The majority of individuals with AD/HD have difficulty falling asleep (sleep-onset insomnia). Children are often unable to settle down in bed and "stop thinking" about things like uncompleted homework, television shows and video games, bedtime fears, and loneliness. Adults with AD/HD often have similar worries at bedtime. For many, moderate afternoon exercise, a consistent bedtime routine, and some type of relaxation technique may be sufficient. If these techniques do not work, a mild sleep aid (clonidine or melatonin) could be helpful.

Another common sleep problem for these individuals is staying asleep. Some are restless; others wake up at the slightest noise. Children with AD/HD also have bedwetting and nocturnal enuresis that may persist until the teen years. This could be resolved by limiting fluids after supper and voiding at bedtime. Medications may be necessary for camps and sleepovers.

It is suggested that parents develop and adhere to a strict bedtime practice. Avoid stimulating activities, such as outdoor play, and choose more relaxing and soothing ones, such as coloring, just before bedtime. Along with these practices, parents should also develop bedtime rules and enforce them. These children should know what they are allowed to do and what they are not allowed to do when getting ready for and going to bed.

Substance Abuse

Youths with AD/HD are at increased risk for very early use of alcohol and then drug abuse. Cigarette smoking is common in adolescents with AD/HD. Youths with AD/HD are twice as likely to become addicted to nicotine as those without AD/HD (CHADD, 2001). Adults with AD/HD have elevated rates of smoking and a particular difficulty in quitting. However, cocaine and stimulant abuse is not more common among AD/HD individuals previously treated with stimulants (CHADD). Growing up taking stimulant medicines does not necessarily lead to substance abuse as these children become teenagers and adults. Adolescents with AD/HD prescribed stimulant medication are less likely to subsequently use illegal drugs than are those not prescribed medication (CHADD).

Allergies

In some children with AD/HD, their behavior and distractibility may be caused by allergic reaction to food or other substances. Each child may be allergic to a different agent (Rapp, 1991). It is important to determine which particular substance the child is allergic to and eliminate that from the diet to examine if attentional issues persist. Rapp determined that allergic symptoms such has hives, allergic shiners, asthma, and rhinitis are more common in AD/HD children. A child suffering from an allergy may present with symptoms such as irritability and distractibility which contribute to the AD/HD behavior or can be mistaken for it.

The relationship between AD/HD and allergies was evaluated by Roth, Beyreiss, Schlenzka, and Beyer (1991) in a study where 81 allergic children were compared to 71 controls. Parents of both groups filled out the Conners' Parent Rating Scale–Revised (CRS–R; Conners, 1997; Long Version), and the children were asked to perform several tests of attention and impulse control, including reaction time tasks and the Matching Familiar Figures test (see Kagan, Moss, & Siegel, 1960). The allergic children scored significantly higher on the Conners' Parent Rating Scale than did the controls.

Research studies have suggested that food allergies cause AD/HD and have advocated restricted diets to treat behavioral problems (Pliszka, Carlson, & Swanson, 1999). Egger, Carter, Graham, Gumley, and Soothill (1985) selected 76 hyperactive children for a study using the **oligoantigenic diet.** Individual foods were introduced in an open fashion by the parents at home to determine if the child's behavior deteriorated. If the parents reported that the child's behavior was worse, it was accepted as evidence that the child was allergic. Twenty-eight of the children were then placed on a double-blind placebo-controlled protocol in which the parents gave the child a placebo or active capsule containing the "allergen." Parents and clinicians filled out the Conners' Rating Scale—Revised (CRS–R; Conners, 1997; Short Version), and a psychologist also rated behavior during a testing session. While the parents and clinicians rated the child as more disturbed when he/she was exposed to the supposedly allergenic substance compared to the placebo, the objective measures of AD/HD, such as the actometric (activity-level) measures and the Matching Familiar Figures Test, showed no changes in the response to the "allergens."

Pediatric allergists advocate skin testing to determine the item or items to which the child is allergic. These items can be removed from the diet and **desensitization** pursued by injecting diluted amounts of the allergen(s) into the skin.

While the research evidence does not favor the allergy-AD/HD hypothesis, the issue is not completely resolved. More well-controlled studies are needed, where AD/HD children with no obvious evidence of allergic disorder are placed on a restricted diet and administered foods or food additives in a double-blind fashion in highly controlled conditions. While the issue deserves further study, at present the data do not support the use of diets or allergy procedures in the treatment of AD/HD. It is not accepted that allergies cause AD/HD; however, comorbidity has been recognized.

Oligoantigenic diet
Elemental diet, it focuses on identifying the foods that may be negatively affecting health and reducing them using the elimination/ challenge approach.

Desensitization
A way to reduce or stop a response such as an allergic reaction to something. For example, if someone has an allergic reaction to something, the doctor gives the person a very small amount of the substance, at first, to increase one's tolerance. Over a period of time, larger doses are given until the person is taking the full dose. This is one way to help the body get used to the full dose and to prevent the allergic reaction.

Autism

Are children with AD/HD the product of autism? Due to similar behaviors of attention, lack of social appropriateness, and awareness of the environment of others, many children with AD/HD often appear in their early years to exhibit characteristics of autism. As they age, and develop better learning and communication skills, they are considered children with AD/HD by the time they enter grade school. The etiological relationship is not clear.

The impairment in communication is also marked and sustained, and affects both verbal and nonverbal skills. There may be delay in, or total lack of, the development of spoken language. To date, there are no data indicating the prevalence of autism in the AD/HD child's early history. Although there are shared symptoms, the degree to which they are manifested clearly differentiates between the two disorders. On the same note, there is a prevalence of Asperger's syndrome, which may co-occur with AD/HD or mask as AD/HD, or vice versa.

Autism is more prevalent today than it was in the early 1980s. Currently, the National Institutes of Health (NIH) estimates that one in 250 children are diagnosed as autistic ("New Approach," 2002). The essential features of autistic disorder are the presence of markedly abnormal or impaired development in social interaction and communication and a markedly restricted repertoire of activities and interests. Manifestations of the disorder vary greatly depending on the developmental level and chronological age of the individual.

The impairment in reciprocal social interaction is gross and sustained. There may be marked impairment in the use of multiple nonverbal behaviors to regulate social interaction and communication. There may be failure to develop peer relationships appropriate to developmental level that may take different forms at different ages. Younger individuals may have little or no interest in establishing friendships. There may be a lack of spontaneous seeking to share enjoyment, interests, or achievements with other people. Lack of social or emotional reciprocity may be present. Often an individual's awareness of others is markedly impaired. Individuals with this disorder may be oblivious to other children, may have no concept of the needs of others, or may not notice another person's distress.

Asperger's Syndrome

The essential features of Asperger's syndrome are severe and sustained impairment in social interaction and the development of restricted, repetitive patterns of behavior, interests, and activities. This neurobiological disorder was named for Hans Asperger, a Viennese physician who, in 1944, described a pattern of behaviors seen in several boys who had normal intelligence and language development, but who exhibited autistic-like behaviors and marked deficiencies in social and communication skills. It was not until 1994 that Asperger's syndrome was added to the *DSM–IV,* and it was not until recently that it has been recognized by professionals and parents. A description of Asperger's syndrome as defined by the American Psychiatric Association (APA; 2000) can be found in Sidebar 2.2, page 38.

It is not yet known what the prevalence of Asperger's syndrome is among individuals with AD/HD. Many youngsters are being reevaluated because the speech-language pathologist has come to see the child's communication pattern as sufficiently aberrant to suggest a diagnosis of Asperger's syndrome.

In contrast to autism, there are no clinically significant delays in language, no clinically significant delays in cognitive development, or in the development of age-appropriate self-help skills, **adaptive behavior,** and curiosity about the environment in childhood.

Adaptive behavior
The ability for an individual to adjust to the natural and social demands of his or her environment.

The most pronounced feature with Asperger's Syndrome is communication inappropriateness, a symptom often found in AD/HD. Here too, the degree to which this behavior is manifested differentiates between the two disorders. However, shared symptoms, albeit different in degree, may suggest similar neurobiological substrates.

Fragile X Syndrome

Individuals with Fragile X syndrome have attention and learning difficulties, but it is not clear whether these difficulties are the result of auditory processing deficits or hearing deficiencies that are interfering with learning. Fragile X syndrome is an X-linked chromosome condition that is estimated to affect one in every 4,000 individuals. It is the most common inherited cause of mental retardation, affecting both males and females. Males have one **X-chromosome** and females have two X-chromosomes. To cause Fragile X

X-chromosome
The female chromosome contributed by the mother. It produces a female when paired with another X-chromosome, and produces a male when paired with a Y-chromosome.

Sidebar 2.2

DSM–IV Description
of Asperger's Syndrome Behaviors

A. Qualitative impairment in social interaction, as manifested by at least two of the following:

- Marked impairments in the use of multiple nonverbal behaviors such as eye-to-eye gaze, facial expression, body postures, and gestures to regulate social interaction
- Failure to develop peer relationships appropriate to developmental level
- A lack of spontaneous seeking to share enjoyment, interests, or achievements with other people (e.g., by a lack of showing, bringing, or pointing out objects of interest to other people)
- Lack of social or emotional reciprocity

B. Restricted repetitive and stereotyped patterns of behaviors, interests, and activities, as manifested by at least one of the following:

- Encompassing preoccupation with one or more stereotyped and restricted patterns of interest that is abnormal either in intensity or focus
- Apparently inflexible adherence to specific, nonfunctional routines or rituals
- Stereotyped and repetitive motor mannerisms (e.g., hand or finger flapping or twisting, or complex whole-body movements)
- Persistent preoccupation with parts of objects

C. The disturbance causes clinically significant impairment in social, occupational, or other important areas of functioning.

D. There is no clinically significant general delay in language (e.g., single words used by age 2 years, communicative phrases used by age 3 years).

E. There is no clinically significant delay in cognitive development or in the development of age-appropriate self-help skills, adaptive behavior (other than in social interaction), and curiosity about the environment in childhood.

F. Criteria are not met for another specific Pervasive Developmental Disorder or Schizophrenia.

syndrome, either parent can pass on an affected X-chromosome to their daughter, but a son would inherit the affected X-chromosome from his mother. (Fathers pass on the **Y-chromosome** to their sons, so a male can only inherit the affected X-chromosome from his mother.)

Symptomatology varies and is more severe in males. Physical symptoms are usually present by age 8, which include an elongated face, large head, and prominent ears. Girls' characteristics are generally normal, but some may have a long face and prominent ears. Most males have intellectual impairment, which can be severe, resulting in mental retardation and other cognitive deficits which appear later in childhood. In addition, both males and females can evidence adaptive, social skill, and behavioral problems that are often seen in children with autism, such as poor eye contact, social avoidance, stereotypic/repetitive behaviors, and hyperactivity. It is the hyperactivity that can be masked as AD/HD. For females, one-third exhibit mental retardation, but the rest have average intelligence with learning disabilities and psychosocial disabilities.

Attention and executive functioning are deficient, along with visual-spatial skills and math achievement, shyness, and social anxiety. Autism has been present in 7 to 25 percent of cases. For speech production, there is often perseverative and repetitive speech, reduced speech intelligibility, and rapid and uneven speech. Phonological delays have been reported (Roberts, Hennon, & Anderson, 2003). Oral motor skills indicate low muscle tone, poor motor planning, and sequencing difficulties with tactile defensiveness. Language issues indicate difficulty in maintaining a topic and retrieving words, with delays in vocabulary and syntax. Higher scores in comprehension than production of syntax and vocabulary are reported (Roberts et al.). There is little interest in social interactions. Adaptive behavior is characterized by social anxiety, gaze aversion, hyperarousal, and hypersensitivity to stimuli. Pragmatic language problems such as disorganized **tangential** language, poor topic maintenance, and delay in initiating conversations, along with difficulty with abstract language, reasoning, and making inferences have been attributed to females with executive function deficits, hyper-arousal, and memory problems. Hand flapping is stereotypic behavior. Short attention span and hyperactivity appear to be pervasive among both males and females.

Y-chromosome
The small chromosome that is male-determining in most mammal species and found only in the heterogametic sex.

Tangential
Of superficial relevance, if any, relating to the theme but not directly connected to the thought at hand.

Attention-Deficit/Hyperactivity Disorder

Neuroimaging studies have found smaller cerebellar vermis and larger caudate, thalamus, and hippocampus regions of the brain in individuals with Fragile X syndrome (Roberts et al.). See Figure 2.1 and Study More 2.1 on the CD-ROM for a Checklist of Comorbid Conditions Associated with AD/HD to serve as a summary for individual children.

Figure 2.1

Checklist of Comorbid Conditions Associated with AD/HD

Client Name: _____ Date: _____

Person(s) Completing This Checklist: _____

Disorder	Suspected	Confirmed	By Whom	Date
Allergies				
Anxiety				
Asperger's syndrome				
Autism				
Conduct disorder				
Depression				
Fragile X syndrome				
Learning disabilities				
Mania/Bipolar disorder				
Memory loss				
Mood disorder				
Oppositional defiant disorder				
Schizophrenia				
Sleep disorders/Disturbances				
Substance abuse				
Tics				
Tourette's syndrome				

Comments:

Summary

When considering the various possible co-occurring conditions, it behooves the professional to understand what the critical markers are for each of the comorbid conditions in order to improve assessment expertise. Being able to differentiate among behavior, mood, anxiety, Tourette's syndrome, learning disability, autism, Asperger's syndrome, and Fragile X syndrome expands the professional's skills and enables one to assess the presence of a concomitant disorder. Often, an anxiety disorder can mask as an attentional disorder. So, too, can a seizure disorder with petit mal seizures mask as "lapses" in attention. It takes an astute professional to raise the question and seek the help of an expert(s) to help sort out the diagnosis for the benefit of the child/client.

Chapter 3

Associated Language and Auditory Processing Problems

Children with AD/HD have measurable problems in processing language, both receptively and expressively, which is often also true for those with a designated auditory processing disorder. (Refer to Figure 1.2 on pages 7–8 for a list of language characteristics of AD/HD subtypes.) Although the latter is considered an input disorder, while AD/HD is considered an output disorder, both groups share many of the same characteristics, which surely impose restrictions on language comprehension. It is often difficult to draw a line between audition and language comprehension, particularly for those individuals for whom perception and comprehension of verbally presented speech is impaired. **Top-down** concept driven factors influence **bottom-up** auditory perceptual events. Auditory perception influences spoken language. The ability to perceive phonemes is not only dependent upon acoustic-feature encoding, but influenced by exposure to and experience with speech sounds of the language, memory, auditory discrimination, and coarticulation. A person does not perceive isolated sounds. Acoustic properties and phonemic processing are interrelated and contribute to a higher-order language process. Experience also impacts speech-sound processing that alters spoken language. Language cues, contextual and otherwise, have an influence on perception. Such cues include knowledge of prosody, semantics, pragmatics, and vocabulary; familiarity with language; and word predictability. In cases where language is easy for an individual to understand, he or she can fill in the missing components. For others, filling in (a cloze task) is not easy.

Processing of language stimuli, like any sensory stimuli, depends on the ability to pay attention adequately. Anything interfering with attending

Top-Down
A model that stresses the influence of the higher levels (i.e., the message which is comprehended) on the processing of words and letters. Processes that use pre-existing knowledge or context to interpret that information. To get the gestalt and then analyze its parts.

Bottom-Up
A model that views the process of comprehension as proceeding linearly from the isolated units in the lower levels (e.g., letters, words) to higher levels of comprehension. Processes that register and integrate sensory information, and are data-driven.

Metalinguistics
Aspects of language competence that extend beyond unconscious usage for comprehension and production; involves ability to think about language in its abstract form.

Metacognition
Awareness and appropriate use of knowledge; awareness of the task and strategy variables that affect performance and the use of that knowledge to plan, monitor, and regulate performance, including attention, learning, and the use of language; second phase in the development of knowledge, which is active and involves conscious control over knowledge.

to the signal will affect auditory processing. A deficiency in the reticular activity system, which mediates overall arousal, can make a listener unaware of a signal. Attention deficits can impact the listener's ability to attend to and process auditory input. Dysfunction in parietal and frontal regions of the brain (as seen in AD/HD) can affect auditory processing in spite of an intact auditory mechanism. When input is affected, so is output. Auditory processing relies on executive functioning which serves to coordinate behavioral responses. Learning, planning, decision-making, and goal-setting comprise executive training. Attention is critical to the process of listening and coordinating. According to Goldenberg, Oder, Spatt, and Podreka (1992), damage in the cortical areas such as the basal ganglia, thalamus, frontal lobe, temporal lobe, and parietal lobe can affect executive functioning and listening skills.

Ultimately, input does affect output—as do many sensory modalities. Many children and adolescents have learning problems that negatively affect the modalities of language. Typical problems cited are in syntax, semantics, pragmatics, and **metalinguistics.** Auditory processing and **metacognition** often are affected. Children may present with short-term auditory memory deficits, difficulty following directions of length, reduced speed of processing, written and spoken language deficits, and problems listening in the classroom or in a room with competing stimuli. Poor reading comprehension, writing, handwriting, and keeping to the point are reported difficulties. Providing tangential information, inability to get to the point, giving unnecessary details, rambling or a verbal mazing in conversation, along with word-finding problems are reported. The ability to infer a meaning from a statement, to understand the nuances or the nonliteral meaning, is often overlooked.

Social language is another deficiency in that these individuals do not often read social cues appropriately, misread social cues, and say the wrong thing at the wrong time. Often the standard battery of speech-language testing does not accurately reflect these difficulties, since they are subtle, or require further probing. Tests that measure metacognitive skills, nonliteral language, and story narratives are more beneficial in disclosing these deficiencies. In fact, if professionals used different, more discerning instruments in assessing these children, or recognized that the children they were assessing had an AD/HD problem, there would be more identification and data on their language issues.

The literature outlines the prevalence of language impairment in this population. According to Cohen, Vallance, Barwick, and Im (2000), language impairments are commonly observed among children referred for psychiatric services. The most frequent psychiatric diagnosis of children with language impairments is attention-deficit/hyperactivity disorder. However, it is not clear whether there are differences between children with AD/HD and comorbid language impairments and children with other psychiatric disorders who are also comorbid for language impairments.

Reading Disability

Often reading impairments are reported along with AD/HD, compounding an already complex problem. In **electroencephalography** (EEG) studies of children with reading disability (RD), researchers (John et al., 1977) found that 87 percent of such children had EEG divergences (i.e., excessive levels of theta activity, excessive delta and theta wave activity in the parieto-occipital regions, and deficiencies in alpha activity). A number of studies have found increased slow-wave activity in the left hemisphere, especially the posterior region. Few studies have investigated EEG differences in AD/HD children with and without comorbid RD.

In a study investigating AD/HD children, AD/HD with learning delays, and AD/HD with dyslexia, the AD/HD group had greater parietal and midline low-frequency beta than the other two groups (Clarke, Barry, McCarthy, & Selikowitz, 2002). In their study of mixed AD/HD children, having either inattentive or hyperactive forms, a different EEG profile was seen. In their study, Clarke et al. found that the group identified as having AD/HD with RD had more relative theta, less relative alpha, and a higher theta/alpha ratio than the group with AD/HD alone.

A number of hemispheric differences were also found in the delta and alpha bands, suggesting that some of the EEG divergences found in the AD/HD+RD group represent an electrophysiological component associated with the reading disability that is independent of the EEG divergences found in AD/HD. This would support the thinking that although RD is often found in children with AD/HD, the disorders are independent. Further, in the EEG of children with inattentive and combined types of AD/HD, the latter group had similar but more extreme EEG divergences than the children with the inattentive type. The extra EEG divergences found in the AD/HD+RD

Electro-encephalograph (EEG) A procedure where electrodes are placed on the scalp to record the electrical activity of the brain.

group represented another electrophysiological component that is associated with RD and more likely independent of the AD/HD diagnosis (Clarke et al.). The differences found between the two clinical groups in this study were similar to the EEG divergences found in other studies that compared children with RD and children without disabilities.

Positron emission tomography (PET) studies involving language tasks have found differences in the left hemispheres of children with RD compared to children without RD (Flowers, 1993). An inferior left parietal component was associated with word meaning in children with RD. In the Clarke et al. (2002) study, the AD/HD+RD group also showed higher left posterior absolute delta than the AD/HD group. Delta activity has been associated with underarousal which is consistent with the studies that found decreased left-parietal-region activation. Such results support the finding that there is an atypical functioning in the left posterior region of the brain in RD. The right posterior region compensates for the left hemispheric posterior difficulties in children with RD (Pugh et al., 2000). The right posterior regions have been associated with affective components of language and with narrative passage reading. The AD/HD group in the Clarke et al. study had more right hemisphere relative delta and less relative alpha. These results suggest underarousal in the right posterior region as well as in the left region. Pugh's recent findings (2004) support more activation in the right hemisphere than in the left for reading-impaired adults. The number of hemispheric differences found between the AD/HD+RD group and AD/HD group support the independence of components of the two groups, indicating that the groups have distinct electrophysiological components. The RD group has components that are different from those found in children with AD/HD, although the two disorders commonly occur together.

In Breier et al. (2001), researchers investigating the comorbidity of reading disorder and AD/HD suggest that these two deficits do not necessarily interact in a synergistic manner. Although children with AD/HD exhibited reduced shallower slopes on category labeling functions for speech and nonspeech stimuli, as seen on a task of **voice onset time** and **tone onset time** continua, they were not significant, and the effects of RD were independent of the presence of AD/HD. Since reading disability is often associated with language impairment, it is not clear whether the language impairments per se are specific to AD/HD or comorbid.

Voice onset time
Time between the stop consonant and the beginning of voicing in the vowel; time required to initiate sound at the vocal cords.

Tone onset time
Nonspeech analog of voice onset time series consisting of two tones that mimic voice onset time.

Language Impairments

The language abilities of children with AD/HD with and without reading disability were investigated in a task requiring recall of lengthy narratives and
in tests assessing knowledge of the semantic aspects of language. A study
with 14 AD/HD only, 14 AD/HD and RD, 8 RD, and 14 controls aged 7–11
(Purvis & Tannock, 1997) found that children with AD/HD exhibited difficulties in organizing and monitoring their story retelling. The task of story
retelling was selected because attention to the incoming information was
required along with extraction of meaning and relevance, encoding into
memory, and reconstruction from memory. This requires judgment to
enable the information to be organized, coherent, and sensitive to the
needs of the listener. The ability to conduct the latter, which requires
effortful organization, planning, and self-monitoring, involves executive
functions (i.e., high-level cognitive skills).

Results indicated that children with AD/HD+RD, and those with RD-only,
had deficits in receptive and expressive semantic language on language processing tests. The deficiencies found in the AD/HD group were consistent
with those found in higher order executive functioning. The deficits found
in the RD children were consistent with basic semantics of language processing. The AD/HD group, regardless of RD status, had difficulty organizing
and monitoring their verbal production. The AD/HD group exhibited a higher incidence of sequence errors, which affected the global organization of
the story. The AD/HD-only group had trouble with ambiguous references with
failure in cohesion, making it difficult to follow the speaker's train of thought.
The AD/HD-only group and the AD/HD+RD group were more likely to misin-
terpret information and to use inappropriate word substitutions, in the
absence of comprehension failure. The authors interpreted this finding as a
failure of test subjects to monitor the accuracy of the information and a pragmatic difficulty with language usage. The inability to relate ideas specifically
and accurately in a logical sequence results in disunity in discourse and
makes comprehension by the listener difficult (Prutting & Kirchner, 1987).
The researchers concluded that the language deficits of AD/HD children without RD seem to reflect difficulties with language use (pragmatics) rather than
deficits with the basic subsystems of language.

Pragmatics

The use of language in social context requires knowledge about the speaker, the listener, and the setting. According to Bloom (as cited in Lahey, 1988):

> The three major aspects of language use (or pragmatics) are: (1) the use of language for different goals or functions, (2) the use of information from the context to determine what we say in order to achieve the goals, and (3) the use of the interaction between persons to initiate, maintain, and terminate conversations. (p. 15)

Communicative competence involves knowing what to say; who says it; to whom, where, and when it is said; and by what means it is said. Pragmatics is a "study of speaker-listener intentions and relations, and all elements surrounding the message" (Nicolosi, Harryman, & Kresheck, 2004, p. 246). Pragmatic difficulties, such as with turn-taking and maintaining a conversation, have been demonstrated in AD/HD children (Humphries, Koltun, Malone, & Roberts, 1994). Such difficulties may be related to deficits in executive functions. Executive functions are **self-regulatory processes** which are responsible for the organization and monitoring of information processing, mobilizing attention, and inhibiting responding (Douglas, Barr, Amin, O'Neill, & Britton, 1988). This finding suggests that children with AD/HD should receive instruction in self-monitoring and awareness of language use in language contexts which require more than mere sentence structure, per se.

Self-regulatory processes
The ability to manage and regulate one's own behavior.

The Children's Communication Checklist (CCC; Bishop, 1998), developed to provide an objective assessment of pragmatic aspects of children's communication, completed by parents and a professional knowledgeable about the child, indicated that the lowest scores were obtained for children with autism, followed by those with Asperger's syndrome, pervasive developmental disorder (PDD), and then AD/HD. The highest scores were obtained for those with a diagnosis of specific learning disability (Bishop & Baird, 2001).

In agreement, Westby and Cutler (1994), reported that children with AD/HD have a secondary language problem that arises as part of the executive function disorder. The vocabulary and syntax appear normal, but language that is used for monitoring or language that requires organization, such as extended discourse, is difficult for these individuals. Typical errors may be in structuring a story, maintaining a topic, or any activity that requires language to monitor their performance. During reading, individuals may fail to monitor their comprehension and be less likely to notice something that is in contradiction with that previously read. The child's ability to use language to plan ahead, problem solve, or produce **narrative** or **expository discourse** is most affected. Thus, work on social skills, organization, and management of behavior will be effective in helping youngsters to function.

The following pragmatic problems are often evident:

- *Difficulties in social context and using appropriate verbal and nonverbal language.* Individuals may not read the social situation at hand, often misreading cues and facial expressions, or neglecting to pick up nonverbal body language. For an example, see Sidebar 3.1.

- *Limited exchange of greetings.* Individuals are often not aware of basic social graces or verbal exchanges that would enable children to enter a social group, or adults to participate in a community group activity. Social graces are often absent. Simple "thank-yous" for presents are often forgotten.

Narrative discourse
Orderly continuous account of an event or series of events.

Expository discourse
Narrations of logic-based knowledge; purpose is for instructing, comparing, explaining, and offering an opinion.

Sidebar 3.1   **Example of Difficulties in Social Context**

Jimmy was celebrating his 10th birthday. To improve his popularity, his parents decided to make him a birthday party for his entire class. They told him to go into class the next day and invite every student in his class. He did that and came home the next day announcing that everyone was coming. The parents prepared a lavish party for the class of 22 children. When Saturday afternoon arrived, no one showed up! When questions were raised to the teacher on Monday, the parents found out that the way Jimmy asked was so off-handed and the way the children responded was so indefinite, that he should not have anticipated that all the children would be attending the party. The result was a big misunderstanding, but a terrible memory for a boy on his 10th birthday.

- *Difficulty expressing intent.* Individuals are unable to express what it is they want to say, often expecting the other person to understand what was meant. This misunderstanding often occurs between couples with "she said" and "he said,"—neither of them express what they want to say, yet expect the other person to know what was intended.

- *Limitations in inquiring.* Individuals often don't ask for clarification or repetition for a direction they did not understand or hear clearly. For an example, see Sidebar 3.2.

Sidebar 3.2   Example of Limitations in Inquiring

Joseph was in the sound booth undergoing auditory training. He was asked to respond to questions following the reading of a story. At the end of the story, when asked what it was about, he responded "I don't know. I couldn't hear you." The microphone was not turned on. Naturally he couldn't hear the speaker. It never occurred to him to say anything.

- *Limitations in requesting information.* Often children will come home from school with an assignment that they don't fully understand. They will not think to ask a buddy or the teacher for a more complete explanation. Sometimes the person feels "stupid" asking for more information.

- *Difficulty initiating/terminating conversation.* Individuals seem to have difficulty starting a conversation or knowing how to end one. This leads to difficulty breaking into groups or affiliating with the group of one's choice. For an example, see Sidebar 3.3.

Sidebar 3.3   Example of Difficulties in Conversation

Lydia, a 13 year-old middle school child, was complaining that she had a great deal of difficulty being accepted by her peers. Her school had all kinds of cliques and she was desirous of being in one particular clique. She didn't know how to "break into their conversation." When role-playing the situation, her behavior was indeed inappropriate. She merely sat there listening as if she was eavesdropping on their conversation.

- *Difficulty maintaining a topic.* Individuals struggle to stay on topic, derailing to other areas, providing a great deal of unnecessary facts or information. This is not to be confused with Asperger's syndrome. The degree to which it occurs is not the same, and the AD/HD person is usually aware of this trait.

Working Memory

Working memory is information maintained for short periods. Such material has a specific temporal context. Rehearsal is critical to actively maintain the information in working memory. In a model described by Honig (1978) and Olton (1979), language is deemed to be the critical determinant of how information is to be remembered, with verbal information processed differently than nonverbal information.

An area often implicated as an area of language impairment is working memory, which is seen as a component of long-term memory that serves for a limited time. It involves storage and processing of information deemed to be an executive process. Cohen et al. (2000) noted that working memory measures used to tap the core cognitive deficit of AD/HD in executive functions were more closely associated with language impairments (LI). That is, those individuals with LI had a propensity for having a working memory deficit. The range of structural language impairments investigated in the literature on AD/HD has been limited to those underlying reading disorders, particularly phonological processing. In a broad-range study of receptive and expressive language characteristics (Cohen et al.), children who had been diagnosed as having both AD/HD and language impairment were found to exhibit more severe receptive language impairment if they had expressive language impairment than did children with AD/HD alone. Low IQ scores and poor visual-motor integration have been associated with both LI and AD/HD. Children with comorbid conditions have more severe problems in general. Deficiencies in cognitive measures of executive function—particularly those that tap inhibitory control—were also implicated. Working memory, an aspect of executive function, is considered to be a necessary component in cognitive measures.

McInnes, Humphries, Hogg-Johnson, and Tannock (2003) investigated listening comprehension and working memory abilities in children with AD/HD, presenting with and without language impairments (LI). They produced a series of basic language and cognitive tests to measure verbal and

Working memory
A set of linked and interacting information processing components that maintain information in a short-term memory store for the purpose of the active manipulation of the stored items (Becker & Morris, 1999).

Verbal span
A listing of words to be repeated.

Spatial span
Ability to perceive, understand, and manipulate objects in space.

spatial working memory and passage-level listening comprehension. Results indicated that children who did not have comorbid LI comprehended factual information from spoken passages as well as did children with typical development. However, they were poorer at comprehending inferences and monitoring comprehension of instructions. Children with AD/HD did not differ from typical children in **verbal span,** but showed significantly poorer verbal working memory, **spatial span,** and spatial working memory. The AD/HD and LI, and LI groups were most impaired in listening comprehension and working memory performance, but did not differ from each other. Listening comprehension skills were significantly correlated with both verbal and spatial working memory and parent-teacher ratings of inattention and hyperactivity/impulsivity. The researchers further concluded that children with AD/HD but no LI showed subtle higher level listening comprehension deficits.

Barkley (1998) postulated that a developmental impairment as a result of the AD/HD is associated with problems in self-directed speech and in internalization of language and its use for self-regulation and mental representation. Thus, children with AD/HD encounter more difficulties in higher order executive functioning, which includes verbal mediation and planning, goal-directed behavioral guidance, than in spontaneous speech (Zentall, 1988). Not only must children understand rules, they must retrieve, organize, and express them. In this way, language structure takes on a greater function as children get older, as development of internalized language for self-regulation comes to depend on adequate receptive and expressive language skills. Language impairments are highly prevalent in a psychiatric population (Cohen, Barwick, Horodozky, Vallance, & Im, 1998).

Given the large component and comorbidity of language impairment in the population with AD/HD, and the fact that some children have a history of language delay (Westby & Cutler, 1994), it is incumbent upon evaluators to investigate language skills when making a clinical diagnosis. Further, language competence impacts the effectiveness of most therapies that are verbally based, such as behavioral and social skills training. It is essential to make a detailed analysis of language functioning in children with AD/HD in view of the potential role that language deficits play in explaining some of the basic underpinnings of AD/HD (Barkley, 1998). The typical speech-language deficits seen in the population of children with AD/HD are organized into input and output disorders and summarized next.

Input Disorders/Receptive Language Problems

Children with AD/HD have a propensity for comprehension difficulties due to:

- *Limited auditory memory.* Individuals have trouble remembering serial numbers and words, or lengthy sentences.

- ***Reauditorization*** *and temporal sequencing deficits.* Individuals have difficulty repeating a sequence as they hear it, or saying it in their heads, which is a common strategy for recall.

- *Linguistic processing deficits, with poor interpretation of ambiguous sentences, idioms, puns, jokes, and analogies.* Individuals have difficulty interpreting jokes or ambiguous remarks, often missing sarcasm, taking comments seriously when meant to be funny, or misjudging the intent of the speaker.

- *Increased latency in responding, and reduced speed of processing.* Individuals do not respond quickly to a question or comment, taking more time than expected, often asking, "What?" as a "stall technique" until the information is processed.

- *Difficulty understanding spoken messages in the presence of competition (e.g., noise, other speakers).* Individuals have trouble hearing in noisy places, at restaurants, during events, and in large rooms with reverberant walls.

- *Mishearing.* Individuals often hear one word for another and miss a fact or command. Interesting examples are provided in Sidebar 3.4.

Reauditorization
Verbal mediation, to repeat to oneself in an inaudible voice.

Sidebar 3.4 **Examples of Mishearing**

These were written by children in Hebrew and Catholic schools and have not been retouched for incorrect spelling, etc.:

- The Egyptians were all drowned in the dessert. Afterwards, Moses went up on Mount Cyanide to get the ten amendments.
- The first commandment was when Eve told Adam to eat the apple.
- The seventh commandment is: "Thou shalt not admit adultery."
- Moses died before he ever reached Canada.
- Then Joshua led the Hebrews in the battle of Geritol.

- *Comprehension difficulties in understanding the main idea or intent of the spoken passage, especially as the passage gets lengthier and more complex.* Individuals have difficulty summarizing what they heard or sorting main ideas from details.

- *Difficulties understanding nonliteral meanings.* Individuals have difficulty distinguishing a literal from a nonliteral phrase or expression, reflecting a concreteness in thinking and in expressions. For example, when Garth heard his mother tell him that he had to "broaden his perspective on life and expand his horizons," he promptly went out and joined the Sailing Club at school. When he arrived home, he proudly told his mother what he did to "broaden his horizon." "I will sail the seas to see the horizon," he said to her.

Output Disorders/
Expressive Language Problems

Children with AD/HD have difficulty communicating and struggle to formulate their thoughts in an organized manner, to get to the point efficiently, and to say what they mean. The individual, whether a child or an adult, often has trouble with concise self-expression, or with finding the right words. Typical problems in expressive language include:

- *Paraphasic errors.* Individuals transpose syllables *(ephelant/elephant, evelator/elevator)* in multisyllabic words, or transpose words in lengthy sentences.

- *Word-finding difficulty.* Individuals have difficulty retrieving the word they want to use, often substituting one word for another, or using "fillers" such as *thing, thingy, stuff.* Word-finding problems are one of the most frequent difficulties reported from clinicians. Individuals do not have a deficiency in vocabulary, but rather in finding the word they want to use.

- *Word substitution errors.* Individuals use one word, often incorrectly, in place of another, sometimes because of mishearing. Some examples are provided in Sidebar 3.5.

Sidebar 3.5   **Examples of Word Substitution Errors**

My father is a vegeternarian. (Veterinarian)
Do I have to read about the Silver War? (Civil War)
The dogs run in place. (The dogs run and play.)
Did you park the cart? (Did you start the car?)

- *Delay in onset of expressive language.* Some children with AD/HD have typically delayed onset of language development (i.e., they're "late talkers" with immature speech for the first few years of life).

- *Difficulty expressing feelings.* Individuals often have trouble expressing emotions, paying compliments, or telling how they feel in intimate relationships or friendships.

- *Poor use of referents.* Individuals do not use appropriate designators, or pronoun identifiers, to indicate about whom they are talking; they use *he, she,* or *it* for different agents; listeners don't know to whom the person is referring, or when the event happened, particularly if it requires an organized sequence of events.

- *Sequencing difficulties.* When telling about a situation, the action is often out of sequence, making it difficult to follow the story.

- *Overshooting the main idea.* When telling a story, or telling about an event, the individual goes on and on, giving details far too over-reaching than need be, going on relentlessly. This is sometimes referred to as "verbal mazing," not getting to the point/main idea, or "verbal logorrhea."

Attention-Deficit/Hyperactivity Disorder

A Language Deficits and AD/HD Checklist is presented as a thumbnail view in Figure 3.1 and included in Study More 3.1 on the CD-ROM. It can be printed from the CD-ROM and used for individual children to document the presence or absence of concomitant language deficits along with AD/HD.

Figure 3.1

Language Deficits and AD/HD Checklist

Client Name: _____ Date: _____

Person(s) Completing This Checklist: _____

Possible Language Deficit	Yes	No
Receptive Language		
Reduced auditory memory		
Poor comprehension		
Poor interpretation of ambiguous language, humor, or puns		
Reduced latency in response		
Asks, "What?" or "Huh?" frequently		
Difficulty understanding nonliteral language		
Expressive Language		
Paraphasic errors		
Word-finding difficulty		
Poor use of referents		
Poor sequencing ability		
Difficulty getting to the point (overshooting the main idea)		
Pragmatic Language		
Does not read social context		
Misreads nonverbal cues		
Limited exchange of greetings		
Limitation in inquiring, exchanging greetings, initiating, and terminating conversation		
Difficulty maintaining conversational topic		

Comments:

Auditory Processing Disorders

The AD/HD population has problems in listening and following directions. In fact, the original definition on the *DSM–III* indicated these auditory behaviors as deficient and listed them as critical components in the diagnosis. The *DSM–IV* refers to some of the same behaviors. Often this population has auditory processing deficits, and many consider the two to be interchangeable, that is, a person with AD/HD struggles with auditory processing problems much the same as an individual diagnosed with central auditory processing disorder ((C)APD) struggle with attentional problems. It is often too difficult to differentially diagnose the two, particularly since the rate of co-occurrence is high (DiMaggio & Geffner, 2003).

The typical auditory processing characteristics occurring in this group are:

- *(C)APD.* According to recent data (Dimaggio & Geffner, 2003), 84 percent of a population of 407 (C)APD children had confirmed or suspected AD/HD, as indicated on the Attention Deficit Disorders Evaluation Scale (McCarney, 1995). The percentage of AD/HD children having (C)APD is not yet known since not all children diagnosed with AD/HD are tested.

- *Normal peripheral hearing.* Individuals usually have normal peripheral hearing.

- *Subacute hearing (hyperacusis).* Hearing levels are often better than 0 dB threshold. For example, parents report that these children hear an airplane before it approaches.

- *Hypersensitivity to loud noise.* Data reveal that children with AD/HD respond with more sensitivity to lower levels of loudness sooner than a non-AD/HD population (Lucker, Geffner, & Koch, 1996). For example, parents frequently reported that their child was unable to sit at a circus or go to a birthday party because it was too noisy.

- *Reduced tolerance for loud noise.* Parents report that their children with AD/HD would often cry when the environment became too loud. For example, a child might put his hands over his ears whenever a fire engine approached. In a study investigating comfort levels of hearing and tolerance levels, children with AD/HD were shown to

Attention-Deficit/Hyperactivity Disorder

have statistically lower levels of comfort and tolerance of loud noises (Lucker et al., 1996).

- *Poor speech discrimination in noise.* Individuals have difficulty listening in noisy situations. Discrimination skills are measurably compromised in the presence of competing auditory stimuli (Geffner, Lucker, & Koch, 1996).

- *Reduced auditory memory for commands and sequences.* Individuals complain that they cannot retain long commands or follow multi-step directions, often forgetting a part. For example, when a child on a subtest of the Test of Auditory Processing Skills–3rd Edition (TAPS–3; Martin & Brownell, 2005), was asked "What would you say if I told you to go to the table, take out your math workbook, turn to page 9, and do all the problems of addition before lunch?", the child responded, "I would say what you just said!"

- *Recalls first or last part of sequence only and forgets what is said soon after.* Because of reduced short-term memory, individuals often recall only part of the multi-step command—the first or the last. Often children are quick to complete the last part of the command first, while still holding it their memory bank. The **recency effect** is when one recalls the item he or she heard last. The **primacy effect** is recalling the first part of the multi-step command.

- *Easily distracted while in background noise.* Individuals are readily distracted by any background noise. They lose their focus and listen to the voices outside the room, rather than to the speaker in the room. This occurrence is similar for visual stimuli. These individuals often focus on the small dot, rather than on the whole design.

- *Auditory figure-ground deficits.* Individuals' hearing discrimination falters when there is background noise. Whenever the signal-to-noise level is reduced, making the listening condition less than ideal, these individuals have trouble discriminating words. This problem is often undetected until the person answers a question incorrectly.

- *Auditory integration deficits for sound blending.* Individuals often have trouble sounding out words when reading or discriminating sound segments or syllable segments in a word, a skill necessary for decoding a reading passage. Phonemic synthesis is often compromised, as is reading phonemically.

- ***Auditory closure.*** The ability to fill in the missing sounds of a word, when frequencies or parts of the word are missing, is compromised, as measured on auditory processing disorder tests.

An Auditory Deficits and AD/HD Checklist is presented as a thumbnail in Figure 3.2 and is included as Study More 3.2 on the CD-ROM. It can be printed from the CD-ROM and used to document the presence or absence of specific deficits.

Auditory closure
Ability to integrate auditory stimuli into a whole (i.e., completion of a word or words by filling in the parts omitted when the word or words are spoken).

Figure 3.2

Auditory Deficits and AD/HD Checklist

Client Name: _____ Date: _____

Person(s) Completing This Checklist: _____

Possible Auditory Deficits	Yes	No
Hypersensitive to noise		
Poor speech discrimination in noise		
Easily distracted in noise		
Deficits in phonological awareness including sound blending and phonemic awareness		
Reduced auditory memory for spoken messages		
Difficulty following multi-step directions		

Comments:

Perceptual Deficits

In addition to the compromising of receptive and expressive language skills, one cannot overlook the perceptual deficits that often accompany this population:

- Unable to read emotions in others
- Social imperception
- Failure to convey emotions
- Trouble perceiving where they are in space, in relation to other people and objects

These individuals have a difficult time in psychotherapy because of an inability to express their feelings or detect the feelings of others. They are often labeled "insensitive" to others, which impacts their ability to be social, engage in relationships, and sustain long-term, meaningful relationships.

They often come into a room and step on toes, overthrow a vase, walk into someone, or bump into a table because they do not judge the distance or notice the objects in their surroundings. It is not clumsiness, but rather an imperception of their body in space.

For a Perceptual Deficits and AD/HD Checklist, see Figure 3.3 and Study More 3.3 on the CD-ROM. This checklist may be printed from the CD-ROM and used with individual children or adults to profile weaknesses and strengths.

Written Language Deficits

Written language skills are often not assessed in youngsters with oral language deficits. As is the case with this population, children with AD/HD presenting with receptive and expressive language disorders are often prone to similar deficits in written language. Only in text can errors of spelling, punctuation, and grammar become apparent. Such seems to be evident. Although not clinically confirmed, it is a frequent occurrence to see syntax and spelling errors in a written sample. Such problems in written language are manifested when the child has difficulty writing, getting started on a writing assignment, writing more than a few sentences, combining paragraphs into a cohesive story, writing the story in an organized sequence of events, producing structures consistent with grade level, and

Figure 3.3

Perceptual Deficits and
AD/HD Checklist

Client Name: _____   Date: _____

Person(s) Completing This Checklist: _____

Possible Perceptual Deficits	Yes	No
Difficulty reading emotions		
Difficulty picking up on social cues and nonverbal language		
Difficulty conveying emotions		
Trouble perceiving self in relation to other people or objects		

Comments:

elaborating on details. Language is often simple, with spelling errors (words are spelled according to how they are heard). There is a paucity of vocabulary with little use of **metaphors** and **similes**. Sentence structures are immature for age level. Examples of written samples are presented on page 62. They include:

- A 12 year-old, seventh grade boy, Billy, was asked to write an expository passage defending an opinion. Note the spelling and punctuation errors (Figure 3.4)

- A spelling list by a 12 year-old boy (Figure 3.5)

- A spelling list by a 10 year-old girl (Figure 3.6)

- An 8 year-old third grade girl was asked to write about the family boat (Figure 3.7)

Metaphor
Implied comparison of two or more objects, which in most respects are totally unlike, without the word *like* or *as*.

Simile
An explicit comparison between two things using *like* or *as*.

Attention Deficit Disorder

Figure 3.4

Dear Bobby,

I think that Kids should have gym. Gym is important because I gets the kids burn of there energy. Which is good because some Kids need to burn of same energy.

My second resone is that if kids sit down all day without moving they could get out of shape. That is not good because we need kids to play after school sports.

last but not least kids grades can as drown because they wouldn't want to listen because they can be get tired. That would give our school a bad reputation. Thats not good.

Sincerly,
Billy

Figure 3.5

Mrs Connor   12/6/03

1. Navaho   Navaho
2. photography   photography
3. traditional   traditional
4. terciose   terquiose
5. jewlry   jewelry
6. bargain   bargain
7. exquisite   exquisite
8. treasure   treasure
9. heritage   heritage
10. vendor   vendor
11. culture   culture
12. perepectue   perspective
13. egypt   Egypt
14. hierogliphs   hieroglyhs
15. harass   harass
16. there   there
17. theyre   theyre
18. their   their
19. gaurantee   gaurantee
20. guidince   guidence

Figure 3.6

Patricia Marie.   x^13/20   8/12

1. ouder order I will ouder a hot Dog   1 funny ✓
2. pretty You're pretty.   2 exaped expect
3. markit market Lets go to the mark it. 3 affter after
4. hello Hello, how are you ok?   4 stuben stubben
5. window Why did you jump out the window?
6. dallon dollar
7. Monday
8. Sudden
9. until
10. forget
11. happen
12. flews Follow

Figure 3.7

It is a left of work to get a Old Bustohe Wallr But My dad had a Bastohe Wallek so My dad know how to yous a Bystoh Waller.

8 yeold 3rd grader

62

A Written Language Deficits and AD/HD Checklist is presented in Figure 3.8 and is included in Study More 3.4 on the CD-ROM. It can be printed and used to document the presence or absence of specific written language deficits.

Figure 3.8

Written Language Deficits and AD/HD Checklist

Client Name: _____ Date: _____

Person(s) Completing This Checklist: _____

Possible Written Language Deficits	Yes	No
Little elaboration or description		
Immature structures		
Spelling errors		
Punctuation errors		
Little elaboration of details		
Paucity of vocabulary		
Poor transitions between paragraphs		

Comments:

Factors Contributing to Attention-Deficit/Hyperactivity Disorder

Early Middle-Ear Infection in Children

Chronic suppurative otitis media (OM) is an inflammation of the middle ear accompanied by pus that persists for more than three months. The child who has experienced recurrent ear infections along with persistent middle ear effusion appears to be at greatest risk for language impairment and auditory processing deficits. The population with severe otitis media is more apt to have language and learning problems by school age. So, too, is a population of AD/HD more apt to report incidences of otitis media. In a study by Hagerman and Falkenstein (1987), 94 percent of children diagnosed with ADD and medicated with psychostimulants experienced 3 or more episodes of chronic otitis media, and 69 percent had experienced more than 10 infections. They found 50 percent of children who experienced school failure but were not hyperactive had had three or more episodes.

Darling and Sedgwick (2003) found a correlation between OM and subsequent auditory processing deficits (SAPD). However, many factors may contribute to the extent of the auditory deficit. The study compared 20 normal hearing individuals without a history of OM and 20 normal hearing individuals (ages 18 to 30) with self-proclaimed childhood history of recurrent OM. The SCAN-A: A Test for Auditory Processing Disorders in Adolescents and Adults (Keith, 1994) was used to obtain the data. The results of the total test standard scores of the SCAN-A suggest that adults with childhood history of OM had a higher incidence of signs of auditory processing disorders (APD) than individuals without significant childhood history of OM. These adults had more difficulty with auditory closure, with listening in the presence of background noise, and with binaural integration tasks.

Table 3.1, illustrates the prevalence of otitis media with effusion among children diagnosed with central auditory processing disorders. Fifty percent had a history of two or more occurrences of otitis media with effusion (OME; Marasa & Geffner, 2003). However, this is not exceptional from a normal population.

Table 3.1 **Prevalence of OME, Reading Disorder, and Neurobiological Indicators in Children with (C)APD**

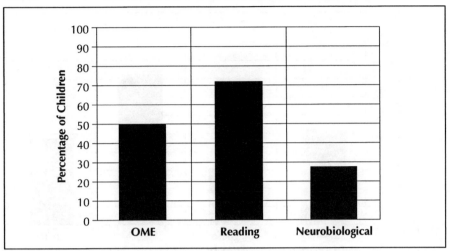

Source: Marasa and Geffner (2003)

Central Auditory Processing Disorders

Often the diagnosis between AD/HD and (C)APD are so interchangeable that it is difficult to differentially diagnose the two disorders from one another. They frequently co-occur. Table 3.2 on page 66 illustrates the outcome of a study of 407 children identified as having (C)APD. Among 407 children identified as having a (C)APD, DiMaggio and Geffner (2003) found that 84 percent had been diagnosed or suspected to have attention deficit disorder. The final word is not out yet regarding the comorbidity or whether these two disorders are in fact separate entities, or if they are part of a larger processing deficiency. Perhaps brain scans and PET scans will put this argument to rest.

Nevertheless, we have some evidence to help us differentiate between the two disorders, primarily the prevalence or prominence of particular behaviors, indigenous to each, as identified by professionals working with these populations.

(C)APD and APD are defined as sensory-perceptual deficits in the processing of information that is specific to the auditory modality (Jerger & Musiek, 2000). Individuals with APD present deficits in one or more of the following behaviors: sound localization/lateralization, auditory discrimination, auditory pattern recognition, temporal aspects of auditory processing,

Table 3.2

Prevalence of AD/HD, Speech-Language Delay, & Familial Indicators in Children with (C)APD

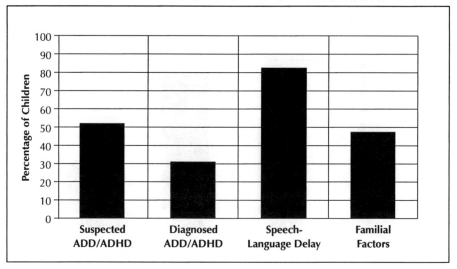

Source: DiMaggio and Geffner (2003)

and performance deficits when the auditory signal is in competing noise or with other acoustic signals, or when the auditory signal is degraded, muffled, or filtered. (C)APD is associated with attentional components that cause difficulty in listening in noise or reverberant backgrounds or following oral directions. Since AD/HD has been conceptualized as an executive function disorder and a disorder of behavioral self-regulation that leads to problems in initiating, inhibiting, and sustaining or shifting attention to tasks, such conceptualization leaves one category of inattention most like (C)APD. The symptoms most associated with AD/HD-inattention share similar behaviors to APD. However, the AD/HD-I subgroup diagnosis is based on behaviors, whereas the APD group diagnosis is based on a battery of behavioral tests and, at times, electrophysiological measures. The former has no empirical markers other than behavioral observations which must be made by physicians. Nevertheless, based on Chermak, Tucker, and Seikel (2002), following an analysis of responses to a questionnaire completed by 100 physicians and 100 audiologists, comparison of behaviors emerged. These are summarized in Table 3.3.

Results indicated that in spite of marked differences in pediatricians' and audiologists' rankings, there was some degree of overlap across the disorders. The differences were explained on the basis that different sources were at the root of similar behaviors, (i.e., cognitive disorder

Table 3.3   **Comparison of AD/HD and (C)APD Behaviors**

AD/HD	(C)APD
Inattentive	Asks for things to be repeated
Academic difficulties	Poor listening skills
Daydreams	Difficulty following oral instructions
Distracted	Difficulty hearing in background noise
Poor listening skills	Academic difficulties
Disorganized	Distracted
Asks for things to be repeated	Reduced rate of information processing
Auditory divided attention deficit	Auditory divided attention deficit
Difficulty hearing in background noise	Auditory selective attention deficit
	Poor memory
	Difficulty discriminating speech

From "Behavioral Characteristics of Auditory Processing Disorder and Attention Deficit Hyperactivity Disorder: Predominantly Inattentive Types," by G. D. Chermak, E. Tucker, and J. A. Seikel, 2002, *Journal of the American Academy of Audiology, 13*(6), pp. 332–338. © 2002 by the *Journal of the American Academy of Audiology.* Adapted with permission.

involving disorganization and executive function in AD/HD-I), whereas the difficulties in (C)APD stem from a perceptual disorder causing deficits in processing information through the auditory channel. It is clear that further research is needed to differentiate the two disorders. Additional differences can be seen in Table 3.4 on page 68.

Interview

To elaborate on the symptomatology that was described in this chapter, "listen in" on an interview with a parent regarding the assessment of her son's language and auditory problems. Sidebar 3.5, pages 69–70, features a shortened transcript of an interview with Mrs. Z regarding her son Ray, a 15 year-old with AD/HD. Read what Mrs. Z says about Ray's inadequacies regarding listening, verbal expression, academics, and communicating. Her comments illustrate the characteristics of language and auditory processing problems associated with AD/HD outlined in this chapter.

Attention-Deficit/Hyperactivity Disorder

Table 3.4   **Additional Differences between AD/HD and (C)APD**

AD/HD	(C)APD
Prevalence is 5 to 10% in school-age population	Prevalence is 2 to 3%
Prevalence in adults is 2 to 4%	Prevalence in older adults is 10 to 20%, 70% in over 60 years old
4:1 male-female ratio	2:1 male-female ratio
Must be manifested in at least two settings	Measured by a battery of standardized audiological tests administered under acoustically controlled environment
Output disorder	Input disorder
Must be present before the age of 7	Should evaluate following auditory maturation (age 7)
Attention deficits are primary and global	Executive dysfunction is secondary source of listening problems
Selective attention, inattention, distractibility, & lack of focus are primary behaviors	Attention deficits are secondary to auditory perceptual deficits
Executive dysfunction	Difficulty organizing, monitoring, and understanding acoustic signals
Excessive talking; interruptive; poor topic maintenance; difficulty producing coherent, extended discourse; difficulty getting to the point	May have associated language processing deficits
Diagnosis is based on observational criteria defined as cluster of behavior	Diagnosis is based on standardized tests
Management includes medication, executive control strategy training, social-pragmatic skills training; contingency management system, & development of learning strategies	Management includes signal enhancement, environmental modification, executive strategies, & learning strategies

Source: Chermak, Hall, and Musiek (1999)

Sidebar 3.5   **Parent Interview**

DG: Mrs. Z, tell me about your son's problems.

Mrs. Z: Ray can't find the words he wants to say to express himself. If he is asked a direct question, he can't get it out of his head. He has the same problem with writing. There is a "poverty of content," as one psychologist named it.

DG: What else is troublesome about his ability to communicate?

Mrs. Z: He has trouble interpreting nonverbal cues. He thought his English teacher was mad at him all semester. He is not intuitive, doesn't know when he is bothering someone. He doesn't read social cues well. He has a few friends. He doesn't want to go to parties because he is afraid he will not fit in. He is not comfortable in social situations. His group of three to four friends are all "different" kids.

DG: Does he understand humor, puns, and jokes?

Mrs. Z: For certain types of humor, he is good at, but for others, the more subtle ones, he had a hard time. It takes awhile for him to get it. He's very literal, he reads things to the "letter of the law."

DG: Does he get to the point when he wants to tell you something?

Mrs. Z: Not exactly. He can answer in several sentences, not quite providing the answer.

DG: What about foreign language? Can he master one?

Mrs. Z: He has a terrible time with a foreign language—Spanish—especially spelling and writing. In fact he has been withdrawn from Spanish; two years were enough. He began to learn Spanish better when he was living with a family in Costa Rica this summer. He learned to communicate better in Spanish.

DG: Is he able to take notes and use technology?

Continued on next page

Sidebar 3.5—Continued

Mrs. Z: No, he can't take notes. It is a disaster. Besides there are grapho-motor problems. He doesn't even write down his homework, which results in his not doing it. He needs a "weekly check-in person" to check out his homework assignments, and see that his big projects are broken down into smaller ones. He needs organizational support to budget his time and plan ahead.

DG: Sounds like he needs executive function training.

Mrs. Z: He does need that and has been receiving training since he was in preschool. He attended a learning center when younger. He has worked with a reading tutor on reading comprehension, vocabulary, and writing skills. He sees a "coach" to help him with his homework assignments. The tutor helps him to plan ahead, stay on track, and write clear essays. It has been a good match. Ray likes the person and will work for him. He is bothered by background noise and has trouble remembering. Having the tutor helps him stay focused and on task. It has also lifted his self-esteem.

DG: How are his grades?

Mrs. Z: They are inconsistent. They range from an A's to F's. He can handle four classes but not five classes, as he proclaimed. The Committee on Special Education (CSE), although they did not say Ray warranted services, said that they would consider the reports of the current, outside clinicians, and those involved in his support, when determining classroom accommodations. We are hoping to provide them with this evidence based on this evaluation.

Summary

This chapter provided an overview of the auditory and language deficits frequently occurring in children with AD/HD. Testimonies from parents and interviews with children help illustrate the nature of the language deficits. Remember that not all children or adults with AD/HD present with all symptoms. There are children though (few in the experience of this author) that have *little or no communication impairments*. The trick is to look for the subtleties in their language and the nonverbal and abstract use of language, in order to reveal the deficits. Traditional testing that involves vocabulary and syntax often does not show these symptoms. If one looks more carefully, the executive dysfunctions and auditory processing deficiencies appear.

Identification and Assessment

If a child or adult presents with attentional problems, it is important to confirm the diagnosis. Diagnosing AD/HD is a multifaceted process. Biological and psychological problems can contribute to symptoms similar to those exhibited by children and adults with AD/HD. For instance, anxiety, depression, and certain types of learning disabilities may cause similar symptoms and are often confused with AD/HD. There is no single test to diagnose AD/HD. A comprehensive evaluation is, therefore, necessary to establish a diagnosis, rule out other causes, and determine the presence or absence of coexisting conditions. A clinical assessment of the individual's academic, social, and emotional functioning, as well as his or her developmental level is key. A history taken from the parents, teachers, and the child (when appropriate), is also useful. Professionals often use checklists for rating AD/HD symptoms and ruling out other disabilities.

The use of the *Diagnostic and Statistical Manual-IV* (*DSM–IV*) criteria is necessary. (The diagnostic criteria were presented in Sidebar 1.1 on pages 5–6.) A medical exam by a physician is important and should include a thorough physical examination, including a vision test, to rule out other medical problems that may be causing similar problems. (Persons with AD/HD may have a thyroid dysfunction, for example.) A hearing test and an auditory processing evaluation conducted by an audiologist should rule out an auditory processing disorder, given its high comorbidity.

Diagnosing AD/HD in an adult population requires an examination of childhood academic and behavioral history as well as a scrutiny of current symptoms, since one does not develop AD/HD in adult years only. The cornerstone of a thorough evaluation consists of the following:

- Review of history and interviews
- Observations
- Rating scales completed by parents, teachers, or the person being evaluated
- Clinic rating scales
- Clinic-based psychological and educational achievement tests
- Review of prior school and medical records
- A standard physical examination or neurodevelopmental screening (to rule out any unusual medical conditions that might produce AD/HD-like symptoms)
- Auditory and language processing tests
- Vision and hearing screening
- Laboratory measures and computer-based tests
- Differential diagnosis

For a useful *Diagnostic Intake Form* refer to Study More 4.1 on the CD-ROM. It can be printed and reproduced for your use. A thumbnail view of it is presented in Figure 4.1.

Review of History and Interviews

There are two interviewing styles. One is an open-ended style. In an open-ended mental health interview, the informant is allowed to set the pace and describe his or her problems. The professional speaks as little as possible, except to ask for clarification. Such a technique places more emphasis on the informant's affect than on the facts of the history. The examiner pays attention to facial expression and emotional responses as the informant speaks. An open-ended interview is a helpful way to uncover psychological processes in the parent, family, or child. The advantages of the open-ended interview include its relaxed style, as well as its ability to make patients feel at ease and listened to. The clients may spontaneously report events to which they attach no importance, but which the clinician might wish to further explore.

Open-ended interviews have their disadvantages, too. Informants vary dramatically in the amount and type of data offered. Some individuals spend a great deal of time describing life events that may not in fact turn out to be relevant. Others fail to mention important symptoms unless

Figure 4.1

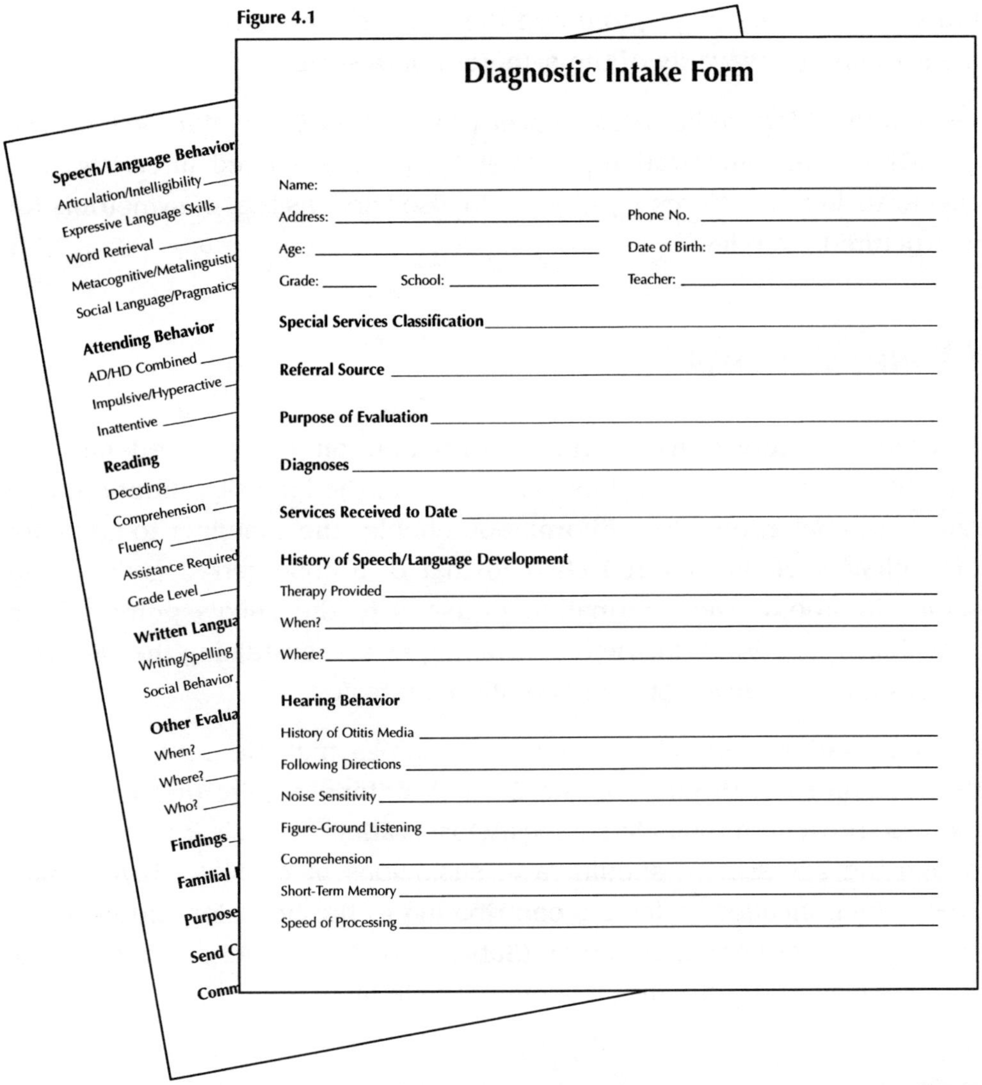

Diagnostic Intake Form

Name: _____

Address: _____ Phone No. _____

Age: _____ Date of Birth: _____

Grade: _____ School: _____ Teacher: _____

Special Services Classification _____

Referral Source _____

Purpose of Evaluation _____

Diagnoses _____

Services Received to Date _____

History of Speech/Language Development

Therapy Provided _____

When? _____

Where? _____

Hearing Behavior

History of Otitis Media _____

Following Directions _____

Noise Sensitivity _____

Figure-Ground Listening _____

Comprehension _____

Short-Term Memory _____

Speed of Processing _____

Speech/Language Behavior

Articulation/Intelligibility ——

Expressive Language Skills —

Word Retrieval ——

Metacognitive/Metalinguistic

Social Language/Pragmatics

Attending Behavior

AD/HD Combined ——

Impulsive/Hyperactive —

Inattentive ——

Reading

Decoding——

Comprehension —

Fluency —

Assistance Required

Grade Level——

Written Langua

Writing/Spelling

Social Behavior

Other Evalua

When? ——

Where? ——

Who? ——

Findings——

Familial

Purpose

Send C

Comm

specifically asked. In an open-ended interview, symptoms may be described in no particular order, making it difficult to keep track of the number and age of the onset of symptoms. Such data are critical in determining the presence of comorbid disorders.

On the other hand, structured clinical interviews lend themselves to a much more reliable clinical assessment. Structured interviews fall into two categories. In the highly structured format, lists of symptoms are presented to the informant who simply states whether or not the symptom is present. In the semi-structured interview, the informant is asked by the professional about a symptom and the professional uses his or her judgment to rate the severity of the symptom on a scale.

See the *Diagnostic Intake Form* provided as Study More 4.1 on the CD-ROM for an organizational format for an open-ended interview. The checklists in Study Mores 3.1–3.4 could also serve as lists of symptoms for a structured interview.

Observations

Behavioral observations provide information on the antecedents and consequences of the behaviors, as well as on the intensity, duration, and rate of the behaviors. Such information enables the examiner to compare the behavior of the referred child to that of a non-referred child in the same classroom. The information is useful to the child's primary care provider in identifying factors contributing to and sustaining the problem behavior, and in developing intervention strategies.

Observations should be conducted across multiple settings and at different times of the day, as the *DSM–IV* criteria require that the symptoms be present in multiple settings. Observations of indicative behaviors during the assessment should raise suspicions of possible AD/HD, and enable identification of factors contributing to the behavior and development of professional intervention (Sattler, 2002). The behaviors that may be indicative of AD/HD are presented in Sidebar 4.1.

Rating Scales Completed by Parents, Teachers, or Person Being Evaluated

Behavioral rating scales might be completed by parents, teachers, and/or the child, adolescent, or adult being evaluated. Analyze and compare the results with established norms, which will provide a baseline so that any changes can be measured at a later date.

The difficulty is in using the findings to make the diagnosis. The results clarify whether the individual is hyperactive, inattentive, or impulsive, but not the reason for these behaviors. The results also report whether a behavior or behavioral cluster is present at a significant level.

Behavioral Observations to Make during Assessment

Sidebar 4.1

Overactivity

- Excessive verbalizations that may or may not be related to the ongoing task
- Lower extremity movements, such as swinging, tapping, or shaking of legs and feet
- Upper extremity movements, such as shaking hands, tapping or drumming fingers, playing with hands, or twirling thumbs
- Whole body movements, such a rocking movements of the whole body or changing seat positions or posture frequently
- Odd noises, such as humming, clicking teeth, or whistling, during a task

Impulsivity

- Fast, incorrect responding, such as quickly responding without first scanning or surveying choices, or responding randomly
- Unsystematic searching, such as looking in the middle of the stimulus first without scanning or surveying in a left-to-right or top-to-bottom direction
- Responding before directions are given or completed
- Failing to look at possible alternatives or prematurely stopping a search

Distractibility

- Playing with own clothing, such as fiddling with shirt collars, threads, zippers, buttons, pockets, pants, or socks
- Touching things in the near vicinity, such as playing with a pencil or edges of a paper, trailing hands on or along the desk or table top, or rubbing pant legs
- Attending to an irrelevant part of the visual task, such as pointing to or commenting in an irrelevant manner during the task
- Attending to an irrelevant part of the environment, such as looking out the window or around the room or gazing or staring, during the task
- Attending to background noises, such as footsteps, voices, or buzzers, that are coming from outside the room

From *Assessment of Children: Behavioral and Clinical Applications (4th ed.,* p. 269), by J. Sattler, 2002, LaMesa, CA: Author. © 2002 by J. Sattler. Reprinted with permission.

Attention-Deficit/Hyperactivity Disorder

Broad-band
Responsive to a wide range of skills, behaviors, or elements.

Narrow-band
Responsive to a limited or select set of skills, behaviors, or elements.

Both **broad-band** and **narrow-band** rating scales help identify appropriate and inappropriate behaviors, including those specifically related to AD/HD. Broad-band scales include questions that survey a wide spectrum of symptoms and behaviors. These include:

Child Behavior Checklist (CBCL; Achenbach & Edelbrock, 1991) is one of the most widely used and psychometrically sound parent rating scales in the assessment of AD/HD. The CBCL is broken down into 20 items which assess Social Competence and 118 items that comprise the Behavior Problems scales. Selected CBCL Behavior Problems scores are excellent discriminators of AD/HD with or without comorbidity (Robin, 1998).

Behavior Assessment System for Children, Second Edition (BASC–2; Reynolds & Kamphaus, 2004) is a comprehensive measure of both adaptive and problem behaviors in the community and home setting consisting of 160 items using a four-choice response format. It enables the clinician to identify whether the child is exhibiting AD/HD, depression, or another behavioral pattern. It is useful for parents of 4 to 18 year-olds and has subscales to measure attention, hyperactivity, and adaptive skills.

Personality Inventory for Children, Second Edition (PIC–2; Wirt, Lachar, Klinedinst, Seat, & Broen, 2002) is a multidimensional test of child and adolescent behavior and emotional and cognitive status. The administrative booklet consists of 600 items to be completed by the child's parent or another rater who knows the child well. The full-length version consists of 20 scales, including 16 standard profile scales and 4 broad-band factor scales. The 16 profile scales include 3 scales that measure informant response (Lie, Frequency, and Defensiveness), a general screening scale (Adjustment), and 12 substantive scales (Achievement, Intellectual Screening, Development, Somatic Concern, Depression, Family Relations, Delinquency, Withdrawal, Anxiety, Psychosis, Hyperactivity, and Social Skills; Lachar, Gdowski, & Snyder, 1984).

Additional scales specifically enable parents to assess their child's behavior and for adults to report on their own behavior. Some narrow-band scales include questions that are designed to measure particular behaviors associated with a specific disorder. These include:

Conners' Rating Scales—Revised (CRS–R; Conners, 1997; Long Version) asks specific questions pertaining to hyperactivity, distractibility, and inattention. In two forms—one for parents and one for teachers—the degree the symptom is seen is indicated. These are the most effective behavioral scales across several categories, such as impulsivity, hyperactivity, and inattention subscales and are effective in discriminating between children with AD/HD and controls. The scales are useful for children between 3 and 17 years of age. The items are well-developed and consistent. One limitation is the underrepresentation of certain minority groups in the normative sample. The long version, offering a broad coverage of behavioral symptoms, is recommended for diagnostic assessment. The short version is not appropriate for diagnosing AD/HD—Inattentive type.

AD/HD Rating Scale–IV (DuPaul, Power, Anastopoulos, & Reid, 1998) diagnoses both AD/HD in children and adolescents, and assesses treatment response. This 18-item scale rates symptoms using a 4-point **Likert scale**, based on the *DSM–IV* criteria for AD/HD. Nine items assess inattentive symptoms and 9 items assess hyperactive/impulsive symptoms. The AD/HD Rating Scale–IV has been developed and standardized as a rating scale specifically for children. The lay-flat manual provides 3 versions of the scale: a parent questionnaire on home behaviors (English), a parent questionnaire on home behaviors (Spanish), and a teacher questionnaire on classroom behaviors. It takes 10 minutes to complete and has subscales.

> **Likert scale**
> A set of attitude statements to which a person is asked to express agreement or disagreement using a specific scale.

Attention Deficit Disorders Evaluation Scale–Second Edition (ADDES–2; McCarney, 1995) has two versions—Parent and School. In each, the observant answers questions pertaining to inattention and hyperactivity. A standard score and percentile are derived to classify a child as either inattentive, hyperactive, or both. Given the need to assess behavior in more than one setting, the school version—a broader measure—fulfills that criterion. It takes 15–20 minutes to complete.

Child Symptom Inventory–4 (CSI–4; Gadow & Sprafkin, 1998) includes two rating scales—one completed by the teacher, one by the parent—to screen 5 to 12 year-olds for symptoms of common childhood psychiatric disorders. This 50-item norm-referenced scale addresses disruptive behavior as well as medication side effects. Based on *DSM–IV* diagnostic criteria, these scales assist both educators and clinicians. Completed and scored before the child sees the examiner, the CSI–4 can be used to conduct a focused, efficient interview, detect comorbid conditions, and make differential diagnoses. The inventory offers both criterion-related cut-off scores and norm-based scores for determining symptom severity (low, moderate, or high) based on teacher and parent ratings of 6 to 12 year-old children.

Brown Attention-Deficit Disorder Scales (Brown, 2001) are user-friendly, self-report measures that tap highly salient, clinically important dimensions of AD/HD symptoms. They can be administered either as a paper-and-pencil measure or a structured clinical interview. Brown created a frequency scale with 40 items that uses expressions to describe behaviors characterizing individuals with AD/HD. Such questions ask whether the person spaces out involuntarily and frequently when reading. It explores executive function aspects of cognition that are associated with AD/HD. This assessment has standardized, validated, clinician-rated, and self-report forms. They tap into 5 clusters of conceptually related AD/HD symptoms:

• Activating and organizing to work
• Sustaining attention and concentration
• Sustaining energy and effort
• Managing affective interference
• Utilizing working memory and accessing recall

The scales can be used for initial screening of individuals suspected of having AD/HD, for comprehensive diagnostic assessment, and for monitoring of treatment responses to medical and psychosocial intervention.

ADD-H Comprehensive Teacher/Parent Rating Scale (ACTeRS; Ullman, Sleator, & Sprague, 1998) helps monitor the efficiency of treatment. It is norm-referenced. There is a teacher and parent form. The limitations include little evidence to support stated goals, and vague information on whom the test was standardized.

Home Situation Questionnaire (Barkley, 1981a) is a self-assessment with 18 symptoms based on the *DSM-III Manual*. There are 15 items addressing problem behaviors commonly occurring at home. Parents are asked to identify the number of problem areas present at home and to rate each problem area by severity on a scale from 1 to 9.

Barkley's Current Symptoms Scale–Self-Report Form (see Barkley & Murphy, 1998) is a scale of 18 items that address symptoms in the *DSM–IV* diagnostic criteria. Odd-numbered items assess frequency of inattentive symptoms and even-numbered items assess hyperactive/impulsive symptoms on a 0 to 3 Likert-type frequency scale. The scale also asks the person to report the age of onset for AD/HD symptoms and to denote how often their symptoms interfere with activities in social arenas like school, relationships, home, and work.

Copeland Symptom Checklist for Attention Deficit Disorder–Adult Version (ADDW–3; Copeland, 1989) assesses whether an adult has characteristic AD/HD symptoms, to what degree, and which areas of functioning are most seriously affected. The checklist covers 8 areas, including inattention/distractibility, impulsivity, activity-level problems, noncompliance, underachievement/disorganization, learning problems, emotional difficulties, and poor peer relations/impaired family relationships.

Conners' Adult ADHD Rating Scale (CAARS; Conners, Erhardt, & Sparrow, 1999) is a 30-item frequency scale with items like "loses things necessary for tasks or activities," and "appears restless inside when sitting still." Symptoms are assessed using a combination of frequency and severity. Patients respond to a 4-point Likert-type scale. All 18 items from the *DSM–IV* can be extrapolated from this scale, validated for both the clinician-administrated and self-rated versions.

Adult ADHD Self-Report Scale–V1.1 (ASRS-V1.1) Screener (World Health Organization, 2003) is an 18-item initial self-screening tool to identify adults who might have AD/HD. Developed by the Work Group on Adult AD/HD of New York University Medical Center, Harvard Medical Center, and Massachusetts General Hospital, it rates symptoms on a frequency basis using a scale of 0 to 4. The screener is composed of six questions which were found to be most predictive of symptoms consistent with AD/HD. The Adult ADHD Self-Report Scale Symptom Checklist modifies this scale, with more descriptions provided for each item. The symptom checklist is composed of 18 questions divided into Part A and Part B. Part A is comprised of the same questions that compose the Screener, and Part B contains the remaining 12 questions which provide additional cues and can serve as further probes into the patient's symptoms. Patients can complete the scale in 5 minutes. Items are phrased like this: "How often do you have trouble wrapping up the final details of a project once the challenging parts have been done?" Nine items assess inattention and nine items assess hyperactivity/impulsivity. Once the scale is completed by the patient, it can be used as a starting point to discuss the individual's clinical history in greater depth. The scores obtained indicate whether the person is likely, highly likely, or unlikely to have AD/HD.

Clinic Rating Scales

Depending on the information collected from the child or adult, parents, and teachers, you may want to include additional narrow-band scales to help evaluate the presence of comorbid disorders. These may include:

- Children's Depression Inventory (Kovacs, 1992)
- Reynolds Child Depression Scale and Reynolds Adolescent Depression Scale (Reynolds, 1989)
- Revised Children's Manifest Anxiety Scale (Reynolds & Richmond, 1985)

Rating scales have limited capacity to render a formal diagnosis and are inappropriate in conducting functional behavioral assessments.

Clinic-Based Psychological and Educational Achievement Tests

Psychological tests are important in the comprehensive assessment of children with AD/HD, even if that role is ancillary. Distinguishing between behavioral and emotional problems is critical in ruling out AD/HD, as anxiety can often manifest itself in fidgety and inattentive behavior. Further, intelligence tests can help establish expectations for school learning and assist in identifying strengths and weaknesses, as well as cognitive ability. Individually administered tests of academic achievement allow accurate measurement of education levels. Children with unique learning problems may reveal the problems during these types of ability and academic tests. These tests are referred to as **psychoeducational tests** or **neuropsychological test batteries.**

The difference between a neuropsychological and psychoeducational test battery is that the neuropsychological evaluation is concerned with inferring brain function based on psychological test results. One such test is A Developmental Neuropsychological Assessment (Korkman, Kirk, & Kemp, 1997). For example, some neuropsychological tests assess the performance of sensory or motor centers in the brain. In a psychoeducational test battery, a child's learning strengths and weaknesses that impact academic performance are revealed. Such tests include the Wechsler Preschool and Primary Scale of Intelligence–3rd Edition (WPPSI–III;

Psychoeducational tests
Measure of an individuals' learning strengths and weaknesses that affect academic ability.

Neuropsychological test batteries
Produce information pertaining to brain function based on results from a psychological test battery.

Wechsler, 2002), The Wide Range Achievement Test–3 (Wilkinson, 1993), and the WIAT–II (Wechsler, 2001).

Individually administered tests help rule out cognitive impairments or learning deficiencies. Such deficits can be confused with AD/HD or co-occur with it. For instance, if a child cannot comprehend information or follow the teacher's discourse because of cognitive deficiencies, then that child will not focus in class. If information becomes unclear or incomprehensible, then the person tunes it out. Attentional problems can be an outcome of learning impairment as well as contribute to it.

Review of Prior School and Medical Records

The clinical history is critical to the diagnosis of AD/HD. A history of behavior is important, as is the pervasiveness of the behaviors. Remember that symptoms must be present for at least six months before they can be considered inherent in the diagnosis. The *Diagnostic Intake Form* (see page 75 and Study More 4.1) provides a vehicle for recording historical data. It is helpful to review prior school and medical records as preparation for interviewing so that information in records can be clarified or elaborated, as needed.

Standard Physical Examination or Neurodevelopmental Screening

Physical assessment, and more rarely, the use of biomedical tests, play important roles in establishing the overall diagnosis of AD/HD, as well as in preparing a treatment plan, despite their limited contributions in detecting AD/HD itself. The purpose of the physical examination and biomedical assessment are:

- To rule out the possibility of a rare biomedical or metabolic condition as the cause of the AD/HD symptom

- To detect additional physical problems that may require treatment

- To establish whether there are contraindications to the use of certain medication (e.g., psychostimulants)

Computerized tomography (CT)
An x-ray technique using a computer to sequentially scan the organ under evaluation and produce radiologic images resulting in a high resolution image of that organ for analysis.

Magnetic resonance imaging (MRI)
A procedure where the individual's brain and spinal cord or entire body is placed in a confined space and a scan is conducted using a very powerful magnetic field resulting in detailed anatomic images.

Positron emission tomography (PET)
A scanning method which produces a cross-section image of cellular activity of blood flow in the brain following an intravenous injection of a radioactive substance.

Empirical studies
A method of research used in psychology that involves observation under controlled conditions.

The physical exam also enables you to measure vital signs, such as blood pressure, and to collect basic physiological values, such as height and weight. Problems that may be detected during examination as part of evaluation for AD/HD may include enuresis (bedwetting), encopresis (problems with bowels), motor incoordination, somatic complaints (body aches), allergies, middle-ear infections, and neurological/epilepsy (seizure activity). Other conditions such as lead poisoning, medication side effects, anxiety disorders, brain damage, oxygen insufficiency, and Lyme's disease may also be possible causes of exhibited AD/HD symptoms (Wodrich, 2000).

None of the medical screening tests—including lead level, thyroid function, brain imaging, neurological screening, continuous performance tests, and studies of electroencephalogram (EEG) patterns—were found by researchers to be useful as diagnostic tools for AD/HD. However, significant differences in brainwave activity between children with AD/HD and control subjects were found on their EEGs (Sattler, 2002).

Unfortunately, diagnostic studies such as electroencephalography, which measures electrical activity in the brain; **computerized tomography** (CT) and **magnetic resonance imaging** (MRI), which both allow detailed study of the anatomy of the brain; and **positron emission tomography** (PET), which measures the brain's use of energy as it performs tasks, do not yield significant information about AD/HD for the vast majority of children with AD/HD. **Empirical studies** involving these techniques have generally failed to detect AD/HD with much precision, to measure its severity, or to determine its cause in the individual child. It can highlight parts of the brain that are active during certain tasks and has shed light on the parts of the brain that are vulnerable in individuals with AD/HD. There are new attempts to objectify behaviors through SPECT scans, which will be described in an upcoming section.

Auditory and Language Processing Tests

Various tests are useful in the assessment of auditory processing and language processing deficits often found in the population with AD/HD. An overview of available tests, areas assessed, and age range is provided in Table 4.1. A description of each test follows.

Overview of Auditory and Language Processing Tests

Table 4.1

Test Name	Age Level	Expressive Language	Written Language	Receptive Language	Pragmatics	Auditory Processing	Phonological Processing
APAT	5–12;11			✓		✓	✓
CASL	3–6; 7–21	✓		✓	✓	✓	
CELF–4	5–21	✓		✓	✓	✓	✓
CTOPP	5–6; 7–21					✓	✓
DTLA–A	16;11–Adult	✓		✓		✓	
DTLA–4	6–16;11	✓		✓		✓	
LAC–3	K–Adult					✓	✓
OWLS	5–21	✓	✓				
PST	6–Adult					✓	✓
SCAN–A	11–Adult					✓	
SCAN–C	5;11–11					✓	
SSW	5–Adult					✓	✓
TACL–3	3–10			✓			
TAPS–3	4–19			✓		✓	✓
TARPS	5–14	✓		✓		✓	
TAWF	12–80	✓					
TLC	4–19	✓		✓	✓		
TOPL	5–13				✓		
TOWL–3	7;6–17;11		✓				
TTFC	3;5–12;6			✓		✓	
TWF	6;1–21.11	✓		✓			
TWFD	6;6–12;11	✓					

Auditory Processing

The Staggered Spondaic Word Test (SSW; Katz, 1986) is a test that measures a student's performance under competing and noncompeting conditions to two-syllable words, reaching the ear in a stagger. The resulting errors can be interpreted in patterns. The Tolerance Fading Memory Pattern is the most related to AD/HD. This pattern is associated with difficulties in reading comprehension, figure-ground listening, short-term memory, distractibility, and expressive language. The other pattern is the Decoding Pattern that is associated with difficulties in reading accuracy, phonics, articulation, and receptive language. This test often predicts a child with a phonemic awareness deficit and reading disorder. Results indicating a Type A pattern are most aligned to reading/learning disabilities; problems in auditory/visual integration; and severe reading, spelling, and phonics difficulties.

SCAN–A: A Test for Auditory Processing in Adolescents and Adults (Keith, 1994) is a four-part test of difficult listening tasks used to identify an adolescent or adult (age 11[+]) at risk for (C)APD. The four parts measure closure skill, auditory figure-ground listening, binaural integration, and binaural summation through dichotic listening tasks.

Individuals with normal hearing are able to understand speech in a wide range of listening conditions. There are those individuals who exhibit difficulty processing auditory stimuli in unfamiliar acoustic conditions, distorted speech, speech in the presence of noise, or listening to speech in a reverberant room. This test presents these adverse listening conditions.

SCAN–C: A Test for Auditory Processing in Children (Keith, 2000) is for younger children ages 5;11 to 11;0 and attempts to identify children at risk for (C)APD. The same four parts as in the SCAN–A measure closure skills, figure-ground listening, binaural integration, and binaural summation.

Auditory Processing Abilities Test (APAT; Ross-Swain & Long, 2004) is a norm-referenced auditory processing battery for children ages 5 through 12;11. Ten subtests quantify a child's performance in various areas of auditory processing. This battery is designed primarily to be used by speech-language pathologists, but may be used by other professionals. The tasks are based on a model devised by the authors which incorporated current theoretical models with the American Speech-Language-Hearing Association's guidelines for assessing auditory processing disorders. The subtests include: Phonemic Awareness, Word

Sequences, Semantic Relationships, Sentence Memory, Cued Recall, Content Memory (immediate and delayed recall), Processing Complex Sentences, Sentence Absurdities, Following Directions, and Passage Comprehension. Individual subtest scores are reported as scaled scores and percentile ranks, and are combined to yield composite scores that may be reported as standard scores, percentile ranks, and age-equivalents. The indices include: an overall Global Index, a Linguistic Processing Index, and a Memory Index. In addition, optional analyses yield three additional indices for Linguistic Processing-Auditory Discrimination, Auditory Sequencing, Auditory Cohesion and four additional Memory Indices— Immediate Recall, Delayed Recall, Sequential Recall, and Cued Recall.

Test of Auditory Processing Skills–Third Edition (TAPS–3; Martin and Brownell, 2005) is newly revised, norm-referenced, and expanded to include the subtest areas: Word Memory, Numbers (forward-reversed), Sentence Memory, Word Discrimination (same/different), Phonological Blending, Phonological Segmentation, Auditory Comprehension, and Auditory Reasoning.

Phonological Processing

Lindamood Auditory Conceptualization Test–Third Edition (LAC–3; Lindamood & Lindamood, 2003) is an individualized measure of auditory perception and conceptualization of speech sounds. It measures the dimension of auditory function judging the identity, the number, and the sequence of sounds in spoken patterns. If a student is unable to make that association, he/she learns to read through rote memory rather than through an understanding of the link between sounds and letters. It produces a grade equivalent score that can be useful in determining if a person has decoding and/or encoding problems. It is normed on kindergartners through adults.

Comprehensive Test of Phonological Processing (CTOPP; Wagner, Torgesen, & Rashotte, 1999) is a two-part test—one for 5 to 6 year olds, and one for 7 to 21 year olds—that aims to evaluate the individual's ability to phonemically decode, using real and nonsense words. The person is asked to tell what sounds make up a word or what word is made up by a series of phonemes. The individual is asked to sound out words phonemically, synthesize words, and discriminate words with sounds deleted. It measures rapid naming skills, a skill strongly aligned with phonological processing.

Phonemic Synthesis Test (PST; Katz & Fletcher, 1998) assesses phonemic decoding ability by measuring the ability to blend sounds to form words. Children with poor decoding have difficulty in class in understanding what is said, making verbal associations, and recalling words. This test offers insights about auditory memory and sequencing. It is composed of 25 test items varying from 2 to 4 sounds and ordered according to level of difficulty. It is normed on first graders through adults. There is also a preschool version with a picture pointing task—the **Phonemic Synthesis Picture Test** (Katz, 1997).

Receptive and Expressive Language

The Token Test for Children (TTFC; DiSimoni, 1978) measures one's ability to follow spoken directions. It is a test of spoken commands requiring the subject to manipulate various colored tokens (square, circles). Each of the five subparts increases in difficulty with more complex directions. A child scoring below two standard deviations is considered at risk. It is normed on 3;5 to 12;6 year olds.

Clinical Evaluation of Language Fundamentals—Fourth Edition (CELF–4; Semel, Wiig, & Secord, 2003) is a comprehensive test of language fundamentals designed to measure receptive and expressive language skills in children ages 5 to 21, providing a percentile score and age equivalence. It is helpful in determining the child's ability in relation to his or her peers. It also has several subparts that are key to the areas of deficit typically found in this AD/HD population, and the newly revised subparts can be used independently. The reader should look carefully at the subparts in Concepts and Directions—a following directions task, a formulating sentences task, an expressive language task, a word association task, a naming skill, and a rapid naming supplemental test, often implicated in phonological processing disorders. The 2003 version has two subparts that measure phonological awareness and short-term memory, both areas often deficient in the AD/HD population. Another supplemental test is the Pragmatics Subtest that measures language use in context. The values of the 2003 edition include the newly standardized norms and percentiles that help recognize a general language disorder.

Detroit Tests of Learning Aptitude–Fourth Edition (DTLA–4; Hamill, 1998) is a 10-part test battery that measures different but interrelated mental abilities pertaining to receptive and expressive language (content and form) in verbal and non-verbal domains; auditory and visual perceptual skills; and short-term memory, cognitive and attentional skills. It is normed on 6 to 16;11 year olds. The adult version is normed on 16 through adult years. Subparts are similar.

For purposes of investigating specific areas that impact attention, the following subtests are pertinent.

Word Opposites—A vocabulary and word-finding task.

Basic Information—A measure of the subject's knowledge of commonly known facts (e.g., information that is usually acquired from everyday events, movies, television, and various other living experiences), rather than from formal school instructions. The subject answers questions regarding information. It helps determine the child's ability to learn and retain information.

Story Construction—A measure of expressive language to determine narrative skills and ability to elaborate and sequence events in a cogent story. The expressive language is evaluated based on the student's ability to provide conceptual information, sequence events, name characters, see inferences, identify the conflict, or recognize humor. It also tells the examiner about the individual's ability to provide narrative discourse.

Sentence Imitation—A measure of short-term memory for connected sentences of increasing length. The student must reproduce each sentence of increasing complexity exactly as it was read aloud. It is a measure of auditory memory related to spoken syntax and grammar.

Word Sequence—A measure of short-term memory for short unrelated words. This is a working memory task whereby the student has to repeat a series of words of increasing numbers. It often identifies a child's discrimination difficulty.

Story Sequence—A measure of nonverbal organizational and sequential skills. It determines a student's ability to follow a sequence nonverbally, demonstrate problem-solving skills, and use and apply reason. A series of cartoon pictures are presented that must be put into order by numbered chips to tell the story. Often the youngster demonstrates better ability on this nonverbal task than on the verbal task. It helps the examiner assess the student's problem solving and cognitive ability. When the corollary is true, the examiner investigates the child's nonverbal/performance IQ, the discrepancy between a verbal and performance IQ, and the possible presence of a nonverbal learning disability.

Comprehensive Assessment of Spoken Language (CASL; Carrow-Woolfolk, 2000) attempts to measure receptive language skills through a series of stand-alone subtests. There are a number of subparts that serve this population well. It is normed on 3 to 6 year olds and 7 to 21 year olds.

Paragraph Comprehension of Syntax assesses the comprehension of language structure. It is composed of short stories containing sentences that are ordered according to the level of syntactic complexity both within the paragraph and from one paragraph to the next. It measures comprehension of syntax by spoken narratives that increase in complexity. The use of pictures ensures that the response is not contaminated by a possible problem in language expression. The test integrates semantics and syntax along with other skills involved in understanding, such as cohesion.

Pragmatic Judgment measures the knowledge and use of pragmatic rules of language by having the examinee judge the appropriateness of language used in specific environmental situations. Pragmatics is assessed by asking the examinee to express a specific communicative intent; to recognize appropriate topics for conversation; to select relevant information for directions; to initiate conversation or turn-take; to adjust the communication level to situational factors; to use language for expressing gratitude, sorrow, and other feelings; and to judge the pragmatic appropriateness of language behavior of others.

Nonliteral Language measures the ability to understand the meaning of words and phrases that are idiomatic or are figures of speech. The examinee is presented with statements that he or she must interpret. It is a measure of the ability to interpret language that is beyond the literal meaning. It requires metalinguistic skill. This subpart is normed for older children.

Ambiguous Language measures the ability to understand the double meaning of a word or expression. It measures one's metacognitive knowledge of language, the ability to play with language, and the ability to see the relationships in words that have more than one meaning or interpretation.

A test that probes a child's nonliteral language, often yields telling responses. Sidebar 4.2, contains a transcript from one child who was tested with a nonliteral subtest. Note the concrete answers.

Test of Language Competence (TLC; Wiig & Secord, 1989) measures metalinguistic and metacognitive skills of language by interpreting humor, puns, double meanings, and situations that have implied inferences. There are

Responses of Inattentive Subtype on
Nonliteral Language Subtest of the CASL

Mrs. S brought her 10 year-old son Joshua for a reevaluation. He was seen three years ago and she needed an update for his IEP. At the initial evaluation, Joshua was identified as having an auditory processing disorder with suspicions of having AD/HD. Over the years, that suspicion was confirmed and medication was prescribed. The following is a transcript of some of the answers Joshua, a student with AD/HD-Inattentive, provided on the Nonliteral Language subtest of the CASL:

Ex. A. After waiting a long time for her friend, Pedro, to come out of the locker room, Maria remarked, "I could have written a book while you were in there." What did Maria mean?

Joshua's response: She was able to talk.

Ex. B. When Mom told her son that astronauts liked applesauce, what did she mean?

Joshua's response: She wanted more applesauce.

Ex. C. After seeing the plate of fresh baked cookies gone, Mom said, "I see a magician was at it again." What did she mean?

Joshua's response: The cookies were baked.

Ex. D. "He moved around like a cat in the dark." What does that mean?

Joshua's response: He looked like a cat.

Ex. E. When Helen told her friend a secret, she asked her to keep a lock on it. What did she mean?

Joshua's response: Lock it.

Ex. F. When Mom heard about the accident, the ground beneath her started to shake. What was happening?

Joshua's response: There was an earthquake.

Ex. G. "Every morning the teacher was the car keys to the class." What does that mean?

Joshua's response: She unlocked the room.

Ex. H. When the teacher handed back the essays to the students to have them correct them, she told them to keep their pencils sharp. What did she mean?

Joshua's response: They should sharpen their pencils.

4 subtests: Understanding Ambiguous Sentences, Recreating Sentences, Making Inferences, and Understanding Metaphoric Sentences. It was normed on 9 to 19 year-olds. The expanded version accommodates 4 to 9 year olds.

Test of Auditory Reasoning and Processing Skills (TARPS; Gardner, 1993) measures the quality and quantity of a subject's auditory thinking and reasoning. It assesses the child's ability to draw conclusions, to make inferences, and to apply and use judgment from what the child auditorily perceives. The test attempts to determine what the child does with what he or she has learned, how he or she thinks logically, conceptually, and abstractly. It taps the ability of a child, from ages 5 to 14, to perceive auditory matter accurately, make sense out of it, and use judgment and common sense to arrive at a conclusion. The child often has to pick out key words in a question or a statement that holds the clue to, or is, the answer.

Oral and Written Language Scales (OWLS; Carrow-Woolfolk, 1996) provides an assessment of written language that may be administered individually or in small groups to persons aged 5 to 21. The scale is designed to measure the ability to use conventions (letter formation, spelling/incorrect words, punctuation, capitalization); linguistic forms (modifiers, phrases, questions); to communicate meaningfully (appropriate content, details, supporting ideas). Oral language problems are frequently manifested in written language as well.

Test of Written Language–Third Edition (TOWL–3; Hammill & Larsen, 1996) includes 8 subtests which are normed for children 7;6 to 17;11 years of age and measure the student's writing competence through both essay-analysis (spontaneous) formats and traditional tests (contrived) formats.

Test of Word Finding (TWF; German, 1989) measures word retrieval by presenting naming tasks for nouns, verbs, categories, and descriptions; sentence completion; and comprehension assessment. It is appropriate for 6;1 to 21;11 year olds.

Test for Auditory Comprehension of Language–Third Edition (TACL–3; Carrow-Woolfolk, 1999) is a test that measures comprehension in three categories: word classes and relations, grammatical morphemes, and elaborated sentences. It is a spoken test normed for children ages 3 to 10 years.

Test of Word Finding in Discourse (TWFD; German, 1991) analyzes word finding in storytelling/narrative tasks for 6;6 to 12;11 year olds.

Test of Adolescent/Adult Word Finding (TAWF; German, 1989) measures word finding in adolescents and adults by providing a quick assessment of various abilities for ages 12 to 80 years.

Test of Pragmatic Language (TOPL; Phelps-Terasaki, & Phelps-Gunn, 1992) measures 5 to 13 year-old students' ability to use pragmatic language effectively.

Vision and Hearing Screening

To begin with, the individual should undergo a vision screening to rule out any problems in seeing and tracking. The individual should be given a hearing screening to rule out any hearing acuity problems. Often a child has a middle ear condition that contributes to listening problems and loss of focus. A child with mild hearing loss will miss soft speech, nuances, and background sounds that can affect his ability to discriminate and attend.

Similarly, an adult can have a high-frequency hearing loss that contributes to uneven hearing acuity and speech discrimination impairment. Both conditions can be remedied and should not be mistaken for AD/HD. Nevertheless, given the considerable overlap with central auditory processing disorder, it would be advisable to refer the individual for an auditory processing work-up.

Often, poor discrimination, figure-ground listening, inadequate decoding, or comprehension skills contribute to inattention and distractibility. If there is a problem on input, such as understanding the spoken message, or hearing clearly in quiet and in noise, then output (expressive language) will often be affected and reflect these deficiencies. The salient language features that often accompany AD/HD include difficulty with word retrieval, with formulating thoughts in a concise manner, with understanding and using nonliteral language, and with listening in noise or competing stimuli. There are tests available that measure nonliteral language such as the CASL (Carrow-Woolfolk, 2000), Detroit Tests of Learning Aptitude (DTLA–4; Hammill, 1998), TLC (Wiig & Secord, 1989), and the TARPS (Gardner, 1993). Tests that measure retrieval include The WORD Test 2: Elementary (Bowers, Huisingh, LoGiudice, & Orman, 2004), Subtest I of the DTLA–4

(Hamill), and subparts of the CTOPP (Wagner, Torgesen, & Rashotte, 1999). Also, such tests as the CTOPP (Wagner, Torgesen, & Rashotte) and the LAC–3 (Lindamood & Lindamood, 2003) reveal poor phonemic awareness. The APAT (Ross-Swain & Long, 2004) and the TAPS–3 (Martin & Brownell, 2005) have a wide variety of subtests that measure many of the skills noted. For a listing of tests available to address these deficits, see Table 4.1, page 85.

Laboratory Measures and Computer-Based Tests

Laboratory measures have increasingly been used to assess inattention and impulsivity as part of the diagnostic process with AD/HD individuals. Such measures have included continuous performance tests (CPT), cancellation tasks, matching familiar figure tasks, subtests of IQ tests, card sort tasks, color associations tests, and direct observations of AD/HD symptoms in laboratory situations. A CPT can measure processing speed in addition to focused, sustained, divided, and alternating attention characteristic in a neuropsychological evaluation. The term CPT was first coined by Rosvold, Mirsky, Sarason, Bransome, and Beck (1956). With CPT researchers use a wide variety of presentation methods (auditory, visual, or verbal) and performance measures such as hit rate, commission (impulsivity), and omission (inattention). Some studies have examined simple reaction time (SRT) to one stimulus while other studies have used choice reaction time (CRT) to two or more stimuli that require different responses to the stimuli or require a response for one stimuli and inhibition of a response for another stimuli. Laboratory measures have great potential as one component of a multimethod assessment because of their objectivity (Tinius, 2003).

Gordon Diagnostic System (GDS; Gordon, 1983) is a popular CPT that has been subjected to careful empirical scrutiny in studies with AD/HD adolescents. It is one of the few laboratory measures that meets the criteria of psychometric validity and practicality in clinical work with adolescents. It is a portable, solid-state, child-proofed, microprocessor-based CPT which can be programmed to administer multiple tasks. Three tasks are commonly administered to adolescents:

- The Vigilance task requires the child to inhibit responding under conditions that make demands for sustained attention.

- The Delay task requires the child to inhibit responding in order to earn points, according to a Differential Reinforcement of Low Responding schedule.

- The Distractibility task is similar to the Vigilance task.

The test records the number of correct responses, the number of omission errors, and the number of commission errors. Extensive normative data have been collected for this test. Research indicates that this CPT effectively distinguishes AD/HD from non-AD/HD children. It is also sensitive to changes produced by stimulant medications, and correlates to a modest extent with other measures of sustained attention and impulsivity. However, concerns have been raised that it may under-identify children with AD/HD (Robin, 1998).

Conners' Continuous Performance Test (CPT II; Conners, 1995) and the ***Test of Variables of Attention*** (TOVA; Greenberg, Leark, DuPuy, Corman, & Kindschi, 1994) are the most frequently used computer-based tests. On each test, vigilance is assessed by having the child respond to an auditory or visual stimulus by pressing a button. The stimulus may be in the background of similar signals. The task is monotonous and requires constant attention. The speed or complexity of the task can be increased. Children or adolescents with AD/HD perform more poorly than do children without AD/HD. They might make some errors of omission or more errors of commission. Errors of omission reflect inattention. Errors of commission reflect impulsivity. That is, they respond too quickly or before a stimulus actually appears.

The Conners' Continuous Performance Test is a CPT that requires subjects to continuously respond for 14 minutes as single letters are flashed on the screen and to inhibit a response when a target stimulus (x) appears. The Conners' CPT runs on a standard microcomputer rather than requiring a self-contained piece of equipment. The youngster responds by using the mouse or the keyboard. This has the disadvantage of introducing equipment variability, compared to the GDS or the Test of Variable Attention (Robin, 1998).

Attention-Deficit/Hyperactivity Disorder

The Conners' CPT yields a variety of scores, which are automatically computed as soon as the software completes administration of the tasks. These scores include omission errors, commission errors, and a variety of reaction time and variability scores. The Conners' CPT was standardized on a large sample. Results indicated that the scores obtained by AD/HD individuals were elevated as compared to controls.

The TOVA (Greenberg, Leark, DuPuy, Corman, & Kindschi, 1994) is a 23-minute CPT administered on a microcomputer that utilizes a special microswitch with which the subject responds. Such usage standardizes the equipment better than the use of a keyboard or mouse. The TOVA is a nonlanguage-based CPT in which the subject watches for designated targets and ignores nontargets. The TOVA provides scores for omission errors, commission errors, response time, variability, and anticipatory errors. Its length of task makes it a more sensitive measure with older adolescents and adults. It has also been found to be sensitive to developmental changes in attention and impulse control in a cross-sectional study of children and adolescents in the normative sample. The test was able to correctly identify 90 percent of AD/HD and 87 percent of the normal controls (Greenberg & Waldman, 1993). The TOVA has also been found to be sensitive to medication effects and it has therefore been suggested that the TOVA be used as a method of monitoring the effects of medication (Corman & Greenberg, 1996).

Intermediate Visual and Auditory Continuous Performance Test (IVA CPT; Sanford & Turner, 1995) can assess auditory and visual attention on the same tasks. The IVA CPT is an integrated 13-minute auditory and visual CPT. In addition to the typical demands of clicking in response to a designated target, the IVA CPT requires the test taker to "shift sets" and to make discriminatory responses to mixed auditory and visual stimuli (e.g., click if you see or hear a "1"; do not click if you see or hear a "2"). The IVA CPT calculates errors of commission **(prudence),** errors of omission (vigilance), as well as response speed and response speed variability. Results for six primary subscales and three validity scales are presented separately for auditory and visual stimuli allowing for a comparison between the two modalities. Full-scale response control (impulsive errors) and attention quotients (inattention errors) are calculated from a combination of select subscales. In addition, a fine motor regulation scale is calculated by summing off-task behaviors with the mouse (e.g., excessive clicking). Three validity scales are included to assess neurological and/or learning problems, poor motivation or motor fatigue, and lack of comprehension, all of which could invalidate the test results.

Prudence
On the IVA computer test, a calculation of errors of commission.

Test results include raw score percentages (percent of correct trials and quotient scores) for all the major variables, as well as a histogram of auditory and visual response speeds. The printout of results does not provide any interpretive notes, thus the clinician must be quite familiar with the guidelines contained in the Interpretation Manual in order to draw conclusions from the test. A step-by-step guide is provided in the manual to assist in the interpretation of the IVA CPT identifying AD/HD (O'Laughlin & Murphy, 2000).

Results of Tinius's (2003) study indicated that visual and auditory full-scale attention and full-scale response-accuracy scales were significantly lower for the AD/HD group than for controls. The scores yielded by the AD/HD group were also significantly lower on the secondary scale for auditory and visual attention and for auditory and visual response accuracy, reaction time, inattention, and impulsivity. His findings indicated that AD/HD groups and traumatic brain injury (TBI) showed similar patterns of performance on the IVA CPT.

Quantitative Electrophysiologic Measures

Brain-scanning techniques are currently being used to better identify AD/HD. While scientists agree that there are striking differences in the brain images of people with AD/HD, most say it's premature and impractical to use brain scans to diagnose the disorder. One such method is called **SPECT (Single Photon Emission Computed Tomography),** which requires the injection of a small amount of radioactive material to illuminate brain activity. Of great concern is that the SPECT scans expose young brains to radioactive material, and there is no research on any long-term effects (Parker-Pope, 2002). Further, scans can cost $1,000 or more and may not be covered by insurance. Other physicians are using MRI scans to compare differences in normal and AD/HD brains. The major advantage of these laboratory measures is objectivity.

Altropane SPECT has been shown to have potential in serving as a diagnostic brain-imaging tool. Altropane, an imaging agent developed by Boston Life Sciences, has been used to identify adults with long-standing AD/HD. Thomas (2003) studied nine men and four women between the ages of 18 to 29, who were injected with radiopharmaceutical I-123 Altropane, a substance that binds to dopamine transporters in the basal ganglia section of the brain. SPECT scans performed on these patients following the injections revealed

Single photon emission computed tomography (SPECT) scan Provides information about blood flow to tissue. It is a sensitive diagnostic tool used to detect stress fracture, spondylosis, infection (e.g., discitis), and tumor (e.g., osteoid osteoma). Analyzing blood flow to an organ (e.g., bone) may help to determine how well it is functioning.

higher binding ratio of I-123 Altropane to dopamine transporters in AD/HD patients than in normal patients. This evidence supports the dopamine deficiency in AD/HD patients. The finding lends support to the theory that patients with AD/HD do not have sufficient neurotransmitter dopamine. The use of I-123 Altropane may have potential to serve as a useful objective diagnostic measure to identify AD/HD in individuals. The author, Carmen Thomas, and colleagues from the Department of Nuclear Medicine at Harbor UCLA Medical Center and the UCLA Neuropsychiatric Institute presented these findings at the 50th Annual meeting of the Society of Nuclear Medicine in 2003.

The Quantitative Electroencephalograph (Q-EEG) measures the ratio between key brain waves. A technician fits a cap with 17 electrodes onto a patient's head. The electrodes pick up different types of electrical activity in many brain regions, and this information is fed into the computer and analyzed. The so-called theta wave represents a mental state of inattentiveness and distractibility, and delta waves are associated with sleep. Beta waves suggest a very alert state, and alpha waves represent alertness, relaxation, and wakefulness. The Q-EEG produced is based on findings from 2,600 people with and without AD/HD. Their brain-wave patterns differ enough that researchers can predict with 90 percent accuracy if a given pattern indicates AD/HD, according to John Drozd, clinical director of Lexicor, a company that developed the diagnostic scan. A computer program analyzes the brain scan and plots the child's brain response on a curve from normal to that seen in children with AD/HD (Talan, 2004).

Another device waiting Food and Drug Administration approval is the DataLex Indicator (Lexicor Health Systems, 2001) developed by Lexicor NeuroAssessment Center, which uses non-invasive technology and takes an hour to complete. It evaluates where a child falls in terms of the AD/HD classification. This objective, physiologic measure used for assessment can classify a person with AD/HD (inattentive and combined) to an accuracy of 90 percent. The neuroassessment evaluation uses the Lexicor Neuro-Search, a 245 quantitative electroencephalographic data acquisition unit. The DataLex database is used in the analysis of the data obtained. The theory is that patients with inattentive subtype AD/HD typically express an increase in the theta-beta ratio or an increase in frontal beta power. A theta-beta ratio is established and compared to normal age groups. A frontal beta power

Kelly, you're such a helper
opening the door for Daddy.

indicator is also derived and compared to normal age groupings. It is thought that those with the AD/HD combined subtype display specific brainwave patterns with a marked increase in frontal beta power relative to normals. The developers caution that when using these data, patient history, clinical interview, and test measures should also be included in a full assessment.

Differential Diagnosis

Given a likelihood of confusion among different but overlapping labels, it would be beneficial to differentiate AD/HD from other "look alikes," such as behavior anxiety, brain injury, auditory processing, and/or learning difficulties. Situational variability also occurs that interferes with the diagnosis and produces an irregular clinical picture. One cannot negate the impact of family disruptions on the child's behavior and attention or on the child's motivation. A number of children recently seen were affected by the World Trade Center shock. Some suffer from a loss of a parent from the home, either by death or divorce. Life events such as birth of a new baby in the family, or a move, affect the child's behavior. These antecedent events

Attention-Deficit/Hyperactivity Disorder

Hyperactivity
Signs of fidgetiness, distractibility, constant movement, abnormal physical action.

Inattention
The inability to hold focus or concentration.

Selective attention
The ability to focus consciousness on a single event in the environment while ignoring other stimuli.

Vigilance
Ability to stay with a task over time.

Divided attention skill
Aspect of attention enabling a person to appropriately allocate focus and time between a series of activities.

contribute to the confusion that clouds the diagnosis of AD/HD. Thus, the need for a differential diagnostic process becomes clear. Attention itself has several components. See Sidebar 4.3 for a list of these components. In making a differential diagnosis, keep the following keystone behaviors as paramount—hyperactivity, inattention, and impulsivity.

In **hyperactivity,** children appear to be fidgety, tapping their fingers, moving their pencils, swinging their legs, and getting up and down from their desk or the dinner table. They are always in motion. Parents may report that the child is equally restless at night, moving about the bed. With adolescents, the fidgety behaviors may be less apparent.

With **inattention,** children are unable to seek out what needs to be attended to, focus on it, maintain the focus during the activity, and stop attending once the task is complete. Children and adolescents who are

---

Behavioral Observations to Make during Assessment

Sidebar 4.3

- Inattention: inability to perform tasks that involve the parameters of attention
- **Selective attention**/selective listening: ability to attend specifically to a given condition and make a response; it may be a motor response (e.g., button press) or some mental counting task of the target stimulus
- Sustained attention **(vigilance):** ability to inhibit interference; requires sustained focus while waiting for a target stimulus to happen
- Divided attention or **divided attention skill:** ability to appropriately allocate focus and time between a series of activities (Delmar Learning, 2000)
- Alternating attention: ability to shift attention between tasks that have different cognitive demands

Source: Mendel, Danhauer, & Singh (1999)

100

anxious, worried, or depressed might have difficulty sustaining their attention after beginning an assignment. Their symptoms produce an inattentiveness that is not diagnosable as AD/HD. If the environment is too noisy or stimulating, children will have difficulty concentrating. On the other hand, if the work is too hard, or not understood, or if the student has difficulty screening out unimportant stimuli, or relevant from irrelevant information, that child will not be able to focus. That, too, is not diagnosable as AD/HD. Nor is a child with an obsessive-compulsive disorder who has difficulty stopping one task to move onto another. Therefore, it is important to look at the many reasons for inattentional behaviors.

Inattention may be categorized into two groups: **internal** and **external.** Internal inattention may be due to daydreaming, an auditory perception disability, and **cognitive disinhibition.** External inattention may be due to environmental overload and/or AD/HD. External inattention is witnessed when children have difficulty screening out unimportant sounds. They seem to hear everything, such as, someone talking in the next room, a phone ringing, or the dog's tail wagging. In school, they may become distracted by the sound of footsteps in the hall. Very often, these children experience sensory overload when in a very stimulating environment. They may become irritable, cry, cover their ears, or want to leave.

Internal inattention is seen when children daydream, which can be quite common among children and adolescents. As students, they escape into their thoughts and then realize that they have not heard what the teacher was saying. The teacher might comment that such a student is not paying attention. However, daydreaming may reflect family or other stress, an emotional disorder, or simply the excitement of an event.

With **impulsivity,** individuals are unable to stop or have difficulty stopping to reflect before speaking or acting. In school, these individuals might interrupt in class, call out before they are called on, blurt out an answer or interrupt a teacher while he or she is working with another student. At home, these individuals interrupt parents while they are on the phone or are talking to someone else. They exhibit "jumping behavior." This is described as having a mind that is busy with many thoughts occurring at the same time. An individual might make a comment from one of these thoughts and it

Internal inattention
Inattention due to one's own distractions.

External inattention
Distractions caused by forces outside one's self.

Cognitive disinhibition
Removal of an inhibitory, constraining, or limiting influence of the mental processes of comprehension, judgment, memory, and reasoning, in contrast to emotional and volitional processes.

Impulsivity
Behavior characterized by acting on impulse, or without thought or conscious judgment.

will have nothing to do with what is being talked about. Jumping behavior confuses others and frustrates the person who has this difficulty. Children who act before thinking might grab something, knock someone else's blocks down, push their way into line, hit someone, or worse yet, run out into the middle of the street.

The main difficulty in diagnosing AD/HD is in differentiating among the many causes of hyperactivity, distractibility, and impulsivity. It is important to document that there is a chronic and pervasive history of these behaviors. For instance, anxiety—the most common cause of hyperactivity, distractibility, and impulsivity—can often be at the root of the behavior. Anxiety can be a reflection of psychological stress or conflict, or due to a specific anxiety disorder as a result of an academic problem. When anxious, children might be physically active. If the child has a learning disability, the child may become anxious when asked to perform in an area of weakness. When working individually, the child might become frustrated and look around the room or out the window.

Depression is another cause of hyperactivity, distractibility, and impulsivity. Depression might reflect a psychological conflict, or stress, or a specific mood disorder. This might be manifested by poor self-image and low self-esteem. Depression has agitated and psychomotor retardation phases. (For a discussion of depression, see Chapter 2.) Another cause can be the child's health. Allergies, congestion, physical or metabolic disorders, and brain injury can cause behaviors that mirror AD/HD symptoms. Motivation is another factor that affects a child's performance on tests, schoolwork, and behavior.

Summary

Without an accurate way to physically diagnose and measure a disorder, one may not be sure whether AD/HD is present. Concern has been raised that physicians are falsely diagnosing children. Critics also comment that schools are overusing medication to deal with children who have discipline problems when behavior modification or other nonmedical therapy may be a better choice.

Nevertheless, AD/HD is a condition that is well defined and recognized internationally in the mental health field. According to the *DSM–IV*, multiple criteria must be met before concluding that AD/HD is present. The first of these guidelines stipulates that a child must frequently display at least 6 of 9 inattention symptoms and/or 6 of 9 hyperactivity-impulsivity symptoms. These symptoms must have an onset prior to 7 years of age, duration of at least 6 months, and a frequency above and beyond that expected of children. Further, it must be observed in at least two settings. Given the clinical presentation, situational variability, and symptomatology that overlaps with other disorders as well as co-occurring disorders, it behooves the examiner to accurately identify AD/HD in the child or adult so that management and treatment can be effective.

The Team Approach to Assessment and Management

Chapter 5

Children with AD/HD, like other children with special needs, benefit from the observation and evaluation of a team of individuals. A team approach in managing attention-deficit/hyperactivity disorder can bring together adults from different disciplines who contribute their expertise, share in decision-making, and provide strategies for intervention. Teams are **interdisciplinary** and may be referred to using various terms (e.g., multidisciplinary, transdisciplinary). The interdisciplinary team concept is not new and is required for special education evaluation in the public schools (PL 108-446, The Individuals with Disabilities Education Improvement Act of 2004; IDEA). Specifically, in the schools, an Individualized Education Program (IEP) team is formed and used to assess and plan for special education services.

> **Interdisciplinary**
> Refers to two or more professionals (educators, psychologists, and others) working together and sharing information in diagnosis, assessment, and treatment.

The needs of an individual child determine what members will make up a team. As a child's strengths and weaknesses emerge during evaluation and observation, additional professionals from other disciplines may need to join the team. The team approach is applicable in medical, educational, mental health, or other settings. Regardless of the setting, the value of a team or collaborative approach for the child with AD/HD is that it offers a well-defined reservoir of data on the child and provides interpretations from varied professional perspectives. Members of the team can include a parent, physician, school nurse, educator(s), (educational) psychologist, speech-language pathologist, audiologist, special education administrator, occupational therapist, and others.

Parents

In all situations involving a child or adolescent, parents are integral members of the team. As soon as the child enters any type of formalized learning experience, the parents begin to be part of an educational process that will continue for many years. The majority of parents never experience being a member of a team focusing specifically on their child, but for parents of a child with special needs, it becomes a reality.

According to Jones (1998b) there are three primary reasons why parents should be involved in the team process:

1. *The parent is the primary caregiver.* The family is the key to the child's growth and development; it provides the primary care for the child through maturation. The ultimate responsibility for the child lies with the parent.

2. *The parent is the decision-maker.* Because of the parent's ultimate responsibility, the parent must be given an opportunity to participate in joint decision-making and in choices affecting the child's growth and development.

3. *The parent is a partner.* There is growing evidence that the home is vital to and intimately linked with school achievement. There is a need for cooperation between all the adults in a child's life to facilitate **acquisition, internalization,** and **maintenance** of new skills.

Informed, organized parents will be stronger advocates for their child. The involvement of parents is an essential component in the development of a team. In helping parents feel comfortable in the team process, one member of the team can meet with the parents first and explain what the team is, how it functions, and what its purpose is in helping the child. Team members could guide parents by showing them how to keep track of critical papers and information about their child.

In the public schools, a designated parent advocate may be available to help parents through the special education process. In addition, to involve parents in the educational process, they should receive written information on legal rights and procedures to read before attending team meetings. See Sidebar 5.1, for an explanation of parent's rights afforded by the federal guidelines and pertaining to public school services.

Acquisition
Something gained, acquired, or added to.

Internalization
To incorporate (as values or patterns of culture) within the self as conscious or subconscious guiding principles through learning or socialization.

Maintenance
In conditioning, administration of occasional reinforcement to keep an already-acquired response at a desired frequency.

Sidebar 5.1   **Parental Rights under Federal IDEA 2004**

Parents have the right to:
- Be members of the IEP (Individualized Education Program) Team
- Receive written notification of their procedural safeguards in their primary language when feasible
- Refer their child for an evaluation
- Be notified whenever the district proposes to or refuses to initiate or change the identification, evaluation, or educational placement or free appropriate public eduction (FAPE) of their child
- Participate in all meetings related to identification, evaluation, and educational placement of their child
- Contribute to the evaluation and IEP process
- Obtain an independent educational evaluation of their child
- Examine their child's records and request changes to the records
- Have an advocate assist them in dealing with the special education process
- Have an opportunity for voluntary mediation of disagreements
- File a complaint with the district within two years regarding the identification, evaluation, educational placement, FAPE, or due process procedures. States must provide a model form to assist parents in filing a complaint
- Invite others with knowledge or special expertise to be part of the IEP Team
- Receive periodic progress reports on IEP goals

Parents must give consent:
- For the child to be evaluated by the IEP Team
- To accept and commence special education services
- To allow an outside agency to review the child's records
- To the use of a multi-year IEP

NOTE: Parental permission may be withdrawn at any time.

Written notification for special education services must include:
- The parents' native language when feasible
- A description of the actions offered or rejected by the district
- An explanation of the proposal or refusal along with supportive evaluation and assessment information
- A statement that the child and parents are protected by procedural safeguards and how to obtain a copy (A copy is provided for initial referrals.)
- Sources for parents to contact to obtain assistance in understanding the proposal and their rights
- A description of other options considered by the IEP Team and why they were rejected
- A description of the factors that are relevant to the district's proposal or refusal

Source: Individuals with Disabilities Education Improvement Act of 2004

The Physician

The complexity of diagnosing AD/HD requires that the child's primary physician collaborate with other professionals. The physician or child neurologist, child psychiatrist, and/or developmental-behavior pediatrician conduct a thorough medical examination with an emphasis on assessing distractibility, attention, concentration, and short-term memory. According to Goldstein and Goldstein (1990): "The physician's role includes directing the search for remedial medical causes of AD/HD, participating in the multidisciplinary diagnostic evaluation, and, when medication is indicated, supervising the medication intervention programs" (p. 52). The gathering of data, diagnostic testing, and interpretation of results is facilitated when a physician is a member of the team. Often, a physician who specializes in AD/HD such as a developmental-behavioral pediatrician is particularly knowledgeable about treatment and psycho-pharmacology. In the educational setting, if a physician is not able to attend team meetings, written correspondence can be submitted and becomes valuable at team meetings.

The School Nurse

The school nurse is a valuable member of the team process. Training in recognizing normal growth and development, observing and recording behaviors, and communicating with physicians and families are skills that make the school nurse an important part of a collaborative effort. The nurse also can offer current information to parents regarding the effectiveness of treatments, identify local physicians with particular expertise in AD/HD, and provide help in forming support groups.

Pharmacological component
Involving the use of drugs.

Once the assessment data have been recorded and the diagnosis established, the school nurse can become significantly involved in any **pharmacological component.** The nurse may participate in speaking or acting as a liaison with the family or physician throughout the therapeutic trial period to assist in achieving the child's correct dosage. The nurse can be helpful in gathering observational data as before-and-after documentation of behaviors, and observing the child for side effects, or this duty may be conducted by the educational psychologist. The nurse or educational psychologist can monitor the child on medication using objective observations of a rating scale, teacher's weekly progress reports, and parent and physician conferences.

Once a successful dosage and schedule is determined, the nurse is responsible for maintaining an effective and organized method for dispensing the medication, including charting of dosages and the child's response. An effective plan achieves a balance between reliable dispensing of the medication without drawing negative or extra attention to the child. As long-acting medications are manufactured and utilized (e.g., Ritalin LA, Concerta), many children are not needing dosages during the school day.

Educators

Regardless of the setting, general and special education teachers are important members of a team of professionals working to serve a child with AD/HD. However, in the public schools, educators are required members of the IEP team and those teachers most closely involved in educating a child must participate in the team process (PL 101-476, The Individuals with Disabilities Education Act; IDEA, 2004).

During the evaluation and assessment process, educators are asked to examine and report on a child's classroom performance. Teachers are intimately familiar with the demands of the curriculum, the expectations of the classroom, and the range of performance from the students they teach. This makes educators valuable members of the team of people who assess the needs of a child with AD/HD. Educators will benefit from the expertise of other team members in developing their understanding of the characteristics of AD/HD and the nature of a given child's AD/HD. Collaboratively the team, with great contribution from the educators, will be able to suggest the academic impact of such a disorder.

While it is critical to involve educators in the diagnostic and assessment phase, they are likely to be even more interested in the educational planning the team will complete. Educators are frequently responsible for dozens of students each day. In fact, middle school and high school teachers often have one hundred or more students in their classroom across a school day. In addition, educators are asked to address the tremendous needs of a wide range of students. These variables frequently make it challenging for educators to participate with ease in meeting the needs of a child with AD/HD. However, when the team process is used appropriately, all team members will feel empowered and successful.

Compensatory strategies, environmental modifications, and other educationally based methods of AD/HD management should be discussed and selected as a team to meet the individual needs of a child. This allows all team members to take ownership of the treatment plan. Educators should be familiar with the compensatory strategies the child is being taught so that the appropriate generalization and use of such strategies in the classroom can be monitored. Monitoring of the educational plan is done by all members of the team. However, a special education teacher may oversee this process. Educators contribute important information as a plan is monitored, as they are the ones who can report on the student's behavior in the educational setting.

The Psychologist

In educational and nonschool settings, a psychologist (or educational psychologist) is an important team member when assessing and planning treatment for a child with AD/HD. Psychologists are involved in many aspects of evaluation and are valuable members for examining pharmacological and behavioral treatment options. The educational psychologist is frequently the case manager for students with AD/HD in the schools. However, that person may not always be the official team leader. This role varies from case to case and is dependent on variables such as age of the child, presence of concomitant conditions (e.g., speech disorder), and system established in a particular school.

Traditionally, psychologists are responsible for giving and interpreting assessments that measure a child's general intelligence. These assessments include tests of attention, vigilance, and behavior patterns. The psychologist can compare the child's performance on intelligence and achievement tests to determine where discrepancies appear. The testing procedures can provide valuable information for understanding how the child focuses with mild frustration and assess to what degree the child may be successful in school and other environments. The psychologists address concerns regarding the student's strengths and weaknesses in academic areas as well as the child's emotional and behavioral status.

In addition to contributing information related to intelligence level, psychologists are trained to use tests to diagnose AD/HD. Indeed, many children who come to school with an AD/HD label often have been diagnosed by someone in the profession of psychology. Many children with

AD/HD, however, may also be under the care of a psychologist for associated symptoms of frustration and depression that occur with continual academic and communicative struggles. Psychologists are important members of the AD/HD team because they can provide valuable information regarding the social-emotional impact of the disorder, as well as **cognitive** and academic functioning. The psychologist can facilitate the information-gathering phase by helping teachers and parents complete questionnaires and checklists; observing the child in school, home, and play environments; calculating results of checklists and rating scales; and formulating patterns of similar observations.

Using data collected, the psychologist, along with the other team members, makes interpretations of educational impact of the AD/HD. This is then followed by treatment planning during which time the psychologist can provide input related to pharmacological and nonmedicine options. The psychologist may, in conjunction with the school nurse, monitor the medication using objective observations, rating scales, teacher's weekly progress notes, and parent and physician conferences. In addition, the psychologist can offer insights for behavioral interventions that occur instead of, or in addition to, pharmacological treatment.

Finally, psychologists may be called upon to provide individual or family counseling services to those children in need of such services. Or, they may act as a referral source to help families and students find appropriate counseling and related services from other agencies. In some schools, the guidance counselor may take the lead in following up and implementing recommendations and/or providing counseling to the student.

The Speech-Language Pathologist

The referral of a child for suspected AD/HD may indicate the need for a speech-language pathologist to join the team for assessment and treatment planning purposes. Or, a child with a previously diagnosed communication disorder may be referred for suspicion of AD/HD.

Studies of the AD/HD population suggest that a higher than average percentage of preschoolers with AD/HD also have speech and language problems (Baker & Cantwell, 1987). Specifically, 10 to 54 percent of children with AD/HD may exhibit expressive language problems, compared to 2 to 25 percent of the general population (Barkley, DuPaul, & McMurry, 1990).

Cognitive
General concept embracing all of the various modes of knowing: perceiving, remembering, imagining, conceiving, judging, and reasoning.

111

Children who have AD/HD may exhibit difficulties in formulation of thought, word retrieval, and use of socially appropriate language. Listening skills are also often poor in these children. They may not attend to relevant stimuli, lack selective attention, and struggle to follow complex directions. They may express tangential, unconnected thoughts, and fail to adapt their behavior to varying contexts. Often their language is literal with little room for humor or abstract references.

The speech-language pathologist is important during the assessment phase to assist with a differential diagnosis. It is critical that AD/HD is contrasted with a speech and language disorder so that the most appropriate diagnosis can be made. The two conditions may be co-occurring, but considering all elements and options is important. The information gathered during the assessment phase by the speech-language pathologist can help the team shape a treatment plan that is comprehensive. In addition, speech-language pathologists often use service delivery that allows them to work one-on-one with a child. These types of teaching opportunities are often critical for a child with AD/HD so that new skills can be taught in a setting with minimal distraction. Finally, the speech-language pathologist may serve as a consultant to the classroom teacher, educational psychologist, or guidance counselor in providing or modeling strategies for effective communication skills with a child with AD/HD and in an effort to transfer new skills to other educational and social settings.

The Audiologist

Since a differential diagnosis is important when AD/HD and a central auditory processing disorder are suspected, an audiologist is an important member of the team. In a school, an educational audiologist can be requested to join the team in order to contribute to the diagnosis and make recommendations for treatment. The audiologist tests hearing and conducts specific and rigorous evaluations to attempt to detect or rule out a central auditory processing disorder. Then, the audiologist can contribute recommendation and accommodation information.

The Special Education Administrator

Unique to the public school setting, special education administrators may be important members of the team. Administrators are responsible for providing the full range of special education services for all qualified children. A principle concern for educational administrators is the need for service delivery. Administrators are likely to have questions regarding the numbers of children affected in their schools or districts, the purpose of each member's involvement in the program, and the time and equipment necessary for implementing a comprehensive AD/HD program. Educational administrators that are team members may need information about prevalence of AD/HD; the academic, communicative, and emotional impact of such disorders; and current state-of-the-art recommendations for service delivery, test modifications, and other accommodations needed in the classroom and school buildings. In this way, the need for AD/HD services, as well as the rationale behind a comprehensive program, can be highlighted for support.

Although responsibility for AD/HD service delivery may be shared among existing school professionals, additional time or funding may be required for the implementation of a comprehensive program. If the presenting difficulties of a given child are deemed by the educational professionals working with the child to require further evaluation or additional services, the special education administrator arranges for additional funding or staffing. Educational administrators, along with other professionals, may develop guidelines for pre-referral interventions and special education referral for AD/HD services in the schools.

The Occupational Therapist

For some children, reduced fine motor skills may necessitate the need for an occupational therapist on the team. Occupational therapists use activity in a person's surroundings to facilitate independent functioning in school, and to minimize the effect of the disabling condition on the student's ability to participate in the educational process. As a member of the team, the occupational therapist identifies the fine-motor problems of the child with AD/HD and makes and carries out recommendations for remediation. A child with suspected or diagnosed AD/HD may be referred for occupational therapy due to difficulty with **visual-motor integration,** difficulty tuning out excessive stimuli in the classroom, or difficulty with motor coordination (Jones, 1998a).

Visual-motor integration
Ability to synchronize vision with the movements of the body or body-parts into a complete and harmonious whole.

The occupational therapist can help the other team members form realistic expectations of the child's current level of functioning in the classroom and set forth a course of action to increase the child's skills so that greater success is more likely. The occupational therapist can address effective posture for learning (e.g., sitting erect in a correctly sized table and chair with books and learning materials placed to facilitate visual tracking of the text), eye-hand coordination that is adequate for copying from the chalkboard, and compensatory strategies for children who have difficulty with visual-motor memory integration. The therapist serves as a resource for adapting and modifying the physical environment of the classroom to meet the child's specific needs.

Other Possible Team Members

Interdisciplinary teams that are formed to diagnose and plan treatment for a child with suspected or previously diagnosed AD/HD may also include professionals such as guidance counselors, physical therapists, or others. The need for other team members will be based on the specific needs of a particular child. As diagnostic and assessment information is obtained, and other professionals are deemed necessary for the team, additions should be made.

Health insurance companies typically do not cover all the different components that may be needed for the diagnosis and treatment of AD/HD. A complete assessment with the necessary professionals is costly and often unaffordable to most families, leading to fragmentation of care, incomplete evaluation, and inefficient management of the condition. Since AD/HD is a chronic disorder that persists into adulthood and comorbidity is the rule rather than the exception, it is likely that referrals to various professionals on this team will continue to be needed over time. The professionals mentioned in this chapter form the basis of a team, but additional professionals may be called upon from time to time. What draws these individuals into a team is the fact that AD/HD brings with it many behavioral, learning, language, auditory, and social issues. See Table 5.1 for a summary of potential team members and their roles.

Table 5.1 **Potential Team Members and Their Roles**

Team Members	Roles
Parents	• Provide insight • Participate in assessment and planning • Approve plan • Carry out suggestions and behavior management
Developmental Pediatrician, Child Neurologist	• Assesses neurobiological integrity • Rules out other health issues • Provides diagnosis • Prescribes medication • May refer to other health professionals • Assesses attention and mental health status
Psychiatrist	• Assesses individual's emotional/behavioral status • Provides diagnosis • Prescribes medication • Counsels child/adult and family in coping strategies • Treats comorbid behavioral disorders
School Nurse	• Gathers information • Observes the child in the class and play • Participates in medication regimen and monitors child on medication

Continued on next page

Table 5.1—*Continued*

Team Members	Roles
Educator	• Assesses academic performance in the classroom and measures academic achievement • Modifies instructional methods
Educational Psychologist	• Evaluates and observes behaviors • Contributes to diagnosis • Designs behavioral management plan • Determines social-emotional impact of AD/HD • Provides counseling
Speech-Language Pathologist	• Assesses language skills (receptive and expressive) • Determines presence of executive language disorder and/or pragmatic language disorder • Makes recommendations for treatment, goals, and classroom modifications
Audiologist	• Tests hearing and evaluates for central auditory processing disorder • Makes recommendations for accommodations • Reviews health record for recurrent otitis media
Special Education Administrator	• Makes range of special education services available • Determines who provides diagnostic and treatment services, and how current caseloads are managed • Authorizes accommodations (test taking and other academic modifications)
Occupational Therapist	• Facilitates child's functioning independently • Identifies fine motor problems • Assesses sensory integration problems and recommends treatment plan • Makes recommendations to remediate including adaptations in the classroom and home to meet the child's physical challenges

Summary

Ideally, all these professionals should interface when possible. The minimal team, in addition to the parent, should consist of a physician (preferably a developmental pediatrician or psychiatrist knowledgeable about AD/HD), a psychologist or guidance counselor, an educator, and a speech-language pathologist.

Educational and Behavioral Management

Treating AD/HD in children requires educational and behavioral management in a multimodal approach. This approach includes:

- Parent training in diagnosis, treatment, and behavior management techniques
- An appropriate educational program
- Individual and family counseling, when needed
- Medication, when required

Behavior management is an especially important intervention with children who have AD/HD. The most important techniques are consistency and positive reinforcement in which the child is rewarded for desired behavior. Management involves using resources, repositioning, relearning, and coping with the environment in order to function successfully.

Treatment for adults is also multimodal but more deficit specific to ameliorate the problem. Education is the paramount issue, followed by structuring the environment to improve management skills, and then specific treatment protocols that help the individual cope with the challenges of AD/HD.

Among the most effective treatment and management methods to date are the judicious use of medication and behavior management. Cognitive self-control programs, when applied carefully and consistently, can also be helpful (MTA Cooperative Group, 1999, 2004).

Given that individuals with attention-deficit/hyperactivity disorder have problems with self-regulation and organization, management of their lives is frequently a challenge. Management deficiencies impact learning in the classroom and behaviors at home.

Educational Management

Challenges that students with AD/HD have in organization are due to memory problems and problems in actively managing their learning in relationship to time and materials. (Memory issues will be dealt with in Chapter 8.) They tend to not keep separate notebooks for their classes, they forget to bring the necessary items to class, or they forget to take home the materials necessary to do their homework. Many of the children are messy and have difficulty finding their things (Minskoff & Allsopp, 2003). These organizational problems are related because they represent the metacognitive skills of coordinating time, materials, and activities.

Time Management

Managing time includes classifying activities into school, work, social, and home responsibilities. In particular, planning using time variables involves advanced cognitive skills (Minskoff & Allsopp, 2003). Many children with AD/HD are helped by using time charts, such as the daily time chart example in Figure 6.1. Enhancing student awareness of time can be facilitated by making sure that they wear watches and keep schedules in their notebooks. To help the child keep track of tests and assignments, it is also beneficial to create a calendar for the month, for the grading period, or for the week to lay out all assignments, tests, and activities (Minskoff & Allsopp). Figure 6.2 on page 120 illustrates a monthly calendar.

One of the major organizational difficulties students with AD/HD have is setting goals and then prioritizing what is most important to complete. To teach students to use their time effectively, they need to think of things they need to do, arrange them into categories (school, home, social), prioritize them, and then do them (Minskoff & Allsopp, 2003). Figure 6.3 on page 121, illustrates a goal-setting chart. A blank *Goal-Setting Chart* can be printed from Study More 6.1 on the CD-ROM. Figure 6.4 on page 122 is an example goal management chart used to help parents focus their child's goals on accomplishing homework with a reward system. A blank *Goal Management Chart* can be printed from Study More 6.2 on the CD-ROM.

Figure 6.1 **Daily Chart**

Time	Activity
7:00 AM	Wake up
7:00–7:20 AM	Shower, brush teeth, get dressed
7:20–7:30 AM	Tidy up room, prepare materials for school
7:30–7:45 AM	Place school bag by the door, eat breakfast
7:45–8:00 AM	TV time
8:00 AM	Leave for school
8:15 AM–3:00 PM	School
3:15 PM	Come home
3:15–3:30 PM	Relax, snack, TV
3:30–5:00 PM	Homework
5:00–6:00 PM	Play time
6:00–6:30 PM	Dinner
6:30–7:00 PM	Free play, reading time, computer time
7:00–7:30 PM	Free play
7:30–7:45 PM	Shower, brush teeth
7:45–8:30 PM	Relax, quiet time, reading time
8:30 PM	Bedtime

Another difficult challenge in school is taking tests. Students with AD/HD have not developed test-wise strategies to perform well on class and standardized examinations. Being test-wise involves knowing how to manage time effectively during testing. These students do not work well under time constraints and must be taught to work quickly on timed tests and accurately on untimed tests. Being test-wise also involves reading questions and directions carefully. Many students who are impulsive do not have a careful analytical approach and, therefore, may not read directions or may read them superficially. Often they read the first and second choice

Figure 6.2   **Monthly Calendar**

Sunday	Monday	Tuesday	Wednesday	Thursday	Friday	Saturday
1	2	3	4	5	6 3:00 baseball practice	7 Billy's birthday party
8 picnic at Bronx Zoo	9 4:00 piano lesson	10 math quiz	11 library trip	12 science test	13 spelling test	14
15 circus	16 4:00 piano lesson	17 math quiz	18	19	20 spelling test	21
22	23 4:00 piano lesson	24 math quiz	25	26	27 spelling test	28

in a multiple choice question, neglecting items 3 and 4. Effective test taking involves use of different strategies to match the format of the test. Children with AD/HD have difficulty activating strategies they use for studying when taking the test. They compartmentalize their thinking and learn strategies related to a specific situation without transferring from the study setting to the test setting. Students with AD/HD find it difficult to meet the challenge of developing independent study skills because of difficulty in integrating the required attention, advanced cognitive processes, and memory skills.

Minskoff and Allsopp (2003) offer the following strategies to help in managing time while taking the test:

- Read the directions carefully.
- Look over the test.
- Answer the easiest questions first.

Figure 6.3   **Goal-Setting Chart**

Goals I Have to Accomplish. Order of priority.	What I'm Going to Do to Accomplish the Goal.	How I'm Going to Accomplish the Goal.	When I'm Going to Accomplish the Goal.	Goal Accomplished
Completing math homework 1	1. Read the entire problem. 2. Re-tell the problem. 3. Think of a solution.	Quietly. I'm going to try to work along and then ask for help if I need it.	After an after-school snack and before dinner	Yes, 6/4/2005
Studying for test in 3 days 2	Study for 10 minutes every day	Recite out loud the information. Write it down in a notebook, underline important information.	Before my favorite TV show at 8 PM	Yes, 10/5/2005

Set priorities. Number the most important goals.

1 = most important goal, must be completed ASAP

5 = least important goal, can wait until later

- Answer questions that are worth more.
- Skip difficult questions.

Many students find it difficult to get started on a task or studying for tests, and, once started, find it difficult to sustain attention. They become dependent on a teacher to get them started and to help them stay on task. Many of these students have their parents study with them at home. This assistance is important in the initial stages of learning, but must be gradually reduced so that the students develop the ability to study independently. Many of these students tend to be passive learners and do not lay out a study plan of how to organize their time and learning. Many times, they simply read the material without imposing an overall structure on the material to increase their understanding and retention. When studying for tests, they fail to apply cognitive strategies to aid their memorization of the material (Minskoff & Allsopp, 2003).

Figure 6.4 **Goal Management Chart**

Weeks	Sun	Mon	Tue	Wed	Th	Fri	Sat
First Week	✔✔	✔✔✔	✔✔✔	✔✔	✔		
Second Week		✔✔	✔		✔✔	✔✔	✔✔
Third Week	✔		✔✔✔	✔	✔✔	✔	
Fourth Week	✔✔✔	✔✔	✔	✔	✔✔		

✔ = 1 point

1 point for completed homework

1 point for homework checked (by parent)

1 point for homework put away and ready to be turned in

Possible Rewards

Go Rollerblading	12 points
Cookie	4 points
Play a board game	6 points
Trip	24 points
Stay up later	15 points
Watch one extra TV show	18 points

Students sit down with the best intentions to study; however, they just can't get started. They stare at their books or out the window. It is recommended that for these students it is best not to impose any study preferences. Students need to identify study environments that are best for them. To develop effective study skills, students must reduce the distractions in their environments, have all necessary equipment nearby, establish rewards, and create checklists of tasks to be done. Often, promise of a reward at the end helps students complete the study period. To keep students focused when studying, set a timer and have periodic checks to assure they are keeping on task. Set small goals or segments to study at one time. Then, reorganize and proceed again.

Materials Management

Students with organizational difficulties seem to lose or misplace items frequently, so it is important to have back-up planners and notebooks.

Enhance student awareness of time by making sure they wear watches and keep schedules in their notebooks.

Teach students with AD/HD the skills of good attendance and punctuality, and instruct them on the consequences of their actions. Good attendance and punctuality are essential for success in school and on a job. Help students analyze the causes of poor attendance and lack of punctuality (e.g., don't like the class, don't like the teacher, don't understand the material), identify the consequences (lower final grade, fail the class, unable to graduate), and set goals to increase motivation.

Many students read textbooks only once or twice. They do not realize that they must interact with the material to comprehend and memorize it. They are reluctant to review the chapters over and over until they master the organization of the material. They need to write main ideas and relevant details in their notebooks, keep margin notes, or underline or highlight parts of the text. Minskoff and Allsopp (2003) propose the following helpful strategies for use when studying from books:

- Copy chapter heading and subheading.
- Organize note cards.
- Number the cards under categories.
- Arrange the note cards in columns and identify each card's correct place.
- Review the note cards.

When managing children in the classroom with AD/HD concerns, see Table 6.1, pages 124–125, for ideas. This table is also included as a reproducible handout on the CD-ROM as Study More 6.3. Additionally, physical adaptations and organizational systems are helpful to many students with AD/HD. Ideas for organizational systems, physical adaptations, and tools for fidgeting are provided in Sidebar 6.1, pages 126–127. These products are available from Abilitations at www. abilitations.com and are highlighted in Study More 6.4.

Curriculum Management

When Attention Affects Reading

Children with AD/HD who do not have learning disabilities or a reading disability may still experience reading difficulties. They exhibit problems with reading as a result of difficulties with attention and working memory (Rief, 2000). This often results in nonreading, or struggles in learning how to read. Many children with AD/HD have poor reading comprehension

Table 6.1   **Managing Children with AD/HD in the Classroom**

Problem	Ideas for Management
The child has difficulty starting an activity.	• Signal child when he/she should begin. • Parcel out work in small units. • Before giving assignment, explain purpose and the number of steps involved. • Give feedback immediately after performance to encourage child. • To help child assess the time an assignment will take, use a timer or digital clock. • Use colored cube (color code cubes) depending on level of difficulty. Place one at beginning of activity. When completed have child drop the cube in a box in the front of the room. • Plan a reward when the activity is completed (playing time, token, point).
The child has difficulty staying on task.	• Keep work area clear and free of distractions. • Position child near a "buddy," preferably one who is attentive. • Use colored markers to reduce the repetition. • Provide immediate reinforcement for every task, then make it intermittent. • Reward child for good eye contact. • Plan activity with steps that are easy and doable to meet with success. • Change activities. Use motor or physical actions to reduce fatigue. • Use colored paper or colored transparencies, or use PowerPoint and change background and foreground colors.
The child has difficulty staying seated.	• Make sure the child understands what is expected of him or her. • Reward the child for sitting. • Have child bring a picture of his/her sitting and hang it up. • Keep child's seat away from distractions, preferably in front of teacher. • Place child's seat in an area where it is not easy to vacate. • Place child in a special seat cushion to reduce fidgetiness. (See Sidebar 6.1 and Study More 6.2 for more about "fidgets.") • Provide a "fidget" for the child to engage his hands. • Promote a hand clasp on the desk position. • Remind child to keep feet on the floor in "listening position."
The child has difficulty following directions.	• Keep directions short. • When giving directions, use visual, auditory, and kinesthetic models. • Repeat directions and provide visual cues. • When repeating directions, paraphrase and reformulate words. • Ask child to retell the directions before beginning. • Pair the child with a "buddy" who knows the directions. • Have child act out what was asked of him/her. • Use a drawing to illustrate what the child has to do. • State how many steps are involved in the direction. • Tell what number in the steps the child is on.

Table 6.1—*Continued*

Problem	Ideas for Management
The child has difficulty working independently.	• Explain how many steps are involved in the task ahead of time. • Make sure the task is age appropriate. • Provide an end goal and show child his progress toward it. • Announce how many steps are left or how much more time is needed. • Make reward immediate. Praise children for concentrating. Always identify the positive attending skills. • Give tasks that are shorter followed by longer tasks that may need assistance. • Encourage independent work and reward for such. • Use fading technique to encourage more independence.
The child calls out impulsively and inappropriately.	• When a child is listening, present reward. • Reward children who do not call out. • Establish classroom guidelines (rules) that are posted in the room. • Point to the rule posted on the cue board on the wall to remind the child not to interrupt. • Alternate leadership positions rotating among the class. • Give each child a chance to speak or role-play. Use small group projects or use plays to act out.
The child has difficulty following classroom rules.	• Keep classroom rules visible and review each morning. Illustrate the chart with photos of children in the class following rules. • State rules simply. • Make a Do and Don't chart. Point to the Don't when the child violates that rule. • Rules need to be followed consistently with consequences for those violating rules. • Give each child a personal list of the rules, where he or she can store it and see it. • Provide stimuli illustrating the rule.
The child has difficulty listening.	• Use visual/pictures along with the story. • Ask child to repeat directions in passage. • Place child in front of teacher. • Have the child act out what was said. • Have the child wear an FM unit or infrared unit to hear the speaker more clearly, or place a hand-held speaker in front of the child's desk (toteable).
The child has difficulty remembering.	• Teach child how to use mnemonics to help with remembering. • Ask child to repeat directions aloud or into a tape recorder for later recall. • Put instructions into a song or a chant, or a rhyme. • Go over and repeat information. • Use colored markers to code important details. Use red for urgent, blue for less urgent, etc. • Teach how to extract critical information from noncritical. • Teach visual/verbal imagery techniques.

Source: Jones (1998b)

Physical Adaptations and Organizational Systems to Help Children with AD/HD

High-Back Bean Bag Chair

T-Stool

Visual Timer

Swiss Disc

Movin' Step

Metronomes

Study-Rite Carrels

Concentration Station Carrels

Sensory Snuggle

Teacher's Hands

Physical Adaptations

- *High-Back Bean Bag Chair*—Provides the advantages of a bean bag chair with the added support for arms and back.

- *T-Stool*—Provides children who need the balance challenge to stimulate themselves enough to pay attention.

- *Movin' Step*—Used under a desk for improving focus by using movement and heavy work. Can adjust the level. Designed to improve coordination, balance, and sequencing.

- *Study-Rite Carrels*—Reduce distractions to help students concentrate while providing personal work environment.

- *Sensory Snuggle*—Horseshoe-shaped pillow enhances postural stability, which increases a child's attention span and organizes arousal for learning. Top pockets for fingers and hands.

- *Visual Timer*—Gives instant feedback on the amount of time remaining for the activity.

- *Swiss Disc*—Round, slightly textured cushion with beveled edges for comfort and support. Helpful in maintaining balance in a seat.

- *Metronomes*—Provides calming effect when set to 60 beats per minute.

- *Concentration Station Carrels*—Minimizes visual distractions and includes a weighted lap pad to help keep the student calm.

- *Teacher's Hands*—A student pager that vibrates when the teacher needs a child to attend to a task.

Organizational Systems

- *Over-the-Chair Storage Buddy*—Fine, colorful storage pockets to fit over the chair to contain utensils (e.g., pens, scissors, etc.).

- *My Personal Data Organizer*—Toy Palm Pilot with touch screen to hold email addresses, schedules, timer, and calculator.

- *Take-Along Clipboard*—Large clipboard that provides storage for loose paperwork and has additional storage space. An effective organizing tool to hold papers, pencils, etc.

- *Oxford 8-Pocket Project Organizer*—Translucent folder protects work with compartments to organize by topic, class, etc.

- *Oxford 4-Pocket Portfolio*—Cover with 4 interior pockets to store and organize papers.

Fidgets

- *Twidget*—Two-handed fidget offers visual input, moving texture, and sound which encourages rhythmicity.

- *Koosh Ball*—A tentacle covered ball.

- *Squidgie Ball*—A crushable, vented surface that floats in water.

- *Squishy Balls*—Soft balls that light up when squeezed or have internal balls within that move around when squeezed.

- *Fidget Pens*—A variety of shapes and movement options seated atop a pen.

Products available from Abilitations, www.abilitations.com.

Over-the-Chair Storage Buddy

Twidget

My Personal Data Organizer

Koosh Ball

Take-Along Clipboard

Squidgie Ball

Oxford 8-Pocket Project Organizer

Squishy Balls

Oxford 4-Pocket Portfolio

Fidget Pens

because they are not actively thinking about the material they are reading and have trouble processing and understanding it. They have difficulty maintaining their focus while reading, struggling to keep their attention. They need to reread repeatedly for clarity and often lose their place while doing so. Table 6.2 (see pages 129–131) includes effective strategies to manage reading problems. This information can also be printed from the CD-ROM: Study More 6.5.

When Attention Affects Writing Skills

Writing is another academic area that causes great struggle for most children with AD/HD. Many AD/HD children are knowledgeable and able to verbalize a great deal of information on a topic, yet have difficulty committing these words to paper, producing few words or simple sentences. Because they are often unable to communicate thoughts and ideas on paper, their writing skills (not handwriting) are often deficient. The process of writing is very complex and involves the simultaneous integration of a variety of skills. Some children may have an expressive language disorder for both oral and written modalities. Language expression, organization, and fluency involve a facility with vocabulary usage and word retrieval. Transcribing and expressing ideas on paper in complete descriptive sentences require proper sentence syntax and paragraph structure. A logical flow and sequence of ideas from start to closure requires organization. Children with comorbid learning disabilities exhibit weak spelling skills, often due to auditory sequential memory deficits and visual sequential memory deficits.

The physical task of handwriting is a difficult task for children with AD/HD as they have poor spatial organization on a page (writing on and within given lines, spacing adequately, lining up numbers in a column as in math addition and subtraction tasks). They may have poor fine-motor control which requires small muscle movements such as holding a pencil properly and writing. Immature handwriting skills (poor letter formation) and speed of output affect their penmanship. Many times they write very rapidly and the product is illegible or the writing is excessively slow and tedious, or they can't write script. For many children, occupational therapy is needed. Table 6.2, pages 129–131, and Study More 6.5, also includes strategies for addressing writing problems.

Table 6.2　　　　　　　　　**Effective Curriculum Strategies**

Academic Concern	Strategies
Reading	• Teach effective reading techniques that engage one's attention and require interaction with the text—before, during, and after the reading. This involves scanning the chapter headings and illustrations, and highlighting the text. • Use graphic organizers to guide thinking and processing through literary and expository text (Wiig & Wilson, 2001). • Model, practice, and encourage predicting and confirming strategies while reading (Wiig & Wilson, 2002). • Model and teach how to ask self-questions about the material, and then have the child read through the text for the answers to those questions. • Have the child find a location to read with as few distractions as possible. Allow and encourage reading aloud to self and have the child summarize what he or she read verbally into a tape recorder. Use ear plugs to block out background noise. • Have the child read in short amounts, paraphrase, retell, summarize, take brief notes, highlight key information, circle, underline, and make quick illustrations. Teach the child how to underline and highlight. • Teach the child to write margin notes on the side of the page to ensure understanding. • After reading the text, have the child review, restate, summarize, and fill in any graphic organizers or study guides. Have the child quiz himself or herself on the main ideas (Wiig & Wilson, 2002). • Provide technology like Reading Assistant (www.reading-assistant.com) or Reading Pen (readingpen.net) to ensure fluency and understanding. Technology holds a child's interest while filling in gaps of information.
Writing	• Help the child pre-plan when it is necessary to generate and organize the ideas prior. Use graphic organizers to pre-plan (Wiig & Wilson, 2001). • Teach the structures and formats for different writing **genres** and papers, providing many models, frames, **rubrics** of expectation, and lists of words (Wiig, Larson, & Olson, 2004). • Use a guide to help with mechanics and punctuation (children with AD/HD are typically inattentive to the details of capitalization and punctuation). • Provide self-editing checklists and direct assistance for editing. Have student write rough drafts on every other line, making it easier to edit and make corrections. • Teach the student to reread what has been written, then to self-edit and correct errors. These steps are particularly difficult for children with AD/HD. • Help the child check spelling (children with attention difficulties are often inattentive to visual detail, not recalling all of the letters in a word, or leaving out a letter without noticing).

Genres
A category of artistic, musical, or literary composition characterized by a particular style, form, or content.

Rubrics
Rules or directions for conducting a routine action.

Continued on next page

Attention-Deficit/Hyperactivity Disorder

Table 6.2—*Continued*

Academic Concern	Strategies
Writing—*Continued*	• Teach and practice spelling words using a variety of motivating, multisensory techniques. • Provide concrete, spatial anchors and models of letter formation to help with handwriting and organization on the page. • Use the technique of fading letters to help the child print letters more accurately. • Teach keyboarding and word processing skills, and provide access to the computer when writing. • Teach the child to use spell-check. • Use AlphaSmart—a small portable keyboard laptop. It allows one to type notes and then transfer stored notes onto the desktop computer for printout (www.AlphaSmart.com). • Use technology for voice-to-text such as "Via Voice," "Write Out Loud," and Draft-Builder (www.DonJohnston.com).
Math	• Use graph paper to set up problems, or use notebook paper positioned so that the lines run vertically down the page to keep numerals better organized and aligned on the paper. • Provide a lot of space on the page between problems. • Have child first color or highlight the math processing signs before beginning the assignment. • Get the child started making sure he or she correctly works on a few problems before proceeding with the rest of the assignment. Check the child's work after completing a limited amount to reduce the frustration of solving several problems incorrectly and having to correct a number of errors. • Provide models of sample problems. • List steps/procedures to multi-step problems and algorithms. • Color, highlight, or underline key words and vocabulary in word/story problems—especially those words that indicate the process that will be used to solve the problem. • Teach efficient techniques for finding the answer to addition and subtraction facts. • Teach multiplication tables and counting using a systematic and multisensory approach. • Teach through melodies, rhythms, and chants to help children with memory difficulties. • Practice and review until the child feels a mastery for each set of facts. • Use software programs for math (e.g., Sound Reading Solutions Math Program). (www.Soundreading.com)

Table 6.2—*Continued*

Academic Concern	Strategies
Homework	• Address homework problems in the early grades to establish early study skills and work habits. • Collaborate strategies with the teacher to determine the amount and type of homework assigned. • Designate a distraction-free, well-organized location to work in, away from other children and noise. • Supply the area with paper, pencil, and other supplies necessary to complete the work. • Set time limits. • Divide homework into manageable chunks. • Negotiate realistic goals with appropriate rewards and penalties. • Consider token reinforcements that can be exchanged for privileges and treats. Positive reinforcement should be given four times more often than penalties. • Focus on positive behaviors. • Involve children in determining the terms of time, accuracy, and completion of tasks.

Source: Rief (1998)

When Attention Affects Math Skills

Many AD/HD and LD children have good mathematical reasoning and conceptualization skills, yet demonstrate very poor computation skills (Minskoff & Allsopp, 2003). Computation is a complex tasks requiring attention to many details, and focusing throughout the problems. Organizational challenges include spatial organization and alignment of numerals on the page, accurately copying the problems from the board or book onto paper, being able to quickly retrieve basic math facts from memory, recalling and following a sequence of multiple steps, and speed and accuracy of output. There is also a strong language component, especially for math word problems. For those youngsters with a language disorder, math skills are frequently compromised. See Table 6.2 on pages 129–131 and Study More 6.5 for strategies to help with math difficulties.

When Attention Affects Homework

Because of the types of symptoms associated with AD/HD, many children with this condition not only have difficulties performing in school, but also have trouble completing their homework assignments. Their weak organizational skills and difficulty in focusing lengthen homework into tedious hours, cutting into play time and quality time with the family. Many of them fail to write down assignments, argue with parents, and avoid doing the work.

It is important to recognize that each child's symptoms are unique, and the help associated with homework should be tailored to each child's individual needs. Thomas Power, PhD, Director of the Center for Management of AD/HD of the Children's Hospital of Philadelphia (CHOP) comments, "Addressing homework problems in the early grades can help establish study skills and work habits that are fundamental to success throughout school" ("Homework Strategies," 2001, p. 11). The strategies for homework management presented in Table 6.2, pages 129–131, are written as strategies for parents and caregivers, and are based on the Homework Success Program at CHOP. (Table 6.2 is provided on the CD-ROM as Study More 6.5.) For a list of helpful supplies for families to have on hand for daily homework see Figure 6.5 and consult Study More 6.6 on the CD-ROM.

Behavioral Management

No one specific behavioral approach works best with children with AD/HD. Behavior management techniques are usually designed by a psychologist to improve children's behavior, which is especially important when the child is not taking medication. These techniques teach parents behavioral strategies to manage noncompliance and defiance.

The basic premise of behavior management is that children learn many of their behaviors from their environment. Children with AD/HD, although compromised by problems with impulse control and attending, learn many behaviors from the world around them. By implementing behavior management techniques, many of these unacceptable behaviors can be unlearned and more-acceptable behaviors can be learned in their place (Wodrich, 2000).

When implementing behavior management, the important factor is to identify the essential behaviors that are primarily symptoms of the AD/HD condition. These behaviors will be difficult, but not impossible, to change by using behavioral strategies. An important factor to consider is the parents' personal or marital problems that may prevent the sound use of

Figure 6.5

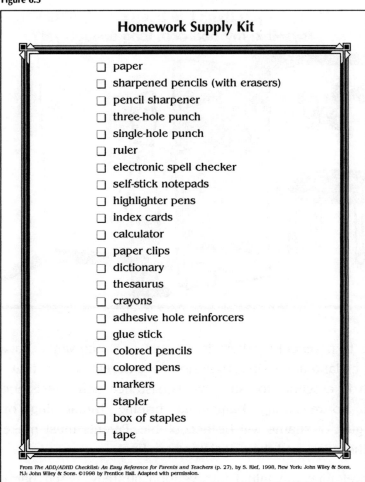

Homework Supply Kit

- ☐ paper
- ☐ sharpened pencils (with erasers)
- ☐ pencil sharpener
- ☐ three-hole punch
- ☐ single-hole punch
- ☐ ruler
- ☐ electronic spell checker
- ☐ self-stick notepads
- ☐ highlighter pens
- ☐ index cards
- ☐ calculator
- ☐ paper clips
- ☐ dictionary
- ☐ thesaurus
- ☐ crayons
- ☐ adhesive hole reinforcers
- ☐ glue stick
- ☐ colored pencils
- ☐ colored pens
- ☐ markers
- ☐ stapler
- ☐ box of staples
- ☐ tape

From *The ADD/ADHD Checklist: An Easy Reference for Parents and Teachers* (p. 27), by S. Rief, 1998, New York: John Wiley & Sons, NJ: John Wiley & Sons. ©1998 by Prentice Hall. Adapted with permission.

behavioral techniques. The emotional environment in the home may make implementation of a plan difficult. If there is disagreement between the parents, the techniques will be hard to use effectively.

The first step is to assess the behaviors and collect data. Based on these data, a plan can be developed and utilized. Any successful plan is based on two concepts espoused by Silver (1999):

1. Changing behavior is more likely to succeed by rewarding desired behavior than by punishing undesirable behavior.

2. Responses to acceptable and to unacceptable behaviors must be consistent. Inconsistent response patterns may reinforce the negative behaviors.

Stress to parents that there is no right or wrong way to raise children. However, collaborating with professionals to develop a plan they're comfortable with is essential for success. Persistence and consistency are also essential. No reasoning, bargaining, bribing, threatening, or trying to provoke guilt or shame will be acceptable. Parents must make the rules, enforce the rules, and their decisions are final.

In developing the initial intervention strategy, teach parents how to collect data on their observations of the behaviors. Each parent should collect data separately because differences between the observations will be useful. Besides, each may have a different perception of what the child did. Encourage them to record what really happens without worrying what someone will think.

Establishing a Plan

After the initial data are collected, analyze them for patterns. First, clearly define unacceptable behaviors that need to be changed which might relate to the child's learning disabilities or sensory integration disorder. Consider whether the child was given too many instructions at once, assigned a chore that was too difficult, or was frustrated with homework. Lastly, study the pattern of consequences. Are they consistent? Are they threatened and then not carried out? Are the consequences enforceable?

Once the behaviors are identified, develop a plan. Work with the parents to define the behaviors and work out consequences that can be implemented consistently and which are compatible with the family's philosophy, culture, and values. After the plan has been developed, present it to the family. The plan should apply to all children, even if they do not cause problems; it will not affect them negatively to be a part of the program and it will decrease the focus on the child for whom the plan was developed. Include ways to reverse the pattern of punishing bad behaviors and usually ignoring or inconsistently rewarding good or positive behaviors. Specifically, include plans to reward positive behaviors and withhold rewards for negative behaviors. Each parent should have planned responses that can be used every time so that the child cannot catch a parent off guard, making the child feel helpless or angry. The parental response should be the same each time the behavior occurs, and both parents must concur. To help parents manage their child's behavior, ask these questions:

1. What is the problem behavior I would like to eliminate?
2. Which behavior would be more acceptable?
3. What are the consequences of the problem and target behaviors?
4. How can I rearrange the consequences to discourage the problem behavior and encourage the target behavior?

Keep a chart of the behaviors discussed, the frequency of occurrence and the rewards distributed. Then plan an outing when they are completely accomplished. For an *Action Agreement* between the parent and child, see Figure 6.6, page 136, and Study More 6.7 on the CD-ROM. To encourage consistency in behavior, ask the teacher to cooperate by completing a questionnaire to track the child's behavior in school. An example questionnaire for the teacher is displayed in Figure 6.7, page 137, and included on the CD-ROM as Study More 6.8.

Coaching

Coaching is another form of management where it is the coach's job to help the client develop skills in the areas of time management and organization and incorporate structures that will improve the overall quality of the child's life. According to Brown (as cited in Horan, 1999, p. 12), a licensed therapist, "A coach helps his/her client create an individualized structure and a best-fit environment that compensates externally for what is weak internally." Coaching involves creating compensatory strategies that cue clients to behave the way they want to behave and motivate them

Attention-Deficit/Hyperactivity Disorder

Figure 6.6

Action Agreement

Student Name: _____ Date: _____

Teacher Name: _____

> **I will work hard to achieve the following goals, using the strategies listed, in order to receive the stated rewards or benefits.**

Goal 1 _____ Date _____

    Strategies: _____

    Reward: _____

Goal 2 _____ Date _____

    Strategies: _____

    Reward: _____

Goal 3 _____ Date _____

    Strategies: _____

    Reward: _____

My progress will be checked (circle one): Daily   Weekly   Monthly

_____ _____

Student Signature   Date   Parent/Adult Signature   Date

From "Action Agreement" by McNeil Consumer & Specialty Pharmaceuticals, (n.d.), www.concerta.net. © 2000–2005 by McNeil Consumer & Specialty Pharmaceuticals. Adapted with permission.

---

to be persistent in a task. A coach's job is simply to support the client in his or her efforts. Coaches can work for children as well as adults.

There is no set formula for developing effective coaching strategies. Many coaches indicate that it is the client's needs that are the focus. Flexibility is needed as goals may change depending upon the project at hand. The coach's role is to devise effective organizing systems. Coaching is a collaborative process where the coach facilitates the goals and serves as a catalyst for accomplishing them (Horan, 1999).

Coaching can be beneficial for individuals with AD/HD since they have trouble with self-direction due to memory problems, impulsivity, or distractibility. Coaching helps these individuals develop a map, focus on the

136

Figure 6.7

Teacher Questionnaire

Teacher Name: _____

Student Name: _____

Tracking/Evaluation Period: _____

Complete each item below by reflecting on the student's performance during the time period indicated above. Mark the box "Usually," "Sometimes," "Seldom," or "Never" to best represent the student's use of each skill described. Consult with the parents or caregivers, as needed.

Skills	Usually	Sometimes	Seldom	Never
Arrives at school on time				
Arrives to class prepared (homework completed and materials on-hand)				
Remains seated without being disruptive to others				
Waits for his or her turn without interrupting				
Gets along with classmates during structured academic times				
Gets along with classmates during unstructured, extracurricular times				
Transitions from activity to activity without misbehavior				
Completes activities in a timely fashion				

Comments:

From "Action Agreement" by McNeil Consumer & Specialty Pharmaceuticals, (n.d.), www.concerta.net. © 2000–2005 by McNeil Consumer & Specialty Pharmaceuticals. Adapted with permission.

"big picture" and choose tools that will help them accomplish their goals (Horan, 1999). Often, successful business people rely on coaches to help them execute their duties. Others have "mothers" or "wives" (or "husbands").

Coaching does not replace either medication or psychotherapy. It provides a missing link that allows individuals with AD/HD to achieve the changes in their lives. Coaching focuses on the practical implementation of a client's goals, and it deals with the actions that need to be taken in order to get things done.

A coach works with the client frequently for brief periods of time, helping the client stay focused on the tasks at hand. The coach also teaches the client to break down large tasks into small, manageable units. Throughout the whole process, it is the client who is accountable for taking these steps and working steadily toward larger, more meaningful goals.

The main goal of AD/HD coaches is to help the individual develop skills and strategies that compensate for the weaknesses that result from having AD/HD. These coaches communicate with their clients on a daily basis either through face-to-face meetings or telephone calls to assure that the client stays on track, maintains focus, and makes steady progress. The schedule set is not for the coach's benefit but rather is dependent upon the person's need for frequent reminders to stay focused on the most important task facing him or her.

AD/HD coaching is a highly flexible process. The initial setting of goals and strategizing takes place in a face-to-face meeting. Afterwards, the contact may be by telephone, fax, or even email. It is important to recognize that the schedule is not for the benefit of the coach but reflects the need of the individual with AD/HD. An AD/HD coach in many ways becomes an integral part of the environment, providing the necessary cues at the appropriate times, which in turn helps the individual make decisions, prioritize, and sequence tasks. The coach requires the client to be accountable, first to the coach and ultimately to himself or herself.

Coaches can be found in directories and often advertise in local CHADD newsletters. It is not a recognized "profession" so therefore it is unregulated. There is no specific educational background or license necessary to become a coach. AD/HD coaches should possess the following skills: ability to engage the client in strategic planning and design implementation; and ability to manage time effectively, organize, and manage projects. Coaches should have a thorough understanding of the complexities of AD/HD and be able to partner with the person's therapists. The National Coaching Network (NCN) is an organization which provides referrals, training, educational material, and networking opportunities for coaches of individuals with AD/HD.

In many cases, a friend or spouse of a family member may serve as the coach, providing encouragement to stay on tasks and accomplish the tasks at hand. This, however, may be an uncomfortable set-up for an individual with AD/HD because someone they know may have a personal interest in changes being achieved. Further, these individuals may not have the necessary skills. Coaching can provide the needed impetus to help a person with AD/HD succeed.

Management between School Years

Although the focus on AD/HD is primarily in school and at home, AD/HD does not cease existing at the end of the school year. It is a part of the child's life during the summer months as well. These children continue to need special support and programs that will allow them to interact with their environment effectively. Sending the child to camp is a common option. Many parents have concerns as to whether the camp will provide an effective environment that will help alleviate their child's AD/HD. Parents should be aware that there are camps specifically structured for children with AD/HD, or other physical or mental disabilities. The staff in these camps are adequately trained to provide a receptive atmosphere and understanding of the whole child in order to provide the best possible camp experience.

In choosing such a specialized camp, encourage parents to consider two important issues to ensure that the child receives the appropriate level of care necessary (Choskey, 2002). These are the policies on the discipline processes and procedures for distributing medication. The parents should also become aware of the camp's philosophy, the types of programs available, and how their child can benefit from the experience.

When choosing a camp, parents should consider the child's particular interests and input. The activities offered should be consistent with the interests of the child. It is important to recognize whether the camp is an "all-weather camp," providing outdoor activities, such as tennis courts, softball, basketball, nature trails, hockey field, rollerblade tracks, mountain biking, climbing wall, soccer, as well as indoor activities, such as arts center, culinary arts program, fitness center, computer labs, music room, and library.

Parents should be familiar with the safety measures and precautions, such as a health supervisor, high staff ratio for enhanced supervision, and a discipline and reward process with logical and appropriate consequences. Positive reinforcement should be helpful in building the child's self-esteem and motivating the child to further increase skills.

Not all types of camps are suitable for all children. Day camps may be suitable for some children while overnight camps may be more appropriate for children who need a longer amount of time to measure success, self-confidence, or acceptance. The following is a list of questions parents should ask when considering summer camps (Choskey, 2002):

- What is the discipline process?
- How is medication handled?
- What are the safety standards at the facility?
- Is the camp American Camp Association (ACA) accredited?
- What are the camp's staff qualifications, philosophy, and training?
- How does this camp for children with AD/HD differ from regular camp?
- Do many children return to the camp after their initial stay?
- How does this camp establish goals for each child, and how is progress charted?
- What types of programs are available?
- Is there a theme or focus to this camp?
- What activities are available? (indoor and outdoor)
- What are the accommodations?
- What incentives do the children receive, if any?
- Can the camp provide a list of references? (Preferably a list of parents whose children attended the camp)
- What should I do, as a parent, to prepare my child for attending this camp?

Camp can be either a positive or negative experience for the child, so it should be chosen wisely and with consent.

Summary

This chapter discussed management strategies from home to school to camp. Behavior management techniques are essential whether the child is medicated or not. Implementing behavior management techniques through environmental alterations, the support of a coach, or adaptations in the classroom or social environment can reduce symptoms of AD/HD.

Medical Treatments

Individuals with AD/HD often rely on medical treatments including medication, complementary alternative medicine (CAM) and controversial treatments to improve symptoms of AD/HD. In this chapter, treatments that work and treatments that do not, or are not proven, are discussed in an effort to provide direction for coping with AD/HD.

Medication

Medication plays an integral part in the treatment plan. Medication is used to improve symptoms of AD/HD to allow the person to function more effectively. It does not cure the behavior, but allows the person to manage the behavior by alleviating the symptoms while the medication is active.

According to the American Medical Association, as reported in Goldman, Genel, Bezman, and Priscilla (1998), the effectiveness of pharmacotherapy relative to AD/HD—particularly stimulants—has been studied extensively. Medication alone can provide significant symptomatic and academic improvement in the short-term, although the "risk-benefit ratio of stimulant treatment must be evaluated and monitored on an ongoing basis in each case, but in general it is highly favorable" (p. 106).

Controlled studies involving more than 6,000 children, adolescents, and adults have been conducted to determine the effects of psychostimulant medications, one of the most researched medications (CHADD, 2003). Although there are no studies on the long term use of these drugs, many individuals have been taking medication for years without negative outcomes.

Is Medication Effective?

A primary multi-modal treatment study of children with AD/HD (Combined type), conducted by the National Institute of Mental Health (MTA Cooperative Group, 1999), found that for many children the most effective way to mitigate AD/HD symptoms is through a combined approach (medication and behavioral treatment). The study followed 579, 7 to 10 year-olds from the United States and Canada. The researchers compared the effects of four interventions: (1) group whereby children were administered medication individually only, (2) group whereby children were administered medication individually combined with behavioral intervention, (3) group administered behavioral intervention only, (4) no interventions but standard community care (i.e., medical care typically provided in the community). The group refers to the number of children, but each child was administered medication individually at home and not as part of a group. The results indicated that the group receiving both medical and behavioral interventions fared better than medical or behavioral intervention alone or community care alone. Multimodal approaches also proved effective in improving social skills for students from high-stress environments and children with AD/HD in combination with symptoms of anxiety and depression. The study also showed that lower medication dosage was effective in multimodal treatments, and higher doses were necessary to achieve similar results in the medication only treatment.

In what is now considered a classic study, Arnold et al. (1997) found that for three groups of youngsters with AD/HD (medication only, medication with behavioral therapy, and behavioral therapy only), that the group receiving both interventions fared better than the other two groups. The medication-only group fared better than behavioral-therapy-only group, thus supporting the notion that medication is an effective form of intervention. The findings in this study apply to a wide range of children and families identified in need of treatment services.

In a follow-up study (The MTA Cooperative Group, 2004), the largest AD/HD treatment study ever conducted with 540 children with AD/HD-combined subtype, children were randomly assigned to 1 of 4 treatments. Those treatment groups were: medication management, behavior management, medication management and behavior modification, and community care. The medication and behavioral treatment provided in the MTA study were more rigorous than what children typically receive in community settings. The behavioral intervention included over 25 parent training sessions, an intensive summer camp treatment program, and extensive support provided by paraprofessionals in children's classrooms. Children in community care received whatever treatment parents opted to pursue for their children in the community. The initial results examined outcomes 14 months after treatment began. The general conclusions indicated that children who received intensive medication management, either alone or in combination with behavior treatment, had more positive outcomes than children who received behavior therapy alone or community care only. There was some evidence to conclude that children who received combined treatment did better overall than children who received medication treatment alone. Sixty-eight percent of the children who were no longer showing clinically elevated levels of AD/HD symptoms were in the combined subgroup, 56 percent were in the medication-only groups, and 33 percent were in the behavior therapy group, with only 25 percent in the community care group. Such figures suggest that intensive medication treatment was more likely to result in a normalized level of core AD/HD symptoms than either behavior therapy or community care. The combined treatment was associated with the highest rate of "normalization."

Other studies also demonstrate that multimodal treatments are more effective for those children for whom treatment with medication alone is not sufficient. In October 2001, the American Academy of Pediatrics (AAP) released the following evidence-based recommendation for the treatment of children diagnosed with AD/HD:

- Primary care clinicians should establish a treatment program that recognizes AD/HD as a chronic condition.

- The treating clinician, parents, and the child, in collaboration with school personnel, should specify appropriate target outcomes to guide management.

- The clinician should recommend stimulant medication and/or behavioral therapy as appropriate to improve target outcomes in children with AD/HD.

The AAP report found that for children, stimulant medication for the management of core AD/HD symptoms is highly effective (2001).

Medication Choices for Treating AD/HD

For children and adults with AD/HD, a review of the literature indicates a clear pattern of symptom improvement with stimulants, with approximately 70 percent of patients responding to treatment. Once dosage is appropriately adjusted or **titrated** in adults, studies show similar patterns of improvement. AD/HD is presumed to stem from dysfunction of the **catecholamine**

Titrate
The adjustment of a medication's dosage in order to obtain the most favorable clinical response.

Catecholamine
Any of a group of chemicals including epinephrine, norepinephrine, and dopamine that are produced in the medulla of the adrenal gland and affect mood and appetite.

Attention-Deficit/Hyperactivity Disorder

Dopamine
A chemical substance (neurotransmitter) manufactured in the brain that transmits messages between neurons (brain cells) involved in the control of movement.

Norepinephrine
Also known as noradrenaline; is a hormone produced by the adrenal glands and also secreted from nerve endings in the sympathetic nervous system as a chemical transmitter of nerve impulses. Many of its general actions are similar to those of adrenaline, but it is more concerned with maintaining normal body activity.

Reuptake
The process in which neurotransmitters are taken up by the same nerves that released them.

Pathogenesis
The formation and development of a disease.

system, particularly **dopamine** and **norepinephrine.** Stimulants enhance the transmission of catecholamines, often blocking dopamine and norepinephrine **reuptake** transporters, with the net effect of increasing attention and decreasing impulsivity (CHADD, 2003).

The **pathogenesis** of AD/HD remains poorly understood. It is thought to be caused by an imbalance in catecholamine metabolism in the cerebral cortex. It is thought that norepinephrine may help control sensory processing by influencing the dopaminergic system, believed to be impaired in patients with AD/HD. Children with AD/HD have problems cognitively inhibiting behaviors.

Medications—First Tier

Psychostimulants are most widely used and were first administered to children in 1937. They derive their name from their abilities to stimulate concentration. Psychostimulants change the levels of transmitter chemicals available to various neurotransmitter systems in the brain. These medications are better termed "neurotransmitter modulators." Of the 70 to 80 percent of children that respond positively to the medication, improvement is seen in attention span, impulsivity control, and on-task behavior, especially in a structured environment. Children often benefit from medication outside of school because it helps them succeed in social settings, peer relations, home environment, and with homework. Consistent use of medication leads to the best long-term results. Psychostimulant medication can also be effective in adults who have AD/HD.

Common psychostimulant medications include methylphenidate (Ritalin), mixed salts of a single-entity amphetamine product (Adderall), and dextroamphetamine (Dexedrine, including one brand with several related compounds). Ritalin is now thought to be a dopamine transmitter blocker that "amplifies dopamine release." Thus, amplification of weak dopamine signals in AD/HD people would enhance task-specific signaling, improving attention and decreasing distractibility. It is thought that dopamine imbalances are related to AD/HD symptoms (Volkow et al., 2001). It often takes a few weeks to determine the proper dosage and medication schedule. Many adolescents and adults continue to respond well to the same dose of psychostimulant medication. Up to 70 percent of children with AD/HD continue to exhibit symptoms into adulthood. For these adults, continuing effective treatment modalities, including medication, can be helpful.

Methylphenidate is the best known stimulant, and is marketed by several pharmaceutical companies in various forms, including brand names Ritalin, Ritalin LA, Metadate CD, and Concerta. Among the available agents, stimulants are the mainstay of treatment for AD/HD.

Rapid-acting methylphenidate starts to work in 15 to 20 minutes and lasts for about $3^1/_2$ to 4 hours. Because of its relatively short action, methylphenidate is discontinued every night and started again in the morning. It improves concentration, memory, and control of frustration and anger. Possible side effects include: appetite suppression, sleep disturbances, transient weight loss, and irritability. **Rebound effect** can occur— anger and frustration—when the effect of medication **dissipates.** When the dosage is too high, motor tics may be unmasked, depression and **lethargy** may occur. Methylphenidate LA 20 (methylphenidate sustained release) is long-acting, and can last for approximately 6 to 8 hours. The dosage is determined on an individual basis. It is administered by mouth and is as effective as Ritalin, with similar side effects.

A Nashville study (Wolraich et al., 2001), revealed that once a day the extended-release methylphenidate (Concerta) was as effective as three times short-acting immediate release methylphenidate. The two formulations worked equally well in addressing the core AD/HD symptoms. Metadate is methylphenidate HCL or CD, extended release, that enhances higher plasma levels at earlier time periods. Metadate CD, when administered in a single morning dose, results in control of symptoms during the school day, relieving the need to visit the school nurse at noon. The United States Food and Drug Administration (FDA) approved revised labeling for Metadate CD to allow treatment of patients older than 6 years to have the option of having it sprinkled over their applesauce. This is beneficial for those individuals who have been unable to swallow solid dosages. It has been cited that approximately 26 percent of patients experience difficulty swallowing a capsule or solid tablet ("Studies," 2002). Sprinkle administration may help patients improve compliance with their dosing regimen.

Amphetamine products include short- and long-acting formulations of dextroamphetamine (Dexedrine, Dexedrine Spansule) and mixed amphetamine salts (MAS; Adderall; Adderall XR). In recent years, short-acting

Rebound effect
Behavior resulting when medication effects dissipate.

Dissipates
To cause to separate; move away from each other.

Lethargy
Weakness characterized by a lack of vitality or energy.

Attention-Deficit/Hyperactivity Disorder

formulations (3.5–6.5 hours) have been overtaken by longer-acting formulas that require less daily dosing. This ameliorates the stigma, inconvenience, noncompliance, and rebound associated with short duration of action. The extended-release agents are effective for as long as 10 to 12 hours. Some patients still require additional short-acting stimulants to extend their treatment time. The current dosages available are often too low for adults, requiring them to take several pills a day and often paying considerably more for the medication. Now, parents have a choice in the duration of the medication between the short-acting, immediate-release, and long-acting, extended-release. For long-acting medication, the treatment can be administered without involving the school personnel. The medication appears to improve the symptoms of AD/HD and may decrease aggression and stubbornness. The side effects are similar to methylphenidate.

In a recent study presented at the American Psychiatric Association Annual Meeting (Wigal, 2004) in one of the largest AD/HD classroom trials, the benefits of Adderall XR were compared to Strattera. Over a three-week period children with AD/HD achieved significantly greater improvement in both their behavior and attention with extended-release MAS (Adderall XR) compared to those with atomoxetine (Strattera). Patients taking MAS (Adderall XR) showed consistently improved behavior scores at weekly intervals as measured by the Wigal, Gupta, Guinta, Swanson (SKAMP) Behavior Rating Scale (Wigal et al., 1998). Those children taking atomoxetine (Strattera) had varied behavior scores from one week to the next. Improvement was noted in week one, but not in weeks two or three. (This study was sponsored by the manufacturer of Adderall XR.)

Generally, stimulant medications are well tolerated, but side effects can occur. Such side effects include insomnia, headaches, weight loss or **anorexia,** tics, **anxiety,** and dysphoria. Cardiovascular effects typically involve mild increases in heart rate and blood pressure, but need to be more closely watched in adults than in children (Bush et al., 1999). Adults who have borderline hypertension may be at risk for cardiovascular problems when taking such stimulant medication; thus, the hypertension needs to be treated before stimulant medication is instituted. For adults, insomnia or sleep disturbance may occur in the form of sleeplessness or delay in the onset of sleep. Stimulant medication is initially administered by titrating the dosage until symptoms are well controlled and side effects are minimized or manageable for the patient.

The dosage must be determined for each individual according to the ranges based on a medication dose per unit of body weight. The patient is monitored both on and off the medication. For children, observations are collected from parents and teachers, coaches, and tutors. The speech-language pathologist plays a key role in monitoring the child's focus and ability to communicate. This feedback helps the physician determine titration.

Psychostimulant medication is the most studied medication in pharmacological history. Yet, there are no long-term studies on the use of psychostimulant medication. Most immediate side effects related to these medications are mild and typically short-term. The most common side effects are reduction in appetite and difficulty sleeping. Some children experience "stimulant rebound"—a negative mood or an increase in activity when medication is losing its effect. These side effects are usually managed by changing the dose and the scheduling for short-acting medications, or by changing to a prolonged-release formulation. Studies suggest that ultimate height and weight are rarely affected, although they may be affected initially. For any child that seems to be lagging behind, height and weight should be closely monitored.

A relatively uncommon side effect of this medication may be the unmasking of latent tics—eye blinking, shrugging, and clearing of the throat. Psychostimulant medications can facilitate the emergence of a tic disorder in susceptible individuals. The medications may cause them to be noticed at the beginning stages of treatment, but they eventually go away in the latter part of the teenage years. Recent research suggests that the development of Tourette's syndrome, a rare tic disorder, in children with AD/HD is not related to psychostimulant medication. New research shows that for children who have AD/HD and uncontrolled tics or Tourette's syndrome may find relief from stimulants. Stimulant drugs may actually minimize the unwanted movements rather than exacerbate them. New findings (The Tourette's Syndrome Study Group, 2002) show both Ritalin and Catapres, especially when used together, are effective in treatment. Researchers found improvement within 136 children (7 to 14 years old) with AD/HD and a chronic tic disorder after four months of treatment. Not only did tics not worsen, but the severity of tics decreased in all groups. The Tourette's Syndrome Study group (2002) found improvements in attentiveness and behavior among those on Ritalin. For those on Catapres, there was less crying, frustration, restlessness, excitability, and impulsiveness. Such findings dispute the notion that children with tics should not take stimulants.

For many children, medication is an integral part of treatment. It is generally understood that children and adults who take medication for the symptoms of AD/HD attribute their successes to themselves, not to the medication. For a summary of the first tier medications, their generic names, types, duration, and side effects, see table 7.1.

Medications—Second Tier

For patients who do not respond to or cannot tolerate stimulant medication, other medications have been the next line of treatment. For example, desipramine (Norpramin), a tricyclic antidepressant that blocks norepinephrine and serotonin reuptake, and bupropion (Wellbutrin), an antidepressant with greater dopamine reuptake block than most antidepressants, have been somewhat effective in the treatment of AD/HD. Therapeutic benefit from these medications is often limited by tolerability problems. Side effects from these agents include drowsiness, insomnia, headache, weight gain, constipation, sexual dysfunction, seizures, and possible cardiac conduction abnormalities (Searight, Burke, & Rottnek, 2000).

Antidepressant medications are used less frequently for AD/HD but have been shown to be effective. Those antidepressants that affect the neurotransmitter serotonin (the serotonin selective reuptake inhibitors, or SSRIs) do not have an effect on AD/HD, but may be effective against coexisting conditions.

Imipramine and desipramine (Tofranil and Norpramin) are antidepressant tablets administered by mouth and doses are determined on an individual basis. Duration of action is variable; however, it often has a 24-hour effect. Lower doses may improve AD/HD symptoms within several days, but may take 1 to 3 weeks for full effect. Doses may improve depressive symptoms and mood swings. Side effects include: nervousness, sleep problems, fatigue, stomach upset, dizziness, dry mouth, accelerated heart rate, and irregular heart rate. It should not be abruptly discontinued.

Bupropion (Wellbutrin) are antidepressant tablets that last for about 4 to 6 hours in short-acting form; 6 to 8 hours in long-acting form. It improves symptoms of AD/HD, and can improve depressive moods.

Table 7.1   **Medication Used in the Treatment of AD/HD**

Medication/ Generic Name	Type	Duration	Side Effects
Adderall Dextroamphetamine	Psychostimulant	4–6 hours	Oversensitivity, headaches, irritability, loss of appetite, poor appetite, weight loss, tics (9% of children, 1% chronic)
Adderall XR Amphetamine	Long-acting psychostimulant	8–12 hours	
Concerta Methylphenidate	Long-acting psychostimulant	8–12 hours	
Cylert Magnesium Pemoline	Psychostimulant	4–6 hours	
Dexedrine Dextroamphetamine	Psychostimulant	4–6 hours	
Metadate Methylphenidate	Short-acting psychostimulant	2–5 hours	
Metadate CD Methylphenidate	Long-acting psychostimulant	8–12 hours	
Ritalin Methylphenidate	Short-acting psychostimulant*	2–5 hours	
Ritalin LA Methylphenidate	Long-acting	6–8 hours	
Catapres Clonidine	Short-acting	3–6 hours	Constipation, dizziness, drowsiness, dry mouth, unusual tiredness, or weakness
Focalin XR Dexmethylphenidate Hydrochloride	Long-acting	Over 8 hours	Stomach pain, loss of appetite, nausea, weight loss
Norpramin Desipramine	Antidepressant	24 hours	Constipation, diarrhea, dizziness, dry mouth, headache, nausea
Strattera Atomoxetine	Nonstimulant	Up to 24 hours	Abdominal pain, decreased appetite, dizziness, fatigue, headache, mood swings
Tenex Guanfacine	Long-acting	6–12 hours	Constipation, dizziness, drowsiness, dry mouth
Wellbutrin Bupropion	Antidepressant	24 hours	Constipation, diarrhea, dizziness, dry mouth, headache, nausea

*Stimulants increase the levels of neurotransmitter dopamine (to reduce hyperactivity), norepinephrine (to improve attention), and serotonin.

Sources: HealthCommunities.com, (2005) and Spencer (2002)

Attention-Deficit/Hyperactivity Disorder

It is important to look for comorbidity of depression because it is better to stabilize the comorbidity before treating the AD/HD since stimulant medications can create major decompensations not readily observed. According to M. Schwarz, MD, Case Western Reserve University, a person with undiagnosed bipolar disorder on stimulants can develop aggressive mania. The antidepressants that work on AD/HD include bupropion (Wellbutrin SR), venlafaxine (Effexor XR), and tricyclic antidepressants (CHADD, 2001). To determine if a child or adolescent is depressed, consult Sidebar 2.1 (page 23) for tell-tale signs.

Atomoxetine is the first nonstimulant agent approved by the FDA that offers a different mechanism of action than the standard therapy. Atomoxetine (called Tomoxetine until the name was changed to avoid confusion with the medication Tamoxifen) was originally studied for the treatment of depression and anxiety. In 1996, Eli Lilly and Company investigated its use with AD/HD. Atomoxetine is a selective presynaptic norepinephrine reuptake inhibitor. It is metabolized via the cytochrome enzyme system. Its plasma half-life varies in patients who are poor metabolizers. It can take one week to see minimal changes and up to four weeks to see the full benefit. It has been approved for use in pediatric and adult patients. It has been found to improve symptom severity, as suggested by their results. Its efficacy was compared to immediate release Ritalin (methylphenidate). Atomoxetine may be administered once or twice daily.

Strattera, its trade name, is dosed according to body weight (up to 70 kg body weight). It is recommended that it be taken with food. It should be taken at a total daily dose of 0.5 mg/kg and increased after a minimum of 3 days to a targeted total daily dose of 1.2 mg/kg administered as either a single daily dose in the morning or as evenly divided doses in the morning and late afternoon or early evening. Clinical studies have found that Strattera reduces AD/HD symptoms by blocking or slowing reabsorption of norepinephrine, a brain chemical considered important in regulating attention, impulsivity, and activity levels. Strattera is not a controlled substance and in an abuse-potential study in adults, it was not associated with stimulant or **euphoriant properties** (Baldinger & Yogman, 2003). Physicians can write for refill prescriptions as they are periodically needed.

The safety and efficacy of Strattera in pediatric patients younger than 6 years of age has not been established. The efficacy of Strattera use beyond 9 weeks of treatment has not been systematically evaluated. The

Euphoriant property
A feeling of happiness, confidence, or well-being sometimes exaggerated.

150

more recent studies seem to question its effectiveness. The most common adverse effects have been nausea, vomiting, fatigue, decreased appetite, stomach pain, dizziness, mood swings, and depression. In adults, the adverse affects also include: constipation, dry mouth, insomnia, decreased **libido,** impotence, urinary hesitation, and/or **dysmenorrhea.**

In just six months, physicians wrote more than 1 million prescriptions for Strattera, the only nonstimulant approved for the treatment of AD/HD, according to an announcement by Eli Lilly and Company (Bailey, 2003). That's the strongest launch ever in terms of total prescriptions for a new medicine, ahead of Concerta and Adderall XR. Eli Lilly's president touted that Strattera is filling an important unmet need. From June 30 through fall 2003, 700,000 patients had taken the medicine. It is the first medication approved for adults with AD/HD that received approval from the FDA in November 2002. The first clinical trials were done on adults for the purpose of providing a medication for adult patients. Atomoxetine (Strattera) lacks cardiovascular toxicity. It does not have abuse potential, minimizing the likelihood that it would be sold as a street drug. It isn't classified as a controlled substance and does not require a special prescription. More than 2 million patients have taken Strattera for AD/HD symptoms. Latest information presented by Lilly suggests that several of the patients using Strattera have developed liver problems. The individuals have recovered normal liver function after discontinuing the medication. However, a warning on the label was placed to alert the medical community of this side effect (Kusmer, 2004). Further, in a recent publication of The Medical Letter (2004), data suggest that Strattera is not as effective as stimulants and should not yet be considered a first line of treatment.

Pemoline (Cylert) is a stimulant medication. This is not the first choice for the management of AD/HD symptoms, due to potential liver damage. These are long-acting tablets administered by mouth. The dosage depends on the individual. It has a slow onset of action and lasts 6–8 hours. The side effects are the same as for Ritalin.

Clonidine, originally an **antihypertensive** medication, seems to be effective primarily on **intrusive** and hyperactive behavior. Taken alone, however, this medication is often not enough help. Clonidine can be administered via patches, applied to the back of the shoulder, with an effect lasting 5 to 6 days. Tablets, administered by mouth, are short-acting, lasting 4 to 6 hours. It improves symptoms of AD/HD as well as decreases

Libido
The desire for sexual activity.

Dysmenorrhea
Difficult or painful menstruation.

Antihypertensive
A medication or other therapy that lowers blood pressure.

Intrusive
To force in or upon someone or something especially without permission or welcome.

facial and vocal tics of Tourette's syndrome. It has a positive side effect on oppositional defiant behavior and is beneficial for management of anger. One major side effect is fatigue; others include dizziness, dry mouth, increased activity, irritability, and/or behavior problems. Dosage is determined on an individual basis. Discontinuation can lead to rebound or other effects. For a summary of second tier medications, their generic names, types, duration, and side effects, see table 7.1 on page 149.

Possible Future Medications

Monoamine Oxidase Inhibitors (MAOIs) are another category of drugs being studied, which metabolize tyramine substance in the body that helps support blood pressure, and dopamine. Preliminary studies suggest that MAOIs are effective in significant reduction of AD/HD symptoms with minimal adverse effects in children. Feigin et al. (1996), found a robust symptom response in children with AD/HD and Tourette's syndrome in the first period of his study. Major limitations associated with MAOIs include dietetic transgressions manifested as **hyperthermia,** rigidity, myoclonic movements, and rarely, death.

Hyperthermia
An increase in the body temperature.

Cholinergic agents, such a nicotine, have been shown to possess cognitive benefits such as improved temporal memory, attention, cognitive vigilance, and executive function (Spencer, 2002). Levin et al. (1998) showed that transdermal nicotine resulted in significant improvement of AD/HD symptoms, working memory, and neuropsychological functioning in adults. Studies also indicate that this type of drug has a low abuse liability and it is adequately safe and well tolerated by the elderly population. These findings are preliminary, but promising in that these agents may provide another useful tool in controlling AD/HD.

How Are Treatments Evaluated?

Treatments may be evaluated in one of two ways: (1) by standard scientific procedure, or (2) by limited case studies of testimonials. Standard scientific procedures include having the study go through a peer review before it is published in a scientific journal—subject to the rigor of clinical trials, statistical analysis, and scrutiny of results. When evaluating treatments via case studies, conclusions are drawn from a limited sample size and are often based solely on testimonials from doctors or patients. In spite of an attempt to rigorously investigate treatments and medications, there are still a number of approaches used by a variety of people (i.e., chiropractors, nutritionists, etc.), that individuals with AD/HD pursue. The efficacy of most of these approaches or CAM (complementary and alternative) treatments has not been scientifically proven or subjected to the same rigorous scrutiny. Nevertheless, several unproven treatments should be considered and evaluated with caution.

Complementary Alternative Medicine (CAM)

The most frequent CAM reported by parents, according to Dr. Chan of the Division of General Pediatrics, Children's Hospital in Boston (Chan, Rappaport, & Kemper, 2003), were vitamins; expressive therapy (sensory integration, occupational therapy, dance/gymnastics, art and music); dietary manipulations including low sugar/sugar-free diets; Feingold/additive-free diet; special exercises such as yoga, tai chi, and meditation; and dietary supplements including evening primrose oil and blue green algae. Other therapies included prayer, massage, biofeedback, chiropractic therapy, herbal remedies, healer/healing touch, and hypnosis. Although only 11 percent of families discussed CAM with their child's physician, they felt that such therapies gave them more control over treatment, and were adherent to their cultural/family tradition. The "CAM users" preferred "natural therapy" as opposed to drugs with possible side effects.

Alternative treatment approaches are usually publicized in books or journals that do not require review of the material by recognized experts in the field. If you are considering an approach that has not been subjected to peer review, questions to ask include:

- Have clinical trials been conducted regarding the approach? Do you have information regarding the results?

- Can the public obtain information about the alternative approach from the Office of Alternative Medicine Clearinghouse (1.888.644.6226 or www.nccam.nih.gov/)?

- Is there a national organization of practitioners? Are there state licensing and accreditation requirements for practitioners of this treatment?

- Is the alternative treatment reimbursed by health insurance?

Suspect an unproven treatment if it:

- Claims it will work for everyone with AD/HD and other health problems
- Uses only case histories or testimonials as proof
- Cites only one study as proof
- Cites a study without a control group
- Comes without directions for proper use
- Does not list contents
- Has no information or warnings about side effects
- Is described as harmless or natural (Remember, most medication stems from "natural" sources.)
- Claims it's based on a secret formula
- Claims that it will work immediately and permanently for everyone with AD/HD
- Is described as "astonishing," "miraculous," or an "amazing breakthrough"
- Claims it cures AD/HD
- Is available from only one source
- Is promoted only in the media, books, or by mail order/website
- Claims that treatment is being suppressed or unfairly attacked by the medical establishment

Develop a healthy skepticism and be sure to watch for red flags when evaluating media reports of medical advances. Besides unproven treatments, there are treatments that lead to equivocal results.

Zinc Supplements

Zinc, which is basic for the production and modulation of melatonin, is thought to help regulate dopamine function and as such could be important factor in AD/HD and treatment (Akhondzadeh, Mohammadi, & Khademi, 2004). Children taking 55 mg a day of zinc supplement with methyphenidate scored higher in behavioral rating than children taking methyphenidate plus placebo. Children taking zinc were more prone to nausea. Further investigation into this treatment regimen is warranted.

154

The Silent "Drug"

For some undiagnosed and untreated adults with AD/HD, the ingestion of several cups of coffee has served as a **"pseudomedicine."** Unbeknown to the person, the caffeine serves as a stimulant and in sufficient doses, can produce similar effects as a psychostimulant. Thus, the adult "self-medicates" by drinking many cups of coffee, cola, or other caffeine products in the course of a day.

A consumer survey (Consumer Reports, 2003) indicates that children can easily consume caffeine through the food products found in many households that leave them jittery and anxious. Caffeine seems to have a similar effect on children and teenagers as it does on adults. Low doses produce an increase in wakefulness, alertness, feelings of energy, and sociability. Increases in dosage lead to feelings of anxiety, insomnia, and tension. Further increase results in nausea and upset stomach. Some experts recommend no more than 3 cans of cola a day (100 mg). The Canadian government has made recommendations of total amount by body weight from 45 mg per day for 4 to 6 year-olds to as much as 300 mg a day for adults (2 to 3 cups of brewed coffee). For examples of caffeine amounts in beverages and food, see Figure 7.1 on page 156 and Study More 7.1 on the CD-ROM.

Pseudomedicine Branch of pseudoscience.

Controversial Treatments

Dietary Intervention

The effectiveness of dietary intervention in treating AD/HD continues to be controversial. One of the questions often asked by parents is whether diet plays a role in AD/HD and whether eliminating certain foods (namely sugars) would reduce hyperactivity. The Feingold Diet (Goldstein & Ingersoll, 2000) made dramatic claims. The diet promoted elimination of most food additives to improve children's learning and attention. A large number of studies have also examined the relationship between sugar and hyperactive behavior, but most of them are difficult to interpret. The bottom line appears to be this: only a small percentage of those with AD/HD seems to be vulnerable to diet or food additives.

Megavitamins and Mineral Supplements

The use of very high doses of vitamins and minerals to treat AD/HD is based on the theory that some people have a genetic abnormality that

Figure 7.1

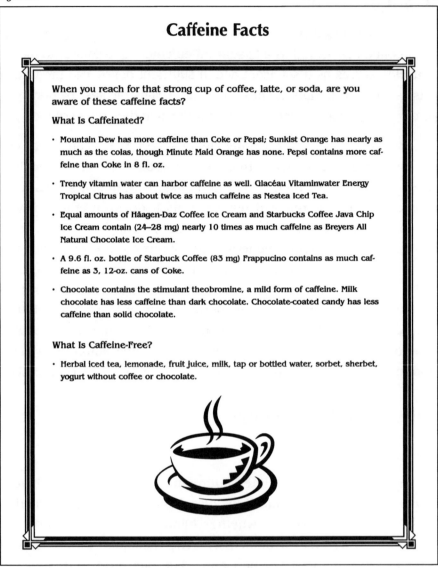

Caffeine Facts

When you reach for that strong cup of coffee, latte, or soda, are you aware of these caffeine facts?

What Is Caffeinated?

- Mountain Dew has more caffeine than Coke or Pepsi; Sunkist Orange has nearly as much as the colas, though Minute Maid Orange has none. Pepsi contains more caffeine than Coke in 8 fl. oz.

- Trendy vitamin water can harbor caffeine as well. Glacéau Vitaminwater Energy Tropical Citrus has about twice as much caffeine as Nestea Iced Tea.

- Equal amounts of Häagen-Daz Coffee Ice Cream and Starbucks Coffee Java Chip Ice Cream contain (24–28 mg) nearly 10 times as much caffeine as Breyers All Natural Chocolate Ice Cream.

- A 9.6 fl. oz. bottle of Starbuck Coffee (83 mg) Frappucino contains as much caffeine as 3, 12-oz. cans of Coke.

- Chocolate contains the stimulant theobromine, a mild form of caffeine. Milk chocolate has less caffeine than dark chocolate. Chocolate-coated candy has less caffeine than solid chocolate.

What Is Caffeine-Free?

- Herbal iced tea, lemonade, fruit juice, milk, tap or bottled water, sorbet, sherbet, yogurt without coffee or chocolate.

results in increased requirements for vitamins and minerals. Both the American Psychiatric Association and the American Academy of Pediatrics have concluded that the use of megavitamins to treat behavioral and learning problems is not justified (Goldstein & Ingersoll, 2000).

Anti-Motion Sickness Medication

Advocates of this treatment believe that there is a relationship between AD/HD and problems with coordination and balance attributed to problems in the inner-ear system (which plays a major role in balance and coordination). They recommend a mixed array of medications including anti-motion sickness medication.

This approach is not consistent in any way with what is currently known about AD/HD and is not supported by research findings (Goldstein & Ingersoll, 2000). Anatomically and physiologically, there is no reason to believe that the inner-ear system is involved in attention and impulse control in other than marginal ways.

Candida Yeast

Candida is a type of yeast that lives in the human body. Normally, yeast growth is kept in check by a strong immune system and by "friendly" bacteria, but when the immune system is weakened, or friendly bacteria are killed by antibiotics, Candida can overgrow. Advocates of this model believe that toxins produced by the yeast overgrowth weaken the immune system and make the body susceptible to AD/HD and other psychiatric disorders. They tout the use of anti-fungal medication and a low-sugar, or elimination diet as treatment. The claim is unproven.

EEG Biofeedback

Proponents of this approach believe that children with AD/HD can be trained to increase the type of brain-wave activity associated with sustained attention and to decrease the type of activity associated with daydreaming and distraction. While the theory underlying EEG biofeedback as a treatment for AD/HD is consistent with what is known about low levels of arousal in frontal brain areas in individuals with AD/HD, its effectiveness has not been demonstrated at this time. This is an expensive, unproven approach, and parents are advised to proceed with caution.

Neural Organization

Advocates of the neural organization technique—also referred to as applied kinesiology—believe that learning disabilities are caused by the misalignment of two specific bones in the skull which create unequal pressure on different areas of the brain, leading to brain malfunction. This misalignment is also said to create "ocular lock," an eye-movement malfunction that contributes to reading problems. Treatment consists of restoring the cranial bones to the proper position through specific bodily manipulations. Cranial-sacral realignment is often the approach used and administered by chiropractors. The Dore Program is based on the theory that people with AD/HD have underdeveloped cerebellums and, therefore, customized exercises can stimulate that part of the brain. The exercises include balancing on machines and repetition that will create new pathways that allow information to be transmitted more efficiently. The program costs $2,500 and takes 9 to 15 months for results. There is no scientific data, however, to substantiate its efficacy (Kelly, 2004).

Optometric Vision Training

Advocates of this approach believe that visual problems—such as faulty eye movements, sensitivity of the eyes to certain light frequencies, and focus problems—cause reading disorders and other maladies. Since reading disabilities are prevalent in children with AD/HD, this treatment is mentioned here. Treatment programs vary widely, but may include eye exercises, educational and perceptual training, biofeedback, and nutritional counseling. There is no empirical evidence to support this theory. Anecdotal evidence suggests that children with reading problems, who were identified as having visual tracking problems, have had them ameliorated by optometric training. Families have reported improvement in reading skills.

Potential for Substance Abuse

Substance abuse is thought to result either from the taking of stimulants, or a comorbid condition that exists independent of AD/HD, regardless of whether the patient is taking any medication. Surely the public, through the media, has been led to believe that individuals who do take "drugs" for their AD/HD are more prone to being addicted to drugs and therefore more likely to try mood enhancers. Although studies vary in findings, there is some evidence that there is a between 10 to 20 percent rate of substance abuse among AD/HD adults. Compared with controls, adults with AD/HD have a 3- to 4-fold higher rate of marijuana and cocaine use, a 3-fold higher rate of alcohol abuse, and utilize tobacco 40 percent more often.

With pharmacotherapy, there is an 85 percent reduction in risk for abuse among adolescents (Ward, Wender, & Reimherr, 1993). Therefore, a child who is appropriately medicated for his or her AD/HD would not become a drug abuser. It is the unmedicated child that becomes more vulnerable to drug use, and addiction to caffeine and alcohol. These products are thought to mask the AD/HD symptoms that have been either undiagnosed or disregarded. Research shows that children with AD/HD and conduct disorders (delinquent behaviors) by age 10, who are smoking cigarettes by age 12, are at a higher risk for substance abuse in the teenage years (CHADD, 2001).

There are reports in the popular literature (Wilens, 2001; Lambert & Hartsought, 1999) that there is potential for abuse with the widespread use of stimulants. An adult who suffers from AD/HD, uses the medication as prescribed, and does not concurrently have a substance abuse problem, will not become addicted. There are reports (Wilens; Lambert & Hartsought) of stimulant medication prescribed medically being diverted for nonmedical recreational use. This is becoming more widespread. Circumspection when prescribing the medication to those whom physicians suspect will "sell" the drug, is warranted. Some studies offer evidence that stimulant treatment of AD/HD may in fact decrease the risk of future substance abuse, including cocaine, among adult sufferers (Wilens; Lambert & Hartsought).

Pharmacotherapy is a central element in the treatment of AD/HD and some studies have shown it to be more effective than behavioral treatment in reducing the symptoms of AD/HD. When prescribed appropriately, stimulant medication is not addictive. Nevertheless, care should be taken for the patients with a comorbid substance abuse disorder.

Summary

The literature is voluminous with reports of treatment efficacy with stimulants as they affect the core features of AD/HD, such as cognition, social function, and aggressiveness. Treatment has expanded from primarily a behavioral focus to addressing executive functions in school and work settings. A new generation of stimulants has made available effective long-acting alternatives. While stimulants have been the most studied, there is a considerable body of knowledge that indicates the important role of other psychopharmacologic agents. There is evidence that new agents being developed may provide even more acceptable alternatives.

It has been found that the combined protective actions of psychosocial and pharmacological treatments are more effective than any one procedure alone. Self regulation—the ultimate goal for this population—results in delayed but greater rewards. The ability to elicit behaviors that bring benefit or are more ethical and reasonable is the desired outcome of treatment.

Chapter 8

Remediation of Language Processing and Auditory Processing Problems

In a presentation before a regional Children and Adults with Attention Deficit Disorder (CHADD) group, Peter Jensen, MD (Director of Columbia University Physicians and Surgeons and former associate director at National Institute of Mental Health (NIMH)), reported that although medication is a critical component, the interventions one receives serve an important function in the management of AD/HD (2004). Therapies are effective in improving social skills, anxiety levels, academic performance, oppositional behavior, and parent-child interaction. Other studies demonstrated that multimodal treatment has value for those children for whom treatment with medication alone is not sufficient (Klein et al., 1997).

The American Academy of Pediatrics (AAP) stresses that the treatment of AD/HD (whether behavioral, pharmacological, or multimodal) requires the development of child-specific remediation plans that describe not only the methods and goals of remediation, but also the means of monitoring over time and specific plans for follow-up. Development of target goals involves input from parents, children, and teachers, as well as other school personnel. Goals should be realistic, measurable, and attainable. For many children, even those who have success with medication, adjunct management through behavioral interventions are valuable as either a primary or an ancillary approach (AAP, 2001).

Since it is known that children with AD/HD typically can have language deficits or difficulty with **language processing** and auditory processing, then it is reasonable to endorse speech-language intervention for those children who have identified speech-language disorders. Intervention requires consideration of the child's auditory processing, receptive and expressive language deficits, pragmatic skills, and executive functions. Intervention and management should specifically address these skills. For

Language processing
The process of hearing, discriminating, assigning significance to, and interpreting spoken words, phrases, sentences, and discourse.

the adult, remediation of executive functions, organization, and planning should serve as the core of a treatment program.

This chapter will address remediation of the language and auditory processing deficits frequently associated with AD/HD. There are general guidelines for treatment that include environmental modifications, followed by recommendations and examples of direct intervention.

Modification of the Environment

General modifications to the environment for children with AD/HD and language deficits are similar to modifications for children with AD/HD without language involvement. However, the modifications are listed here again specifically for individuals with language processing and/or auditory processing disorders combined with AD/HD.

Home

To modify the home environment:

- Reward good behavior.
- Be the child's advocate.
- Develop self-esteem in the child.
- Provide "coaching support."
- Promote routines and schedules to meet deadlines.
- Alter the room to reduce distractions and noise interference.
- Be consistent when modifying behavior.
- Apply consequences.
- Use aids and devices for recall and planning.
- Limit noise or insulate study areas.

School

To modify the child's school environment:

- Alter the classroom to reduce distractions.
- Promote an atmosphere that allows student to ask for repetition.
- Use learning aids.
- Allow for physical needs and movement.
- Teach **visualization** strategies.
- Take into account the student's interests.

Visualization
Use of guided or directed imagery, using visual stimuli.

- Break assignments into small steps, or assign the student a buddy, and give both students visual and verbal directions.

- Provide a model for the student.

- Periodically remind the student of assignments and check on the child's progress.

- Insulate the environment by reducing the noise source, removing distracting sounds and treating the walls with curtains, the ceiling with acoustic tiles, or the floors with carpeting to reduce reverberation. A ceiling height less than 12 feet is optimal.

- Treat the environment around the school, like landscaping with hedges, which abate the noise.

- Reduce noise levels and distractions in the classroom.

- Insulate walls and windows by hanging plants or students' work. Improve lighting and ventilation.

- Improve classroom acoustics. Children with AD/HD should be in smaller sized classes, with no more than 18 to 20 children in the class. If there are other problems like learning disabilities, then the class size could be further reduced, with an assistant or consultant teacher available in the room.

- Install an FM system to improve signal-to-noise level. There are three choices: a personal unit, a classroom speaker unit, or an individualized toteable unit.

  1. A personal unit includes placing headphones (receiver) on the child while the teacher wears the transmitter with a microphone. Another variation would be to use ear-level receivers in place of a headset.

  2. The classroom speaker unit, or sound enhancement unit, involves placing a speaker in the classroom at the teacher's desk or on the ceiling so that everyone in the class benefits from improved figure-ground listening. A recent ASHA position statement (ASHA, 2005) and the American National Standards Institute (ANSI, 2002) advocated for a noise level in the unoccupied classroom no louder than 35 dBHL, with a signal-to-noise level of +15. (The speaker should be 15 dBHL louder than the background noise.) This is a useful system when a personal unit is not desirable (i.e., child feels stigmatized).

3. An individual, toteable desktop unit is useful when the child feels uncomfortable wearing something on his ears or being "singled out." This "lunch box" sits on the child's desk and delivers the amplified voice of the teacher, who wears the transmitter.

- Install an infrared sound system to beam sound to a light sensitive receiver. These devices enable the signal to be louder than the background noise, thereby enhancing the signal-to-noise level of the room. This favorable listening environment is certainly superior for listening and attending. In fact, Rosenberg (2005) contends that enhanced listening systems do promote better attending and eye contact, not to mention improved auditory discrimination.

- Another device is the Facilitator (Kay Elemetrics Model 3500), developed by Daniel Boone, which has 4 different modes, some of which are useful for the individual with AD/HD. Its four modes include sound enhanced, delayed auditory feedback, direct audio feedback, and metronome pacer. The sound enhanced mode is useful in developing attention and improving figure-ground listening.

Remember that a smaller class size, located in a quiet area, with little distractions is a better placement for these children. For the same matter, adults should place themselves in an environment that is restricted from distractions and noise in the background. An adult needs to be conscience of sitting away from windows and avoiding the middle of large, high ceilinged rooms. For example, sitting in a booth or against a wall is preferable, especially in a restaurant.

Workplace

Adults can modify their work environment as well. Here are suggestions:

- Alter the workspace to allow for movement.
- Limit distractions.
- Work away from doors that are open.
- Use aids and devices to keep on task (e.g., using Post-it notes, pocket-talker memo recorder, calendar).
- Break down large projects into smaller steps.
- Allow for breaks.
- Use a coach or buddy to keep on track.

- Learn to prioritize.
- Keep a notepad and pen handy.
- Become knowledgeable about your issues.
- Engage the help of a cohort.

Other helpful tips are addressed in *Driven to Distraction* (1994) by Hallowell and Ratey.

Direct Intervention

For a review of typical language problems of AD/HD, see Chapter 3.

Expressive Language Skills

Word Retrieval

Word retrieval refers to the mental activity of selecting or retrieving from memory the words that are known to express ideas. A disruption in the mental activity of retrieving known words from memory is called **word-finding difficulty.** Often a person with AD/HD may fare well on vocabulary measures but have a hard time retrieving the words he or she wants to use. A test score from an evaluation in an isolated setting often does not match the individual's performance in the classroom, home, or other setting. This word-finding difficulty is often seen with people who have rapid naming and recall issues typically associated with phonological processing disorders.

German (2001) identifies three types of word finding errors:

- *Slip of the Tongue*—Substituting or interchanging names and words related to the target word (e.g., *washer* for *dryer*, *Bob* for *Joe*); mispeaking the name of a place, person.

- *Tip of the Tongue*—Losing a word temporarily, but the word is imminent. The word is in mind, but can't be said, even with a sense of the first sound (e.g., "The coach's name is...").

- *Twist of the Tongue*—Omitting or exchanging sounds or syllables of long names or words that are known (e.g., *merious* for *mysterious*).

Building vocabulary is helpful, but the skill of finding the word at the time of usage is more challenging. For that there are a number of word

Word retrieval
The mental activity of selecting or retrieving from memory the words one knows in order to express ideas.

Word-finding difficulty
A disruption in the mental activity of retrieving known words from memory.

retrieval strategies. First, develop a wide selection of words from which to choose. That comes from exposure to words, reading, and experience with naming activities. Develop cuing strategies, such as first letter or sound cues that help stimulate the word search. German (2001) provides many cuing strategies such as:

- Association cues (e.g., *bread* goes with...; *milk* goes with...; *red, white,* and...)
- Same-sound cues
- Familiar word cues
- Pausing
- Syllable dividing (visual and rhythm syllable dividing)
- Alternate word (synonym or category name substituting)
- Self-correction
- Rehearsal (rehearse the word out loud)
- Alternate word switching (switch to a another known word)

There are computer software programs available to assist with these skills as well, if one has access and can use a keyboard.

There are many commercially available word games that stimulate word-finding skills. Some of them are: Word Burst, Password, and Scategories (for children and adults). Other resources are:

- *HELP for Word Finding* (Lazzari & Peters, 1995)

- *It's on the Tip of My Tongue* (German, 2001)

- *Word Retrieval Exercises for Adolescents and Adults* (Academic Communication Associates, 1996)

- *Word Joggers* (Krassowski, 2001)

Formulation of Thoughts

One of the most difficult challenges for AD/HD individuals is to gather their thoughts and express them in a cohesive manner that is to the point. Often the person rambles on and on, with the listener fatiguing rapidly. The speaker, of course, has little awareness of his or her audience's reaction and continues to talk.

The challenge is to get the person to say what he or she wants to say succinctly, and to say what is intended. The Mad Hatter in *Alice in Wonderland* uttered, "Say what you mean and mean what you say," to Alice's bewilderment who responded, "But that's the same thing." "No," replied the Mad Hatter. That skill in saying what you mean requires efficiency of thought. The ability to mean what you say reflects **veracity.** Doing so in an efficient manner is a skill and a challenge for the person with AD/HD.

Veracity
Unwillingness to tell lies. A truthfulness.

For the older child, adolescent, and adult, the focus should be on formulating thoughts and doing so successfully. Use of feedback via tape recorders, videotape, and transcripts can help. The speaker, often unaware of the rambling, does not take the listener into consideration. The person needs help **telegraphing** thoughts to present the most salient points, with activities such as asking the person to serve as listener and discern what is important from unimportant information; giving the person the opportunity to select the salient from the nonsalient features; and highlighting and underlining key points. Teaching the person to highlight the most critical pieces of information (eliminating nonessential points) can carry over into improved note taking skills. Practice improving note taking should be a goal.

Telegraphing
Reducing a message to its essential components, leaving out function words.

Sample formulation of thought activities include these:

- *Sentence completion tasks*—Complete a sentence by filling in the most appropriate word for the situation.

- *Semantic development*—Vocabulary mapping may be an early activity to increase awareness of alternate word choices.

- *Getting to the point*—Describe how to send an email message using only important details, write an ad in 50 words or less, or write an abstract of a story in 75 words or less.

- *Sequencing cards*—Select picture cards in the appropriate order of the story, from beginning to end.

- *Use of referents*—Use appropriate names to designate the actors of the action, reducing the use of nondescript pronouns *he, she, it*. Learn to use discrete designators so the listener knows about whom you are talking, or to whom you are referring.

Executive Function

Executive function includes five general components that impact school performance (Barkley, 1998; Brown, 2000). They are:

1. *Working memory and recall*—Holding facts in mind while manipulating information, accessing facts stored in long-term memory

2. *Activation, arousal, and effort*—Getting started, paying attention, finishing work

3. *Emotion control*—Tolerating frustration, thinking before acting or speaking

4. *Internalizing language*—Using self-talk to control one's behavior and direct future actions

5. *Complex problem solving*—Taking an issue apart, analyzing the pieces, reconstructing and organizing it into new ideas

Executive functions require the skill to transform knowledge into behavioral strategies. They involve task analysis, planning, and decision-making.

Activities may include:

- *Problem-solving tasks*—Finding the solution to problems presented, selecting the best solution, making decisions; using problem-solving cards that depict situations that could be hazardous

- *Describing consequences*—Solving if-then problems; doing analogies; explaining ambiguous sentences, puns, jokes, idioms; using resources such as *Saying One Thing, Meaning Another* (Spector, 1997), *Cartoon Cut-Ups* (Hamersky, 1995), *Come Back, Amelia Bedelia* (Parish, 1995), *or* any of the *Amelia Bedelia* books.

- *Planning and organizing parts into a whole*—Recognizing words such as *fat/skinny* regardless of the size of the letters (i.e., upper or lower case) (e.g., "fat/SKINNY; fat/skinny; Fat/Skinny; fat/SKINNY; FaT/skinny") to improve concentration; or organizing a task such as planning a class trip or a party, and listing things to do and when to do them.

Executive functions require metacognition, which involves active monitoring and consequent regulation of attention, memory, listening, learning, and language processes to achieve some goal. An appropriate intervention involves a cognitive approach with an emphasis on functional strategies such as those suggested by McMahon (2002):

- Use of self-efficacy
- Regulation of strategies
- Development of self-monitoring

Self-monitoring is the act of maintaining a level of self-awareness and self-regulation of behavior. Through self-instruction, the person is trained to adapt and self-direct verbal statements before and after a task or situation, to listen, and to manage impulsive behaviors. The person conducts the activity while self-verbalizing aloud. This may take many trials in actual life activities. Videotaping the person for later self-analysis may be helpful. The professional can co-support the person by verbalizing as well. The person eventually reduces the self-reporting behavior to a whisper, then to **covert** behavior.

Covert
Not openly shown, engaged in, or avowed, not readily apparent.

Cognitive problem solving is a systematic process to resolve difficult situations, while also learning self-control, with the professional's support. The person learns to address the problem, employ executive functions in analyzing the situation, and generate a variety of responses that will resolve the situation. It involves a level of cognition, comprehension, and critical thinking and questioning. Tendencies to jump to conclusions and respond impulsively are pointed out. This process helps reduce fear and anxiety. Problem solving involves understanding the entire nature of the problem, generating possible solutions, evaluating all possible solutions, predicting outcomes and benefits, and selecting the best solution. Then it is followed by monitoring of one's own performance regarding solving the problem. Throughout this process, **cognitive rehearsal** can help identify potential problems, obstacles, solutions, and preventive measures. Then, using real-life situations, the person is helped to generalize the new behavior.

Cognitive problem solving
Person addresses a problem by analyzing it and finding solutions that are thought out.

Cognitive rehearsal
Thinking to oneself. Weighing possible alternatives to arrive at a solution.

Self-regulation can be developed through self-control (Whitman, Burgio, & Johnson, 1984). Self-regulation involves self-monitoring, self-evaluation, and self-reinforcement. Training begins with an increasing awareness of the desired behavior to control, goal setting, and developing self-monitoring skills needed to effect behavioral change. Self-regulation training promotes active listening by encouraging the listener to monitor comprehension processes to determine if they are meeting his or her needs. When they do not, the listener must modify the behavior to handle the inconsistencies.

Reasoning skills include evaluating arguments, drawing inferences and conclusions, and generating and testing hypotheses (Nickerson, 1986). Effective listening requires reasoning to evaluate and reconstruct messages as well as to select behavior appropriate to the situation. Ambiguity and imprecision—as seen in phonemic confusions, verbal ambiguities, figurative language, idioms, metaphors, and proverbs—can create challenges in listening, inferring, and making an interpretation that is beyond the literal meaning. Training in "reading between the lines," and recognition of nuances, tone of voice, ambiguities, and abstractions helps promote the development of reasoning skills.

Receptive Language Skills

Comprehension

Comprehension involves the ability to understand the spoken message and interpret the information with accuracy. For those individuals with receptive language and auditory processing deficits, comprehending and listening to lengthy passages is a challenge, as is getting the main idea, the salient points, or the intent of the message. Often the person will remark, "You never said it," "I didn't hear it," or simply "I misheard." Frequently, individuals will hear one word for another and not be aware of the difference. What one person says and what another person hears may not be the same.

There are a variety of techniques to improve comprehension of the spoken message. One of the more successful methods is a visualization approach—to have the listener think in pictures. This works well if the listener is a "visual person." Such a person is able to "see" an auditory event by formulating a picture. The pictures of the landmarks seen previously can leave an indelible memory image. For example, if he or she travels to a place using the landmarks on the streets, not by street names, that person is likely a visual learner. Such a person can hear and translate the words into a visual image. A technique of transferring words to images is known as Visualizing and Verbalizing (V & V), first identified by Bell

(1991) of Lindamood-Bell Learning Processes. Bell is responsible for promoting this method, which has been successful for particular types of learners. Another technique promoted by the Lindamood-Bell learning processes is *Seeing Stars* (Bell, 1997), which uses symbol **imagery** for phonemic awareness, sight words, and a spelling approach to comprehension and reading proficiency. It involves training in the ability to visualize letters. Symbol imagery is related to literacy development which requires a gestalt analysis of the reading process. Reading comprehension requires concept imagery. "Concept imagery is the ability to image basic concepts and visualize the gestalt—or whole from what is read or heard" (Bell, 1997, p. 3). Grasping only parts, one may get the few details, names, and dates, but miss the essential idea of what was read, the gestalt. Many may be good decoders, read fluently in context, and be savvy with phonological awareness, but not comprehend oral or written language. For those people, there is a lack of ability to do the kind of reasoning and critical thinking that results from imagining the gestalt. Reading involves:

> **Imagery**
> Generally, all figurative or non-literal language. Specifically, imagery suggests visual and tangible pictures by using words, refers to the use of language to represent things, actions or abstract ideas descriptively. In its most common use, imagery suggests visual pictures, but it can also denote other sensory experiences.

- *The auditory code*—The ability to accurately sound out a word, put all the sounds into the right place, and apply "phonics to reading," along with good word-attack skills

- *The visual code*—The rapid naming of a word, and having a memorized sight-word base (which requires a base of phonological processing and visual memory)

- *The language circle*—The contextual cues and oral vocabulary that involve understanding the meaning of words (comes into play after phonics and sight word instruction)

According to Bell (1997), phonemic awareness is a skill primary to decoding, and concept imagery is a skill primary to comprehension. Weakness in these areas may manifest itself in reading difficulty, low self-esteem, poor expressive language, the label of dyslexia, hyperlexia, and attentional issues. Children and adults with phonemic awareness weakness have difficulty sounding out words accurately and fluently, and with self-correcting errors in reading and spelling. They have difficulty getting the words off the page. Those with concept imagery weakness have difficulty comprehending and interpreting what is read and what is heard, and in following directions and thinking logically. They have difficulty in getting the gestalt meaning off the page, and understanding and interpreting oral or written language. Efficacy data are readily available and show measurable improvement following use of *The Lindamood Phoneme Program for Reading, Spelling and Speech (LiPS;* Lindamood & Lindamood, 1998) and *Seeing Stars* (Bell).

Attention-Deficit/Hyperactivity Disorder

Another technique to improve comprehension is to have the person sketch the meaning on paper after hearing the paragraph read aloud. After the reading, have the individual draw (sketch) the passage in 20 seconds. That encourages a visual imagery that enables the meaning to be "pictured" by the listener. Such techniques work well with visual and **kinesthetic** learners. Often the person knows if he or she is a visual learner. If it is not known, one simple nonscientific test is to ask how he or she got to the office or school. If the person describes the landmarks and not the street names, it is likely that he or she is a visual learner!

Following Directions

The ability to follow directions is linked to short-term memory ability. The longer the direction, the harder it is to remember. Visualization, repetition, clarification, and reduction into smaller steps are helpful strategies.

The ability to repeat the directions and self-auditorize (say it to oneself quietly) are effective for those learners who are not visual. These people can sit at a lecture and not take a note, but can listen and take it all in. For some, listening and writing are too difficult to do at the same time.

Having a child follow sequenced directions to successfully complete a task, in a game format, is good practice, as long as the child repeats the directives before acting to enhance reauditorization and transference to a motor act. The Telephone Game and others that require children to repeat what they have heard or that require following directions that result in a product (drawing) are effective listening exercises. Oral directives can become more complex by the addition of adjectives (big blue), prepositions (on the table) and number (three of ____). More complicated directions can be posed such as: "If you like broccoli, count to 10. If not, say the first 3 letters of the alphabet." Commercial resources are available for practice with following directions (e.g., *The Processing Program—Level 1* (McKinnis, 2000a) and *The Processing Program Levels 2 and 3* (McKinnis, 2000b); *Make-It-Yourself Barrier Activities* (Schwartz & McKinley, 1987); *Working Out with Listening* (Larson, Sterling-Orth, & Thurs, 2002); *The Deciders Take On Concepts—Missions I, II,* and *III* (Thinking Publications, 2001–2002); *Following Directions: Left and Right* (Semel, 1999) and *Following Directions: One and Two Level Commands* (Semel, 2000)).

Nevertheless, the ability to follow complicated directions may not be possible unless they are broken down into smaller steps, or are accompanied by printed instructions. Repetition is always helpful, and making the individual comfortable with asking for repetition is a necessity. In fact, training the person to ask for repetition is a goal in and of itself. Assertiveness training can be helpful in teaching one to self advocate. Such statements as "I didn't understand that," "Can we move to a quieter place?", "Can you repeat that please?" are important self-help tools.

Using Prosody and Suprasegmentals

The meaning conveyed through timing and durational cues help in the reception of a spoken message. **Prosody** involves the suprasegmental aspects of spoken language and is the melody, timing, rhythm, and amplitude changes of speech. Prosodic information guides attention to the informative parts of the message (Cutler & Fodor, 1979; Chermak & Musiek, 1997). Similarly, intonation can convey meaning. Intonation and timing of the spoken message can shift meaning. Changes in temporally cued sentences change the message entirely (e.g., "Visiting relatives can be fun").

Train the individual to recognize that by placing the stress on a given syllable or word, one can change the meaning, change the word class, and take on another meaning or implication. If one puts the stress on the first syllable in the word *contract*, it serves as a noun, and means an agreement. If one places the stress on the second syllable, it makes it a verb, implying an action. The use of stress juncture can change the entire sentence meaning. It involves the auditory ability to pick up on duration, contrasts, temporal cuing, and acoustic features. However, such cues are not readily available or discernable for those with AD/HD.

Intervention ideas include:

- Supply practice with differentiating sentences that have subtle durational cues (Cole & Jakimik, 1980). For example:

    He gave her a dress for a friend.
    He gave her address for her friends.

    A sign at the front window of a Hair Salon read, "If your hair is not *becoming* to you, you should *be coming* to us!"

    They saw the snow drift by the window.
    They saw the snowdrift by the window.

- Read poetry with appropriate stress to emphasize meaning.

- Study words affected by stress juncture. There are changes that occur when one places the stress on another part of the word, or

> **Prosody**
> Involves the suprasegmental aspects of spoken language and is the melody, timing, rhythm, and amplitude changes of speech.

uses a similar sounding word, such as: affect/af*fect*, combine/ com*bine*, commune/ com*mune*, conserve/con*serve*, conduct/con*duct*, console/con*sole*, contract/con*tract*, converse/con*verse*, defect/ de*fect*, desert/des*sert*, intern/in*tern*, proceed/pro*ceed*, refuse/ re*fuse*, object/ob*ject*.

- Demonstrate the effects of suprasegmental alterations with the use of cartoons, jokes and puns, or idioms. They go beyond the literal meaning of the word or expression. By changing a sound or the stress on a syllable, a joke or humorous story can be created. See the cartoon example in Figure 8.1 and the humor examples in Table 8.1 on page 175. To learn more, see the examples in Study More 8.1 on the CD-ROM.

- Have fun with language. These are the likely result of mishearings: What is a fibula? **A:** small lie. What does varicose mean? **A:** Nearby. (See Study More 8.1.)

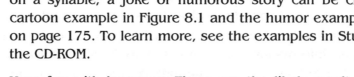

Figure 8.1   **Humor Created by a Change in Stress**

From *Cartoon Cut-Ups: Teaching Figurative Language and Humor* (p. 105), by J. Hamersky, 1995, Eau Claire, WI: Thinking Publications. © 1995 by Thinking Publications. Reprinted with permission.

Table 8.1 **Creating Humor by Changing Sound or Syllable Stress**

Change	Humor
Stress and Pausing Changes	Q. What did the termite say when he walked into the tavern? A. Is the bar tender here? Q. Could Christmas trees grow in Los Angeles? A. No, but Hollywood. Q. What did the sad little girl say when her puppy ran away? A. "Doggone." Teacher: What is the capital of Alaska? Student: Juneau. Teacher: Of course I do, but I'm asking you.
Switching Words or Sounds	Q. What's the difference between a coyote and a flea? A. One howls on the prairie and the other prowls on the hairy. "Smith," said the coach, "Get in there and tackle 'em." Smith went into the game. Soon the opposing team was doubled over with laughter. The game had to be stopped. "What are you doing?" asked the coach. "Why aren't you tackling the other team?" "Oh, tackle!" said Smith. "I thought you said tickle!" Q. If a dog has fleas, what does a sheep have? A. Fleece.
Jokes	Georgia: Where were you born? Annie: England. Georgia: What part? Annie: All of me, silly!
Multiple Meaning Words/ Phrases	Paul: I know a restaurant where we can eat dirt cheap. Matthew: Who wants to eat dirt? Jayne: I can't sleep. What should I do? Jonathan: Lie near the edge of the bed and you'll drop right off.

Sources: Gorman-Gard (2002); Spector (1997)

Pragmatics

This aspect of communication is most critical because it explains why some individuals with AD/HD have difficulty with social language, relating to peers, and making friends. Pragmatics is often explained to parents as *knowing what to say, when to say it, and to whom.* Other components

include being able to start a conversation; terminate a conversation; say what is intended; request information; clarify, request, and express intent.

Suggested pragmatic intervention ideas are presented in Sidebar 8.2. They are also printable from Study More 8.2 on the CD-ROM.

Auditory Processing

The goals to address include attending to an auditory or spoken message, understanding it, hearing the message from the background competition (figure-ground discrimination), extracting the essential information, telling where the sound is coming from, and interpreting the message accurately. There are many approaches. The first should include management, followed by treatment specific to the areas of deficit (deficit-specific approach).

Management of Auditory Processing Deficits

Noise is a major factor to consider when managing auditory processing deficits. It is important that the classroom is conducive to learning. Noise, hallway distractions, open doors, moveable walls, and unsealed windows vulnerable to street traffic create a poor learning environment. ASHA's Task Force on Acoustics in Educational Environments recommends conditions consistent with ANSI (2002) Acoustical Performance Criteria (ASHA, 2005). Table 8.2 on page 178 lists the limitations to background noise in unoccupied and occupied classrooms.

Pragmatic Intervention Ideas

Sidebar 8.2

- Ask questions or make suggestions to help a child use language for different purposes.

- Respond to a child's intended message rather than correcting the pronunciation or grammar, but provide an appropriate model in one's own speech. For example, if a child says, "That's how it doesn't go," respond, "You're right. That's not how it goes."

- Take advantage of naturally occurring interactions to increase use of different language functions. For example, practice greetings at the beginning of a day; have children ask peers what they want to eat for snacks; have children request necessary materials to complete an art project.

- Role-play conversations that might occur with different people in various situations.

- Encourage use of effective persuasion techniques (e.g., polite request through expansion of the phrase, such as, "Would it be OK if I... ?").

- Comment on a child's topic of conversation before introducing a new topic. Add related information. This will help a child say more about a particular topic.

- Provide visual prompts such as pictures, objects, or a story outline to help a child tell a story in sequence.

- Encourage a child to rephrase or revise an unclear word or sentence. Provide an appropriate revision by asking, "Did you mean... ?"

- Show how nonverbal signals are important to communication. For example, talk about what happens when a facial expression does not match the emotion expressed in a verbal message (e.g., using angry words while smiling).

- Watch a videotape of people conversing, particularly in conflict situations, and comment on their communication skills.

Table 8.2   **Recommended Classroom Acoustics**

		Allowable Levels
Signal-to-Noise Level	**Unoccupied Classroom**	35 dBA
	Occupied Classroom	15 dBA
Reverberation	**Small Classroom**	.6 sec
	Large Classroom	.7 sec

Source: ASHA (2005)

These recommendations were adopted as policy in 2003. They are being reviewed by the American National Standards Institute (ANSI). Since children spend 45 to 60 percent of their days focused on listening, the listening environment is critical. We do know that the ability to hear in noise improves with age until age 13. Adults need at least a +6 dB signal-to-noise level in communication.

Malapropisms
Misuse of a word leading to confusion and misinformation.

These general intervention techniques should be used:

- *Improve listening behavior*—Identify mishearings, **malapropisms,** and poor listening-in-noise behavior. Reduce background noise. Make the listening environment more conducive to hearing accurately. Utilize sound enhancement devices, and self-advocacy skills (e.g., teach the youngster to ask for repetition and to realize that what he or she heard may not be what was said).

- *Teach lip-reading cues or "look and listen" behavior*—One possible device is the AudiSee (Gagne, 2001), a visual and auditory device that projects the teacher's face and voice onto a personal screen placed at the child's desk.

For more general management tips, see Sidebar 8.3, which provides management tips for teachers, and Sidebar 8.4, which provides tips for parents. Both sidebars are included as Study Mores 8.3 and 8.4 on the CD-ROM.

Sidebar 8.3 **Management Tips for Teachers**

- Gain bi-sensory attention (audio and visual) before speaking with a student.
- Speak at eye level; get close to the student.
- Assign a class "buddy" to assist the child in getting assignment and project information.
- Announce transitions, name each new activity, and the number and sequence of steps.
- Use cuing to alert the student, or gentle tapping.
- Summarize and review before going on to a new activity.
- Help students with note taking; provide notes or study guide ahead of time.
- Speak clearly with gestures.
- Repeat directions and allow response time.
- Encourage students to ask for repetition, then rephrase and check for comprehension.

Source: Florida Department of Education (2001)

Sidebar 8.4 **Management Tips for Parents**

- Plan to work alone with your child, without competing activities.
- Have the child look and listen while you give instruction.
- Give short and simple directions. Divide multi-step directions into brief steps.
- Ask your child to repeat directions to check for understanding.
- To assist with sequencing tasks, use pictures or key words.
- Praise the child for smallest successes.
- Slow down your rate of speech and use pauses.
- Do not just repeat, rephrase.
- Give time for the child to transition from school to home.
- Create a quiet study area for the child, away from noise and distractions.

Source: Florida Department of Education (2001)

Deficit-Specific Treatment

Short-Term Memory

Short-term memory deficit has been identified as one of the most common problems among the AD/HD population. For one, short-term memory requires attending to the auditory stimuli in order to retain it. Ordinarily, when information is presented, it is processed in short-term memory. Here is where attention problems surface. The person must continue to pay attention while working on the information to store it into long-term memory. Repetition and rehearsal are used to remember the information, but with more complex information, concentration is required to be able to organize, categorize, and associate it with previously learned material. Children with AD/HD have difficulty sustaining attention to the stimulus, either due to underarousal or interference. Others, when concentrating, have difficulty figuring out what is relevant because they cannot organize or categorize. Still others are distracted by a competing stimulus. Long-term memory comes into play when information is rehearsed, organized, associated, and stored into the "file drawer" of the mind. To retrieve information, the individual must think about it and efficiently call it forth and relate it to previously learned information. Retrieval becomes easier as one learns to associate and make the information meaningful. Making associations is a learning strategy that requires more organization and well-developed thought processes.

Having a deficit with short-term memory implies that the person has trouble recalling recent facts and information, affecting recall and productivity. Working memory is the ability to hold facts in mind while manipulating information and accessing facts stored in long-term memory. For one with a limited working memory, weak short-term memory can produce a sense of forgetfulness. That is, the person can't keep things in his or her mind, leading to poor recall and ability to follow instructions. Memorizing math facts, spelling words, and remembering dates is hard to do. Doing mental computation work and requiring one to hold a piece of information while retrieving another piece of information, is a challenge, as is the summarizing and paraphrasing of information. Difficulty holding events in mind affects ability to be on time and to prepare for upcoming events and the future. The inability to judge the passage of time and estimate how much time it takes to finish a task leads to poor planning and judgment. All these characteristics diminish one's self-awareness, resulting in poor ability to examine or change one's behavior. Thus, the student often lives in the present, focusing on the here and now.

Retrieval is another matter and a more prevalent problem in this population. The outputting of information after it is stored is a processing skill. Children and adults with AD/HD lose that ability to develop learning strategies to make material meaningful for retrieval. Typically, these individuals tend to not sort information, but rather bounce it about without reflecting on its relevance or association. They do not reflect on the structure. Thus, many youngsters can provide details, but cannot relate the details or explain how details relate to one another. It has been said that these individuals have difficulty separating the forest from the trees. This is often evident when they are asked to tell the main idea, or listen in background noise. Such inefficiency leads to inconsistency in performance, an inconsistency resulting from inefficient information processing.

To improve short-term memory, there are a several approaches, some of which involve recognizing learning style (i.e., whether one is a visual, auditory, or kinesthetic learner). For instance, if one is a visual learner, then developing a strategy to visualize and use imagery of the whole **"gestalt"** is helpful. If one is an auditory learner, then hearing the information repeated, or re-auditorized is helpful. If one is a kinesthetic learner, then feeling the sensation, or writing the number or letter in the air is helpful.

Gestalt
A configuration or pattern of elements so unified as a whole that it cannot be described merely as a sum of its parts.

A visual learner remembers a story, event, or a word by its picture or image. The image method works in the following way: Picture a scene described through the use of words. Take a picture of the item or items in your mind's eye. Create an image of the items together and store it as a photograph in your brain. See the colors, shapes, and forms. Relate it to a picture you have seen before. Many individuals remember numbers by picturing the numbers, or putting a color, form, or fabric on them.

An auditory learner hears the names/words. The auditory method works in the following way: Hear the message, the words, the numbers. Repeat what you heard by either **subvocalizing** them (i.e., saying them to yourself in a low audible voice) or reauditorizing them (i.e., recollecting a sound on a thought-level). By self-repetition, subvocalization, and verbal rehearsal, the acoustic image can be held in short-term memory long enough to be stored.

Subvocalizing
Repeat to oneself in a low, audible voice.

A kinesthetic learner feels the experience by using hands, fingers, mouth, or other sensory receptors. The method works in the following way: Listen to the message and draw an image or word with your hand. Invoke a motor response, touch, or feel the image. Remember the sensation and feel of the response.

Other techniques to improve memory include:

- *Chunking*—A memory strategy in which the child is encouraged to recall specific words through association or clusters of related words. It may be modified to include volume and intonation.

- Mnemonics—A device to assist the memory, such as a formula, or rhyme, or using the first letters of a group of words which will be easily stored into one's memory bank. These codes, rhymes, or acronyms trigger the target word or sentence to one's memory. For example, ROY G BIV = the colors of the rainbow (red, orange, yellow, green, blue, indigo, violet).

- *Verbal Imagery*—Recalling a series of events by attributing meaning to them through the use of words or story sequences. Put a series of words or tasks together into a story framework (silly or not) to remember and recall the items in the story. The story will trigger the individual words or events. A story in context is easier to recall than a series of isolated words or items.

- *Note Taking*—Capturing the main ideas and relevant details. Taking salient notes and learning what is relevant from irrelevant can be taught, often with the use of technology. Taking in the information and capturing it instantaneously is a "speed of processing" skill, which can be supported through the use of technology. This is addressed later in the chapter. For additional helpful hints to improve memory skills, see Sidebar 8.5.

Auditory Attention

Auditory attention can be described as the ability to maintain focus on an auditory stimulus over a period of time for an intended purpose. Issues such as neurology, **volition**, and interest become relevant variables. Ability to sustain attention to auditory information appears related to other skills such as memory, maturation, interest, and attention. A sound enhancement system, as discussed earlier, is useful to focus attention.

Volition
The capability of conscious choice, decision, and intention.

Activities for auditory attention may include:

- *Listening to tapes of stories.* Books on tape are available through Recordings for the Blind and Dyslexic, Learning through Listening. This nonprofit volunteer organization serves people who cannot read standard print because of visual impairment, dyslexia, or other physical disability. Visit www.rfbd.org.

Sidebar 8.5   **Hints for Improving Short-Term Memory**

- Have the student read the information to be memorized out loud into a tape recorder so it can be replayed.
- Let students make a visual picture or schematic.
- Ask students to retell or describe information to be memorized out loud so that he/she can focus attention on the facts.
- Create a card category set and store parts of information on durable cards to create a flexible system on recall.
- Break information down into manageable units.
- Include attention and stretch breaks.
- Underline key phrases and words.
- Have students repeat and rephrase directions.
- Give students review material at the end of instruction.

Source: Fowler (1992)

- *Engaging in vigilance tasks.* Use the Simon Patterning Game, which uses sound and light to develop vigilance. See Attention Module 1 from the *Captain's Log* software (BrainTrain, 1995). This is a computer software program in which the individual focuses on changes that occur on the screen. Such changes include color patterning, sound patterning, and foreground and background changes, all within a given time frame. This program is available for purchase, on a trial basis, or is "rentable" online for six months. Also play Simon Says or Bop It for timing and vigilance training.

- *Transcribing from tape recording.* Listen to a tape or book on tape and write the transcript. One can do a transcription of words from a song.

- *Listening to broadcasts.* Listen to various broadcasts for specific information or words, or listen to passages from Guinness World Records, 2005 (Guinness World Records, 2005) read aloud and answer key questions.

- *Listening to a series of numbers and letters read aloud.* Then pick out or signal only when a designated letter or a specific letter, number, or word is heard.

Attention-Deficit/Hyperactivity Disorder

Speed of Processing

Often youngsters with AD/HD have a problem processing information auditorily at the same speed as other individuals. There is often a lag in response, resulting in such fillers as "What?" or "Huh?" These are often delay tactics until the information is received by the brain and understood. The person knows the question, but only after a few seconds. The individual often has the answer, but well after the question has been asked, subsequently asking, "What?" This is due to delayed temporal processing skills, often found to be deficient in this population. Such a temporal integration problem is related to timing of the acoustic signals, slow connectivity, or delayed neurotransmission.

Intervention activities may include:

- Listening to compressed speech
- Listening to adjusted speech to interpret a message, such as with *The Processing Program, Level 1* (McKinnis, 2000a) and *Levels 2 and 3* (McKinnis, 2000b)
- Utilizing computer programs such as *Fast ForWord* (Scientific Learning, 2001) to improve temporal integration skills

Auditory Cohesion

Auditory cohesion involves the ability to interpret, organize, and synthesize auditory information on a higher order level of functioning. This includes pulling all the auditory cues together; listening to a story, a tape, or a lecture and understanding their meaning. Activities may include:

- *Integrating and organizing tasks*—Sequencing pictures, events, or sentences into a cohesive story
- *Listening comprehension tasks*—Listening to stories or passages read aloud and telling what they are about
- *Categorizing tasks*—Placing words or items into corresponding categories
- *Naming a title of a story*—Selecting the best title for the story
- *Solving math word problems*—Analyzing the language of math to problem solve
- *Reading aloud tasks*—Reading a story or passage aloud (use an easier book for more fluency) to stimulate the auditory feedback loop

- *Solving riddles and analogies*—Completing tasks like, "Give two words that rhyme and mean an overweight kitten" (*fat, ca*t), and "Sugar is white, grass is _____."

- *Responding to contingencies*—Completing tasks like "If you like cookies, add 6 and 9, otherwise subtract 6 from 7."

- *Participating in reasoning, inferencing, and problem-solving tasks* (Kelly, Lee, Charrette, & Musiek, 1996)

Materials should come from the student's curriculum whenever possible. Collaboration with the classroom teacher is essential.

Additional auditory cohesion activities include:

- *Engaging in binaural separation and integration skill-building tasks* (**dichotic digits,** dichotic words), on tapes, using a dual track tape recorder. (Available from Auditec of St. Louis). The child listens through headphones and repeats what he or she hear in both ears.

Dichotic digits
A pair or sets of numbers presented to both ears at the same time.

- *Performing interhemispheric transfer of information activities (hold an object in one hand and draw it with the other)*. For example, the professional says one word in the right ear through ear phones, the student points to its picture with the left hand, or points with the right hand, then both hands, depending on the directions. Then the professional says the word in the left ear with the same response protocol, while the stimuli arrive at quicker rates (Masters, Stecker, & Katz, 1998). Repeating words such as "fat/skinny," according to the size of the print of the word and not the word itself.

- *Closure skills*—Filling in the missing pieces in a story or word (e.g., tel _ _ _ one), to derive meaning and make predictions

Figure-Ground Listening

The ability to discern the figure from the background noise is typically challenging for the person with AD/HD. This speech discrimination in noise skill enables one to focus on the speaker and not on the background distractor.

Training in this area primarily involves desensitization to noise. One technique would be to have background noise set to a given level while the speaker gives directions. The professional maintains a high level of foreground information (e.g., directions to complete a puzzle or drawing) with low-level background noise (white noise) gradually increasing. The clinician switches the foreground stimulus to a less interesting task and makes the background sound more interesting (e.g., tape reading of the *Harry Potter* series (Rowling, 1998–2005)), while raising its intensity level. This challenges the individual's attending skills. One learns to "desensitize" the background distraction. Adaptation and desensitization to the background noise occur over time.

Tapes are available from commercial vendors such as Auditec of St. Louis and The Psychological Corporation (replicas of the original *Developmental Learning Materials* (1970) tape series). For a listing of auditory processing programs, see Table 8.1, page 187.

Reading Difficulties

The population with AD/HD is at risk for reading problems. Given the high level of language and auditory processing deficits seen in this group of youngsters, and the high comorbidity of learning disabilities, it behooves the professional to investigate the youngster's phonological processing ability. **Phonological awareness** is the ability to perceive and identify the number of and order of sounds. It is primary in the early stages of reading that a youngster is able to associate sounds with letters, understand that sounds make up a word, associate words with their component sounds, sound out words, blend sounds together to form a word, and manipulate sounds within the word. It relies on auditory discrimination ability.

Decoding is the ability to hear and associate individual speech sounds with the printed letters. It involves the knowledge that words are made up of sounds and that by changing one sound, you can change the word. Developing these abilities, and learning that sounds come together to form words (around the second grade), are necessary skills for the youngster who is learning to read. Decoding the symbols occurs before comprehension of the read material. If one does not make the association between the sound and the printed letter, then that person will not be able to decode and understand the word.

Programs available to help the person develop decoding skills involve a multimodality approach. A sound-symbol approach such as the Orton-Gillingham method (Gillingham & Stillman, 1997), the *Wilson Reading System* (Wilson, 1998), LiPS (Lindamood & Lindamood, 1998), *Sound Reading Solutions* (Howlett, 2001), *Lexia Reading System* (Lexia Learning Systems, 2000), and the *Phonological Awareness Kit*

Phonological awareness
The ability to perceive and identify the number of and order of sounds.

Table 8.1 **Programs Available to Develop Auditory and Phonological Awareness Skills**

Program	Publisher
125 Ways to Be a Better Listener	LinguiSystems
A Metacognitive Program for Treating Auditory Processing Disorders	Pro-Ed
Auditory Processing	Slosson Educational Publications
The Central Auditory Processing Kit	LinguiSystems
The Deciders Take On Concepts (CD-ROMs)	Thinking Publications
Earobics (CD-ROMs)	Cognitive Concepts
The Emotion Game	LinguiSystems
Figurative Language	Thinking Publications
The Following Directions Series	Laureate Learning Systems
Help for Auditory Processing	LinguiSystems
Help Handbook for Exercises for Language Processing	LinguiSystems
It's Time to Listen: Metacognitive Activities for Improving Auditory Processing in the Classroom (2nd ed.)	Pro-Ed
Listening and Following Directions	Super Duper
The Listening Game(s)	Super Duper
Memory Stretch	Pro-Ed
No-Glamour Auditory Processing Cards	LinguiSystems
Phonological Awareness Kit	LinguiSystems
Phonological Awareness Success	Thinking Publications
Processing Auditory Directions	Super Duper
The Processing Program Level 1 and Levels 2 & 3	Thinking Publications
Responding to Oral Directions	Pro-Ed
Sound Smart	BrainTrain
Sounds and Symbols	American Guidance Service
Story Comprehension to Go	LinguiSystems
Understanding and Following Directions (CD-ROM)	Singular Publishing
Warm-Up Exercises	Thinking Publications
Word Joggers	Thinking Publications
Working Out with Listening	Thinking Publications
Working Out with Phonological Awareness	Thinking Publications

(Robertson & Salter, 1995), are all valuable. Some are more demanding in time and instruction than others. Some have home program interactive CDs available. One example is *Earobics* (Cognitive Concepts, 1999) that trains phonological and auditory processing skills. Many have efficacy data available (e.g., *LiPS, Sound Reading Solutions, Wilson Reading System, Earobics*).

After decoding skills have been mastered, then comprehension of the written material is expected. By the end of third grade the child stops learning to read and uses reading to learn. To improve comprehension, the 5Ws (who, what, why, where, when) approach can be helpful. That is, the youngster learns to ask the five *Wh* questions in order to derive the essential meaning from the paragraph read:

- *What* is the story about?
- *Who* is it about?
- *Where* does it take place?
- *When* is it happening?
- *Why* is it happening?

Training in understanding these key elements can be accomplished through tutoring with a reading specialist, special education teacher, or a speech-language pathologist. The youngster needs to focus his or her attention on the key points in the story. He or she can also be taught to sketch the story to visualize it. Another approach is the *Lindamood Visualizing and Verbalizing* program (Bell, 1991), which uses gestalt imagery.

Written Language Deficits

Mayes and Calhoun (2000) identified written expression as the most common learning problem among students with AD/HD. Nearly 65 percent of the population has reported deficits in written language. As a result, writing essays, drafting book reports, or answering questions on tests or homework are often challenging for these students. When attempting to write an essay, these students have trouble holding ideas in mind; acting upon and organizing ideas; retrieving grammar, spelling, and punctuation rules from long-term memory; manipulating the material in a logical sequence; and reviewing and correcting the errors.

To help with written language it would be useful to dictate information to a scribe, a parent, or a computer using a program such as voice recognition. Graphic organizers help provide visual prompts. Post-it notes help to promote brainstorming ideas which can later be placed into the essay. Use of technology such as grammar check and spell check on a keyboard, or software programs that teach writing skills such as *Write:OutLoud* or *Draft:Builder* (Don Johnston, 2004) are helpful. Assessment of writing skills could be conducted with the Test of Written Language–Third Edition (TOWL–3; Hamill & Larsen, 1996), and the Written Subpart of the Oral and Written Language Scale (OWLS; Carrow-Woolfolk, 1996).

Helpful accommodations for writing problems include:

- Request that the teacher reduce the amount of written assignments.
- Give the child extended time to complete longer written assignments.
- Suggest a grading differentiation for mechanics and for ideas or content.
- Encourage and develop computer skills.
- Use software programs, such as *Type to Learn Junior: Grades K–2* (Sunburst Technology, 1999), New Keys for Kids: Grades 1–3 (Sunburst Technology, 2001a), and *Type to Learn 3: Grades 3–Adult* (Sunburst Technology, 2001b) that helps children in kindergarten through grade 12 learn keyboarding.
- Help child to brainstorm ideas and put key words down on sticky notes. When the child starts the writing process, arrange the notes so the child can refer to them and recall thoughts.
- Use semantic web strategies and graphic organizers to help generate thoughts for writing. Place the main topic in the center of the "web." Then on lines extending from the center write the supporting details.
- Use a thesaurus for alternate words.
- Have the child express thoughts into a tape recorder to be later transcribed.
- Teach the child simple short-hand symbols so note taking can be quicker and more efficient.
- Break writing tasks into manageable chunks. Set a timer when writing and write until it rings. When it rings, take a short break for a change of pace.
- Use bright-colored paper and/or interesting pens for the writing task, to add novelty.
- Reward completion of written tasks.

Many of these recommendations can be included in the child's accommodation plan or on his or her Individualized Education Plan (IEP).

Organizational Skill Deficits

Use changes in the environment to help the individual stay organized. Organization is one of the most prominent problems, along with planning ahead. It can be termed an executive function disorder (EFD). Inherent in an EFD is difficulty not only with organization, memory and planning, but language formulation efficiency and retrieval. Children struggle with personal organization skills. Helping a child develop such skills involves establishing routines for the major tasks to be accomplished and obtaining or using aids, devices, timers, calendars, and appointment date books.

Helpful hints include:

- Use colored baskets, notebooks, and folders to organize schoolwork and papers.

- Use visual reminders around the house to help the child remember what he or she has to do.

- Break down tasks into smaller steps; set a timer for a specific length of time for each step.

- Write down a schedule for the child's activities, both at home and in school, on weekends, and after school.

- Praise the child for positive organization behaviors.

- Make rules and instructions clear and repetitious.

- Help remove clutter (See Sidebar 8.6 for suggestions on ways to clean-up).

Time management strategies are also critical for children and adults with AD/HD to acquire. Ideas for intervention include:

- Select a compatible day-planner, keep it accessible, refer to it often, enter basic information, carry it at all times, and write in all appointments.

- Construct a "To Do" list and refer to it often. Prioritize a daily "To Do" list and act in accordance with these priorities.

- Generate long-term goals, but break them into small manageable units and allocate each unit to a given daily or weekly task (Robin, 2001).

- Plan ahead.

Sidebar 8.6 **Ways to Clean-Up Clutter**

1. Ask yourself "What does this do for me and can I live without it?" Come up with ways to make do without it.

2. Clean off surface area. Make an area where you keep things you need.

3. If you work with an item regularly, keep it handy in a container.

4. Keep a wastebasket in each room to be ready to discard unnecessary items.

5. Do a check everyday to remove unwanted things. Put things away daily.

Source: Maynard (2004)

As mentioned, these suggestions are useful for adults as well. The advantage for adults is that there is a wealth of technology aids and devices such as personal data assistant (PDA), and Palm Pilots to help one stay on task. The use of a coach is also valuable. A coach can help with decision making, planning, sorting, and meeting goals. For more information on finding an organizational coach, go to www.additudemag.com or contact the National Association for Professional Organizers (www.napo.net). Figures 8.2 and 8.3 (see page 192) show a weekly planner of an adult with AD/HD, before organizational therapy and two months into therapy with a coach.

Note-Taking Deficits

The ability to extract the salient points from what is being said or read is one of the challenges facing a person with AD/HD. This occurs mainly because the person is either not attending to the material or not processing it to understand it. Thus, the ability to know what is important from unimportant becomes questionable, rendering note taking a disastrous experience. It is not unusual to see children write down some insignificant detail and miss the main point. They simply do not know the main point from a detail. The individual needs to be taught how to capture the 5 Wh questions—What, When, Who, Where, Why—mentioned previously.

Attention-Deficit/Hyperactivity Disorder

Figure 8.2   **Weekly Calendar before Therapy with Coach**

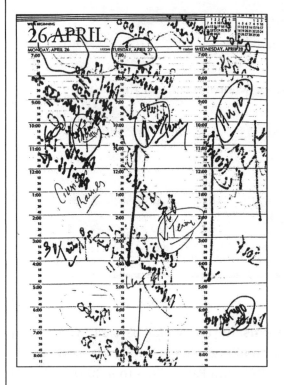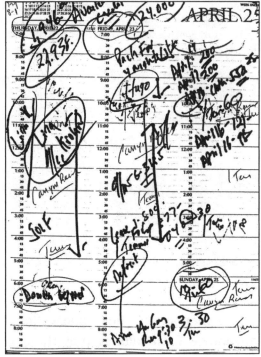

Figure 8.3   **Weekly Calendar after Therapy with Coach**

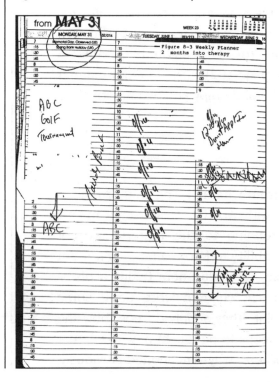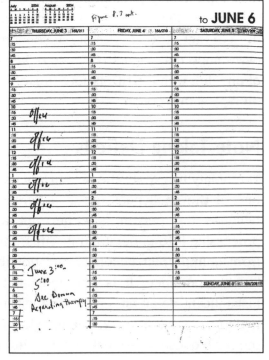

The person needs to ask for help in note taking or use a buddy with a Palm Pilot or an AlphaSmart (2004) to take notes. AlphaSmart is an electronic keyboard that allows the person to type notes which are later downloaded to a computer for a print-out. It is a lightweight portable writing pad. The person should have access and use of a copy of the buddy's notes, or verify one's own notes against the teacher's or a good note taker's. Teacher notes provided ahead of class lecture are useful, and a request for such can be placed on the student's accommodation plan. Use of wireless technology such as Bluetooth can be used to send notes to other mobile devices. Bluetooth is a wireless device that allows linkage between a person's PDA and other operating networks. This emerging radio technology lets electronic devices communicate back and forth, without wires, to anywhere. A two-way communication system allows the transmission immediately from one device to another (e.g., to a computer for storage, and spell-grammar checks). (See Sidebar 8.7 for its application with 12 year-old Gabriella.)

Social Skills Deficits

Children with AD/HD often have difficulty mastering social skills because of impulsivity, inattention, distractibility, nonverbal and verbal language difficulties, and processing problems. Such processing problems make it difficult for the individual to figure out social signals and cues. However, social skills can be taught.

Sidebar 8.7   Technology Application Example

One of my patients, Gabriella, a 12-year-old girl with significant auditory and language processing deficits, has a wireless cell phone that transmits her voice to a Bluetooth chip (an earpiece) that is placed in her mother's ear. The mother can give her instruction as she goes to the store for her. The mother reminds her what to buy and how much money she has given her. Gabrielle then reports back to her mother through her cell phone how much the item costs and how much change she is receiving. It helps keep Gabrielle on track, remembering what she has to do. The mother also guides her crossing the street. With this support and reminders, the child can practice independence.

It is important to:

- Identify what social skills need to be learned (e.g., make eye contact with the person who is speaking).

- Teach the child what he or she did right in a social situation. This is motivating.

- Take photographs of the child performing the desired skill as a visual reminder. Point to the picture when the child does an undesirable behavior and remind him or her to use the desired skill instead.

- Create positive opportunities for the child to interact. Arrange play dates, but limit the time spent to what the child can handle.

- Create social situations around activities the child can do well, and have the child plan the activity.

- Build coping strategies into activities, especially when an activity doesn't turn out the way it was expected.

- Help the child find the words to express how he or she is feeling. Help to develop social language and the vocabulary of feelings. Help the child name specific feelings. Help the child by having the adult express feelings for him or her.

- Help the child identify social cues and read other people. Have the child observe interactions between other people, or watch a videotape to study body language, facial expression, body gestures, and tone of voice.

- Rehearse special events. For example, prepare for a party, and ask the child to practice how to greet, share toys, take turns, and thank guests for their presents. If the individual is older and permits, use videotapes for viewing and critiquing.

- Allow the child time to play and have fun with other children. Provide more opportunities for the child to make friends and practice friendship-making skills.

- Provide a social skills training group with other children with similar issues, moderated by a professional.

There are computer programs to address social skills, such as:

- *Sanford's Social Skills* (Sims Baran, 1996)

- *FACE to FACE: Facilitating Adolescent Communication Experience* (Hess, 1993)

- *Nickel Takes On Teasing* (2003), *Nickel Takes On Stealing* (2004a), *Nickel Takes On Anger* (2004b), *Nickel Takes On Disrespect* (2005) (Thinking Publications)

Other social skill resources can be found on pages 227–228. Professionals should not lose sight of the human capacity and motivation for personal growth. To encourage one to be a better communicator, see Sidebar 8.8 and Study More 8.4 for guidelines and suggestions.

General Guidelines for Good Communication Skills Development

Sidebar 8.8

- When talking to the child, minimize distractions (e.g., turn off television).
- Get the child's attention before speaking.
- Make eye contact and expect the child to make eye contact.
- Help the child to get to the main point and stick to it.
- Simplify language used with the child; give simple directions.
- Confirm understanding; ask the child to repeat what was asked or said.
- Take turns when speaking to the child.
- Praise the child for speaking and trying to listen.
- Avoid talking over noise or other people talking.
- Avoid looking away when speaking.
- Avoid pressuring the child to do something when he or she may not be capable.
- Keep focused on a topic.
- Practice role-playing and acting out situations. Watch for appropriate language and behavior.
- Give clear and consistent choices and consequences.
- Get the services of a professional speech-language pathologist to evaluate the child and determine any need for intervention.

Source: Florida Department of Education (2001)

Use of Technology

The attention span of children with AD/HD is much longer when they are engaged in high-interest activities—a phenomenon that has been coined the "Nintendo effect" (Barkley, DuPaul, & McMurry, 1990). Therefore for programs to become more interesting, they should be couched in contexts for which students show interest. Variables include interaction among student, teacher, and or instruction. There are many ways to modify lesson material, such as changing the lesson length or format, the type of seatwork, the activity, and the difficulty of lessons. However, with the age of technology, there are visual and interactive programs that provide high motivation, demonstration, clear and corrective feedback, and reinforcement through visual and or auditory presentations. Technology can improve the timing of the response as well as the accuracy. For this population, it can be the solution to many struggles. Teaching good keyboarding and computer skills is a critical component.

The use of computers to assist with instruction increases the on-task and work production behaviors of students with AD/HD, as the instructional features of such allow students to focus their attention on academic stimuli (Torgesen & Young, 1983). Usually, computer-assisted instruction (CAI) provides instructional objectives, highlighting of essential material, large print, color, and multi-sensory modalities. The content is usually broken down into smaller pieces of information, and immediate feedback is provided regarding response accuracy. CAI limits the nonessential features that may distract. In a research study involving math, 18 students diagnosed with AD/HD were given a readable display format and self-paced instructional work. Results indicated that students completed almost twice as many problems and spent more time working in the CAI condition than in the paper-and-pencil condition (Kleiman, Humphrey, & Lindsay, 1981). Other researchers (Ford, Poe, & Cox, 1993) found that students were more attentive when the CAI included a game format with animation. In the "drill" format, nonattending behaviors increased. No increase in nonattending behaviors were seen in the CAI material with a game format.

A sample listing of available technology programs appropriate for use with this population follows. Please note that for some programs, efficacy has not yet been established but the first *two* listed do have efficacy data.

- *Earobics* (Cognitive Concepts, 1999)—This program is useful for children ages 4–7 (Step 1), 7–10 (Step 2), and 10+ (adolescents and adults) with deficits in speech-language processing, phonological awareness learning, and reading. Each level includes 5 or 6 interactive games focusing on auditory skills, blending, sensory integration, and phonological awareness training techniques. Automatic goal writing, performance tracking, and data collection are provided. Activities include exercises for auditory memory, sequential memory, attention and vigilance, figure-ground discrimination, identification of phonemes, rhyming, and recognition of word endings and beginnings. (www.earobics.com)

- *Fast ForWord* (Scientific Learning, 2001)—This computer-based program uses research and technology to improve learning skills. The first program, designed for 4 to 12 year-olds, purports to help with basic elements of speech and language by altering the acoustic properties of speech signals to aid in differentiation of phonemes leading to mastery of natural speech sounds and the ability to process language. There are four programs available, depending upon age of the student and need (Language basics, Language, Middle and High School, Language to Reading). (www.scientifi-clearning.com). There are also new software programs available: Reading Preparation, Reading 1, Reading 2, Reading 3, Reading 4, and soon to be released Reading 5 to strengthen reading skills in elementary school children.

- *Captain's Log* (BrainTrain, 1995)—This is termed the "complete computerized mental gym." This software program helps adults and children with AD/HD, brain injury, psychiatric disorders, and learning disabilities learn faster, improve memory, and become better thinkers. It consists of 33 multi-level programs arranged in 5 modules. (www.braintrain.com)

- *Sound Smart* (BrainTrain, 2001)—This software program builds auditory attention and helps children (age 4+ through adults become better listeners and readers. The program targets phonemic awareness, listening skills, working memory, mental processing, speech, and self-control. Four distinct behavioral "tracts" include: speed, patience, listening, and challenge. There are 3 modules. (www.braintrain.com)

- LocuTour Multimedia Software—This company produces numerous software programs addressing areas of literacy, attention and memory, phonemic awareness, spelling, language learning, and phonology. The software is appropriate for ages 3 to adult and some programs are available in Spanish as well. In *Attention and Memory* (Scarry-Larkin, 1994–2001), there are 35 comprehensive exercises in 6 submodules to address attention and memory. (www.locutour.com)

- *Brain Builder* (Advanced Brain Technologies, 1999)—When auditory activities are presented, a different voice is used with each sequence presentation allowing the ear and the brain to tune-in to voices with pitches and tonal qualities in the sound spectrum. The individual responds to a variety of brain training exercises, like remembering a sequence of numbers in reverse order. This program uses number sequences at random in order to avoid repetition. (www.brainbuilder.com)

- *AlphaSmart* (AlphaSmart, 2004)—This small, lightweight hand-held keyboard allows the youngster to take notes and carry it about during the school day. All the notes taken on the keyboard are stored until the child returns home and downloads it onto his or her computer. The information saved in the AlphaSmart can be stored and retrieved on the child's home computer program. (www.alphasmart.com)

- *Write:OutLoud* (Don Johnston, 2004)—This computer program is recommended for those youngsters who have difficulty writing their thoughts and getting them onto paper. One speaks into the computer and the computer generates notes from that utterance which can later be used to generate a composition in written format. It is most useful for those that are stronger orally but have problems in written language.

- *Draft:Builder* (Don Johnston, 2004)—This computer program allows the student to draft a message and put it into a story format by adding thoughts, converting them into sentences, and then sequencing the sentences into a paragraph unit, thereby producing a whole composition. The ultimate goal is to produce a written document.

- *Soliloquy Reading Assistant* (Soliloquy Learning, 2003)—This software program assists the child who is struggling with reading. The student reads the written passage aloud. When he or she gets stuck on a word, or mispronounces, or has a problem understanding the word, then the Reading Assistant will pronounce it, read it aloud, and provide access to finding out the meaning. (www.reading-assistant.com)

- *Listening Programs* (Advanced Brain Technologies, 1999)—This compilation of audio CDs allows one to listen to electronically treated music through headphones. It is designed to improve listening skills and attending. The CDs can be used at home, at school, or in clinic settings. The theory is that this "therapeutic listening" has a soothing effect on the hearing mechanism by delivering high frequency filtered and non-filtered sound to the ear and the brain. Low frequencies have been filtered out to avoid the grating sounds and "enhance the ear's ability to hear the information." There are a number of programs commercially available, each usually tailored to the person. (www.thelisteningprogram.com)

- *Bluetooth* (Bluetooth, 2005)—Bluetooth is a radio technology that lets electronic devices interface wirelessly with mobile phones, computers, personal hand-held devices, etc. It can travel through walls, doors, and other barriers. A Bluetooth interface can transmit data from a cell phone or computer by processing them into radio signals which flow from the unit's antenna to the antenna of the receiving device. There the data are decoded back to their original form. The two-way communication enables one to transmit data from a deskbound PC or laptop screen to a classroom, testing device, and back again. (www.bluetooth.com)

These low-technology multimodal options might also be considered during intervention:

- *Interactive Metronome* (Interactive Metronome, 1993–2004)—This technology assesses and enables individuals to systematically practice and improve timing, rhythmicity, and related motor sequencing and planning capabilities. Rhyming and timing seem to play a role in motor planning, sequencing, and cognitive functions such as attention and academic achievement. Timing has been found to play a role in academic achievement in math, reading, and language. Timing and rhythmicity have been found to be related to self-control and gross motor behavior. (www.interactivemetronome.com)

- *Balametrics* (Balametrics, 1980–2004)—This program is based on the understanding that the role of the vestibular system combines the inertial information from the three semicircular canals with the gravitational orientation provided by the otolith organ (i.e., the perception of the world as a three-dimensional space). Activities involve physical balancing to bring inertial movements under control and establish balance of the organism. With improved balance, the person can focus better. (www.balametrics.com)

- *NeuroNet Kit* (Balametrics, 1980–2004)—This program includes a number of materials, such as a rotation board to help develop the ability to organize space auditorily. "These types of spatial organization problems are present in people who have problems in math." It includes a balance board, rotation board, and a pendulum. (www.balametrics.com)

Parent Organizations and Support Groups

Parents and families need to know that they are not alone in seeking help for their child. Adults need to know that they are never too old to seek assistance and remediation for these needs. There are support groups. Such groups serve an enormous function of providing education, enlightenment, and resources. The following are some agencies that have served in that capacity. For a more comprehensive list, see Resources (Chapter 14).

- CHADD (Children and Adults with Attention Deficit Disorder)
  301.306.7070   800.233.4050
  www.chadd.org

- ADD Consults-AD/HD online e-clinic, offers a variety of resources and services
  www.addconsults.com

- ADDAPPT: Attention Deficit Disorder Association of Parents and Professionals Together
  PO Box 293
  Oak Forest, IL 60452

- CESD: Council of Educators for Students with Disabilities
  512.219.5043
  www.504idea.org

- Adult ADD—This website designed by Eli Lilly and Company provides AD/HD information relevant to adults.
  1.800.LILLY.RX
  www.adultadd.com

- "Experts on Call"—This program, hosted by Shire US Inc., helps families and caregivers better understand attention-deficit/hyperactivity disorder. Its purpose is to dispel myths about the condition. Experts at a national toll-free telephone hotline (888.ASK.ADHD) on a specific date provide access to English- and Spanish-speaking experts, including physicians, school nurses, educators, and advocates who answer questions about the disorder. In addition, a confidential one-on-one online forum is made available (www.adhdsupport.com) throughout the day. Information provided includes topics such as how teachers can approach parents if they suspect a student has AD/HD, how parents can approach teachers about their child's related needs, proper diagnosis and treatment, and common misconceptions about the disorder. For example, Kathy Baker, Emmy Award winning actress, took part in the fifth annual "AD/HD Experts on Call" program ("Actress Kathy Baker," 2003). Her interest was related to her own 13-year-old son diagnosed with AD/HD when he was 9.

Some Final Words on Remediation

Research in neural plasticity indicates that the younger we are the more plastic the brain is, and plasticity extends throughout one's lifetime. By example, adults learn new information, and those who have been affected by a stroke do recover. Evidence shows that functional changes occur after treatment, and such changes can be viewed as alterations in neurophysiologic responses. Tremblay, Kraus, and McGee (1998) found that adults were able to be trained to discriminate phonemic contrasts not found in their native language. These changes were measured on event-related potential reflecting new ability.

The key to maximizing neuroplasticity is through frequent, challenging, and intense activities focusing on the specific deficits. Much has been cited about keeping the brain alert. Recent functional brain scans (fMRI) reveal activation in areas of the brain following intense treatment. Utilizing activities such as integration tasks, and interhemispheric transfer of information whereby both hemispheres are activated, may help preserve auditory and related functions in a similar way that auditory stimulation may partially counteract the loss from aging. Keeping the brain sharp and engaging in activities may help to preserve function. We know that auditory stimulation through the use of hearing aids may partially alleviate or suspend the growth of presbycusis hearing loss (Willot, Hnath, & Lister, 2001).

In the same token, stimulation, training, and behavioral modification plans can alter one's abilities to meet challenges. For speech-language and

auditory processing skills, the evidence is not completely in. From brain scans (functional MRI and PET Scans), activation of certain areas of the brain can be seen during activities. Increased activation in areas of the temporal lobe are noted following intense auditory training (Temple et al., 2003). The capacity to look at the brain while doing an activity (using fMRI) unleashes information that was previously unknown. This is hopeful and supports clinical findings that training and intervention can make it better. We have more yet to learn. But we know this about brain functioning: Use it or lose it!

Summary

This chapter presented the language and auditory deficits indigenous to the population of children and adults with AD/HD. Suggestions for management and treatment as they relate to general and specific areas of deficit were presented. Much can be done to treat language and auditory processing disorders and short-term memory in this population. Other areas not to be neglected include organization, note taking, reading, written language, and social skills. Specific intervention suggestions and technology aids were described. There is much to be done to remediate and improve communication skills in this population.

Attention-Deficit/ Hyperactivity Disorder in Adults

The symptoms of inattention, impulsivity, and hyperactivity as noted in earlier chapters pertaining to children, are also manifested in adults. Although the symptoms of hyperactivity diminish into adulthood, the National Institutes of Health note that 80 percent of children with AD/HD continue to exhibit the symptoms of inattention and impulsivity during adolescence and about half of these continue to struggle with the disorder throughout their lives (Hart, Lahey, Loeber, Applegate, & Frick, 1995). About 5 percent of people in the U.S. have AD/HD (although less than 1 in 4 knows that he or she has it). Statistics indicate that about 30 to 50 percent of children with AD/HD continue to show some form of the disorder in adulthood. Data suggest that adults have more inattentive symptoms and fewer hyperactive-impulsive symptoms (Hart et al.).

Characteristics of Adults with AD/HD

Adults with AD/HD describe symptoms of fluctuating attention. Most of the time, these individuals are inattentive and have difficulty focusing or concentrating during home, work, and social activities. They are easily distracted either by external noises or an array of internal thoughts, and often seem to be daydreaming. Adults with AD/HD begin a project, and as they either try to prepare for or begin their tasks, they soon find themselves off-task, doing something related, but unintended. They are usually "in the middle of" several projects all at once. Frequently they make careless mistakes, inconsistently follow through on serial instructions, and

Attention-Deficit/Hyperactivity Disorder

Novel
New and not resembling something formerly known or used, of a kind not seen before.

have a poor sense of time. Adults with AD/HD are easily bored and drawn to **novel** stimuli, often at the expense of the desired object of their attention (Accardo, Blondis, Whitman, & Stein, 2000). They frequently lose things like keys. Emotionally they may feel "wired" and appear to be on edge. Mood swings can occur and some adults can appear to be "hot tempered." Usually temper outbursts are short lived and quickly forgotten. Difficulty managing stress is also common among adults with AD/HD. Because of this difficulty, they may become overwhelmed and may dart from activity to activity without putting enough effort into any one task.

Symptoms of hyperactivity-impulsivity in adults with AD/HD are often evident in the context of their relationships. There is a long history of social difficulties. They appear aloof as if they are not paying attention, or they may appear self-centered when they interrupt or make socially inappropriate comments. Interpersonal conflicts in close relationships, such as marriage, arise when the adult with AD/HD impulsively makes decisions without consulting his or her spouse, or without considering the impact it would have on the spouse. Making major purchases or buying on impulse will leave the other spouse feeling left out or insulted. These individuals do not slow down enough to consider their spouse's perspective. The idea of planning or taking another person's schedule or needs into account might not occur to adults with AD/HD, not because they are neglectful intentionally, but because they respond without thinking. These difficulties carry over into communication. They may speak before thinking. They may be overly blunt or even insulting and will respond with surprise when their partner is hurt or angry.

Adults with AD/HD generally have a sense of urgency in their daily lives and have little tolerance for frustration, delay, or planning. They are often easily irritated as they wait in lines and usually make decisions without proper consideration of alternatives. Often they have difficulty collaborating with others and can alienate friends and colleagues. Hyperactivity in adults also takes the form of fidgeting, restlessness, and inability to remain seated.

Many of these adults often change their place or type of employment, and they may resolve job conflicts by working for themselves. They commonly describe their work difficulties as stemming from dissatisfaction, boredom, disorganization, outbursts of anger, and impulsiveness.

AD/HD affects an estimated 15 million people, 3 to 4 percent of the U.S. population (Putnam, 1998; Szegedy-Maszak, 2004). Individuals with

AD/HD often function well in the health care arena, for example, because of positive traits like creativity, a high activity level, resourcefulness, warm heartedness, flexibility, and good sense of humor. An individual with AD/HD may be a physician, hospital CEO, allied health clinician, or department supervisor. Many of these individuals are hard working and have trusting and forgiving attitudes.

On the other hand, people with AD/HD may be easily distracted, fail to give attention to details, have difficulty in organizing tasks, have trouble waiting for their turns, and avoid tasks like paperwork. People with the disorder have the option of telling their coworkers about their conditions. The advantage of telling a few select people is that it helps to establish a buddy system in the workplace.

Left untreated or unrecognized, adults with AD/HD are likely to experience serious functional problems affecting personal relationships, school or job performance, daily activities, personal safety, and self-esteem. This can result in serious consequences such as family problems (separation, divorce, multiple marriages), low career achievement, and increased risk of personal injury (e.g., car accidents). Adults with AD/HD also are likely to suffer from comorbid conditions such as depression, anxiety, and substance abuse. The high rate of comorbidity increases the complexity of diagnosing AD/HD, often masking the AD/HD as an underlying condition, causing it to be overlooked or misdiagnosed.

Once properly diagnosed, AD/HD can be highly treatable. Typically, adults diagnosed with AD/HD:

- Had a history of poorer educational performance and were underachievers

- Had more frequent school disciplinary actions

- Had a higher rate of repeating grades and dropping out of school

In work-related settings, adults diagnosed with AD/HD:

- More frequently make change in employment and perform poorly, quit, or are fired from their jobs

- Have fewer occupational achievements, independent of psychiatric status

- Often have social-related adaptive impairments compared to controls

Attention-Deficit/Hyperactivity Disorder

- Have lower socioeconomic status

- Are more likely to be cited for speeding; have their licenses suspended; are involved in crashes; and rate themselves and others using poorer driving habits

- Use illegal substances more frequently

- Are at increased risk for cigarette smoking, and quit at a lower rate

- Are likely to self-report psychological **maladjustment** more often

Adults diagnosed with AD/HD also display impairments that are relationship-related, which include:

- More marital problems and multiple marriages

- Higher incidence of separation and divorce

Most of this functional impairment diminishes with remission of the disorder and can be mitigated by appropriate treatment. **Pharmacotherapy** of AD/HD has specifically shown to protect against later substance abuse and reckless driving. Nearly 75 percent of adults with AD/HD have a comorbid condition, and 77 percent of this population has had at least 1 of the 17 comorbid psychiatric disorders (Weiss, Murray, & Weiss, 2002). Marks, Newcorn, and Halperin, state "Among adults, AD/HD does not appear to be an **artifact** of symptoms shared with other psychiatric disorders, such as major depression, bipolar disorder, generalized anxiety disorder, nor are these comorbidities themselves the result of symptomatic overlap with AD/HD" (2001, p. 229).

Adults with AD/HD are at considerable risk for substance abuse, especially marijuana and smoking, but this risk is diminished by appropriate treatment. Studies indicate that the rate of abuse disorders among adults with AD/HD is about 10 to 20 percent. Compared with controls, adults with AD/HD have a 3- to 4-fold higher rate of marijuana and cocaine use, a 3-fold higher rate of alcohol abuse (32 to 53 percent of people with AD/HD), and use tobacco 40 percent more. With pharmacotherapy, there is an 85 percent reduction in risk for substance abuse among adolescents (Ward, Wender, & Reimherr, 1993). In childhood, learning disabilities and disruptive behavior disorder are the two comorbid conditions most prevalent. The more concurrent problems that appear in childhood—like dyslexia or learning disability—the more likely that AD/HD will continue into adulthood (Szegedy-Maszak, 2004).

Maladjustment
Poor, faulty, or inadequate adjustment.

Pharmacotherapy
The treatment of disease, and especially mental illness, with drugs.

Artifact
Something characteristic of or resulting from a human institution or activity.

Diagnosis of AD/HD in Adults

In addition to taking a history of symptoms exhibited in the past 6 to 12 months, self-report rating scales are valuable for assessing the patients' current level of functioning and their concerns about this level of functioning, including the impact of behaviors in areas of occupation, family, and relationships. While the scales are helpful screening tools, none are capable of definitively establishing a diagnosis and should not be used exclusively. Because many disorders manifest with symptoms of inattention and impulsivity, care needs to be taken in use of the self-report rating scales in diagnosing AD/HD.

A useful scale is the ***Conners' Adult ADHD Rating Scale*** (Conners, Erhardt, & Sparrow, 1999)—available either in 26- or 42-item versions—perhaps one of the best scales available to discriminate between patients with AD/HD and those with other conditions. Internal reliability and validity ratings are high. Available are also *DSM–IV*-based rating scales that list the 18 items of *DSM–IV* AD/HD, including those for oppositional defiant disorder and conduct disorder, along with a 4-point scale: 0=not at all or never; 1=somewhat or sometimes; 2=pretty much or often; 3=very much or very often. Scores of 2 or 3 are usually considered to be in the clinical range. If 6 of the 9 items of inattention and/or hyperactive/impulsive symptoms are rated 2 or 3, this would be considered to have met the *DSM–IV* categorical cutoff. Several versions of this scale are available, and one is available on the Internet. Barkley has also used and adapted the *DSM–IV* criteria to develop his adult scale (Barkley, 1998).

Given the high levels of comorbidity—especially comorbidity with other developmental disorders such as learning disabilities, behavior disorders, or autism spectrum disorders that are unfamiliar to adults—it may be useful to administer a broadband scale to screen the patient and informant for a guide to a full, clinical mental status exam. The ***Adult Inventories–4*** (ASRI-4; Gadow, Sprafkin, & Weiss, 2004) includes assessment of AD/HD, ODD, CD, learning problems, autism, personality difficulties, mood disorders, anxiety disorders, and other relevant *DSM–IV* disorders.

The ***Adult ADHD Self-Report Scale (ASRS–V1.1) Screener***, developed by the World Health Organization (2003) in collaboration with other experts helps primary care physicians in the diagnosis of AD/HD in adults. The ASRS–V1.1 consists of two nine-question sections. One section evaluates

inattentiveness and the other evaluates hyperactivity/impulsivity. The questions asked are relevant to adults, like "How often do you have problems remembering appointments or obligations?" or "How often do you leave your seat in a meeting?" The *Adult ADHD Self-Report Scale (ASRS-V1.1)* is provided as Study More 9.1. It can be printed and reproduced.

A recent survey conducted by the New York University (NYU) School of Medicine Institutional Board of Research Associates (2003) showed that 85 percent of primary care physicians would play a more active role in diagnosing and treating adult AD/HD if they had access to a simple patient-administered scale that would aid in the diagnosis of the condition. Of the 400 physicians completing the survey, 34 percent considered themselves to be "very knowledgeable" about AD/HD, 65 percent would refer a patient with suspected AD/HD to a specialist, while only 2 percent of physicians would refer a patient with suspected depression, and 3 percent would refer a patient with suspected anxiety disorder.

In a 2003 Harris Poll on physician perceptions of adult AD/HD, prepared by NYU School of Medicine, 77 percent of physicians said adult AD/HD was not very well understood by the medical community. Seventy-two percent said it was more difficult to diagnose adults with AD/HD than it was to diagnose children with it (Szegedy-Maszak, 2004).

Other measures such as neuropsychological assessments performed on adults with AD/HD reveal deficits in speed, memory, and attention. These measurements demonstrate that the spectrum of deficit functions associated with AD/HD is not consistent across the various neuropsychological tests available for adults. Therefore, neuropsychological testing of adults may contribute to an overall evaluation, but should not be used as the sole diagnostic measurement.

It is important to recognize that *DSM–IV* criteria were written for children and have never been validated for adults, yet they are still used as the key diagnostic criteria for adults. These criteria may be too stringent in standards for age onset (age 7) and for the required thresholds for diagnosis (6 from either category). Assessment should include a wide range of measurement, including symptom-rating scales, diagnostic interviews, history forms, broadband symptom screens, and rating scales that measure functioning, mental status, developmental history, family psychiatric history, medical exam, and psychological testing. Future research should focus on development of more sensitive and specific criteria for adult diagnosis of AD/HD, especially around the implication of subtype diagnosis and the overlap with other disorders.

The major classification systems—ICD–9 and *DSM–IV*—include an age-of-onset criterion that requires a history of clinically relevant symptoms before the age of 7 years in order for an AD/HD diagnosis to be confirmed. Overall prevalence of psychopathology or psychiatric comorbidity does not differ between early and late-onset patients. There also is no difference between early and late-onset of AD/HD in terms of age, gender, or severity of symptoms. "We do not question the fact that clinically relevant AD/HD symptoms are present before that age of 7 in the majority of cases; however, it should be considered that there might be a subgroup of patients in whom AD/HD presents later" (Hesslinger, Tebartz van Elst, Mochan, & Ebert, 2003, pp. 222–223).

According to Harvard Medical School Professor of Psychiatry, Dr. Stephen Faraone, although no one knows what causes AD/HD, it is generally thought to be a complex alchemy of genetics, environment, and biochemistry. "Some people can have a stronger genetic load to their condition, some a stronger environmental load, and for others, obstetric complications at birth could contribute to the disorder" (Szegedy-Maszak, 2004, p. 56). Such obstetric complications include the mother's smoking or oxygen deprivation at birth. Recent studies in brain imaging are pointing to brain circuitry failure in the cerebellum, which plays a role in cognitive processing, coordination, and movement.

How Can Adults Effectively Manage AD/HD?

Individuals with AD/HD benefit from working in an area away from windows and doorways to minimize distractions. A sheltered environment is a positive support feature and provides a safe place for the individual to take deep breaths and relieve stress.

The following five-step program, advocated by Dr. Edward Hallowell (Hallowell & Ratey, 2005), is an attempt to cope with AD/HD and distractions.

Step One: Adequate Diagnosis

It is never too late to be diagnosed. Since AD/HD occurs with other conditions like depression, substance abuse, anxiety disorders, or learning disabilities, it is important to determine what the true condition is.

Step Two: Education

Adults can learn from their doctor, books, lectures, and talking with other people who have AD/HD, what the syndrome is about and get the right information.

Step Three: Lifestyle Changes

Exercise is wonderful treatment for AD/HD. Proper amounts of sleep, proper nutrition, and intake of omega-3 fatty acids may help. Adding structure to the environment, and using lists, reminders, and alarm clocks are helpful. Finding the right job, and having a successful marriage provide major structure. A small-scale structure is placing a basket near the front door to put keys in when arriving home to not have to look for them frantically every morning.

Step Four: Coaching

Adults should enlist help with implementing structure. It is hard work doing it alone. Working with a coach or a psychotherapist, or engaging in couples therapy or family therapy, can be helpful.

Step Five: Medication
Medication is only one step in the program, but it is an important element in the five steps.

General Coping Strategies for Adults

The following strategies may help individuals with AD/HD in their workplace and daily life. When working with adults with AD/HD, consider which strategies to share with each client.

- *Write it down!*
  Use an appointment book or calendar to keep track of appointments. Keep the appointment book and calendar in a visible place. Write a checklist of what needs to be done each day. Leave notepads in strategic places (beside the bed, by the phone, in a jacket).

- *Know (and accept) your limitations.* Do what you are capable of doing. Do not accept projects beyond your expertise or time limitation.

- *Set realistic goals.*
  Make them challenging, yet not impossible to achieve.

- *Educate yourself.*
  Read books about AD/HD. Talk to professionals and other adults with AD/HD. Self-awareness of your disorder is critical to your success.

- *Have a coach.*
  A friend, colleague, spouse, or therapist can help you get organized, stay on task, and provide encouragement.

- *Join (or start) a support group.*
  Find others like yourself to form a support group or inquire at your local CHADD group if there is an adult group. Often members of that local group themselves have, or know others with, AD/HD.

- *Try to free your mind of negative thoughts.*
  If necessary, consult a knowledgeable psychotherapist to help dispel feelings of negativity.

- *Recognize the importance of external structure.*
  External structure is the key to nonpharmacological management of AD/HD. Forms of external structure include the following: lists, notes to self, color-coding, rituals, reminders, filing systems. Keep notepads handy at all times.

- *Make deadlines.*
  Consider deadlines to be motivators rather than potential failures.

- *Divide and conquer!*
  Divide large tasks into smaller ones, and assign deadlines to each part. This makes for a more manageable task.

- *Prioritize.*
  When life gets hectic, put tasks in order of importance. Do not procrastinate! The trick is to be able to discern what is most important.

- *Realize your optimal working conditions.*
  Get to know how, where, and when you work best. Make sure to work under whatever conditions suit your needs (environment, time of day, body position). Save this place and time for more demanding tasks. Many people with AD/HD succeed at doing two things at once (e.g., jog and plan a business meeting). If you fall into this category, realize that this behavior is acceptable as long as you meet your goal.

- *Give yourself extra time.*
  Be sure to leave time between appointments. Take mini-breaks to alleviate any transitional anxiety.

- *Plan structured "blow-out" time.*
  Schedule sessions whereby you engage in a safe activity that allows you to simply "let go" (e.g., going to the movies, listening to music, engaging in meditation or exercise).

- *Beware of over-focusing on something.*
  Understand the danger involved in obsessing over a problem that exists in your imagination only.

- *Employ memory aids.*
  Use visual prompts. Carry a daily planner for note taking in meetings, during telephone calls, and at conferences. Provide work communication in a written format. Sticky notes can also be used as visual reminders.

- *Use auditory cues*
  Read aloud to focus attention and assist in retention. Electronic reminders, such as alarms, can also be useful.

- *Develop routines*
  Routines can relieve pressure of having to remember to do something. Devise a schedule for all activities, including responding to email and telephone calls and daily meetings.

- *Schedule breaks.*

  Frequent short breaks can remedy restlessness associated with AD/HD. Use a clock to set designated time intervals.

- *Consider **flextime**.*

  Flextime may be an option when coming to work on time is not essential. Work past breaks and quitting time, or come late to work.

- *Utilize "talking" computers, calculators, and other technological devices.*
  Computer software that reads a document (i.e., converts text to speech) may help in reading comprehension. Record meetings and important conferences on videotape or audiotape, or use your computer to record and store digital audio files. Graphic presentation including flow charts and diagrams may assist in comprehension. Palm Pilots and similar devices help with scheduling reminders. Provide adequate computer software for reviewing documents. Computer spelling and grammar checks are useful.

Flextime
A system that allows employees to choose their own times for starting and finishing work within a broad range of available hours.

Coping in a Relationship

There are a number of strategies that can help increase relationship satisfaction among adults with AD/HD and their partners. A structured format for problem solving often will keep the adult with AD/HD on track. The following are a series of steps that can help couples communicate (Searight, 1999):

1. State the problem.

2. Brainstorm a range of possible options.

3. Review the list of options generated.

4. Discard those options that are unrealistic.

5. Further narrow the range of available options in a systematic way.

6. Select one or two options to implement.

7. Show your partner that you respect and understand what he or she has to say. Repeat what was said to make sure you understood it.

8. Observe the partner's body language as she or he speaks for clues of feelings or emotions.

It is also helpful for the couple to set aside a structured time every day to address family issues. Keeping a large calendar with all appointments and family activities scheduled as many months in advance as possible is helpful. It should be kept in a central location to provide frequent reminders.

It is important that the partner with AD/HD not use the disorder as an excuse for failing to follow through on important relationship commitments. Even if there is an area of weakness, there are no excuses for failing to follow through.

A helpful suggestion when giving feedback to a partner with AD/HD is using I-statements rather than you-statements. Instead of saying, "You just don't seem to care about me," it is more helpful to say, "I become disappointed when you arrive late for our lunch appointment." Instead of calling the person inconsiderate, indicate how you feel. Avoid name calling. Provide a solution like, "Call me ahead when you know you are running late for our appointment."

Often adults with AD/HD feel guilty that they have wronged their spouse or their children or employers. It is important for the adult to take responsibility for his or her action and for the inappropriate behavior that has been harmful to others. They should also realize that they are now in a better position to be more responsive and sensitive to others that are important in their lives. It is more productive to focus on what they will do in the future and what they would like their relationships to look like in the future. See Sidebar 9.1 and Study More 9.2 for helpful tips for AD/HD couples.

How to Work It Out at Home Living with an AD/HD Person

Determine who is responsible for each chore in the household. Make a list. Create structure and specify times for meals, maintaining consistency each day. Don't expect too much. Refrain from disappointments.

Designate one area that is "off-limits" to anyone but the AD/HD partner. Let the person have this area all to him or herself. Common trouble areas include these:

Credit Cards: Use credit cards that require a deposited balance to avoid overcharging. Be sure they are paid off each month.

Driving: Avoid the higher rate of accidents among young AD/HD adults by encouraging the person to take extra driver education classes. Consider "safe" cars, not motorcycles.

Sidebar 9.1 **Helpful Tips for AD/HD Couples**

- Have an accurate diagnosis.
- Keep a sense of humor.
- Declare a truce.
- Set up a time for talking.
- Spill the beans.
- Write complaints and recommendations.
- Make a treatment plan.
- Follow through on the plan.
- Make lists for each other.
- Use bulletin boards.
- Keep notepads in strategic places.
- Write daily To-Do lists for your spouse.
- Take stock of your sex lives.
- Avoid mess-maker/cleaner-upper pattern.
- Avoid pesterer/tuner-outer pattern.
- Avoid victim/victimizer pattern.
- Avoid the **sadomasochistic** struggle.
- Watch for control/dominance/submission.
- Break the tapes of negativity.
- Use praise freely.
- Learn about mood management.
- Let the organizer organize.
- Make time for each other.
- Don't use AD/HD as an excuse.
- Don't bring up old mistakes.

From *Answers to Distraction* (pp. 120–125), by E. M. Hallowell and J. J. Ratey, 1996, New York: Pantheon Books. © 1996 by Pantheon Books. Adapted with permission.

Sadomasochistic The derivation of pleasure from the infliction of physical or mental pain, either on others or on self.

Alcohol and Drugs: Adults with AD/HD are more likely to have problems with drugs. Address ways in which such abuse can interfere with judgment and coordination. Nicotine is highly addictive and tobacco smoke is detrimental to health. Avoid smoking. Utilize medication to relieve the need for alcohol and other stress triggers.

Self Esteem: Most adults with AD/HD have taken big hits on their self-concept. Point out their areas of strength and success. Praise and be proud of their accomplishments. Set realistic goals to meet with success and enjoy one's accomplishments. Use a coach to help get there.

AD/HD in Older Adults

When older adults seek treatment for depression, anxiety, obsessive/compulsive behavior, or substance abuse, few medical and mental health professionals consider possible comorbidity of AD/HD. Symptoms are often attributed to aging, stress from losses, retirement, and memory decline. Adults with AD/HD are often misdiagnosed and treated for anxiety disorder or other psychiatric conditions in ways that can actually worsen AD/HD symptoms. Until 1980, AD/HD was considered a childhood disorder normally outgrown by adolescence. Older adults with AD/HD have the same symptoms as children with it, requiring counseling, pharmacology, and treatment. The symptoms that are particularly prevalent are:

- Difficulty sustaining attention and concentration
- Frequent mood swings and short tempers
- An inability to organize or plan ahead

Anyone 50 years or older who has children or grandchildren who have been diagnosed with AD/HD should examine his or her own symptoms and those of one's parents. Since we know the disorder runs in families, the grandparent and/or parent could have the disorder as well. The questions in Table 9.1 are helpful to ask parents in this search. These questions can be printed from Study More 9.3. See Sidebar 9.2 for the parent's story.

These symptoms usually worsen when extreme sustained attention or mental effort is required. Compounding these problems with physical losses, retirement, depression from aging issues, memory loss, and lack of focus because of too much leisure, often clouds the diagnosis. Further, mild cognitive impairment from aging or early Alzheimer's disease can mask or exacerbate the behaviors. These conditions can cause AD/HD-like symptoms. It is important not to confuse the issue of AD/HD with aging. Such issues as disorganization, difficulty traveling to new places, and problems with complex tasks, may be the result of AD/HD. A search across the life-span of the person yields a clearer diagnosis. These AD/HD symptoms occur throughout the life-span. They aren't recent events. Thus, family and

Table 9.1   **Helpful Questions to Ask Parents**

Questions	Yes	No
1. Do you seem not to listen when spoken to?		
2. Do people often have to repeat what they say to you?		
3. Is it difficult to finish tasks, even if you know how to do them?		
4. Is it difficult for you to plan and organize your work assignments?		
5. Is it difficult for you to sit still?		
6. Did you experience any of the symptoms of hyperactivity, distractibility, impulsivity, and inattentiveness as a child?		
7. Did you struggle in school?		

Sidebar 9.2   **Patient: Mr B.**

It is not unusual for a parent to tell me in the interview session that he or she had the same symptoms as the child. In fact, when the AD/HD is confirmed in the child, the parent often has it diagnosed in himself. Often the parent takes the child's medication. I had one parent who did that. Mr. B was a stockbroker and had trouble making a go of his job. He could take orders over the phone, but could not follow through with writing up the order for his company. After experimenting with his son's Ritalin, he found himself working three times as hard, taking more orders, and following through on the write-ups. He tripled his salary! Needless to say, he was thrilled that we discovered his problem. (He was subsequently referred to a psychiatrist for appropriate diagnosis and medication.)

school history are important. Education, job, sleep, and physical histories are important in the diagnostic profile. AD/HD does not begin in later life. It is present throughout life.

Persons with AD/HD are often aware of their disability. They grieve over losses of opportunity and feel angry out of frustration. They may feel flooded by their environments. These individuals can benefit from the same help as other adults, that is medication and psychotherapy, and/or counseling to lead a fuller, more productive life. It is not too late for someone in his or her later years to find help from the negative effects of AD/HD.

The ability to identify AD/HD in adults is growing. With the heightened awareness among physicians, medications for adults, specific programs, counseling, public awareness, and willingness toward accommodations, there is new hope for those adults who have carried a heavy load on their shoulders for years. Once AD/HD is under control, the person owns the energy and regains the benefits that come with it to face life's challenges. After all, if Einstein, Dali, Edison, Neeleman, and Carville could succeed, so can others.

David Neeleman   Salvadore Dali

Summary

This chapter discussed the prevalence, symptomatology, and comorbidity of AD/HD in adults. The limited diagnostic tools available (since the

DSM–IV addresses symptoms commonly found in children), and the late discovery of AD/HD in adults have led to misdiagnosis, and mistaken identity with comorbid look-alikes. If it weren't for their own children being diagnosed, many adults would never be identified, or learn of their condition. Some people may even go through life thinking that they are only depressed or lazy. For many adults, failure to understand this condition has led to frustration, depression, employment struggles, and social failure. Strategies have been offered, along with suggestions for aids and devices to help one cope and manage attention problems. Of course there are coaches, many of whom have been self-selected and not aware they indeed serve as a "coach" (e.g., wife, husband, buddy, girlfriend). It will be interesting to learn more about AD/HD and aging, but that will have to come with time as current adults or newly identified adults grow older. After all, AD/HD is not for children only. As there is help for the young, so too is there help for older individuals.

Counseling and Coping

Chapter 10

Given the behaviors accompanying AD/HD and the trials and tribulations that children and adults undergo in their effort to maintain academic grade averages, friendships, and jobs, there is a need for individual counseling or psychotherapy to deal with the social and emotional problems faced by these individuals. It is generally assumed that structure is good. It is a myth that little can be done about the social problems these individuals face. Specially designed school services, behavior management at home, and medication are the most typically used and most widely accepted interventions for AD/HD. This chapter, however, discusses other approaches that exist as well, namely, counseling and/or psychotherapy.

Individual Therapy

It would be unreasonable to expect that a series of sessions of psychotherapy would address all of the AD/HD symptoms because not all are caused by internal conflicts, misdirected motives, lack of self-worth, or similar issues that individual therapy addresses. However, individual therapy can be beneficial because individuals with AD/HD experience similar self-doubts, conflicts, worries, and confusion. After all, don't they experience rejection from peers, complaints from teachers, and frustration from parents? They are more prone to experiencing these emotions more frequently and more harshly than their peers without AD/HD because of their histories of failure and their lack of self-control. A therapist may prove beneficial when the individual is in need of a caring, supportive, or understanding person, who can offer help that is unavailable

221

elsewhere. Therapy can aid in dealing with problems such as frustration caused by recurring peer rejection, feelings of rejection from parents and siblings as a result of repeated misbehavior, or poor judgment.

Cognitive Behavior Therapy

Cognitive behavior therapy involves working directly with the child or the teenager rather than with the parent or the teacher to train the child to exercise better self-control or to respond reflectively as opposed to impulsively. It involves helping the individual change the cognition that underlies unacceptable behavior. In doing this, children may be instructed in the skill of self-monitoring by being provided with feedback about their behavior and then by learning to rate their own behaviors accurately. After all, isn't an inability to self-monitor a defining characteristic of AD/HD? Children with AD/HD fail to monitor their own behavior closely enough, and, when this happens, they are apt to behave in a poorly controlled fashion. Thus, instructing them on how to analyze, plan, and predict the outcome of their behavior is beneficial.

Along with this training, rewards are dispensed based on how accurately the child learns to evaluate his or her own behavior. Impulsive, poorly planned behavior may give way to more-reflective and better-planned behavior. In this therapy, the child usually participates in a series of training sessions, possibly 10 to 20, in programs that are often sequential and quite detailed. The training usually moves from simple to complex skills. Some programs teach detailed problem-solving skills where children are taught to identify problems, plan a strategy, define a solution, and then rate themselves on the effectiveness of the solution. Later, the child is encouraged to guide his or her own behavior with verbal direction that is spoken aloud. Later still, the child learns to employ internal or cognitive direction toward engaging in acceptable actions.

Throughout this training, the child is rewarded for mastery of the training steps. Since the steps are methodical and help the child to slow his or her responses and be more reflective, cognitive behavior therapy is successful in promoting better problem-solving skills. However, proof of the technique's effectiveness is generally lacking and questions remain about whether the child retains the skills after training stops, or whether the skills generalize to other settings. The child has the best chance to retain the skills and generalize when parents and teachers are aware of training and are capable of rewarding children when real-world applications are made. Cognitive training cannot be regarded as a principle treatment for AD/HD; it is merely an approach in dealing with the behavioral aspects.

Neurocognitive Psychotherapy

This therapeutic approach attempts to foster understanding, reframing, and accepting AD/HD through environmental changes, structure, and support. It has developed over years of clinical work primarily with adolescents and adults. Neurocognitive therapy addresses psychological distress and concrete problems in daily living (Nadeau, 2003).

Coaching

Coaching is a newer approach to working with AD/HD individuals—primarily adults—in helping them cope with their socialization, work, and leisure activities due to poor time management and organizational skills. Some personal coaches specialize in helping people manage their symptoms, succeed in the workplace, set goals cooperatively, and manage their time. As a coach, one offers insight, provides motivation and feedback, and serves as a listener in helping the client know what he or she needs.

The individual and the coach establish a bond based on constructive feedback, reinforcement, and monitoring of progress. Both the individual and the coach cooperatively agree on goals, which can be altered and redefined. The results of coaching are teaching survival skills, setting academic goals, developing problem-solving skills for social/behavioral difficulties, such as reducing outbursts, and increasing work productivity.

Coaching should help with:

- *Setting realistic goals*—Teens, with AD/HD in particular, need strategies to help them set long-term goals (e.g., "What career do I want to pursue?") and the short-term goals they need to reach them (e.g., "How can I pass physics?"). Teens need help with examining the challenges they face as they work toward reaching their short- and long-term goals (e.g., "You are failing physics which makes it difficult to get into a medical school"). They need to ask, "What do I need to do to turn this around?" Once these challenges have been addressed, the teen needs problem-solving techniques that will help overcome weaknesses (e.g., "Let's get a physics tutor").

- *Increasing independence and self-reliance*—A coach should begin with "other-directed" monitoring and move to "student-directed monitoring." Step 1 includes teacher-monitoring and reinforcement for completed assignments on a daily basis. Step 2 involves self-monitoring on the part of the teen (e.g., the student keeps track of the due dates for homework assignments). This step also involves self-reinforcement (e.g., "I got the homework done on time!"). All self-monitoring/reinforcing should be done with teacher supervision. Step 3 involves a time-extension program whereby the teacher reduces the level of monitoring from morning/afternoon to daily, then weekly checking.

- *Reinforcing time management skills*—The coach prepares a weekly list of "Things to Do," and instructs the teen to prepare a daily list of "Things to Do." Using a colored highlighter, those items that must get done that day are highlighted; others that can wait are highlighted in another color. Proper scheduling is a key to success in time managing. Academically demanding courses should be taken early in the day, and a study period should be scheduled before or after.

Family Therapy

Family therapy is a therapeutic approach that involves working with the entire family. This may be beneficial as family discord often results from the stresses of living with a child or spouse with AD/HD. Such scenarios include stress between parents who accuse each other of mishandling their child's behavior or possibly promoting it. Parents often differ on how to handle the disciplinary actions. Also affected are siblings who may harbor deep feelings of resentment because their needs have been over-looked in an effort to help the most difficult or demanding child in the family. Occasionally, these children themselves begin to misbehave as a way to seek attention.

Several contemporary approaches to child behavior management call for unwavering parental acknowledgment that the child has little or no ability to conform to parental expectations. This emphasis is on working with parents to accept and adapt to the child's nature. Engineering a calmer, disability-friendly environment fosters decreased explosive behavior in children and a climate in which the child can have small, progressive demands placed on him or her. Proponents argue that many behavior-change goals are unrealistic given the child's deficits, and that reward and consequence are too confronting for many of these children. The treatment goal is to restore family order and reduce the damaging, demoralizing effect that negative patterns of interaction have on the family. Negativity begets negativity. For *General Tips for Parents* see Sidebar 10.1, and for a *Child's Tips for Parents* see Sidebar 10.2 on page 226. Both Tip Sheets are printable from the CD-ROM as Study Mores 10.1 and 10.2.

What does it take to be a good counselor? One should be an emphatic listener; that is, one should follow a way of listening and speaking that respects and values the other.

Study More on the CD-ROM

Sidebar 10.1 **General Tips for Parents**

- Emphasize strengths when giving feedback. Praise the part of the job that was well done.
- Keep to the facts of an incident.
- Don't forget to praise your child's effort often, regardless of the result.
- Solicit a punishment from your child.
- Don't call it a "punishment," ask "How can you make up for this?"
- Give your opinion, but don't put down theirs; grant that it's alright to disagree.
- Don't be contradicting.
- Be consistent.
- Know that you can't solve all your child's problems, especially those occurring in the social context. Such human struggles build character.
- Don't give a real meaningful consequence that was not discussed or planned.
- Think before you say "yes" or "no."
- If a child is talking about his or her concerns, stop what you are doing and listen.

From "I Scream You Scream: Communication Strategies to Temper the Temperamental Child," by M. Hurley, 2004, *ADHD Research Symposium*, p. 6. © 2004 by ADHD Research Symposium. Reprinted with permission.

Sidebar 10.2   **A Child's Tips for Parents**

- Don't yell!
- Give me a chance to disagree without telling me that I'm "talking back."
- Praise me if I do OK.
- Let me finish! Nothing frustrates me more than being interrupted.
- Don't think you always know what is best for me. Let me see for myself.
- Don't pressure me. Tell me to slow down sometimes and enjoy life.
- Don't try to solve all of my problems. Half the time I just want to tell you about what happened; I'm not looking for a solution.

From "I Scream You Scream: Communication Strategies to Temper the Temperamental Child,"
by M Hurley, 2004, *ADHD Research Symposium*, p. 9.
© 2004 by ADHD Research Symposium. Reprinted with permission.

Group Therapy

Group therapy has been used to teach social skills to individuals with AD/HD, since they report having limited friends, poor ability to mingle among peers, and difficulty sustaining relationships. Many children find that they have only a few friends, often younger or older than themselves. Few have consistently sustaining friendships that function through the years. Many have problems getting along with others their own age. Often these individuals have little awareness of themselves in space, or in relationship to others in a room and can easily overlook someone, bump into something or someone, or knock something over without realizing that their actions and behaviors are inappropriate. Many are not able to express the social amenities that often "break the ice" in a group or get a conversation going. Many are not able to sustain a conversation and thus avoid group social activities. It is not uncommon to find youngsters alone, at their computers, or participating in activities by themselves. Even if they wish to, and with all good intentions, many children with AD/HD have problems getting along with others their own age. The high activity, talkativeness, social intrusiveness, and poor frustration tolerance that characterize these children alienate peers.

Many children remain isolated even after being treated properly with medicine, special school services, or behavior management at home. Most of these children are capable of learning to get along better but they simply find these skills hard to learn. Using a social skills teaching approach, groups of same-age and same-sex children can function as an environment to teach social skills that most children learn naturally. Children move through training curriculum that teaches, step-by-step, how to get along with their age-peers. Unacceptable behavior such as bragging, bossing, belittling peers, and dominating conversation can be isolated and reduced by direct feedback in the group setting. Skills that are essential for acquiring and maintaining friendships are encouraged in a group setting by using rewards, modeling, role-playing, and practicing over a period of weeks.

Important skills that are addressed in this fashion include initiating a conversation, sustaining a conversation without dominating, selecting a suitable topic, complimenting peers, taking turns, giving and accepting feedback, and handling teasing and disappointment. A speech-language pathologist can devise this type of activity in a group setting. Most social skills development programs are practical where group members work together with the therapist to develop a list of dos and don'ts, practiced in contrived role-playing situations within the group and then are tried outside the group. To maximize the effect, inform parents and teachers of the particular skills developed and encourage them to reward or prompt skill usage outside the group. Homework and monitoring of skill usage in the real world can also be included.

Ideally, social skills groups should meet weekly. Because these skills are expected to develop in slow increments, many should participate in these groups on an ongoing basis. For younger children, such a group may also offer support, a chance for acceptance, and fraternity. For professionals, there are many resources to help conduct groups including:

- *My Community* (Social Skill Builder, 2004)
- *Nickel Takes On Anger* (Thinking Publications, 2004)
- *Nickel Takes On Teasing* (Thinking Publications, 2003)
- *Sanford's Social Skills* (Sims Baran, 1996)
- *Scripting: Social Communication for Adolescents* (2nd ed.; Mayo & Waldo, 1994)
- *Scripting Junior: Social skill Role-Plays* (Miller, 2004)

- *Social Communication: Activities for Improving Peer Interactions and Self-Esteem* (Marquis & Addy-Trout, 1992)

- *Social Communication Skills for Children* (McGann & Werven, 1999)

- *Social Skills Intervention Guide: Practical Strategies for Social Skill Training* (Elliott & Gresham, 1991)

- *Social Skills Strategies: A Social-Emotional Curriculum for Adolescents (Books A & B;* Gajewski, Hirn, & Mayo, 1998a, 1998b)

- *Social Star (Books 1, 2, & 3;* Gajewski, Hirn, & Mayo, 1993, 1994, 1996)

Biofeedback Therapy

Feedback
Auditory or visual cues provided while tuning into events as they are happening (i.e., physiologic body actions) which yields understanding of physiological functioning.

Biofeedback refers to a variety of techniques used to teach individuals to control their bodies through the use of a **feedback** device. For example, patients with extreme tension in the frontalis muscles of the forehead often benefit by learning to relax those muscles. A laboratory apparatus that measures changes in tension can be integrated with feedback mechanisms (a light or tone) so that muscle-tension changes in the desired direction can be signaled to the patient.

For children with AD/HD who are motorically overactive and lack either sufficient nervous system arousal or inhibition, biofeedback may help them learn to control their impulses and attend well. Underarousal suspected in individuals with AD/HD is detectable on an electroencephalogram (EEG; Lubar, 1991). Based on this information, some researchers have suggested that biofeedback may play a significant role in treating AD/HD. Using sophisticated EEG devices, patterns of electrical activity are altered to produce enhanced arousal. Individuals are connected to an EEG device through leads attached at the scalp so that some aspects of the brain's electrical activity can be measured. The individual looks at the computer screen that provides feedback. As waves reflecting higher levels of arousal appear, the computer screen provides an encouraging signal—such as a circle that grows in size—to the individual. Gradually, children learn to increase the amount of desired brain waves, and correspondingly, decrease undesirable waves. Case studies suggest that as EEG changes occur, AD/HD symptoms abate. Academic status improves, contributing to the individual's newly acquired capability to arouse attention and sustain concentration (Lubar).

Biofeedback is relatively new and not widely used to treat AD/HD. However, use of EEG biofeedback is being promoted as a nonpharmacologic approach. It is still unclear how effective biofeedback is in treating AD/HD. The training is quite lengthy, requiring 40 to 80 sessions, spread over several months. Often such treatment is not covered by insurance.

Biofeedback has also been called Neurofeedback. This approach, which allows a person to view his or her brain waves on a computer, teaches the person to produce the brain wave patterns associated with a relaxed, alert, focused state, and maintain such a state. As a result, many AD/HD symptoms diminish after 40 to 60 sessions. Scientists, however, do not believe such claims have been sufficiently verified (Rabiner, Palsson, & Freer, 2003).

Building Therapeutic Relationships

Teens, in particular, because of the social and academic adjustment problems they face, are in need of support from a caring and nurturing adult. A therapeutic relationship marks the foundation of an AD/HD management program. Teens who succeed in spite of adversity need support. When asked what was the most significant factor that helped to overcome AD/HD, teens respond, "I had someone who cared, someone who believed in me, someone who never gave up on me, someone who challenged me to do better, someone whom I could talk to when things were bothering me, and someone who made me feel like I could be somebody." Such a person can be a parent, relative, teacher, clinician, coach, or friend.

In my clinical experience, the parents who persisted in finding a better diagnosis, exploring all the avenues of treatment to address all the areas of concern, were the most successful in helping their child succeed. These parents often faced battles with the school district along that journey.

Sidebar 10.3, pages 230–231, may be helpful in deciding what one should say to a youngster regarding his or her attentional issues. These tips are printable from the CD-ROM as Study More 10.3

Sidebar 10.3

Tips for Discussing the Symptoms of AD/HD with Children

For Younger Children (Ages 5–7)
Because of concreteness in thinking, it helps to discuss specific problems the child is experiencing. Such problems can be:

- Raising one's hand too frequently
- Waiting for a turn in class, waiting to be called on
- Difficulty completing class work on time

For Older Elementary School Students (Ages 8–12)
These children understand cause and effect. The counselor should be able to introduce the definition of AD/HD and list related behaviors and can generalize from verbal explanations.

Examples of basic definitions include:
- Distractibility—Trouble staying focused on work
- Disorganization—Difficulty keeping track of belongings, losing items, handing in work on time

For Middle School Students
As children age, emotional issues emerge. Children with AD/HD are vulnerable to feeling inferior to their peer group. Discuss behaviors typical of AD/HD and offer coping strategies.

Examples include:
- Forgetfulness—Before you leave school in the afternoon, check the list in your locker for materials you need to bring home.
- Over-reacting to peers—Discuss and rehearse different noninflammatory responses to another child's teasing.

It is also important that the child's learning skills be evaluated. Often these youngsters have learning disabilities that have been overlooked, or masked by the inattentiveness. They must undergo a thorough examination of their learning skills in preparation for intervention and accommodations in the school. Such programs are essential in improving the child's sense of self-worth and productivity. Too often a learning disability, or reading disability has been overlooked, at the child's emotional expense.

Sidebar 10.3—*Continued*

For High School Students

At this age, the child begins to question conventional ideas about medication and deny any difference with peers. Such issues that arise include the following:

- *The teen decides to stop taking medication.* Have the youngster discuss with the pediatrician the possibility of a time-limited trial without medication, followed by a discussion of the outcome, using feedback from teachers and close friends.

- *The youngster finds that he or she has trouble controlling outbursts and temperament.* Personality shifts affect the ability to be accepted by his or her peers. Discuss the importance of coming to terms with one's own temperament as part of becoming an independent adult.

Discuss the coping skills the youngster has developed to date and the coping skills that may need to be improved and added. Examine specific strengths that can be employed by the child to improve stronger character and deal with future challenges.

Counseling, whether it be through a counselor, psychotherapist, social worker, speech-language pathologist, school psychologist, clinical psychologist, or psychiatrist, can assist the individual in coping with behaviors that interfere with quality-of-life issues that pervade the lifestyle of the person with AD/HD.

Source: Stern & Ben-Ami (2000)

Strategies for Structuring the Classroom to Build Coping Skills

Structure is one of the most critical elements to help the individual with AD/HD in the classroom. A structured class is not to be mistaken for a traditional, rigid, no-nonsense classroom. The most creative, colorful, active, and stimulating classrooms can be structured. Structure needs to be provided through clear communication, expectations, rules, and consequences. Academic tasks must be structured by breaking long-term assignments into manageable increments. Teachers need to carefully structure the schedule—alternating active and quiet periods/activities. Students with AD/HD require assistance structuring their materials and workspace.

Suggestions for educators include:

Proximity
The region close around a person or thing.

- *Use **proximity** control.* Move up close and among the students; make direct eye contact and use physical cuing; review and practice rules and expectations with high frequency; be generous with positive reinforcement (try hard to catch students engaged in appropriate behavior and praise specifically when they are doing something "right"); signaling; and redirecting.

- *Use signals to warn or cue students.* Hand signals or words that are agreed upon privately, or a pager, can warn or cue students (to calm down, get up and stretch, stop talking out, sit appropriately). An observant teacher can redirect students by asking them to do certain tasks.

- *Face transitional times by signaling.* It is important to use a variety of strategies and multisensory techniques to reach all students' learning styles in the classroom, such as flashing the lights, ringing a bell, and playing music.

- *Utilize visual strategies.* These include outlining; diagramming; high-lighting the text; use of films, videos, and pictures; modeling; gestures; graphic organizers; and use of pointers and colored pens/chalk. The overhead projector is one of the most essential tools.

- *Implement auditory strategies.* Discussion group; music/rhythm; verbal games; paraphrasing; and oral reading, reports, and tests all help.

- *Include tactile-kinesthetic strategies.* Use manipulatives, computers, games, movement, role-playing, projects, hands-on activities, writing in the air, and demonstrations.

To maintain the attention of the student with AD/HD, allow active participation in the lessons. Strategies such as unison responses, "Turn to your partner and share or write" techniques, and cooperative learning techniques in the classroom work well. Cooperative learning is particularly beneficial for students with AD/HD in the classroom because it allows for high-response opportunities, shorter wait time, increased structured peer interactions, and a perfect vehicle for teaching social skills in an **authentic** setting and context.

Environmental modifications in the classroom may also make a significant difference for students with AD/HD. Teachers should be mindful of these modifications:

- Seat the students away from distractors such as the door, learning centers, noisy heaters, air-conditioners, etc. Try to seat these students up front within cuing distance and among well-focused students.

- Encourage use of study carrels/office areas, privacy boards, earphones, and earplugs as options for students to block distractions during seat work and test-taking times.

- Allow extra time for verbal responses to questions and provide more working desktop space and distance between desks. Students with AD/HD need more time and more space.

- Accept alternative methods of assessing skills and mastery of concepts beyond written work. AD/HD students often have extreme difficulty with written expression. It is critical to modify assignments and cut the written workload for these students. Allow printing and encourage the use of word processing/typing (e.g., AlphaSmart (www.alphasmart.com)). A similar new product (by AlphaSmart) is Neo. It has a 50 percent larger screen, new font technology, and larger storage capacity. The Neo can beam to Palm and Danas devices (AlphaSmart, 2005).

- Teach organization and study skills. Require students to use three-ring notebooks (with subject dividers, extra paper, and a pencil pouch).

The following techniques might be needed for some children with AD/HD:

- Establish and maintain eye contact with the child while giving directions to help the child attend to and follow those directions.

- Once directions have been given, check with the child to ensure that he or she has understood the directions.

- Utilize a FM sound enhancement system to improve auditory attention.

- Reduce assignment lengths or insert breaks when repetitious or tedious work must be completed, especially if the child can master the skill with a briefer assignment.

Authentic
Taking place in a real world environment or a facsimile thereof.

Attention-Deficit/Hyperactivity Disorder

- Concentrate on novel presentations and stimulating subject matter as much as possible.

- Consider providing the student with reasonable choices about which activities he or she will complete and the order in which they will be completed.

- Provide a computer to enhance work completion and rate of learning.

- Identify and use a child's strengths while avoiding his or her weaknesses.

- Use a peer tutor to increase work completion and learning of material.

- Use programs to monitor a student's behavior, incorporating praise as warranted. Use a system of rewards and incentives to increase work productivity and improve behavior.

Reprimands
An act or expression of criticism and censure.

- Use verbal **reprimands** and redirection to promote on-task behavior, productivity, and appropriate classroom behavior. Avoid severe reprimands.

- Develop a penalty technique involving loss of privileges, rewards, or tokens based on the occurrence of unacceptable behavior, if warranted.

- Use time-out for children with AD/HD but perhaps not in a classroom environment. Modifications of traditional time-out by withholding eligibility for rewards (token economy) may be required.

- Employ a home-school incentive program based on a daily report to assist classroom teachers in helping children become more productive and learn to control their behavior.

Because suspensions fail to influence many children with AD/HD, school personnel should try alternative behavior management techniques first. To help increase motivation, teachers should view the grading system with flexibility and consider each student's unique circumstances and capabilities. Teachers could improve in-class productivity and keep homework assignments within reasonable bounds.

Teachers with training in behavior management or behavior problems are the most suitable instructors. The child's progress during the transition from self-contained elementary instruction to departmentalized middle school or junior high instruction should be monitored. If necessary, a person capable of adding organization, consistency, and structure to the child's day should be employed. For a look-at-a-glance list of classroom tips for teachers, see Sidebar 10.4, which is also Study More 10.4.

Sidebar 10.4   **Classroom Guidelines Tips**

- Use a timer.
- Use cuing techniques.
- Use postcards.
- Use travel cards.
- Make contracts.
- Keep a journal.
- Use color and visuals.
- Develop a metacognitive journal—"What I learned, how I learned it."
- Develop a reflective journal—"What happened, how I felt, what I learned."
- Give structure, tell what is coming (e.g., "There are nine directives for this project").

Coping Strategies for Adults

Many of the issues that impact the performance in school of a child with AD/HD persist into adulthood and become issues in the workplace and in personal relationships. Adults with AD/HD are described as impulsive, self-absorbed, intrusive, inattentive, irresponsible, rude, and insensitive in social settings. One of the bigger issues is that of self-control, or lack thereof. **Self-control** is defined as "the ability to engage in behaviors that result in delayed reward and doing something less immediately pleasurable than an alternative" (Strayhorn, 2002a, 2002b). Difficulties with self-control result in poor regulation of emotion, inability to attend to verbal and nonverbal cues in a social situation, inability to control exaggerated **temperament**, or over-reactivity to social situations.

> **Self-control**
> Individual's ability to control behavior, emotion, actions, and to engage in behaviors that result in delayed reward.

> **Temperament**
> A person's typical way of responding to his or her environment.

In adulthood, poor self-control may lead to:

- Sexual adjustment problems (earlier sexual experimentation, more sexual partners, and increased possibility for sexually transmitted diseases)

- Higher divorce rates and less marital satisfaction

- Frequent job changes and fewer advancements

- Reduced educational attainment (Goldstein & Teeter-Ellison, 2002)

To help adults deal with their issues, the following suggestions may be effective:

- Individual counseling therapy to help develop better judgments and interaction skills

- Specific training in anger management to help develop emotional control

- Practice in self-control by setting achievable goals

- A personal coach to facilitate the process of structuring, monitoring, and providing feedback when setting goals and learning new skills

- Treatment for other comorbid psychiatric problems (anxiety, depression, and comorbid alcohol and drug use/abuse)

- Pharmacotherapy as part of the multifaceted approach, since medication may prevent substance abuse

- Seek neurocognitive psychotherapy to build inner awareness and rational thinking (Goldstein & Teeter-Ellison, 2002)

For general coping strategies for adults see Chapter 9.

Summary

This chapter provided an array of different counseling models, behavior modification suggestions, and coping strategies to help individuals with AD/HD. Selecting an approach that most effectively fits for a given child or family is essential. Regardless of the program, it is important to set behavioral expectations and consequences. Without empathic listening and skillful communication, no program will be effective. Suggestions and modifications have value if they are carried out consistently. Suggestions for coping provided here and in a previous chapter are meant to be used for guidance and support. There can never be enough!

Educational and Legal Rights for Children and Adults with AD/HD

Two federal laws—the Individuals with Disabilities Education Improvement Act of 2004 (IDEA) and Section 504 of the Rehabilitation Act of 1973 (Section 504)—guarantee children with attention-deficit/hyperactivity disorder (AD/HD) a **free and appropriate public education (FAPE).** Both laws also require that children with disabilities be educated to the maximum extent appropriate with children who do not have disabilities. Another law, the Americans with Disabilities Act (ADA) provides protection against discrimination for individuals with disabilities in a variety of settings beyond school.

FAPE
Free and appropriate public education.

Eligibility for IDEA mandates that a child must have a disability requiring special education services. Eligibility for Section 504 may occur when the child needs special education or related services. Children covered under Section 504 include those who typically either have less severe disabilities than those covered under IDEA, or have disabilities that do not neatly fit within the categories of eligibility under IDEA.

Historically, children with AD/HD did not qualify for special services unless they met eligibility criteria developed for other disabilities, such as a specific learning disability or serious emotional disturbance. The United States Department of Education issued a "Policy Clarification Memorandum" on September 16, 1991. This memorandum made clear that children with AD/HD might qualify for special education and related services solely on the basis of the AD/HD when it significantly impairs educational performance. On March 11, 1999, when the regulations for the IDEA Amendments of 1997 were completed, AD/HD was formally listed in the IDEA Regulations under the category "Other Health Impairment." The law states that:

Other health impairment means having limited strength, vitality or alertness, including a heightened alertness to environmental stimuli, that results in limited alertness with respect to the educational environment, that (i) Is due to chronic or acute health problems such as asthma, attention deficit or attention deficit hyperactivity disorder, diabetes, epilepsy, a heart condition, hemophilia, lead poisoning, leukemia, nephritis, rheumatic fever, and sickle cell anemia; and (ii) Adversely affects a child's educational performance. (IDEA, 300.7(c)(9))

Section 504 automatically covers any child who qualifies for IDEA; however, the opposite is not true. It should be noted that state laws may not restrict the provisions of these federal laws.

Individuals with Disabilities Education Improvement Act (IDEA 2004)

Eligibility

IDEA 2004 provides federal funding to states to support special education and related services in their school systems. IDEA provides special education for those children who meet the eligibility criteria for one of ten categories. Under IDEA, children with AD/HD may be eligible for special education services under three categories defined by IDEA: (1) Other Health Impaired, (2) Specific Learning Disability, and (3) Emotional Disturbance.

Other Health Impaired applies to children with AD/HD "where the AD/HD is a chronic or acute problem that results in limited alertness to the educational environment which adversely affects educational performance" (34 C.F.R. 300.7(c)(9)). Children can receive services on the basis of this disorder solely, without having to qualify under other categories, if the AD/HD is severe enough to require special education and related services.

Specific Learning Disability may provide a suitable category if the child with AD/HD has a coexisting specific learning disability, or what is sometimes termed "minimal brain dysfunction."

Emotional Disturbance may serve as a category if the child with AD/HD exhibits an unexplained inability to learn; inability to build or maintain satisfactory personal relationships with teachers and peers; inappropriate behavior and feelings under normal circumstances; general pervasive mood of unhappiness or depression; or a tendency to develop physical symptoms or fears associated with personal or school problems. To be eligible, a child must exhibit these symptoms, which affect academic performance over a long period of time and to a marked degree. It does not apply to children who are socially maladjusted without emotional disturbance (34 C.F.R. 300.7(c)(4)).

Evaluation

A team evaluation procedure is required to determine if a child is eligible for special education under IDEA (i.e., has a disability that requires special education and related services). The evaluation team must also collect information that will assist in determining the content of the individualized education program (IEP). This includes consideration of special factors such as positive behavioral interventions and supports, and whether or not the child needs assistive technology devices and services.

Parental consent is required before any evaluation begins. If an evaluation is warranted, it must be provided at no cost to the parents; parents are not financially responsible for the evaluation. IDEA requires that the school district consider the findings of outside evaluators and have a policy for determining when and how independent educational evaluations (IEE) will be funded by the district.

Provisions in the Law

The child is entitled to have an IEP that includes annual measurable goals that is developed with the participation of the parents. Parents or the school can request changes to it, but no changes can be made without the parents being informed and having an opportunity to request an impartial due process hearing to challenge the decision. The IEP must be reviewed at least annually, but may be revised as often as needed. Parents are members of their child's team(s) determining eligibility, the content of the IEP, and placement.

IDEA specifies that a child must be educated in the general education class and curriculum, as close to home as possible. In the first 15 years of special education, the concept of mainstreaming moved children from special education to general education. That is, children with a disability would be placed in a special education environment, and as the child demonstrated grade-level competencies in math or in reading, he or she would gradually move to a general education classroom. In the last decade, there has been a reconsideration of this concept, and now the philosophy of inclusion is being applied. To the maximum extent appropriate, the child is educated in a general education setting with supports or special services to help the child succeed in the placement. Only when it is clear that individualized or small-group instruction is necessary is the child taken from the class and provided help through resource room instruction or another educational placement.

The Code of Federal Regulations (United States Department of Education, 1999) states that "each public agency shall insure that a continuum of alternative placements is always available to meet the needs of children with disabilities for special education and related services" (34 C.F.R. § 300.551 (a)). Placement options include the following:

- Full-time general education classroom in the child's neighborhood school.

- General education curriculum with in-class support, such as instruction from a speech-language pathologist or teacher of children who are deaf or hard of hearing, or a special education teacher.

- General education curriculum, with pull-out sessions held in another classroom.

- Part-time general education classroom; part-time special education in a resource room.

- Full-time special education curriculum in a separate or self-contained classroom taught by a special education teacher with a small number of other children, often in the child's neighborhood school.

- Full-time special education curriculum in a separate facility (often called a **center-based program**), not necessarily in the child's neighborhood.

Center-based program
One location that provides services for district schools.

242

- Residential school, with a large number of children with similar disabilities. Some children can either live on campus during the week or attend as day students.

Even when suspended or expelled, children covered by IDEA are still entitled to FAPE (i.e., services described by an IEP). These services may be provided in an interim alternative education setting. The IEP Team must determine if the child's behavior that resulted in discipline was a manifestation of the child's disability or a failure to properly implement the IEP. A functional behavioral assessment must examine the factors that led to the behavior, and the IEP must incorporate any needed positive behavioral interventions and supports designed to prevent a recurrence of the behavior. Parents can request an impartial due process hearing when they disagree with the school's decisions in such matters.

According to the U.S. Department of Education, children diagnosed with AD/HD who meet the eligibility criteria under the Other Health Impaired (OHI) category have always been eligible for special education services. The IDEA Amendments of 1997, for the first time, explicitly incorporate ADD and AD/HD. In order for a student to qualify for special education under the OHI category, the following criteria must be met: (1) the student must be diagnosed with AD/HD by the school district, or the school must accept the diagnosis rendered by another qualified professional; (2) the AD/HD must result in limited alertness to academic tasks, due to heightened alertness to environmental stimuli; (3) the effect of AD/HD must be chronic (long-lasting) or acute (have a substantial impact); (4) this must result in an adverse effect on educational performance; (5) the student must require special education services in order to address the AD/HD and its impact.

All aspects of the child's functioning at the school are incorporated into the consideration of adverse effect of educational performance of the student. These can be manifested through grades or achievement tests; behavioral difficulties at school; impaired or inappropriate social relations; impaired work skills—such as being disorganized, tardy, having trouble getting to work on time, and difficulty with following the rules. Special education is required to prepare students for employment and independent living by addressing the effects of a child's disability in all areas of functioning, including academic, social/emotional, cognitive, communication, vocational, and independent living skills.

Attention-Deficit/Hyperactivity Disorder

In order to qualify for special education, the child does not need to be failing. Under the IDEA regulations released in 1999, the fact that the child is progressing from grade to grade is not by itself a basis to determine that he or she does not have a suspected disability. Failing grades may be evidence of a disability, but they are not a prerequisite.

Placement in special education does not necessitate that the child be put into a "special education class." Special education services are defined in the statute as specially designed instruction to meet the unique needs of the child, which may be available within a range of settings, as previously described. Special education refers to services, not a place or a classroom.

A personal doctor's diagnosis of AD/HD does not automatically qualify the child for special education. The school district is required to consider the outside evaluation, but is not obligated to act on it. If the school decides not to conduct an evaluation, they must notify the parents of their decision, inform them of their reasons behind the decision, and provide information regarding the right to request a due process hearing to challenge that decision. If the child is referred for an evaluation, the school must conduct a multidisciplinary evaluation, which must include consideration of any outside evaluations obtained. The IEP Team will determine if the child meets eligibility criteria for OHI. An evaluation must be completed within 60 days of receiving parental consent for evaluation, unless a state has established a different time frame. School districts will provide information on this timeline as part of the procedural safeguards information for parents.

The following information should be considered in determining an adverse effect on education performance: (1) an interview with the child; (2) an interview with the parent; (3) an observation of the child in the learning environment; (4) a review of grades; (5) a review of academic records; (6) a review of disciplinary records (if any) and other school records; (7) behavioral rating scales by the parents, the teachers, and sometimes the student; and (8) the child's current and historical functioning.

Parents, the state education agency, other state agencies, or local school staff all have the right to make a referral for special education evaluation. If the school agrees to do the evaluation, it must be done at no cost to the parents. Parents are informed of the referral and are part of the IEP Team that considers what testing is available and/or needed. Some schools may require a medical evaluation as a component of the school evaluation. Parents have the right to obtain a private evaluation at any time, at their own expense. Parents may request a private evaluation at district expense, if the district has conducted an evaluation with which the parents are dissatisfied. Procedures for requesting independent educational evaluation (IEE) must be made available by the district. Parents may request mediation or an impartial due process hearing if they disagree with the district's decision on the IEE.

A medical evaluation is not required to determine if the child has AD/HD. The school must pay for any medical evaluation it requires as part of the evaluation process. The school district may use its IEP Team, including a psychologist or other professional qualified to diagnose AD/HD, to make the determination for educational purposes. A medical evaluation may be desirable as it can rule out other physiological causes for behaviors and determine the appropriate medication.

The school district cannot require the child to take medication or to take it as a prerequisite for getting special services. Parents have the exclusive legal right to determine if their child should receive medication.

SECTION 504

Who's Eligible?

Section 504 is a civil rights statute requiring that "No otherwise qualified individual with a disability in the United States...shall, solely by reason of his or her disability, be excluded from the participation in, be denied the benefits of, or be subjected to discrimination under any program or activity receiving federal financial assistance" (Section 504 of the *Rehabilitation Act of 1973;* Public Law 93-112). In schools, reasonable accommodations must be made which allow students to access and participate in a FAPE in the general education environment to the greatest extent possible. "Appropriate education" means that regular or special education and related aids and services are designed to meet the individual educational needs of handicapped persons as adequately as the needs of nonhandicapped persons are met.

Eligibility for services under Section 504 is based on the existence of an identified physical or mental condition that substantially limits a major life activity. As learning is considered a major life activity, children diagnosed with AD/HD are entitled to the protections of Section 504 if the disability is substantially limiting their ability to learn. The definition of substantially limiting a child's ability to learn is interpreted in a variety of ways among school districts. A growing number of districts interpret a substantial limitation as the need for special instruction (i.e., special education). These districts follow IDEA procedures to determine eligibility, provide FAPE, and ensure the required procedural safeguards are followed. Other districts interpret the substantial limitation on learning to include effects that do not rise to the level of a need for special education. These districts have established Section 504 compliance procedures that are more streamlined than IDEA and include provision of accommodations that are accomplished through general education staff and services. Since Section 504 is a civil rights legislation meant to protect against discrimination, it mandates accommodations. It does not dictate services as IDEA 2004 does. Services may be provided (i.e., resource room, OT, SLP) at the discretion of the school district.

The Office of Civil Rights administers compliance with Section 504. If a district violates the requirements of Section 504, then it is subject to possible curtailment of federal funding. In some cases, the district may be sued by the student and family for monetary damages and attorney's fees. Often Section 504 accommodations are negotiated with the school district on behalf of the student.

Who Can Apply for Section 504 Services?

Anyone can refer a child for evaluation under Section 504. However, while anyone can make the referral, the school district must also have reason to believe that the child is in need of the services due to a disability. Thus, the school district does not have to act solely on the demand of the parent, but can act on its own accord. The key to pursuing the referral is whether the school district staff suspects that child is suffering from a mental or physical impairment that is substantially limiting his or her life activities and is in need of educational support or special education and related services. If parents request a referral for evaluation and it is refused by the district, then the district must provide the parents with notice of their procedural rights under Section 504.

Evaluation

Section 504 requires an initial evaluation prior to placement, evaluation before significant changes to the plan, and periodic reevaluation. It does not address the role outside evaluations may play. It requires notice but does not require parental consent for testing before any changes are made to the plan.

Section 504 requires a school district to evaluate a student if that student is believed to have a disability and is believed to be in need of special education or related services. Federal Department of Education regulations for implementing Section 504 requirements, found in the Code of Federal Regulations Evaluation 34 C.F.R. Part 104.35, recommend using procedures of IDEA as one way to comply with evaluation requirements.

What Does the Law Provide?

The school district must develop a Section 504 plan if the child is eligible under Section 504. Common classroom adaptations for children with AD/HD include:

- Tailoring homework assignments
- Providing a structured learning environment
- Simplifying instructions about assignments
- Supplementing verbal instructions with visual instructions
- Using behavioral management techniques
- Modifying test delivery
- Using tape recorders
- Providing computer-aided instruction
- Providing nursing services to supervise administration of medication
- Providing counseling or other forms of therapy

See Table 11.1 on page 248 for a more comprehensive listing of general classroom accommodations, assignment accommodations, testing and assessment accommodations, and grading alternatives. This table is printable from the CD-ROM as Study More 11.1.

For a description of the policies and documentation needed to obtain testing accommodations for nationwide tests administered by the Educational Testing Service, see Sidebar 11.1 on pages 249–250.

A copy of the federal regulations that implement Section 504 in education is available at: http://www.ed.gov/policy/rights/reg/ocr/edlite-34cfr104.html.

Attention-Deficit/Hyperactivity Disorder

Table 11.1 **Classroom Accommodations for Students with AD/HD**

Areas to Address	Possible Accommodations or Alternatives
General Classroom Activities	• Materials read aloud • Materials provided on audiotape • Simplified materials, modified textbooks or workbooks • Alternative materials • Supplementary materials (i.e., visual materials) • Study guides or outlines of main ideas and vocabulary words • Strategy cards to remember rules • Notes on overhead or board • Copies of notes; "Note taker" • Note-taking buddy, use of peer tutor • Outline of class discussion, outline of key vocabulary words • A buddy phone system to call when not sure of the assignment • Highlighting of main facts in reading material • Preferential seating or grouping • Use of AlphaSmart, tape recorder, or laptop in class
Assignment	• Verbal and written assignment directions • Extra time on assignments; advance notice of due dates for assignments • Shortened assignments • Alternative assignments or projects • Partner assignments • Extra skill reinforcement and practice assignments • Modification of nonacademic time • Use of tape recorder to complete assignments • Use of calculator • Use of computer or similar assistive technology • Check off on assignment sheet to monitor daily assignments • Alternative grading scale • Use of handheld spellers • Use of copy notes from buddy's Palm Pilot • Provision of an extra book (or set of books) for at-home use (one book is at home and one is in the classroom)
Testing and Assessment	• Directions read aloud • Tests read aloud • Tests provided on audiotape or computer • Alternative test options (i.e., oral testing) • Dictation of test answers • Use of notes on tests • Use of strategy cards to remember rules • Alternative grading scale
Grading Alternatives	• Pass/fail, instead of points or letter grades • Contract grading based on expectations for quantity and quality of work • Grade for effort and improvement • Regular education and special education teacher give combined grade • Change grading emphasis (e.g., more points for homework than tests) • Points for on-task behavior or being organized and prepared

From *The LD Teacher's IDEA Companion: Grades K–5* (p. 17), by L. M. Brown, 2000, East Moline, IL: LinguiSystems. © 2000 by LinguiSystems. Adapted with permission.

Policy and Documentation Needed
for Testing Accommodations

Sidebar 11.1

The following is the documentation needed to validate the existence of and impact of AD/HD on the individual's educational performance and the need for accommodations for candidates registering with the Educational Testing Service (ETS).

To establish that an individual is eligible under the Americans with Disabilities Act (ADA), the documentation must indicate that the disability limits some major activity, including learning. The following elements are considered:

- *Qualifications of the evaluator*
  Determination must be made by a professional who has direct experience in the comprehensive training and diagnosis and indirect experience with AD/HD persons, such as psychologists, psychiatrists, or a team.

- *Recency of documentation*
  Diagnostic evaluation must have been completed within three years.

- *Comprehensiveness of the documentation to substantiate AD/HD*
  Relevant historical information is needed to substantiate the presence of AD/HD, including a clinical summary of objective historical information as gathered from report cards, teacher comments, psychoeducational testing, and third party interviews.

- *Rationale to support the need for accommodations*
  Evidence that there is significant impairment in social, academic, and occupational functioning must be provided.

- A statement that symptoms do not occur in the course of a pervasive developmental disorder, or any psychotic disorder (mood, anxiety, personality disorder).

- A specific diagnosis and an interpretative summary in which professionals must demonstrate that other explanations have been ruled out, the disorder substantially limits learning and testing, and a justification as to why accommodations are needed.

Continued on next page

- *A rationale*
  A multidisciplinary evaluation must include information regarding intensity and frequency of symptoms and whether the impairment is a major life limitation.

For diagnosis of adolescent and adults:

- Provide retrospective confirmation of AD/HD.

- Establish relevant developmental and academic markers.

- Determine other coexisting disorders.

- Rule out problems that may mimic AD/HD.

- Address symptoms over early years, showing impairment over time.

- Provide relevant medical information.

- Determine what accommodations alleviate the symptoms in the past or present settings.

Source: Office of Disability Policy, Educational Testing Service (1999)

Further readings on Section 504 protections and procedures are available at: http://www.ed.gov/about/offices/list/ocr/publications.html#section504.

Which Law Should Apply?

In some districts, under both laws, a child is entitled to a FAPE. This means that both can offer a range of interventions, from minor accommodation in the classroom (such as preferential seating), to substantial services (such as social work services). Section 504 provides a faster, more flexible, and less stigmatizing procedure for obtaining some accommodations and services for children with disabilities. By virtue of the looser eligibility criteria used by these districts, some children may receive protection who are not eligible for services or protection under IDEA. Section 504 can provide an efficient way to obtain limited assistance without the stigma and bureaucratic procedures attached to IDEA.

Under Section 504, there is no "stay-put" provision keeping the child in his current placement until a placement or discipline dispute is resolved. Procedural safeguards—including parental notice and participation—are less well-defined than in IDEA, which can have unexpected consequences for students and parents. See Study More 11.2 on the CD-ROM for a complete explanation of the procedural safeguards under IDEA.

On the other hand, a district's standard for eligibility under Section 504 may be broader and more flexible than the standard under IDEA. To qualify for IDEA services, the child must need special education services. The child may be considered eligible under Section 504 if he or she has a diagnosed physical or mental impairment, including AD/HD, which affects learning. This includes children who need accommodations such as preferential seating, untimed tests, or help in taking medication from the school nurse.

IDEA offers some advantages to school districts because they are reimbursed for a substantial portion of their cost by the state and federal governments (40 percent approximately); no Section 504 expenses are reimbursed with either state and federal funds. Section 504 contains little detail on implementation of the Section 504 plan, but federal regulations recommend the IEP process from IDEA as one way to comply with requirements (34 C.F.R. 100.33 (a)(2)).

Depending on the needs of the child and the district's procedures, parents may prefer to use the district's Section 504 or IDEA procedures. Some children with AD/HD do not need services under either Section 504 or IDEA or may receive appropriate accommodations in general education without a written plan. If accommodations provided under a district's Section 504 guidelines are sufficient for the child, Section 504 may be an easier way to get the help the child needs. Some parents and/or school districts may prefer the more comprehensive procedures and protections of IDEA. Sidebar 11.2, page 252, details how parents can ensure services for their children. This information can be printed from the CD-ROM as Study More 11.3.

Who Has Responsibility to Pay for Special Education/Special School?

The mounting controversy over who pays has led to disputes and mediation between school districts and parents. Districts vary as to philosophy;

Mediation
A method of alternative dispute resolution in which a neutral third party helps to resolve a dispute.

Advocate
A person who pleads for a cause or propounds an idea, specifically of behalf of the child who may be displaying a disability.

Sidebar 11.2
How Parents Can Ensure Services for Children with AD/HD

- Meet with the child's teacher(s). Develop regular, positive communications.

- Seek written documentation from the teacher(s) describing behavioral or academic concerns. Obtain appropriate behavior rating scales from a clinical or school psychologist or physician for the school staff.

- Request an evaluation of the child at any time. Requests should be made in writing.

- Play an active role in preparing the IEP or Section 504 plan. Keep careful records. All letters sent to the school should be copied and filed.

- Be aware that findings of the evaluation team may be appealed by the parent. The school is required to provide information about appeal procedures.

- If disputes arise, consider using **mediation** for informal dispute resolution.

- If necessary, retain an attorney to appeal a school's decision. The school district will likely have its own legal counsel. A parent **advocate** service may be able to help locate a qualified attorney.

Source: Jones (1999)

---

expenditures for funding; allowance of outside reports and evaluations; and the people who sit on the committees, as well as the persons who conduct and make decisions regarding outcome and services. Some districts will allow far more services within the school, while others will release children to more specialized educational settings. A 1991 survey by Hawkins, Martin, Blanchard, and Brady, revealed that of teachers surveyed, 85 percent had taught children with AD/HD, but the majority had received no training to do so. Of those who claimed specific training, the majority received a maximum of 3 clock hours, and only 16 percent had been trained to use a variety of techniques.

A landmark case which led to the term "charter funding" created opportunities and challenges for both school districts and families (along with their attorneys). The Supreme Court ruled unanimously in Florence County School District No.4 v. Carter (1994) that courts can order school districts to reimburse parents for private school tuition and related expenses if the public school fails to provide an appropriate education. The case involved reimbursing $36,000 in private school expenses to the parents of Shannon Carter, a teenager with a learning disability and AD/HD. School evaluations at first failed to identify either condition and misdiagnosed Shannon as "lazy, unmotivated, and a slow learner" who should "work harder." After the child's problems were identified and she was found to be eligible for special education services, her parents rejected the school's IEP because its goals were inadequate. This decision does not allow parents to expect school districts to pay for all private schools when parents unilaterally place their child in a private school. However, in the Carter case, the court ruled that the public school placement did not provide FAPE and the private placement did provide FAPE. Advocates of special education law see this as a landmark case. This Supreme Court ruling was a wake-up call for school districts to provide knowledgeable teachers and accurate evaluations.

Guidelines from the Carter case were incorporated into the IDEA Amendments of 1997. At an IEP Team meeting, parents must inform the IEP Team that they are rejecting the proposed placement, provide their reasons, and express their intent to enroll the child in a private school at public expense. Parents must provide this information to the school in writing at least 10 business days prior to removing the child from the public school.

Suspending and Expelling Children with AD/HD

Schools fail to provide FAPE if they suspend or expel students with an IEP for more than 10 days, or stop education services during any long-term suspension or expulsion. This is important information for school disciplinary officers, since children with AD/HD frequently exhibit disruptive, oppositional, or defiant behavior, and have been found to have high rates of suspension and expulsion.

Attention-Deficit/Hyperactivity Disorder

The U.S. Supreme Court, in Honig v. Doe (January 20, 1988), ruled that IDEA prohibits state or local authorities from unilaterally excluding children with disabilities from school for disruptive or even dangerous behavior associated with their disabilities. In this ruling, the Court supported Congress's intent to prohibit the exclusion of students with disabilities from school, particularly students who are emotionally disturbed (Tucker & Goldstein, 1992). Parent involvement and due process procedures must be followed, even in cases dealing with severe behaviors.

Under IDEA, the child may be suspended for up to 10 days for violations of the school code of conduct. Removal for more than 10 days is considered a change of placement. Students must continue to receive FAPE even when suspended or expelled. When a change of placement is being considered because of discipline procedures, the child's current placement remains in effect until a final resolution of the case, unless the school and parents jointly agree to a change. The IEP Team must meet to make a manifestation determination. If the child's behavior was directly caused by or related to the child's disability, or if the district had failed to properly implement the IEP, then the child is not subject to regular disciplinary actions. A functional behavioral assessment must be used to develop a behavior intervention plan designed to prevent the behavior from recurring. A change in placement might be a component of this new IEP, if all members agree to its necessity.

Whether or not the behavior was a manifestation of the child's disability, districts may place a student in an interim educational alternative setting (IES) for up to 45 school days for the following behaviors at a school or school functions: carrying or possessing a weapon; knowingly possessing or using illegal drugs; selling or soliciting the sale of a controlled substance (including AD/HD medication); and inflicting serious bodily injury upon another person. If the misconduct is determined not to be related to the disability, the child can receive the school's usual disciplinary measures with FAPE provided in an IES. Parents who disagree with that determination may request a due process hearing, and the child must remain in the current placement, with suspension or expulsion delayed, until hearings are completed. Districts may request an expedited hearing when it is believed that a child's current placement is substantially likely to result in injury to the child or others. The hearing officer may place the child in an IES for up to 45 days.

Other Legislation

The Americans with Disabilities Act (ADA)

The Americans with Disabilities Act gives civil rights protections to individuals with disabilities similar to those provided to individuals on the basis of race, color, sex, national origin, age, and religion. It guarantees equal opportunity for individuals with disabilities in public accommodations, employment, transportation, state and local government services, and telecommunications. The Title I employment provisions apply to private employers, state and local governments, employment agencies, and labor unions with 15 or more employees. The ADA prohibits discrimination in all employment practices, including job application procedures, hiring, firing, advancement, compensation, training, and other terms, conditions, and privileges of employment. It applies to recruitment, advertising, tenure, layoff, leave, fringe benefits, and all other employment-related activities. Employment discrimination is prohibited against "qualified individuals with disabilities." This includes applicants for employment and employees. An individual is considered to have a "disability" if he or she has a physical or mental impairment that substantially limits one or more major life activity, has a record of such an impairment, or is regarded as having such an impairment. Persons discriminated against because they have a known association or relationship with an individual with a disability also are protected.

The ADA applies to persons who have impairments that limit major life activities such as seeing, hearing, speaking, walking, breathing, performing manual tasks, learning, caring for oneself, and working. An individual with epilepsy, paralysis, HIV infection, AIDS, a substantial hearing or visual impairment, mental retardation, or a specific learning disability is covered. An individual with a minor, nonchronic condition of short duration, such as a sprain, broken limb, or the flu, generally would not be covered.

Individuals with a record of a disability include, for example, a person who has recovered from cancer or mental illness. Individuals who are regarded as having a substantially limiting impairment, even though they may not have such an impairment, may include persons who are mistakenly believed to have cancer or HIV. This provision would also protect a

Attention-Deficit/Hyperactivity Disorder

Facial disfigurement
Facial anomalies due to genetic factors or accidents.

qualified individual with a severe **facial disfigurement** from being denied employment because an employer feared the negative reactions of customers or coworkers.

Reasonable accommodation must be made for an employee or customer to access or participate in employment, goals, or services. Any modification or adjustment to a job or the work environment that will enable a qualified applicant or employee with a disability to participate in the application process or to perform essential job functions are included. Reasonable accommodation also includes adjustments to assure that a qualified individual with a disability has rights and privileges in employment equal to those of employees without disabilities.

The ADA prohibits discrimination against individuals with disabilities at work, school, and in public settings. It is not limited, as is Section 504, to those organizations and programs that receive federal funds. ADA requires schools to make reasonable accommodations for handicapped persons and applies to both public and private nonsectarian schools, from daycare to graduate schools.

**For answers to additional questions,
contact the ADA Information Line:**
800.514.0301
800.514.0383 (TTY)
website: www.usdoj.gov/crt/ada/adahom1.htm or ada.gov

Supplemental Social Security Income

Supplemental social security income (SSI) is a national program administered by the Social Security Administration which provides monthly payments to individuals whose income and resources are limited and who are at least 65 years old, blind, or disabled under the Social Security rules. SSI is not only a program for adults, but also for children with disabilities under the age of 18. For these children, the program provides monthly cash payments based on the family income, provides Medicaid health care services in many states, and ensures referral into the system of care available under state Title V programs for children with special health care needs (CSHCN). To receive SSI services, the child must meet financial criteria based on the income and resources of the child and family, and meet medical criteria about the impairment or combination of impairments.

For children who have AD/HD, the decision makers will compare the child's functioning to that of same age children with no impairments. They will look at how the child initiates, sustains, and completes all sorts of activities independently compared to children without impairments. They will consider whether the child needs more support and structure in the classroom and at home, including help or prompting, alternative teaching methods, or one-to-one assistance.

One of the six domains used to evaluate a child's impairment is labeled "attending and completing tasks." It relates to the child's ability to focus and maintain attention. This includes how effective the child is in beginning an activity, filtering distractions when engaged in an activity, focusing long enough to finish it, working or playing at a pace appropriate to the activity or tasks, and shifting focus once the activity is completed.

The state team must also consider whether the impairment or combination of impairments affect the child's functioning in virtually all areas of life. When considering and evaluating the child's limitation in the domain of "attending and completing tasks," the state agency team considers how independently the child functions as well as how this limitation affects the child's abilities in more than one setting. Given the nature of AD/HD, several settings are often affected.

For information and an application for SSI contact the Social Security's toll-free number at 800.772.1213 to speak to someone Monday through Friday between 7:00 AM and 7:00 PM (ET), or visit their website, www.ssa.gov.

Legal Rights and Provisions for Adults with AD/HD in the Workplace

Adults with AD/HD that substantially limits a major life activity such as learning or working are considered individuals with disabilities (for the purposes of legal protection) and enjoy the right to be free from discrimination in the workplace. The bar against discrimination applies to recruitment; advertising and job application procedures; hiring; upgrading; promotion; award of tenure; discharge; demotion; transfer; layoff; rehiring; compensation; leave; and various benefits. The two laws which dictate these rights are: The ADA and the Rehabilitation Act of 1973 (RA).

To invoke the protection of these federal statutes, the individual must establish that the statute applies and that he or she (1) is an individual with a disability; (2) is otherwise qualified with or without reasonable accommodation for the job, promotion, employment benefit, or privilege being sought; and (3) was denied it by reason of the disability. To obtain these protections, however, one must disclose that he or she has a disability. The individual may decide if and when to disclose. When the individual decides to disclose the information, he or she must be prepared to submit professional documentation of the disability.

The RA applies to the federal government, federal government contractors, and federal grant recipients. The ADA applies to virtually all employers except those with fewer than 15 employees.

Any individual who has a physical or mental impairment that substantially limits one or more major life activity qualifies as an individual with a disability. AD/HD has been recognized in cases, letters of findings, and

U.S. Department of Education memoranda. The impairment must substantially limit a major life activity to qualify as a disability. In addition to learning and working, in 1995, the U.S. Equal Employment Opportunity Commission (EEOC) recognized concentrating, thinking, and interacting with others as major life activities.

Individuals with AD/HD are entitled to reasonable accommodation in the workplace. A reasonable accommodation is one that does not create an "undue hardship." An employer making accommodations might do the following:

- Reduce distractions in the work area.
- Give instructions orally and in writing.
- Break tasks down into manageable parts.
- Give frequent and specific feedback.
- Provide training course accommodations.
- Provide test accommodations (e.g., extra time, quiet room).
- Provide job restructuring.
- Allow job reassignment.

In addition, each state has a federally funded rehabilitation office (i.e., Office of Vocational Rehabilitation) that provides services such as counseling, job training, education, job placement, assistance in meeting work goals, and development of the necessary tools to make one employable. A person may be eligible for vocational rehabilitation if special education services or other help was provided in school because of a disability. However, provision of special education is not the only criteria. Anyone with a disability is eligible. The need is determined by an agency counselor, and services may be prioritized according to severity of need.

With federal laws of patient confidentiality, the information regarding one's disability is held in confidence unless one gives permission to reveal personal information. Patients are asked to sign releases under the new Health Insurance Portability and Accountability Act of 1996 (HIPAA) to allow health care professionals to release information regarding an individual's medical condition (United States Department of Health and Human Services, 1996). For further information, please visit www.hhs.gov/ocr/hipaa. Sidebar 11.3 on page 260 also provides helpful hints.

Sidebar 11.3 **Helpful Hints**

Adults with AD/HD are usually well-advised to avoid work with high paperwork and record-keeping requirements, considerable supervisory and monitoring responsibilities, high stress, demands for rapid performance, and expectations for rapid learning, especially in large group situations.

Certain career areas seem to work better such as these: the media, the arts, trades, sales, law enforcement, professional athletics, and fire safety. A career with a high degree of autonomy may work better than one that involves close supervision, although a degree of structure is often necessary.

There are many paths to success, but the adult with AD/HD must consider a range of options and determine what works best. Vocational aptitude and interest assessments can be helpful in guiding one's career choice.

Summary

This chapter presented information regarding the legal rights of persons with AD/HD to seek a free appropriate public education, to work in a nondiscriminatory environment, and to have entitlements equal to those of persons without a disability. Federal and state laws make such provisions and protect individuals with disabilities, including AD/HD. Recommendations for educational programs and accommodations for children and alterations in the work setting were discussed with the intention of providing the person with AD/HD, be it a child, adolescent, or adult, with enough knowledge and information to enlighten them and to justify accommodations and other entitlements that are within one's legal rights.

Profiles of People with AD/HD

This chapter presents the growth and development, the appearance, the etiology, and the correlational factors associated with people with AD/HD. You will gain insight into the wide diversity yet similarity among people with AD/HD. Lastly, the people come to life through their stories.

What Are Their Personalities?

Research on the personalities of people with AD/HD and any subtypes, conducted by Robin, Tzelepis, and Bedway (1998) found that of 233 adults with AD/HD, 3 types of personality clusters emerged based on the Millon's Index of Personality Styles (MIPS):

1. Half of the adults with AD/HD were characterized by pessimism, negativity, passivity, self-centeredness, introversion, and disorganization.

2. Slightly less that half were characterized by optimism, assertiveness, extroversion, nurturance of others, and relatively less disorganization.

3. Five percent of adults with AD/HD were motivated by a balance between seeking pleasure and avoiding pain; they were rugged and self-centered.

The researchers concluded that there is not one single "AD/HD personality." Understanding these traits and the variance helps one to understand why some people with AD/HD are more successful in life than others.

What Do They Look Like Externally?

Are People with AD/HD Really Shorter?

There have been long-standing concerns about growth deficits in children with AD/HD. Early studies linked growth deficits with stimulant medication. The Massachusetts General Hospital (MGH) studied growth in boys and girls with AD/HD (Spencer et al., 1996). This study indicated that among the 124 male children and adolescents with AD/HD and 109 controls, using appropriate correction by age and parental height measures, small, but significant, differences (2.1 cm age-corrected) were identified between AD/HD children and controls. Height deficits were evident in early, but not late, adolescents and were unrelated to **psychotropic medication**.

Psychotropic medication
Drugs prescribed to stabilize or improve mood, mental status, or behavior.

There was evidence of weight deficits in children with AD/HD relative to controls and no relationship between measures of malnutrition and short stature. There was no evidence of delayed pubertal development.

These results suggest that AD/HD may be related to temporary deficits in growth in height through mid-adolescence. This may normalize by late adolescence.

In their sample (Spencer et al., 1996), 89 percent of children with AD/HD had received pharmacologic treatment at some time in their life. Over the preceding 2 years, 45 percent had been treated with stimulants at an average daily dose of methyphenidate. Observed height deficits were only evident in early adolescence and were not related to stimulant treatment. The children with AD/HD in the study were slightly heavier than in the normal population, but there was no evidence of stimulant-associated growth-in-weight suppression. They suggest that boys with AD/HD may experience temporary deficits in growth-in-height that are mediated by AD/HD and not by its treatment.

In a parallel study of girls with AD/HD (124) and controls (116) (Biederman et al., 2003), no deficits in age-adjusted height and height-adjusted weight were found. No association between growth measurements and psychotropic treatment, malnutrition, short stature, pubertal development, or family history of AD/HD was detected.

No meaningful differences in any height measurement were detected between psychopharmacologically treated and untreated girls with AD/HD. Medicated girls with AD/HD were consistently taller and heavier than their nontreated counterparts, which suggest that no growth deficits occur or are associated with AD/HD or its treatment in females.

In similar studies with the drug Concerta, a slight loss of weight over time—relative to the normal population—was seen, and age-specific height scores revealed a slight loss of height growth over time, relative to the normal population (Spencer, 2003). Most of the small lag in height occurred in the first nine months, suggesting that the rate decreases with increasing time on the medication. The mean height difference was .52 cm, less than a clinically significant change.

With Adderall XR, height deficits were greater in the first 18 months than over the last 6 months (Biederman et al., 2003). There were negligible height deficits. The authors conclude that growth parameters should be monitored in treated children, but for the majority of children treated with mixed amphetamine salts, growth deficits should not be a clinical concern. Despite reassuring results, until more is known, the authors recommend monitoring growth in children on stimulants.

Do People with AD/HD Develop Tics?

In a recent study of tic disorders in boys with AD/HD, a small sample unselected for tics or any other comorbid disorder, a total of 128 boys with AD/HD and 110 boys without AD/HD were evaluated at baseline and four years later. The overall rate of tic disorders was significantly greater in children with AD/HD versus controls (6 to 34 percent), with an average duration of tic disorders of 4.9 years (Spencer et al., 1999). The onset of tics was much later than the onset of AD/HD (7.1 versus 2.6 years). Treatment with stimulants had little impact on the rate of onset or offset of tic disorders, and the comorbidity of a tic disorder had a limited impact on the AD/HD outcome.

There has been concern about the effects of stimulant medication on tics. Spencer et al. (2001) found that stimulants do not precipitate tics that would not have occurred without the stimulants. These researchers found that a similar proportion of children with AD/HD developed **de novo** tics on both an active drug and placebo. Stimulant exacerbation of preexisting tics in children with AD/HD is hard to disentangle from the naturally waxing and waning of tics. A temporary worsening of tics occurred in 20 percent of children on methyphenidate and 22 percent on placebo.

De novo
Out of nowhere.

Caveat
A warning; a note of caution.

In a measure of long-term effects of stimulant medication on tics, for those children taking medication for 12 months or longer with prior history of tics, few had worsening of tics (Spencer et al., 1999). Very few of the children with no known history of tics reported new onset of tics. Long-term treatment appeared to have a minimal effect on tics in this sample of children with AD/HD. However, there is a **caveat:** Despite reassuring results, some individual patients may experience significant worsening of tics associated with stimulant treatment.

What Do They Look Like Internally?

Are People with AD/HD More Prone to Illness?

Recent studies (Wilens et al., 2003) indicate that vital signs in children and adolescents with AD/HD receiving stimulants indicate a variable but small effect on blood pressure and pulse. While some investigators reported no changes in vital signs associated with methyphenidate treatment, others have reported small but significant changes in heart rate and systolic and diastolic blood pressure. In a report from a large study, 563 children, aged 6 to 12 years, treated with mixed amphetamine salts XR, showed no statistically documented changes in systolic blood pressure, diastolic blood pressure, pulse, or electrocardiogram (ECG) (Wilens et al., 2003). However, effects of long-acting stimulant medication did affect vital signs with significant but minor changes in systolic and diastolic blood pressure and heart rate (Goldman, Genel, Bezman, & Priscilla, 1998). Short-term studies (Gadow, Sverd, Sprafkin, Nolan, & Grossman, 1999) all showed only small, clinically insignificant changes in blood pressure and heart rate in children with AD/HD. However, one long-term study showed minor changes in blood pressure and heart rate, suggesting the need for initial monitoring with less frequent monitoring over time.

Are Their Brains Wired Differently?

Attention-deficit/hyperactivity disorder is known to be a neurological condition. With subsequent research study, the neural substrates that emerge continue to support a neurological base.

Research suggests that 80 percent of children with AD/HD continue to exhibit the symptoms of inattention and impulsivity during adolescence. About half of these continue to struggle with the disorder throughout their lives (Barkley, DuPaul, & McMurry, 1990; Ingram, Hechtman, & Morgenstern, 1999). Shafritz, Marchione, Gore, and Shaywitz (2004) have identified a chemical imbalance in the brain that accounts for the easy distraction—and consequent loss of attention—that is the hallmark of those with AD/HD. Researchers also believe that this imbalance is inherited. Magnetic Resonance Imaging (MRI) scans indicate that the **caudate nucleus** is significantly smaller in children with AD/HD than in controls (Shafritz et al., 2004), a finding that is associated with executive network. MRI scans also indicate that the frontal area of the brain is smaller in children with AD/HD than in controls (Shafritz et al., 2004). According to Sandson, Bachna, and Morin (2000), right hemisphere dysfunction has been attributed to AD/HD for the past 15 years, and is based on the observation that attentional deficits seen in patients with right hemisphere lesions are similar to those with AD/HD. Their **neuropsychological** and **neurophysiological neuroimaging** studies have suggested that the right hemisphere is dominant for attention. Functional and **morphometric neuroimaging** studies have found right hemisphere abnormalities and **anomalous** cerebral symmetry in patients with AD/HD. MRI views have shown reduced right anterior-superior frontal volume and anomalous asymmetry of the caudate nucleus in persons with AD/HD.

When other researchers (Stuss, Binns, Murphy, & Alexander, 2002) investigated the brains of patients with specific lesions (e.g., lesions caused by trauma, hemorrhage, surgery) the **monolithic** concept of attention was broken down into three distinct processes that appear to be functionally and anatomically different. When response patterns to different tasks such as pressing a button when a target stimulus appeared, and measuring speed of response in the face of increasing distractions and redundant information, different types of attentional problems associated with different injuries in different parts of the brain were seen. It was thus concluded that attentional problems are associated with several different parts of the brain and that attention rests on at least three building blocks, each in different parts of the frontal lobes. Donald Stuss of the Rotman Research Institute (Stuss et al.) proposes a cognitive architecture of attention with three systems of attention in the frontal lobe:

Caudate nucleus A brain structure within the basal ganglia responsible for regulating and organizing information in the brain.

Neuropsychology The branch of psychology that is concerned with the physiological bases of psychological processes.

Neurophysiological neuroimaging Techniques using X-ray, magnetic fields, or other tools to produce images of the brain, especially related to physiologically based psychological processes.

Morphometric neuroimaging Imaging techniques for measurement of the size and shape of biological structures.

Anomalous Deviating from the general or common order or type.

Monolithic Characterized by total uniformity.

- *Superior medial (top, middle) frontal regions*
  This system helps maintain a general state of readiness to respond. Patients with lesions in this area were slower to respond than other patients and the control subjects.

- *Left dorsolateral (front side) region*
  This system sets our threshold for responding to an external stimulus. Patients with lesions in this area had trouble setting up the criterion levels, so they made errors by considering most stimuli to be targets.

- *Right dorsolateral region*
  This system helps us to both attend to targets or stimuli defined by some individual schema and to inhibit responses to competing targets or stimuli. These patients could not filter out competing stimuli effectively and responded erroneously at a greater rate to both the desired and competing targets.

According to Stuss et al. (2002), it is possible to separate more specifically the types of attentional disorders, especially those in the frontal lobes (see Figure 12.1). This has implications for diagnosis and treatment in addressing the specific attentional disorder. He and his associates

Figure 12.1   **The Brain**

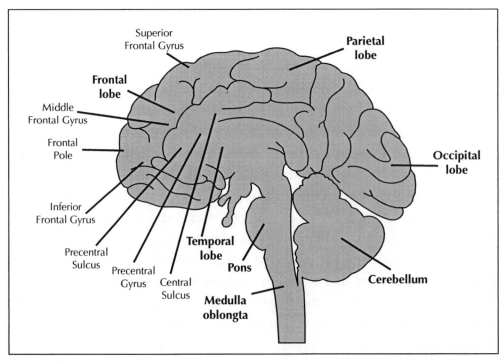

contend that considering the multiple roles played by different parts of the brain, these lesions could also affect a variety of tasks that might not be viewed as attentional, such as verbal fluency, categorization, and sequencing. What is yet to be known is the interactive complexity of the entire brain's attentional system.

Further support for frontal lobe involvement are Position Emission Tomography (PET) scans of men taken while they performed an auditory arithmetic task. Efficient use of the prefrontal cortex was seen in the controls but less use of the prefrontal cortex was noted in the subjects with AD/HD. Schweitzer et al. (2000) postulated that the prefrontal region is responsible for working memory. In the controls, it was evident that focal, localized task-related neural activity was present in the prefrontal area. In the subjects with AD/HD, PET activation was scattered and occurred primarily in the occipital regions, an area associated with visual processing. It was then thought (Iskowitz, 1998) that individuals with AD/HD use visuo-spatial strategies to compensate for verbal weakness. Thus, the use of verbal along with visual strategies should be used by teachers to help children process information.

Genetic studies provide further support for the neurological component to AD/HD (Valente, 2001); studies show a 92 percent concordance in monozygotic twins and 33 percent in **dizygotic twins.** However, a signal marker for genetic transmission has not been found. Other causes have been postulated as delayed due to an abnormal formulation of the brain's frontal lobes and/or complications of pregnancy, such as prematurity, smoking, alcohol or drug use, long labor, malnutrition, and lead poisoning. Having one child with AD/HD increases the risk that another child in the immediate family will have the disorder (Valente).

Dizygotic twins
Children born at the same time but developed from two separately fertilized eggs.

Castellanos et al. (1996) revealed through imaging studies that the basal ganglia and the right prefrontal cortex, as well as the **cerebellar vermis,** were of subnormal size in the children with AD/HD. These specific areas of the brain are used to regulate attention, awareness of self and time, and to coordinate input from different regions of the cortex. Barkley, Fischer, Edelbrock, and Smallish (1990) found that younger children with AD/HD demonstrate elevated rates of developmental deficits (e.g., enuresis, speech and language delays, and "soft" neurological signs). Physical anomalies that have been reported include a longer index finger than the middle finger, adherent earlobes, maternal health and perinatal complications, recurring respiratory infections, allergies, sleep difficulties, and asthma.

Cerebellar vermis
Part of the cerebellum lying in the midline between the two cerebellar hemispheres.

Attention-Deficit/Hyperactivity Disorder

In recent preliminary findings, Castellanos et al. (2003) found evidence of prefrontal striatal impairments in the pathophysiology of attention-deficit/hyperactivity disorder. The findings published in the *American Journal of Psychiatry* were the result of a study of MRIs of monozygotic twin brains. Nine pairs of twins (one of each pair had AD/HD) were scanned. MRI scans revealed that twins with AD/HD had significantly smaller caudate nucleus volumes than their unaffected twin. No other brain areas showed significant differences between affected and unaffected twins. Such anatomic difference appears consistent with selective vulnerability of the striatum to adverse prenatal environmental factors (i.e., hypoxia).

The latest finding by Sowell et al. (2003) provides support for structural changes occurring in areas which control impulsive behavior. Sowell et al., observed abnormal brain structure in the frontal cortices of the brain of children with AD/HD, after studying high resolution MRI scans. Reduced regional brain size was localized to inferior portions of dorsal prefrontal cortices on both sides of the brain. Brain size was also reduced in anterior temporal cortices on both sides of the brain with increases in gray matter recorded in portions of the posterior temporal and inferior parietal cortices. Such regions subserve impulse control.

Neuroinhibitor
Blocking the transmission of impulses from chains of nerve cells.

Neurotransmitter
Biochemical impulses that carry signals to and from cells.

Courvoisie, Hooper, Fine, Kwock, and Castillo (2004) found a two-and-one-half increased level of glutamate, an excitatory brain chemical that can be toxic to nerve cells. Their data suggest a decreased level of gamma-aminobutyric acid (GABA), a **neuroinhibitor.** Such a combination may explain the poor impulse control behavior of children. Such altered levels of **neurotransmitters** (biochemicals that carry signals to and from cells) in the frontal region of the brain may help in the understanding of the underlying neurology of AD/HD. Although the neurobiological basis of AD/HD is not yet fully understood, there is evidence pointing to dysregulation of the dopamine neurotransmitter system as an underlying factor.

Genes of the dopamine system are considered as candidates for involvement. Such genes are the ones encoding the five receptors in the brain (D1–D5) through which dopamine acts. Misener et al. (2004) found involvement of two of these receptor genes, those encoding D4 and D5 receptors. The dopamine receptor D1 (DRD1) gene is implicated in the genetic risk for inattentive symptoms. Such findings need further replication.

Are People with AD/HD Late Bloomers?

Those who have AD/HD often experience late physical maturation. Such "late bloomers" remain behind in typical growth schedule until they reach late adolescence. Some are low-weight babies who struggle with underdeveloped digestive systems. Immune systems cannot fight off infection and allergies during their early years. Tooth development is often late, with baby teeth not shed until age 7 or later, and front permanent teeth not in until age 8 or later. They may be too immature to handle mainstream class work successfully in the first several years of school. They behave much like a younger child, even after they enter high school. Hormone production that starts the cycles of puberty and adolescence is usually quite late. These "late bloomers" seldom have the physical and sexual maturity of their age-mates. They are rarely mature enough at the age of 16 to drive the family car safely on their own. They are not ready to begin practicing romance when their classmates are going out on dates. They are usually well into their early twenties before they have the social maturity typically expected of teenage students. However, most of these "late bloomers" blossom into successful individuals as they leave those first 22 years of struggle behind them.

It may be hard for them to change their image when they are seen as immature. When late bloomers prefer to play with younger children than with their age-appropriate peers, parents feel embarrassed. But late bloomers mature at different stages. At age 14, changes emerge, particularly as they enter high school. They begin to need less supervision, take more interest in their appearance, and respond better to notes, reminders, and daily schedules. They want to grow up in sharp contrast to previous years. At age 16, they show more interest in their grooming, have increased memory for details, stay on schedule with less reminding and less forgetting, and engage in better study habits. By age 18, these late bloomers catch up to their 16 year-old peers, which is an attempt to close the gap. The break-through comes at age 20 to 22. Maturation can occur at age 24. Most individuals with AD/HD do catch up later than their peers without AD/HD.

After a person with AD/HD finds his or her niche, a career of interest, and a job of worth, the late bloomers appear to catch up. Adults with AD/HD can become hyper-focused on their careers and often become workaholics.

Are Females with AD/HD Different from Males with AD/HD?

The most prevalent *DSM–IV* subtype in girls is the combined subtype (Quinn & Wigal, 2004). The second most common subtype in girls is the inattentive subtype. The same findings were found in boys.

Many women are in their late thirties or early forties before they are diagnosed with AD/HD (Nadeau & Quinn, 2002a). The most common pathway to diagnosis is that one of their children is diagnosed. Women with AD/HD present with problems in time management, chronic disorganization, longstanding feelings of stress, and being overwhelmed. They experience difficulties with money management, troubles in their marriage, and feelings of low self-esteem, anxiety, and depression. There is a history of AD/HD in children or siblings.

According to Rucklidge and Kaplan (2000), women with AD/HD are more likely to have a "learned helplessness style" of responding to negative situations than were women without the disorder and tend to blame themselves when bad things happen. They are likely to believe that they can't control the outcomes of life's events. Women are less likely to make efforts to finish more challenging tasks due to the belief that they have no power to change a negative outcome. By further giving up, they reinforce that they are incapable of accomplishing things in life. Women with AD/HD are more likely to report a history of depression and anxiety. Many report being in psychological treatment more often and receiving more psychotropic medication than do women without AD/HD.

As a result of classroom trauma over a span of years, some women develop a set of symptoms that look like "post-traumatic shock" (Adelizzi, 2003). These symptoms are similar to AD/HD. It is not clear what comes first, the post-traumatic stress symptoms, the AD/HD symptoms, or the trauma. The panic and anxiety are triggered years later if the woman decides to return to school.

Mothers with serious mental health conditions are four times more likely to have a child with AD/HD, according to the Centers for Disease Control and Prevention (CDC). Their study analyzed data for over 9,500 mother-child pairs from the 1998 National Health Interview Survey (Lesesne, Visser, & White, 2003). Of the mothers interviewed, 1 percent had a serious mental health condition, such as mood disorder or anxiety disorder. Among these mothers, 20 percent had a child with AD/HD, compared to 5 percent of mothers without a serious health condition. The results of this study are correlational and do not speak to the cause of the relationship. It is thought that perhaps genetics play a part with the mother's condition serving as a **precursor** to having a child with AD/HD, or that the mother's health results from having a child with AD/HD. Research indicates that mothers of children with AD/HD more often had complications during pregnancy, such as toxemia, lengthy labor and delivery, excessive nausea, and excessive weight gain or loss (Jensen & Cooper, 2002). Pre- and post-natal care may be a factor. Other factors include environmental exposure to toxins such as lead, or exposure of the fetal brain to alcohol and nicotine. Food additives such as sugar and food allergens may also be factors, but that remains controversial. However, many children exposed to these factors do not develop AD/HD. Perhaps it is the combination of trauma, toxin exposure, or subtle brain insult, along with susceptible genes that produce a full AD/HD syndrome (Swanson & Castellanos, 2002).

Single mothers and less affluent mothers were significantly more likely than married mothers to report a chronic, activity-limiting mental health condition. It is estimated that single-parent families of lower income may be most affected (Swanson & Castellanos, 2002).

According to Quinn (2002) women with AD/HD are frequently subjected to fluctuating hormone levels that further complicate the picture by worsening attention and focus or contributing to coexisting mood or behavior disorders. Research has confirmed that the brain is a target organ for estrogen and that estrogen's **neuronal** effects have functional consequences. Estrogen has been found to stimulate certain populations of dopamine and serotonin receptors in the brain. At the neuronal synapse, estrogen increases the concentration of neurotransmitters such as serotonin, dopamine, and norepinephrine. The cyclical production of estrogen may increase symptoms of AD/HD by down-regulating dopamine activity that contributes to mood disorders as decreasing estrogen levels exert their effects on serotonin.

Other studies (Huessy, 1990) indicate that girls with AD/HD may have increasingly severe problems with the onset of puberty. There are expected high-functioning levels in women during periods of high estrogen (pregnancy) and lower functioning during low levels (menopause). It has

Precursor
One that precedes and indicates the approach of another.

Neuronal
Of or pertaining to nerve cells and transmission of impulses.

been thought that when brain estrogen levels fall, brain dysfunction may follow. Symptoms shared by women in low estrogen states include depression, irritability, sleep disturbance, anxiety, panic, difficulty concentrating, and memory and cognitive dysfunction. In addition, many women experience mood and behavior disorders. Authors conclude that in addition to long-acting stimulants to address core AD/HD symptoms, it may be valuable to use pharmacological management for women, which would include a selective serotonin reuptake inhibitor (SSRI) to address premenstrual syndrome, premenstrual dysphoric syndrome (PMDD), anxiety and depressed mood, and to use hormone stabilization or **hormone replacement** therapy.

Hormone replacement
Medication containing one or more female hormones, commonly estrogen plus progestin.

Given the right employment setting (health care, social, athletics, etc.), adults with AD/HD can be successful. Adults with AD/HD are keen on picking up nonverbal cues during conversations with others. This helps them process the auditory message and relate well socially with others. Thus, they can perform well in jobs that require socializing.

Are People with AD/HD More Prone to Having a Learning Disability?

It is known that learning disabilities exist in 50 to 70 percent of cases of AD/HD. The National Institute of Mental Health estimates that 4 million school-age children, including 5 percent of public school children, have some form of learning disorder. There are many undiagnosed children as well (National Institute of Mental Health, 1993). The major types of learning disorders include:

- Dyslexia, also known as developmental reading disorder
- Dyscalculia, a math disorder
- Dysgraphia, a handwriting disorder
- Nonverbal learning disorder, a spatial reasoning deficit

The International Dyslexia Association (IDA) says 15 to 20 percent of the population has a language-based learning disability, of which dyslexia is the most common.

Dyslexia is the most common disorder affecting as many as one in every five children (Shaywitz, 2003). Dyslexia reflects a difficulty in attaching the written letters of language to the spoken sounds they represent. The problem is not in understanding the written words, or seeing words backwards, but rather being able to sound out the word that is on the page. Treatment includes the sounding out of individual sounds, and learning how letters represent sounds. According to Shaywitz, people can be highly intelligent and still be dyslexic.

The specific signs of dyslexia, both weaknesses and strengths, in any one individual will vary according to the age and educational level of that person. The five year-old who has difficulty learning his letters becomes the 6 year-old who can't match sounds to letters and the 14 year-old who can't read and dreads reading aloud. The earliest clues involve spoken language. Often the child is delayed in language onset. Sidebar 12.1 (page 274) lists clues across the age spans.

Stories

The people you are about to meet have traveled a journey to reach their diagnosis of AD/HD. For some, the journey has just begun. Share with them their experiences, their struggles, failures, and successes. You will also learn about the pain experienced by parents in search of the cause of their child's frustration and failure. Often these children were found to have more than just AD/HD, like language impairments and auditory processing deficits. Although their roads were less traveled than by others, they arrived at the diagnosis of AD/HD through an arduous journey. How they got there and what they did are the stories that are about to unfold. The reader is also referred to the DVD, *Attention-Deficit/Hyperactivity Disorder DVD: The Journeys—The People and Their Stories* (Geffner, 2005), to meet some of these individuals and their families and hear their stories.

Jared

Jared was a 10-year-old boy when he was brought to my office for an auditory processing work-up. Apparently, he was not doing well in school and was not "meeting his potential," as it was clear he was bright and sharp. He was in a private school with only 12 children in his class. He required a tutor twice a week and was having a hard time getting down to do his homework. He was not a reader, and picking up a book was hard for him.

Attention-Deficit/Hyperactivity Disorder

Glibness
Artfully persuasive in speech.

The mother, after having brought him to many doctors and evaluators, was beside herself. Someone referred her to me. It was clear to me that Jared was suffering from the hyperactivity form of AD/HD. He also had auditory processing problems, particularly listening in background noise. His language skills were good, except for the nonliteral and figurative pieces.

He did well on all tests of language function, yet when asked to retrieve words rapidly and get to the point, he could not do so. Read more about Jared in Study More 12.1.

Jimmy

Jimmy, age 10½, was referred to me by the child psychiatrist. He was having a hard time communicating with his peers, lacked friendships and good humor to get along and play with others. His parents were concerned and brought him to me to investigate his language skills. They thought that he was not able to use good social language. Read more about Jimmy in Study More 12.1.

Kathy

Kathy was 6½ when her mother brought her to me. The mother believed that the school did not pick up on Kathy's learning issues. They had her in a school which followed a multisensory approach, for two years, until she completed kindergarten. A test conducted by the school district, at the parents' request, did not show any speech or language issues. But the mother was not convinced, and given the fact that the child would be starting first grade in a parochial school, she wanted to be certain that Kathy would be able to learn to read and communicate effectively. Read more about Kathy in Study More 12.1.

David Neeleman

David Neeleman, age 44, is the Chief Executive Officer and a member of the Board of Directors of JetBlue Airways. He has served in both capacities since August 1998. He was named Chairman of the Board of Directors in May 2003. Mr. Neeleman was a cofounder of WestJet, and from 1996 to 1999 served as a member of WestJet's Board of Directors. From October 1995 to October 1998, Mr. Neeleman served as the Chief Executive Officer and a member of the Board of Directors of Open Skies, a company that develops and implements airline reservation systems, which was acquired by the Hewlett Packard Company. From 1988 to 1994, Mr. Neeleman served as President and was a member of the Board of Directors of Morris Air Corporation, a low-fare airline that was acquired by Southwest Airlines. For a brief period, in connection with the acquisition, he served on the

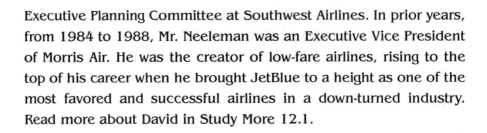

Executive Planning Committee at Southwest Airlines. In prior years, from 1984 to 1988, Mr. Neeleman was an Executive Vice President of Morris Air. He was the creator of low-fare airlines, rising to the top of his career when he brought JetBlue to a height as one of the most favored and successful airlines in a down-turned industry. Read more about David in Study More 12.1.

Gabriella

Gabriella (Gab) is the daughter of a Hispanic, American Indian woman and an Arabic father, exposing her to many languages and cultures. She is being raised by her mother and attends a special school for learning disabled children. She was first evaluated in 1997, by another agency because of presenting auditory processing problems. All previous auditory evaluations indicated normal hearing. Previous speech-language evaluations indicated delayed skills. Her birth history indicated jaundice. She had a total of 4 to 5 ear infections. The mother brought her for her first auditory processing evaluation because of "disassociate expression of thoughts, and concerns regarding her attention, listening, and focusing" as cited by her neurologist. Read More about Gabriella in Study More 12.1.

Summary

Although this chapter has not demonstrated any particular neuro-biological cause of AD/HD, it is known that the etiological basis is a multi-factorial group of biological variables that include neuroanatomical sites of brain dysfunction, plus genetic and environmental determinants. This chapter looked at a variety of factors that have been associated with the population of AD/HD. The stories of people with AD/HD provided on the CD-ROM are compelling and tell of the personal pain and ambition that make every day a challenge.

Benefits of Attention-Deficit/Hyperactivity Disorder

After you have read about all the disadvantages, problems, challenges, comorbidity, and conditions associated with AD/HD, there is a happy and hopeful ending to this book! There are lots of advantages to having AD/HD. It has been said that AD/HD has the "ADD-ed advantage." After all, it isn't every day that a person can juggle two things at the same time—often more than two—or keep many pans on all four burners.

The ADDed Advantage

What are the benefits of AD/HD? Consider these:

- People with AD/HD have heightened awareness. They are the "eagle-eyed" observers of the world.

- They are creative and innovative—the **divergent** thinkers of the world.

- They are persistent. They keep trying until they get it right. Despite setbacks, students with AD/HD show up for school every single morning ready to try again. They are determined. Once they make up their minds to so something, they will.

- They have high energy that can be channeled for good use.

- They are **resilient.** They have a willingness to keep working to improve, to come back again, to take setbacks in stride and keep right on going.

- They have a desire to fit in and to be successful.

Divergent
Distinctly separate or increasingly different ideas.

Resilient
An occurrence of rebounding or springing back; a trait that allows one to keep going.

Attention-Deficit/Hyperactivity Disorder

Abandonment
To leave behind cares, worries, or responsibilities.

- They want to please their parents and teachers.

- They have a wonderful sense of humor, often on the delightfully devilish side.

- They live life with gusto. They have a capacity for huge enjoyment of their experiences, and plunge into things with wonderful **abandonment.**

- They are great fun to talk to (one-on-one).

See Sidebar 13.1 for more positive traits.

Adults with AD/HD can become hyper-focused on their careers, and often become workaholics. Although this can be disruptive on one's personal life, it can lead to success in a career. There are noted

Sidebar 13.1	**Positive Traits of AD/HD**
Energetic	Highly verbal
Spontaneous	Creative
Exciting	Persistent
Innovative	Imaginative
Risk-taker	Tenacious
Warm-hearted	Ingenious
Compassionate	Accepting and forgiving
Inquisitive	Resilient
Fun to be around	Sensitive to needs of others
Resourceful	Empathetic
Good-hearted	Gregarious
Not boring	Often high intelligence
Humorous	Outgoing
Good at improvising	Have an interesting perspective
Are able to find novel solutions	Inventive
Observant	Full of ideas and spunk
Caring	Helpful
Can think on their feet	Good in crisis situations
Willing to take a chance and try new things	

From *The ADD/ADHD Checklist: An Easy Reference for Parents and Teachers* (p. 21), by S. Rief, 1998, New York: John Wiley & Sons. © 1998 by John Wiley & Sons. Reprinted with permission.

"AD/HD-friendly professions" such as dentistry, general surgery, obstetrics/gynecology, oncology, reconstructive surgery, neurosurgery, anesthesiology, nursing, instructing, and consulting. People with AD/HD work well in health-care fields (Cambell, 1999). From clinical experience, individuals who have responsibility for many people, offices, or tasks may not do well.

For example, Tom was stage manager for a Broadway play. Unfortunately, he became distracted during a scene where he was to lower a curtain and instead, sent out a table on a rolling stage that hit the lead in the middle of a moving love scene. Needless to say, he wasn't stage managing long after that. And Bill, who was the night manager for a large Manhattan hotel, was responsible for an important set of keys that opened doors to rooms, lobbies, dining areas, and hallways. Of course, one day, he threw his keys down and lost the index to them and had no idea what key led to what room. What a fiasco! Needless to say, he wasn't doing hotel managing after that. Mark was a videographer who could not meet his deadlines and stayed up all night to complete the script and produce the corresponding video. When asked how he did it and what he produced, he astonished the interviewer by reporting that his latest series was on PBS, and won a Pulitzer Prize. Some people have to work at their own pace, but for Mark, it was a very painful experience.

Putnam (1998) summed up the positive traits associated with people with AD/HD this way: creativity, high activity level, resourcefulness, warmheartedness, flexibility, good sense of humor, forgiving, trusting, sensitive, empathic, inventive, spontaneous, fun loving, not secretive, quick/intense, original, have high standards, and will focus for long periods of time on projects they enjoy. Also added to this list are the following traits: enhanced sensitivity, capable of feeling deeply, see things in a unique perspective, perceptive, eager for acceptance, responsive to positive reinforcement, quick to understand complex concepts, unable to be deceived, down to earth, networker, observant, original, loyal, intense when interested, looks past surfaces to the core of people. These characteristics are similar to those cited by Rief (1998; see Sidebar 13.1 on page 278). Reading these traits kind of makes you want to have someone like this for a friend, or an office mate, or a housemate, doesn't it?

Barton Goldsmith (Goldsmith, 2002) suggests that the incidence of AD/HD is higher in innovators than implementers by a ratio of eight to one. He describes innovators as entrepreneurs—more frequently CEOs—because they have the ability to learn and apply new thinking. The ability

Attention-Deficit/Hyperactivity Disorder

to learn and apply new tasks is more of an implementer trait. High innovators tend to have more disadvantages and advantages than high implementers, which implies that innovators have a more complex personality, with more traits—some better, some worse. Implementers have the ability to attend to detail in ways that innovators sometimes find impossible to do.

Taxonomy
The science of classifying things into categories.

According to Goldsmith (2002), the advantages and disadvantages of both innovators and implementers are equally weighted. Each is capable of running a business and creating wealth, but those with higher innovation tend to be less able to work for someone else. Among 10,000 business owners classified according to Goldsmith's **taxonomy,** those with higher innovator scores tend to be in start-up businesses or investments. Those with lower scores tend to be in second and third generation family businesses and are more conservative investors. He goes on to say that innovation is needed to solve problems, and to create new products and services. Often creativity is confused with artistic ability. Artistic ability can be seen in fields as diverse as accounting, cabinetry, and teaching. Creativity involves the ability of the brain to change, renew, and recombine our life experiences. When we are afraid of new ideas, we can miss opportunities that can change our lives. The key is to be intuitive—to bring ideas to consciousness, to sense trends, danger, and potential problems. Creative people, artistic people, and innovative people have ideas and a vision, but may not be able to express it to others in a socially acceptable way. In his group of innovators, most had AD/HD. This subgroup also tended to be the most successful entrepreneurs, having more than one income stream or business. They also confessed to being C or B students, most likely due to their difficulty in dealing with detail.

How Can a Person with AD/HD Succeed in the Workplace?

Adults with AD/HD can succeed in the workplace by developing a buddy system, by asking coworkers to be mindful of their activities, and by establishing a signal that tells them when they are going beyond the work boundaries. It is also suggested that the person with AD/HD work in an area that is away from open windows and doors to avoid distractions.

Sidebar 13.2   **Tips for Succeeding in the Workplace**

- Take notes during meetings to avoid distractions.

- Divide large projects into smaller parts and reward yourself as each part is completed.

- Devise a simple filing system to organize work.

- Avoid overloading yourself by learning how to say "no"; set limits with others.

- Use a datebook/daily planner to help organize yourself.

- Keep the planner/datebook in the same place every day.

- Check the datebook/planner at least three times a day.

- Ask others for assistance.

- Tape-record important conversations/meetings for reports that you may have to write later.

- Conduct a daily planning session with yourself to schedule the upcoming events for the day.

- Tell others about your AD/HD.

People with AD/HD are keen on picking up nonverbal cues during conversations with others. This serves to counteract the auditory difficulties that people with AD/HD have during conversations (they often fail to process the entire auditory message set forth by a conversational partner).

If adults with AD/HD were to concentrate on their accomplishments, rather than on the failures, they would be more successful and feel better about themselves. Sidebar 13.2, page 281, includes tips for succeeding in the workplace.

How is AD/HD Advantageous for Children?

It is difficult to envision AD/HD benefits to children who are struggling to learn and fit in. However, many are gifted artists, musicians, and videographers. I often ask a child to build with complex building blocks while I talk to his or her parents. I am often amazed to see the results—a sophisticated village or building complex. Such talents ought to be recognized and fostered. Children's behavior should be evaluated based on what they can do as opposed to what they can't. It is important that parents foster self-esteem in their children so that the benefits and advantages are highlighted rather than the negative aspects. Parent suggestions are captured in Sidebar 13.3.

Sidebar 13.3   **How Parents Can Build Self-Esteem**

- Give your child reasonable, developmentally appropriate responsibilities. This is important for developing self-confidence.

- Take care to avoid sarcasm, humiliation, or criticism of your child's character or intelligence when correcting behaviors.

- Tell your children as often as possible how much you appreciate them for who they are.

- Show unconditional love and unwavering belief in your child.

- Save your child's projects or work that he or she is proud of and make a portfolio collection, or take photos of them to keep in a memory book.

- Instill in your children a sense of obligation and responsibility for helping others. Get them involved in volunteering in some community service.

From *The ADD/ADHD Checklist. An Easy Reference for Parents and Teachers* (p. 203), by S. Rief, 1998, New York: John Wiley & Sons. Adapted with permission.

When someone has been diagnosed or thinks he or she has AD/HD, it is important to rule out other "Look-Alikes." Sidebar 13.4 presents a checklist of other conditions that mimic AD/HD. Keep in mind that some of these conditions cause some of the symptoms that contribute to the appearance of AD/HD.

Sidebar 13.4   **AD/HD Look-Alikes**

The following can cause some of the symptoms that may look like AD/HD.

Learning disabilities	Sensory impairments
Depression	Substance abuse
Oppositional defiant disorder	Conduct disorder
Allergies	Post-traumatic stress
Mood or anxiety disorder	Obsessive-compulsive disorder
Sleep disorders	Bipolar disorder
Hyperthyroidism	Rare genetic disorder
Seizure disorders	Fetal alcohol syndrome
Chronic illness	Language processing disorders
Tourette's syndrome	Pervasive developmental disorder
Developmental delays	Low intellectual ability
Severe emotional disturbance	Side effects of medication
High-stress situations	Central auditory processing disability
Chronic otitis media with effusion	Hypoglycemia
Lead poisoning	

From *The AD/HD Checklist: An Easy Reference for Parents and Teachers* (pp. 16–17), by S. Rief, 1998, New York: John Wiley & Sons © 1998 by John Wiley & Sons. Adapted with permission.

Sidebar 13.5   **Great Things about AD/HD**

- Insomnia makes for more time to stay up and surf the Net!
- The drive of hyperfocus
- Resiliency
- A sparkling personality
- Generosity with money, time, and resources
- Ingenuity
- A strong sense of what is fair
- Willingness to take a risk
- Making far-reaching analogies that no one else understands
- Spontaneity
- Possessing the mind of a Pentium—with only 2 MBs of RAM
- Always being there to provide a different perspective
- Willingness to fight for what you believe in
- Pleasant and constant surprises due to finding clothing (or money) you had forgotten about
- Being funny
- Being the last of the romantics
- Being a good conversationalist
- An innately better understanding of intuitive technologies, such as computers and PDAs
- Honestly believing that anything is possible
- Rarely being satisfied with the status quo
- Compassion
- Persistence
- Joining the ranks of artists, musicians, entrepreneurs, and other creative types
- Excellence in motivating others

From "50 (or So) Great Things about Having ADD" by B. Sea, 2001, *GRADDA Newsletter*, Spring 2001. © 2001 by GRADDA Newsletter. Adapted with permission.

Summary

In conclusion, individuals with AD/HD need to keep a positive attitude, a sense of humor, and surround themselves with supportive, caring people. So keep in mind what having AD/HD can mean for the person. See Sidebar 13.5 for 25 great things about AD/HD.

Resources

AD/HD Internet Resources

http://adhd.mentalhelp.net The Mental Help Net is an excellent collection of annotated and rated websites related to AD/HD.

http://childdevelopmentinfo.com This website provides information on diagnosis, medication, classroom management, and parent education on the topic of AD/HD.

http://Christianadhd.com "ADHD of the Christian kind" is dedicated to Christian children and adults with AD/HD and related disorders, including depression, Tourette's syndrome, OCD, and others. This website stresses the fact that these disorders are not punishments from God. In addition, this website encourages people with these disorders to look to God for hope and guidance when dealing with their personal limitation. Also included are online support groups, articles, Bible stories, and related links.

http://kidsource.com Kidsource is a great site for information related to helping young people, from infants to adolescents. To search the site for information on AD/HD, go to the Kidsource home page, click the "Search the Site" button, and type in "ADD" and "ADHD."

http://newideas.net "The ADD Information Library" is a comprehensive website that organizes AD/HD information into 10 lessons. These lessons cover topics such as diagnosis, treatment options, alternatives to stimulant medication, parent resources, teacher resources, family issues, and current research.

www.aap.org/policy/paramtoc.html This site is the home of the American Academy of Pediatrics. It provides guidelines for the diagnosis and evaluation of school-age children with AD/HD, from the American Academy of Pediatrics Committee on Quality Improvement. Created in March 2001, the guideline is intended for use by primary care clinicians working in primary care settings. Topics include child and family assessment, school assessment, use of rating scales, and conditions seen frequently among children with AD/HD.

www.addclinic.com This site is "the Source for ADD Information." It contains numerous links to other AD/HD websites. Also contains information on various AD/HD clinics, AD/HD-related products, support groups, and current research.

www.addhelpline.org ADD helpline is a nonprofit organization that holds weekly meetings every Tuesday at 9 PM (EST). You'll find up-to-date information on research, products, and organization tips.

www.add.org This is the website of the Attention Deficit Disorder Association (ADDA). Topics on this website include: ADD research, ADD therapy, ADD coaching, career and work, family issues, legal issues, school and ADD, and women and ADD; also features a 'Teens Area" devoted to teen interests, questions, and contributions. A "Kids Area" is also featured, which provides information for children with ADD. A listing of ADD support groups is included, as well as personal stories written by children and adults with ADD. The Professional Yellow Page section provides names of health care professionals, coaches, attorneys, counselors, advocates, and other individuals who provide services for people with AD/HD. An online bookstore containing ADD-related materials is also available.

www.addwarehouse.com This website provides over 300 AD/HD-related products that may be purchased by parents, educators, and health professionals to assist children with AD/HD.

www.adhdinfo.com You'll find helpful links and information for parents and professionals at this website.

www.adhdnews.com Solutions for teachers and parents regarding AD/HD can be found at this website. It also contains links for parents related to school/homework management, behavior management, and success stories. Book references are included. The link for teachers includes classroom management techniques, multisensory teaching techniques, and home/school intervention plans.

www.adultadd.com A website dedicated to providing help and resources specifically for adults with AD/HD.

www.biopsychiatry.com/add.htm At this website you'll find information on treatment for AD/HD. Contains the article "Current Drug Therapy Recommendations for the Treatment of ADHD" by Cyr M. Brown, originally featured in the August, 1998, issue of *Drugs*. Includes information on the effectiveness of stimulants, tricyclic antidepressants, and third-line agents such a bupropion and clonidine; also features the article "Pharmacotherapy of AD/HD in Adults" taken from the *Journal of Clinical Psychiatry*.

www.breggin.com/ritalin.html This site will inform visitors of the side effects of Ritalin. You'll also read about cautions and alternatives. This is Dr. Breggin's personal website and expresses his views. He founded the International Center for the Study of Psychiatry and Psychology, a non-profit research and educational network and has been informing the media about the potential dangers of drugs.

www.chadd.org This is the website of Children and Adults with AD/HD, a parent-based nonprofit organization formed in 1987 to better the lives of individuals with AD/HD and their families. People can go to this website to become a CHADD member. The "Member Site" allows CHADD members to post on message boards. This website also contains articles and interviews from *ATTENTION!*, CHADD'S premier magazine for people with AD/HD, and information regarding CHADD's annual conference, as well as a listing of all the national CHADD chapters. Position papers set forth by CHADD regarding issues such as school discipline and legislation may be downloaded. Current research studies are posted, as well as a listing of related AD/HD web links. Each month CHADD holds an open chat with an expert in the field of AD/HD. A calendar of CHADD events is also posted, as well as the CHADD Shoppe, where books and related AD/HD materials may be purchased online.

www.childdevelopmentinfo.com At this website, you'll find information on child development, psychology, parenting, learning, health, and safety, as well as information on childhood disorders such as attention-deficit disorder, dyslexia, and autism. It includes information and suggestions for parents covering toddlers to teens.

www.guilford.com/cgi-bin/search.cgi Guilford Press sells an array of resources on AD/HD. The site contains detailed descriptions of their books and videos, including reviews, descriptions of contents, and the intended audience for each.

www.help4adhd.org This site is the National Resource Center on ADHD Associated with CHADD. 800.233.4050.

www.iser.com The website provides a nationwide directory of professionals who work with children and adults with learning disabilities. This website also assists parents and caregivers with access to local special education professionals serving clients with learning disabilities, attention-deficit disorders, and other special needs. Also contains information on assessment, treatment, and parent-advocacy issues.

www.learningdisabilites.com This is the Kurtz Center's website for treatment on learning disabilities, including AD/HD. It provides information on assessment measures, training and educational opportunities, research articles, and a bookstore featuring online products.

www.nimh.nih.gov At this site, you can view the activities and research on AD/HD, and child and adolescent health supported by the National Institute of Mental Health (NIMH). NIMH is a nonprofit organization dedicated to providing information and support to parents and educators dealing with AD/HD. Scheduled chats are held every Tuesday at 9–11 PM (EST). Information sharing is up-to-date regarding research, products, and organization tips. A "Parents Menu" provides info for parents of children with AD/HD, while an "Educators Menu" provides info for people working with individuals with AD/HD. Message boards allow people to post their ideas online. Full-text articles on AD/HD-related issues such as: (1) general info, (2) AD/HD and education, (3) stimulant medication, (4) nonmedication approaches, (5) parenting articles, (6) adult AD/HD, and (7) comorbid conditions. Also featured is a monthly newsletter featuring AD/HD-related articles. The AD/HD Helpline Special Needs Store features products for parents/teachers working with children with AD/HD, as well as books and products for children.

www.oneaddplace.com This site contains a collection of resources, including information on famous people who have AD/HD. This site also includes a listing of professional services, products, and a community library.

www.thefunplace.com This "Families United on the Net" website contains message boards which feature book lists on AD/HD, autism, and other disorders. Users may post messages regarding AD/HD and read messages posted by other web users.

www.ThinkingPublications.com This website contains products that can be used to develop auditory processing skills, phonological processing skills, and social skills for school-age individuals with AD/HD.

Coexisting Disorders

www.adaa.org This is the site of the Anxiety Disorders Association of America. It features information about anxiety disorders, consumer resources, and information for professionals working with individuals with anxiety disorders. Clinical trials and current news regarding anxiety disorders are also featured. The ADAA Bookstore features books and products that may be bought online. Message boards allow visitors to post their ideas, as well as participate in online chats.

www.bpkids.org The Child and Adolescent Bipolar Foundation educates families, professionals, and the public about early-onset bipolar disorders; supports families to maximize the well-being of the child while minimizing the adverse impact of bipolar disorders on the family; and advocates for increased services to families and research on the nature, causes, and treatment of bipolar disorders in the young.

www.ccbd.net The Council for Children with Behavioral Disorders (CCBD) is a division of the Council for Exceptional Children (CEC) that is committed to promoting and facilitating the education and general welfare of children and youth with emotional or behavioral disorders. The mission of the CCBD is to enhance the education and treatment of students with emotional/behavioral disorders (EBD) and their families by supporting activities in four priority areas in the field: supporting classroom practitioners, providing professional development, recognizing leaders in the field, and funding scholarships.

www.interdys.org The International Dyslexia Association (IDA) is an international nonprofit, scientific, and educational association dedicated to the study and treatment of dyslexia. This website features information on the "ABCs of Dyslexia" (including common signs and symptoms). A listing of all IDA branches, both national and international, is also available. IDA membership may be completed online. Also featured is information on research, technology, upcoming conferences and seminars, and public policy related to dyslexia; and an online bookstore is available. The "Web Discussion Area" allows people to post ideas and share information. There is also an IDA members only subsite.

www.ldaamerica.org The Learning Disabilities Association (LDA) is a national nonprofit association of volunteers that advances the education and general welfare of children and adults with learning disabilities and their families. Also included is a resource index, which lists books, audiotapes, videotapes, and other learning disability websites. News and upcoming events, such as the annual LDA conference, an online bookstore containing materials related to learning disabilities, and online membership to the LDA are also available. LDA publishes two periodicals, *Learning Disabilities: A Multidisciplinary Journal* and *LDA Newsbriefs*, which may be ordered online.

www.ncapd.org The National Coalition on Auditory Processing Disorders, Inc. is a nonprofit organization supported by parents and professionals to assist families and individuals affected by auditory processing disorders. The NCAPD provides education, support, and public awareness of the disorder as well as promoting auditory access of information for those affected by auditory processing disorders.

www.ndmda.org The National Depressive and Manic Depressive Association website was created to educate patients, families, professionals, and the public concerning the nature of depressive and manic-depressive illnesses as treatable medical diseases. The site features online screening for bipolar disorder (Mood Disorder Questionnaire) and online depression screening. Other topics addressed include adolescent depression, advocacy, clinical trials, and news releases. Also included are patient/consumer support information, patient assistance program information, and tips on how to start a support group. A bookstore catalog allows for online purchasing. Also featured are success stories written by patients who have overcome their disorders.

www.psych.org At the website of the American Psychiatric Association you can get news, education, resources, and information for depression, OCD, and phobias.

www.rfbd.org Recording for the Blind and Dyslexic is an organization where recorded textbooks on tape and in digital formats are available for students and professionals who are challenged by print materials.

www.SchwabLearning.org Schwab learning is a parent's guide to helping kids with learning difficulties, providing free information on how to identify the child's problem, manage the child's challenges, and connect with other parents for support. Resources are provided.

www.SparkTop.org This unique website was created only for kids ages 8–12 with learning difficulties and Attention-Deficit/Hyperactivity Disorder. Games, activities, and creativity tools help kids learn about the brain, how to succeed in school and life, showcase their creativity, and connect with other kids sharing the same issues. This is free and compliant with the Children's Online Privacy Protection Act (COPPA).

www.tsa-usa.org Tourette's Syndrome Association (TSA) is a national, voluntary nonprofit organization founded to identify the cause of, find the cure for, and control the effects of Tourette's syndrome. Included at the website are articles on treatment and research. A listing of resources, including books and videos, are available. Membership to the TSA may be done online. Also included are recent news items, especially legislative issues regarding the disorder, and the group's annual conference dates.

Special Education, Disability, Health Issues

www.aacap.org American Academy of Child and Adolescent Psychiatry

www.aap.org American Academy of Pediatrics

www.ahrq.gov Agency for Healthcare Research and Quality

www.cec.sped.org Council for Exceptional Children

www.copaa.net Council of Parent Attorneys and Advocates

www.dredf.org Disability Rights Education Defense Fund

www.dssc.org/frc Federal Resource Center for Special Education

www.ericec.org ERIC Clearinghouse on Disabilities and Gifted Children

www.healthlaw.org National Health Law Program

www.ldonline.org Learning Disabilities Online

www.nasponline.org National Association of School Psychologists

www.nichcy.org National Information Clearinghouse on Children and Youth with Disabilities

www.parentadvocates.org An online newsletter written to empower parents and their children

www.protectionandadvocacy.com National Association of Protection and Advocacy

www.specialeducationmuckraker.com A website run by professionals who care about kids with disabilities in the schools

www.webmd.com WebMD and WebMD Health

www.wrightslaw.com Dedicated to special education legislation and law (website of Peter W. D. Wright and Pamela Darr Wright)

Government Sites

www.ed.gov United States Department of Education

www.eeoc.gov Equal Employment Opportunity Commission

www.hcfa.gov Health Care Financing Administration

www.hhs.gov/ocr/hipaa Health Insurance Portability and Accountability Act information

www.insurekidsnow.gov Insure Kids Now

www.nichcy.org/index.html National Dissemination Center for Children with Disabilities

www.ssa.gov Social Security Administration

www.usdoj.gov/crt/ada Americans with Disabilities Act

Legislative and Legal Resources

http://thomas.loc.gov/home/thomas2.html Thomas Legislative Services

www.findlaw.com A website that provides legal resources

www.visi.com/juan/congress An online directory for contacting the 109th Congress

State Legislative Resources

www.csg.org National Council of State Governments

www.nga.org National Governors Association

www.ncsl.org National Conference of State Legislatures

www.piperinfo.com/state/index.cfm State and Local Government on the Net

AD/HD Support and Advocacy Groups

ADDult Support Network
Mary Jane Johnson
2620 Ivy Place
Toledo, OH 43613

American Academy of Audiology
11730 Plaza America Drive, Suite 300,
Reston, VA 20190
1.800.AAA.2336; 703.790.8466
www.audiology.org

American Academy of Child and Adolescent Psychiatry
3615 Wisconsin Avenue, N.W.
Washington, DC 20016
202.966.7300
202.966.3007 (Fax)
www.aacap.org

American Academy of Pediatrics
141 Northwest Point Boulevard
Elk Grove Village, IL 60007-1098
847.434.4000
847.434.8000 (Fax)
www.aap.org

American Psychiatric Association
1000 Wilson Boulevard, Suite 1825
Arlington, VA 22209-3901
703.907.7300
apa@psych.org
www.psych.org

American Psychological Association
750 First Street, NE
Washington, DC 20002-4242
800.374.2721; 202.336.5500
202.336.6123 (TDD/TTY)
www.apa.org

American Speech-Language Hearing Association
10801 Rockville Pike
Rockville, MD 20852
1.800.638.8255
actioncenter@asha.org
www.asha.org

Anxiety Disorder Association of America (ADAA)
11900 Parklawn Drive, Suite 100
Rockville, MD 20852
301.231.9350 (Voice)
301.231.7392 (Fax)
www.adaa.org

Association on Higher Education and Disability (AHEAD)
University of Massachusetts–Boston
100 Morrissey Blvd.
Boston, MA 02125-3393
617.287.3880 (Voice)
617.287.3882 (TTY)
617.287.3881 (Fax)
www.AHEAD.org

Attention Deficit Disorder Association (ADDA)
PO Box 543
Pottstown, PA 19464
484.945.2101
610.970.7520 (Fax)
mail@add.org
www.add.org

Attention Deficit Disorders Association of Parents and Professionals Together (ADDAPPT)
P.O. Box 293
Oak Forest, IL 60452
312.361.4330

Attention Deficit Resource Center
1344 Johnson Ferry Road, Suite 14
Marietta, GA 30068
800.537.3784

Children and Adults with Attention Deficit Disorder (CHADD)
National Headquarters
8181 Professional Place Suite 201

Landover, Maryland 20785
301.306.7070
800.233.4050
national@chadd.org
www.chadd.org

Council of Educators for Students with Disabilities (CESD)
9801 Anderson Mill Road, Suite 230
Austin, TX 78750
516.219.5043
www.504idea.org/about-us.html

Council for Exceptional Children
1110 North Glebe Road
Suite 300
Arlington, VA 22201-5704
888.CEC.SPED (Toll-free)
703.620.3660 (Local)
866.915.5000 (Text only) (TTY)
703.264.9494 (Fax)
www.cec.sped.org/

International Dyslexia Association
8600 LaSalle Road, Chester Building, Suite 382
Baltimore, MD 21286-2044
410.296.0232
410.321.5069 (Fax)
800.ABCD.123
www.interdys.org

Learning Disabilities Association of America
4156 Library Road
Pittsburg, PA 15234
412.341.1515
412.344.0224 (Fax)
www.ldanatl.org

National Information Center for Handicapped Children and Youth
PO Box 1492
Washington, DC 20013
800.695.0285 (V/TTY)
202.884.8441 (Fax)
nichcy@aed.org
www.nichcy.org/

Recording for the Blind & Dyslexic (RFB&D)
20 Roszel Road
Princeton, NJ 08540
609.452.0606
1.800.221.4792
609.520.7990 (Fax)
www.rfbd.org

National Newsletters

Attention! (A bimonthly magazine published by
CHADD for families and adults with AD/HD)
8181 Professional Place, Suite 150
Landover, MD 20785
attention@chadd.org
800.233.4050

Attention Please, (A newsletter for children with AD/HD)
2106 3rd Avenue, N.
Seattle, WA 98109-2305

Challenge (A newsletter on AD/HD)
P.O. Box 2001
West Newbury, MA 07985
508.462.0495

CHADDER (A bi-annual publication of CHADD)
499 N.W. 70th Avenue, Suite 308
Plantation, FL 33317
305.587.3700
305.587.4599 (Fax)

Focus (A publication of Attention Deficit Disorder Association)
P.O. Box 543
Pottstown, PA 19464
484.945.2101
610.970.7520 (Fax)

Newsletters for Adults

ADDendum
5041-A Backlick Road
Annandale, VA 22003

ADDult NEWS
2620 Ivy Place
Toledo, OH 43613

The ADDvisor (by the Attention Deficit Disorders Association)
19262 Jamboree Blvd.
Irvine, CA 92715
800.487.2282

Vocational Resources

Division of Vocational Services (Call your state Department of Education and ask for the office of the Director of Vocational Services.)

National Association of Vocational
Education Special Needs Personnel (NAVESNP)
American Vocational Association
2020 14th Street
Arlington, VA 22201
703.522.6121

National Center for Research in Vocational Education
1960 Kenny Road
Columbus, OH 43210
800.848.4815

Suggested Reading Materials

Barkley, R. A. (1997). *ADHD and the nature of self-control.* New York: Guilford Press.

Barkley, R. A. (1998). *Attention deficit hyperactivity disorders: A handbook for diagnosis and treatment.* New York: Guilford Press.

Children and Adults with Attention Deficit Disorder. (2000). *The CHADD information and resource guide to ADHD.* Landover, MD: Author.

Fowler, M. (1995). *Educators manual—Attention deficit disorders.* Plantation, FL: CHADD.

Hallowell, E., & Ratey, J. (1994). *Driven to distraction.* New York: Pantheon Books.

Jones, C. B. (1998). *Sourcebook for children and adults with attention deficit* (2nd ed.). San Antonio, TX: Psychological Corporation.

Jones, C., Searight, H., & Urban, M. (1999). *Parent articles about ADHD.* San Antonio, TX: Psychological Corporation.

Kelly, K., & Ramundo, P. (1993). *You mean I'm not lazy, stupid or crazy?* Cincinnati, OH: Tyrell and Jerem Press.

Lakein, A. (1973). *How to get control of your time and life.* New York: Amsterdam Library.

Morris, J. (1998). *Facing ADHD: A survival guide for parents of children with ADHD.* Champaign, IL: Research Press.

Ramer, L., & Gordon, D. (2001). *How to help students with ADHD succeed in school and life.* San Jose, CA: Authors Choice Press.

Richards, G., & Russell, J. (2001). *The source for ADD/ADHD.* Moline, IL: LinguiSystems.

Weiss, G., & Hechtman, L. T. (1986). *Hyperactive children grow-up.* New York: Guilford Press.

Weiss, L. (1992). *Attention deficit disorder in adults.* Dallas, TX: Taylor Publishing.

Wender, P. (1987). *The hyperactive child, adolescent, and adult: Attention deficit disorder though the lifespan.* New York: Oxford University Press.

Videotapes

Neurology Learning and Behavior Center
230 S. 500 E., Suite 100
Salt Lake City, UT 84102

- *It's Just Attention Disorder* (a video for kids) by Sam Goldstein and Michael Goldstein, MD.
- *Why Won't My Child Pay Attention?* by Sam Goldstein, PhD.

Guilford Press
72 Spring Street
New York, NY 10012
800.365.7006

- *ADHD, What Can We Do?* by Russell Barkley, PhD.
- *ADHD, What Do We Know?* by Russell Barkley, PhD.

Pro-Ed
8700 Shoal Creek Boulevard
Austin, TX 78758
800.897.3202

- Face to Face: *Facilitating Adolescent Communication* by Lucille Hess

ADD Warehouse
300 Northwest 70th Avenue, Suite 102
Plantation, FL 33317
800.233.9273

- *ADHD in the classroom: Strategies for Teachers by* Russell A. Barkley, PhD.

Professional Advancement Seminars
1 Dix Street
Worchester, MA 10609
508.792.2408

- *ADHD in Adulthood: A Clinical Perspective,* by Arthur Robin, PhD.

Info-Link Videotape
Salt Lake City, UT
801.544.1388

- *Differential Diagnosis of CAPD and ADD* by Donna Geffner

Product Resource List/Learning Materials

Hand-Held Spellers, Dictionaries, and Thesauruses
Franklin Learning Resources
122 Burrs Road
Mt. Holly, NJ 08060
800.525.9673

American Heritage Dictionary (Hand-Held)
Houghton Mifflin
One Beacon Street
Boston, MA 02180

Attention-Deficit/Hyperactivity Disorder

Hand-Held Day Schedulers
Available at office supply stores such as Office Mart, or at
Day-Timers
One Day-Timer Plaza
Allentown, PA 18195
610.266.9000

Hand-Held Tape-Recorders
Available at electronic retail stores (e.g., Radio Shack)

Easy Listener Listening Aid
PhonicEar
3880 Cypress Drive
Petaluma, CA 94954-7600
707.769.1110
800.227.0735
707.769.9624 (Fax)

Post-it Tape Tabs and Post-it Notes
Available at stationery and drugstores everywhere.

Catalog of Books and Videotapes
ADD Warehouse
300 Northwest 70th Avenue, Suite 102
Plantation, FL 33317
800.233.9273

Books on Audiotape
Recording for the Blind and Dyslexic (RFB&D)
20 Roszel Road
Princeton, NY 08540
609.452.0606

Talking Books
National Library Services for the Blind and Physically Handicapped (NLS)
The Library of Congress
1291 Taylor Street, N.W.
Washington, DC 20542
202.882.5550

Dictionary on Computer
Franklin Add-On Software
Franklin Software

3511 N.E. 22nd Ave
Ft. Lauderdale, FL 33308
900.344.7000

Voice Output Calculator
Talking Calculator with Clock and Alarm
Sharp Electronics
Sharp Plaza
20600 S. Alameda Street
Carson, CA 90810
310.637.9488
310.603.9627 (Fax)

WordPerfect Library (IBM)
(Personal Planner/Notebook)
Word Perfect Corp.
1555 N. Technology
Orem, UT 80457
801.225.5000

Glossary

ABANDONMENT. To leave behind cares, worries, or responsibilities.

ACQUISITION. Something gained, acquired, or added to.

ADAPTIVE BEHAVIOR. The ability of an individual to adjust to the natural and social demands of his/her environment.

ADVOCATE. A person who pleads for a cause or propounds an idea, specifically of behalf of the child who may be displaying a disability.

ANOMALOUS. Deviating from the general or common order or type.

ANOREXIA. Anorexia nervosa (often referred to as just anorexia) is a very serious, pathological loss of appetite and self-induced limiting of food intake. Anorexia nervosa can lead to severe psychological, emotional, and physical problems, including death. This disorder most often affects females (although males do suffer from anorexia as well), and is typically associated with a tremendous amount of concern for and misperception of one's own body image.

ANTIDEPRESSANT. An agent that stimulates the mood of a depressed patient, including tricyclic antidepressants and monoamine oxidase inhibitors.

ANTIHYPERTENSIVE. A medication or other therapy that lowers blood pressure.

ANTIPSYCHOTIC. Tranquilizer used to treat psychotic conditions when a calming effect is desired.

ANXIETY. A feeling of unease and fear that may be characterized by physical symptoms such as palpitations, sweating, and feelings of stress.

ARTIFACT. Something characteristic of or resulting from a human institution or activity.

AUDITORY CLOSURE. Ability to integrate auditory stimuli into a whole (i.e., completion of a word or words by filling in the parts omitted when the word or words are spoken).

AUTHENTIC. Taking place in a real world environment or a facsimile thereof.

BOTTOM-UP. A model that views the process of comprehension as proceeding linearly from the isolated units in the lower levels (e.g., letters, words) to higher levels of comprehension; processes that register and integrate sensory information, and are data driven.

BROAD-BAND. Responsive to a wide range of skills, behaviors, or elements.

CATECHOLAMINE. Any of a group of chemicals including epinephrine, norepinephrine, and dopamine that are produced in the medulla of the adrenal gland and affect mood and appetite.

CAUDATE NUCLEUS. A brain structure within the basal ganglia responsible for regulating and organizing information in the brain.

CAVEAT. A warning; a note of caution.

CENTER-BASED PROGRAM. One location that provides services for district schools.

CEREBELLAR VERMIS. Part of the cerebellum lying in the midline between the two cerebellar hemispheres.

CLINICALLY SIGNIFICANT. Scores falling above or below one standard deviation from the mean score.

COGNITIVE. General concept embracing all of the various modes of knowing: perceiving, remembering, imagining, conceiving, judging, and reasoning.

COGNITIVE DISINHIBITION. Removal of an inhibitory, constraining, or limiting influence of the mental processes of comprehension, judgment, memory, and reasoning, in contrast to emotional and volitional processes.

COGNITIVE PROBLEM SOLVING. Person addresses a problem by analyzing it and finding solutions that are thought out.

COGNITIVE REHEARSAL. Thinking to oneself. Weighing possible alternatives to arrive at a solution.

COMORBID. The presence of coexisting or additional diseases with reference to an initial diagnosis or with reference to the index condition that is the subject of study. Comorbidity may affect the ability of affected individuals to function and also their survival; it may be used as a prognostic indicator for outcome.

COMPUTERIZED TOMOGRAPHY (CT). An x-ray technique using a computer to sequentially scan the organ under evaluation and produce radiologic images resulting in a high resolution image of that organ for analysis.

CONCOMITANT. Accompanying, joined with another.

COVERT. Not openly shown, engaged in, or avowed, not readily apparent.

De novo. Out of nowhere.

Defiant. The act or an instance of challenging, disposition to resist or contradict, willingness to contend or fight.

Delusional disorder. A paranoid disorder where the delusions are characteristically systematized and not bizarre, other characteristics of the active phase or schizophrenia are absent or only fleetingly present, personality functioning remains relatively intact outside the area of the delusional theme, and overall impairment remains less than in schizophrenia.

Desensitization. A way to reduce or stop a response such as an allergic reaction to something. For example, if someone has an allergic reaction to something, the doctor gives the person a very small amount of the substance, at first, to increase one's tolerance. Over a period of time, larger doses are given until the person is taking the full dose. This is one way to help the body get used to the full dose and to prevent the allergic reaction.

Dichotic digits. A pair or sets of numbers presented to both ears at the same time.

Dissipates. To cause to separate; move away from each other.

Divergent. Distinctly separate or increasingly different ideas.

Divided attention skill. Aspect of attention enabling a person to appropriately allocate focus and time between a series of activities.

Dizygotic twins. Children born at the same time but developed from two separately fertilized eggs.

Dopamine. A chemical substance (neurotransmitter) manufactured in the brain that transmits messages between neurons (brain cells) involved in the control of movement.

DSM–IV (Diagnostic and Statistical Manual of Mental Disorders [4th ed.]). The American Psychiatric Association's guide to diagnostic terms and codes.

Dysmenorrhea. Difficult or painful menstruation.

Dysphoria. A psychological state that causes someone to experience feelings of anxiety, restlessness, and depression.

Dysthymic disorder. A chronic type of depression that occurs on most days and lasts for a period of two or more years. In children and adolescents, mood can be irritable and duration must be at least one year. Also, the person has to display at least two of the following symptoms during the two year period: poor appetite or overeating, insomnia or hypersomnia, low energy or fatigue, low self-esteem, poor concentration or difficulty making decisions, or feelings of hopelessness.

ELECTROENCEPHALOGRAPH (EEG). A procedure where electrodes are placed on the scalp to record the electrical activity of the brain.

EMPIRICAL STUDIES. A method of research used in psychology that involves observation under controlled conditions.

ESCAPE BEHAVIOR. Operant conditioning based on the idea that a behavior is more likely to be repeated if it results in the cessation of a negative event.

ETIOLOGY. The study of factors of causation, or those associated with the causation, of disease or abnormal body states.

EUPHORIANT PROPERTY. A feeling of happiness, confidence, or well-being, sometimes exaggerated.

EXECUTIVE FUNCTION. Component of metacognition; set of general control processes that coordinate knowledge and metacognitive knowledge, transforming such knowledge into behavioral strategies, which ensure that an individual's behavior is adaptive, consistent with some goal, and beneficial to the individual (Chermak & Musiek, 1997).

EXPOSITORY DISCOURSE. Narrations of logic-based knowledge; purpose is for instructing, comparing, explaining, and offering an opinion.

EXTERNAL INATTENTION. Distractions caused by forces outside oneself.

EXTROVERSION. Personality style where the individual prefers outward focus and group activity as opposed to inward focus and individual activity.

FACIAL DISFIGUREMENT. Facial anomalies due to genetic factors or accidents.

FAPE. Free and appropriate public education.

FEEDBACK. Auditory or visual cues provided while tuning into events as they are happening (e.g., physiologic body actions) which yield understanding of physiologic functioning.

FLEXTIME. A system that allows employees to choose their own times for starting and finishing work within a broad range of available hours.

GENOME. All the genetic information possessed by any organism (for example, the human genome, the elephant genome, the mouse genome, the yeast genome, and the genome of a bacterium). Humans and many other higher animals actually have two genomes—a chromosomal genome and a mitochondrial genome—that together make up their genome.

GENRES. A category of artistic, musical, or literary composition characterized by a particular style, form, or content.

GESTALT. A configuration or pattern of elements so unified as a whole that it cannot be described merely as a sum of its parts.

GLIBNESS. Artfully persuasive in speech.

HORMONE REPLACEMENT. Medication containing one or more female hormones, commonly estrogen plus progestin.

HYPERACTIVITY. Signs of fidgetiness, distractibility, constant movement, abnormal physical action.

HYPERTHERMIA. An increase in the body temperature.

HYPOMANIC EPISODE. Marked by similar characteristics present in a manic episode but not so severe as to cause marked impairment in social or occupational functioning or to require hospitalization, even though the mood change is clearly different from the subject's usual nondepressed mood and is observable to others.

ICD–9. The International Statistical Classification of Diseases and Related Health Problems (10th Rev.); the latest in a series that was formalized in 1893 as the Bertillon classification or International List of Causes of Death. While the title has been amended to make clearer the content and purpose and to reflect the progressive extension of the scope of the classification beyond diseases and injuries, the familiar abbreviation "ICD" has been retained.

IMAGERY. Generally, all figurative or nonliteral language. Specifically, imagery suggests visual and tangible pictures by using words, refers to the use of language to represent things, actions, or abstract ideas descriptively. In its most common use, imagery suggests visual pictures, but it can also denote other sensory experiences.

IMPULSIVITY. Behavior characterized by acting on impulse, or without thought or conscious judgment.

INATTENTION. The inability to hold focus or concentration.

INHIBITORY CONTROL. To regulate one's need to suppress or restrain behavior, an impulse, or a desire consciously or unconsciously.

INTERDISCIPLINARY. Refers to two or more professionals (educators, psychologists, and others) working together and sharing information in diagnosis, assessment, and treatment.

INTERNAL INATTENTION. Inattention due to one's own distractions.

INTERNALIZATION. To incorporate (as values or patterns of culture) within the self as conscious or subconscious guiding principles through learning or socialization.

INTROVERSION. Personality style where the individual has the tendency to focus energy inward resulting in decreased social interaction.

INTRUSIVE. To force in or upon someone or something especially without permission or welcome.

KINESTHETIC. Pertaining to sensations, feelings, tactile sensations on surface of skin, proprioceptive sensations inside the body, including vestibular system or sense of balance.

LANGUAGE PROCESSING. The process of hearing, discriminating, assigning significance to, and interpreting spoken words, phrases, sentences, and discourse.

LETHARGY. Weakness characterized by a lack of vitality or energy.

LIBIDO. The desire for sexual activity.

LIKERT SCALE. A set of attitude statements to which a person is asked to express agreement or disagreement using a specific scale.

LOW FRUSTRATION TOLERANCE. Reduced threshold or capability to tolerate apparently stressful situation.

MAGNETIC RESONANCE IMAGING (MRI). A procedure where the individual's brain and spinal cord or entire body is placed in a confined space and a scan is conducted using a very powerful magnetic field resulting in detailed anatomic images.

MAINTENANCE. In conditioning, administration of occasional reinforcement to keep an already acquired response at a desired frequency.

MALADAPTIVE. The imperfect action or process of adapting, fitting, or suiting one thing to another.

MALADJUSTMENT. Poor, faulty, or inadequate adjustment.

MALAPROPISMS. Misuse of a word leading to confusion and misinformation.

MEDIATION. A method of alternative dispute resolution in which a neutral third party helps to resolve a dispute.

METACOGNITION. Awareness and appropriate use of knowledge; awareness of the task and strategy variables that affect performance and the use of that knowledge to plan, monitor, and regulate performance, including attention, learning, and the use of language; second phase in the development of knowledge, which is active and involves conscious control over knowledge.

METALINGUISTICS. Aspects of language competence that extend beyond unconscious usage for comprehension and production; involves ability to think about language in its abstract form.

METAPHOR. Implied comparison of two or more objects, which in most respects are totally unlike, omitting the word *like* or *as*.

MONOLITHIC. Characterized by total uniformity.

MOOD STABILIZERS. A psychiatric medication used in the treatment of bipolar disorder to suppress swings between mania and depression.

MORPHOMETRIC NEUROIMAGING. Imaging techniques for measurement of the size and shape of biological structures.

NARRATIVE DISCOURSE. Orderly continuous account of an event or series of events.

NARROW-BAND. Responsive to a limited or select set of skills, behaviors, or elements.

NEUROBIOLOGICAL. Encompassing neuroanatomy, physiology, neurochemistry, and neuropharmacology (Chermak & Musiek, 1997).

NEUROINHIBITOR. Blocking the transmission of impulses from chains of nerve cells.

NEURONAL. Of or pertaining to nerve cells and transmission of impulses.

NEUROPHYSIOLOGICAL NEUROIMAGING. Techniques using x-ray, magnetic fields, or other tools to produce images of the brain, especially related to physiologically based psychological processes.

NEUROPSYCHOLOGICAL TEST BATTERIES. Produce information pertaining to brain function based on results from a psychological test battery.

NEUROPSYCHOLOGY. The branch of psychology that is concerned with the physiological basis of psychological processes.

NEUROTOXIC. Poisonous or destructive to nerve tissue.

NEUROTRANSMITTER. Biochemical impulses that carry signals to and from cells.

NOREPINEPHRINE. Also known as noradrenaline; is a hormone produced by the adrenal glands and also secreted from nerve endings in the sympathetic nervous system as a chemical transmitter of nerve impulses. Many of its general actions are similar to those of adrenaline, but it is more concerned with maintaining normal body activity.

NOVEL. New and not resembling something formerly known or used, of a kind not seen before.

OLIGOANTIGENIC DIET. Elemental diet; it focuses on identifying the foods that may be negatively affecting health and reducing them using the elimination/challenge approach.

OPPOSITIONAL DEFIANT DISORDER. A type of disruptive behavior disorder characterized by a pattern of recurrent, disobedient behavior toward those in authority (American Psychological Association, 2000).

PATHOGENESIS. The formation and development of a disease.

PERIMENOPAUSAL. Relating to, being in, or occurring in perimenopause (i.e., the time during which a woman no longer or intermittently menstruates).

PHARMACOLOGICAL COMPONENT. Involving the use of drugs.

PHARMACOTHERAPY. The treatment of disease, and especially mental illness, with drugs.

PHONOLOGICAL AWARENESS. The ability to perceive and identify the number of and order of sounds.

PLACEBO. A treatment condition used to control for the placebo effect where the treatment has no real effect on its own. An inactive substance which may look like medicine but contains no medicine; a "sugarpill."

POSITRON EMISSION TOMOGRAPHY (PET). A scanning method which produces a cross-sectional image of cellular activity of blood flow in the brain following an intravenous injection of a radioactive substance.

PRECURSOR. One that precedes and indicates the approach of another.

PREDISPOSITION. Tendency; susceptibility; an inclination towards.

PRIMACY EFFECT. The tendency for the first items presented in a series to be remembered better or more easily, or for them to be more influential than those presented later in the series. If you hear a long list of words, it is more likely that you will remember the words you heard first (at the beginning of the list) than you will the words that occurred in the middle.

PROSODY. Involves the suprasegmental aspects of spoken language and is the melody, timing, rhythm, and amplitude changes of speech.

PROXIMITY. The region close around a person or thing.

PRUDENCE. On the IVA computer test, a calculation of errors of commission.

PSEUDOMEDICINE. Branch of pseudoscience.

PSYCHIATRIC DISORDERS. Medical disorders concerned primarily with mental illness.

PSYCHOEDUCATIONAL TESTS. Measure of an individual's learning strengths and weaknesses that affect academic ability.

PSYCHOMOTOR AGITATION. Inability to sit still, pacing, hand-wringing, pulling or rubbing of the skin.

PSYCHOMOTOR RETARDATION. Slowed speech, thinking, and body movements; increased pauses before answering; speech that is decreased in volume, inflections, amount, or variety of content.

PSYCHOSTIMULANTS. Pharmacological substances with potent actions of affect and motor activity, they affect how the brain controls impulses and regulates behavior and attention by influencing the availability of certain chemicals, called neurotransmitters, in the brain.

PSYCHOTROPIC MEDICATION. Drugs prescribed to stabilize or improve mood, mental status, or behavior.

REAUDITORIZATION. Verbal mediation, to repeat to oneself in an inaudible voice.

REBOUND EFFECT. Behavior resulting when medication effects dissipate.

RECENCY EFFECT. The principle that the most recently presented items or experiences will most likely be remembered best. If you hear a long list of words, it is more likely that you will remember the words you heard last (at the end of the list) than words that occurred in the middle.

REMISSION. Diminution of force or effect; lowering or decrease of a condition or quality.

REPRIMANDS. An act or expression of criticism and censure.

RESILIENT. An occurrence of rebounding or springing back; a trait that allows one to keep going.

REUPTAKE. The process in which neurotransmitters are taken up by the same nerves that released them.

RUBRICS. Rules or distractions for conducting a routine action.

SADOMASOCHISTIC. The derivation of pleasure from the infliction of physical or mental pain, either on others or on self.

SCHIZOPHRENIA. A functional psychosis characterized by apathy, withdrawal from reality, excessive fantasy, and also, in some cases, delusions and hallucinations. There are several different diagnostic types.

SCHIZOPHRENIFORM DISORDER. Diagnosis for people who have all the symptoms of schizophrenia, except that the disorder lasts more than two weeks but less than six months.

SELECTIVE ATTENTION. The ability to focus consciousness on a single event in the environment while ignoring other stimuli.

SELF-CONTROL. Individual's ability to control behavior, emotion, actions, and to engage in behaviors that result in delayed reward.

SELF-REGULATORY PROCESSES. The ability of one to manage and regulate one's own behavior.

SENSORY ADDICTIONS. A phenomenon linking the behaviors seen in individuals with AD/HD to the frequent sensory stimulation from TV programs, movies, computers, and other technological advances that may affect biological or neurological development, especially at a time when the brain is just forming connections and synapses, that may result in, but is not limited to, AD/HD.

SEQUELAE. Conditions or events which follow, as a consequence of, a disease or injury.

SIMILE. An explicit comparison between two things using *like* or *as.*

SINGLE PHOTON EMISSION COMPUTED TOMOGRAPHY (SPECT) SCAN. Provides information about blood flow to tissue. It is a sensitive diagnostic tool used to detect stress fracture, spondylosis, infection (e.g., discitis), and tumor (e.g., osteoid osteoma). Analyzing blood flow to an organ (e.g., bone) may help to determine how well it is functioning.

SPATIAL SPAN. Ability to perceive, understand, and manipulate objects in space.

STIMULANT. An agent or remedy that produces stimulation.

STREAM OF STIMULATION. Constant exposure to external stimuli.

SUBVOCALIZING. Repeat to oneself in a low, audible voice.

TANGENTIAL. Of superficial relevance, if any, relating to the theme but not directly connected to the thought at hand.

TAXONOMY. The science of classifying things into categories.

TELEGRAPHING. Reducing a message to its essential components, leaving out function words.

TEMPERAMENT. A person's typical way of responding to his or her environment.

TIMIDITY. Hesitating or state of being hesitant, awkwardness or lack of self-confidence in the presence of others.

TITRATE. The adjustment of a medication's dosage in order to obtain the most favorable clinical response.

TONE ONSET TIME. Nonspeech analog of voice onset time series consisting of two tones that mimic voice onset time.

TOP-DOWN. A model that stresses the influence of the higher levels (e.g., the message that is comprehended) on the processing of words and letters; processes that use pre-existing knowledge or context to interpret that information; to get the gestalt and then analyze its parts.

VERACITY. Unwillingness to tell lies; a truthfulness.

VERBAL SPAN. A listing of words to be repeated.

VIGILANCE. Ability to stay with a task over time.

VISUALIZATION. Use of guided or directed imagery, using visual stimuli.

VISUAL-MOTOR INTEGRATION. Ability to synchronize vision with the movements of the body or body-parts into a complete and harmonious whole.

VOICE ONSET TIME. Time between the stop consonant and the beginning of voicing in the vowel; time required to initiate sound at the vocal cords.

VOLITION. The capability of conscious choice, decision, and intention.

WORD-FINDING DIFFICULTY. A disruption in the mental activity of retrieving known words from memory.

Word retrieval. The mental activity of selecting or retrieving from memory the words one knows in order to express ideas.

Working memory. A set of linked and interacting information processing components that maintain information in a short-term memory store for the purpose of the active manipulation of the stored items (Becker & Morris, 1999).

X-chromosome. The female chromosome contributed by the mother; it produces a female when paired with another X-chromosome, and produces a male when paired with a Y-chromosome.

Y-chromosome. The small chromosome that is male-determining in most mammal species and found only in the heterogametic sex.

References

Academic Communication Associates. (1996). *Word retrieval exercises for adolescents and adults.* Oceanside, CA: Author.

Accardo, P. J., Blondis, T. H., Whitman, B. Y., & Stein, M. A. (2000). *Attention deficits and hyperactivity in children and adults.* New York: Marcel Dekker.

Achenbach, T. M. & Edelbrock, C. (1991). *Child Behavior Checklist.* Burlington, VT: Author.

Ackerman, P. T., Dykman, R. A., & Gardner, M. Y. (1990). ADD students with and without dyslexia differ in sensitivity to rhyme and alliteration. *Journal of Learning Disabilities, 23,* 279–283.

Actress Kathy Baker participates in ADHD experts on call program. (2003, September, 1). *Advance, 13,* 16.

Adelizzi, J. (2003). ADHD in the news. *CHADD of Nassau County.* (E-newsletter).

Advanced Brain Technologies. (1999). Brain Builder (Computer software). Ogden, UT: Author.

Advanced Brain Technologies. (1999). Listening Programs (Computer software). Ogden, UT: Author.

Akhondzadeh, S., Mohammadi, M. R., & Khademi, M. (2004). Zinc sulfate as an adjunct to methyphenidate for the treatment of attention deficit hyperactivity disorder in children: A double blind and randomized trial. *BMC Psychiatry, 4*(1), 9.

AlphaSmart. (2004). AlphaSmart (Computer software). Los Gatos, CA: Author.

AlphaSmart. (2005). Neo (Computer software). Los Gatos, CA: Author.

American Academy of Pediatrics. (2000). Clinical practice guideline: Diagnosis and evaluation of the child with attention-deficit/hyperactivity disorder. *Pediatrics, 105,* 1158–1170.

American Academy of Pediatrics. (2001). Clinical practice guideline: Treatment of the school-aged child with attention deficit-hyperactivity disorder. *Pediatrics, 108,* 1033–1044.

American National Standards Institute. (2002). *Acoustical performance criteria, design requirement and guidelines for schools.* ANSI S12.60-2002. Melville, NY: Acoustical Society of America.

American Psychiatric Association. (1994). *Diagnostic and statistical manual of mental disorders* (4th ed.). Arlington, VA: Author.

American Psychiatric Association. (2000). *Diagnostic and statistical manual of mental disorders* (4th ed., text revision). Arlington, VA: Author.

American Speech-Language-Hearing Association (2004). *Pragmatic Language Tips.* Retrieved June 2005, from http://www.asha.org/public/speech/development/Pragmatic-Language-Tips.htm

American Speech-Language-Hearing Association. (2005). Acoustics in educational settings: Position statement. *ASHA Supplement 25,* in press.

Arnold, L., Abikoff, H., Cantwell, D., Conners, C., Elliott, G., Greenhill, L., et al. (1997). NIMH collaborative multimodal treatment study of children with ADHD (MTA): Design challenges and choices. *Archives of General Psychiatry, 56,* 865–870.

Bailey, E. (2003). *ADHD in the news.* Retrieved July 30, 2004, from http://www.add.about.com/cs/addthebasics/a/inthenews.htm

Baker, J. J., & Cantwell, D. P. (1987). A prospective psychiatric follow-up of children with speech/language disorders. *Journal of the American Academy of Child Psychiatry, 26,* 546–553.

Balametrics. (1980–2004). *Balametrics.* Port Angeles, WA: Author.

Balametrics. (1980–2004). *NeuroNet Kit.* Port Angeles, WA: Author.

Baldinger, S. L., & Yogman, M. W. (2003). Atomoxetine. *Formulary, 38,* 85–100.

Barkley, R. (1981a). *Home Situations Questionnaire.* Minneapolis, MN: National Computer Systems.

Barkley, R. (1981b). *School Situations Questionnaire.* Minneapolis, MN: National Computer Systems.

Barkley, R. (1998). *Attention deficit hyperactivity disorder: A handbook for diagnosis and treatment* (3rd ed.). New York: Guilford Press.

Barkley, R., DuPaul, G., & McMurry, B. (1990). A comprehensive evaluation of attention deficit disorder with and without hyperactivity. *Journal of Consulting and Clinical Psychology, 58,* 775–789.

Barkley, R., Fischer, M., Edelbrock, C., & Smallish, L. (1990). The adolescent outcome of hyperactive children diagnosed by research criteria: I. An 8-year prospective follow-up study. *Journal of the American Academy of Child & Adolescent Psychiatry, 29,* 546–557.

Barkley, R., & Murphy, K. R. (1998). *Attention-deficit hyperactivity disorder: A clinical workbook.* (2nd ed.). New York: Guilford Press.

Becker, J. T., & Morris, R. G. (1999). Working memorie(s). *Brain and Cognition, 61*, 1–8.

Bell, N. (1991). *Lindamood visualizing and verbalizing.* San Luis Obispo, CA: Gander Publishing.

Bell, N. (1997). *Seeing stars.* San Luis Obispo, CA: Gander Publishing.

Biederman, J., Faraone, S. V., Monuteaux, M., Plunkett, E., Gifford, J., & Spencer, T. (2003). Growth deficits and ADHD revisited: Impact of gender, development and treatment. *Pediatrics, 111*, 1010–1016.

Bishop, D. V. (1998). Development of the children's communication checklist (CCC): A method for assessing qualitative aspects of communicative impairment in children. *Journal of Child Psychology and Psychiatry, 39*(6), 879–891.

Bishop, D. V., & Baird, G. (2001). Parent and teacher report of pragmatic aspects of communication: Use of the children's communication checklist in clinical setting. *Developmental Medicine in Child Neurology, 43*(12), 809–818.

Bluetooth. (2005). Bluetooth (Computer software). Overland Park, KS: Author.

Bowers, L., Huisingh, R., LoGiudice, C., & Orman, J. (2004). *The WORD Test 2: Elementary.* East Moline, IL: LinguiSystems.

BrainTrain. (1995). Captain's Log (Computer software). Richmond, VA: Author.

BrainTrain. (2001). Sound Smart (Computer software). Richmond, VA: Author.

Breier, J. I., Gary, L., Fletcher, J. M., Diehl, R. L., Klass, P., Foorman, B. R., et al. (2001). Perception of voice and tone onset time continua in children with dyslexia with and without attention deficit hyperactivity disorder. *Journal of Experimental Child Psychology, 80*, 245–270.

Brown, L. M. (2000). *The LD teacher's IDEA companion: Grades K–5.* East Moline, IL: LinguiSystems.

Brown, T. E. (2000). *Attention deficit disorders and co-morbidities in children, adolescents, and adults.* Washington, DC: American Psychiatric Press.

Brown, T. E. (2001). *Brown Attention-Deficit Disorder Scales.* San Antonio, TX: The Psychological Corporation.

Bush, G., Frazier, J. A., Rauch S. L., Seidman, L. J., Whalen, P. J., Jenike M. A., et al. (1999). Anterior cingulated cortex dysfunction in attention deficit hyperactivity disorder revealed by fMRI and the counting stroop. *Biological Psychiatry, 45*(12), 1542–1552.

Cambell, D. (1999, July 26). Shifting perceptions. *Advance, 9,* 10–12.

Carrow-Woolfolk, E. (1996). *OWLS: Oral and Written Language Scales.* Circle Pines, MN: American Guidance Service.

Carrow-Woolfolk, E. (1999). *Test for Auditory Comprehension of Language* (3rd ed.). Circle Pines, MN: American Guidance Service.

Carrow-Woolfolk, E. (2000). *Comprehensive Assessment of Spoken Language.* Circle Pines, MN: American Guidance Service.

Castellanos, F. X., Giedd, J. N., March, W. I., Hamburger, S. D., Vaituzis, A. C., Dickstein, D. P., et al. (1996). Quantitative brain magnetic resonance imaging in attention deficit hyperactivity disorder. *Archives of General Psychology, 53*(7), 607–616.

Castellanos, F. X., Sharp, W. F., Gottesman, R. F., Greenstein, D. K., Giedd, J. N., & Rapaport, J. L. (2003). Anatomic brain abnormalities in monozygotic twins discordant for attention deficit hyperactivity disorder. *The American Journal of Psychiatry, 160*(9), 1693–1696.

Chan, E., Rappaport, L. A., & Kemper, K. J. (2003, February). Complementary and alternative therapies in childhood attention and hyperactivity problems. *Journal of Developmental & Behavioral Pediatrics, 24(1),* 4–8.

Chermak, G. D., Hall, J. W., & Musiek, F. E. (1999). Differential diagnosis and management of central auditory processing disorder and attention deficit hyperactivity disorder. *Journal of the American Academy of Audiology, 10*(6), 289–303.

Chermak, G. D., & Musiek, F. E. (1997). *Central auditory processing disorders: New perspectives.* San Diego: Singular Publishing Group.

Chermak, G. D., Tucker, E., & Seikel, J. A. (2002). Behavioral characteristics of auditory processing disorder and attention deficit hyperactivity disorder: Predominantly inattentive type. *Journal of American Academy of Audiology, 13*(6), 332–338.

Children and Adults with Attention-Deficit/Hyperactivity Disorder. (2000). *The CHADD information and resource guide to ADHD.* Plantation, FL: Author.

Children and Adults with Attention-Deficit/Hyperactivity Disorder. (2001). *AD/HD and co-existing disorders—CHADD fact sheet #5.* Retrieved December 15, 2004, from http://www.chadd.org/fs/fs5.htm

Children and Adults with Attention-Deficit/Hyperactivity Disorder. (2003). *Evidence-based medication management for children and adults with AD/HD—CHADD fact sheet #3.* Retrieved December 15, 2004, from http://www.chadd.org/fs/fs3.htm

Children and Adults with Attention-Deficit/Hyperactivity Disorder. (2005). *The disorder named AD/HD—CHADD fact sheet #1.* Retrieved January 10, 2005, from http://www.chadd.org/fs/fs1.htm

Choskey, J. S. (2002, February). Understanding the pitch when setting up camp. *Attention!, 8*(4), 33–35.

Clark, C., Prior, M., & Kinsella, G. J. (2000). Do executive function deficits differentiate between adolescents with ADHD and oppositional defiant/conduct disorder? A neuropsychological study using the six elements test and hayling sentence completion test. *Journal of Abnormal Child Psychology, 28*(5), 403.

Clarke, A. R., Barry, R. J., McCarthy, R., & Selikowitz, M. (2002, May/June). EEG analysis of children with attention-deficit hyperactivity disorder and comorbid reading disabilities. *Journal of Learning Disabilities, 35*(3), 276.

Code of Federal Regulations (C.F.R.). Assistance to States for the education of children with disabilities and the early intervention program for infants and toddlers with disabilities; Final regulations, C.F.R., Title 34 § 300, 301, and 303 (1999).

Cognitive Concepts. (1999). Earobics (Computer software). Evanston, IL: Author.

Cohen, N. J., Barwick, M. A., Horodozky, N. B., Vallance, D. D., & Im, N. (1998). Language, achievement, and cognitive processing in psychiatrically disturbed children with previously unidentified and unsuspected language impairments. *Journal of Child Psychology and Psychiatry and Allied Disciplines, 39*(6), 865.

Cohen, N. J., Vallance, D. D., Barwick, M., & Horodozky, N. B. (1997). *Language, achievement, and cognitive characteristics of children with attention deficit hyperactivity disorder and with other psychiatric diagnoses.* Unpublished manuscript.

Cohen, N. J., Vallance, D. D., Barwick, M., & Im, N. (2000, March). The interface between ADHD and language impairment: An examination of language, achievement, and cognitive processing. *Journal of Child Psychology and Psychiatry and Allied Disciplines, 41*(3), 353.

Cole, J., & Jakimik, J. (1980). A model of speech perception. In R. Cole (Ed.), *Perception and prediction of fluent speech* (pp. 133–160). Engelwood Cliffs, NJ: Lawrence Erlbaum.

Conners, C. K. (1995). *Conners' Continuous Performance Test.* North Tonawanda, NY: Multi-Health Systems.

Conners, C. K. (1997). *Conners' Rating Scales* (Rev. ed.). San Antonio, TX: The Psychological Corporation.

Conners, C. K., Erhardt, D., & Sparrow, E. P. (1999). *Conner's Adult ADHD Rating Scales.* New York: Multi-Health Systems.

Consumer Reports. (2003, July). *Caffeinated kids*. Retrieved from http://www.consumerreports.org/main/content/display_report.jsp?FOLDER%3C%3Efolder_id=344065&bmUID=1106341318282

Copeland, E. (1989). *Copeland Symptom Checklist for Attention Deficit Disorder—Adult Version*. Fort Lauderdale, FL: Specialty Press.

Corman, C., & Greenberg, L. (1996). *Guidelines for medication titration with the TOVA*. Unpublished manuscript.

Coury, D. (2001, May). *Biologic influences on brain and behavior*. Symposium conducted at the annual meeting of the Pediatric Academic Societies, Baltimore, MD.

Courvoisie, H., Hooper, S. R., Fine, C., Kwock, L., & Castillo, M. (2004, February). Neurometabolic functioning and neuropsychological correlates in children with ADHD-H: Preliminary findings. *Journal of Neuropsychiatry and Clinical Neurosciences, 16*, 63–69.

Cutler, A., & Fodor, J. A. (1979). Semantic focus and sentence comprehension. *Cognition, 7*, 49–59.

Darling, R. M., & Sedgwick, R. M. (2003, April). *Signs of auditory processing disorders in adults with a childhood history of otitis media*. Paper presented at the annual meeting of the American Academy of Audiology, San Antonio, TX.

DiMaggio, C., & Geffner, D. (2003, November). *Prevalence of attention deficit hyperactive disorder, speech & language delay, reading difficulties, and familial factors associated with CAPD in children*. Paper presented at the annual convention of the American Academy of Audiology, Salt Lake City, UT.

DiSimoni, F. (1978). *The Token Test for Children*. Austin, TX: Pro-Ed.

Don Johnston. (2004). Draft:Builder (Computer software). Valo, IL: Author.

Don Johnston. (2004). Write:OutLoud (Computer software). Valo, IL: Author

Douglas, V., Barr, R., Amin, K., O'Neill, M., & Britton, B. (1988). Dosage effects and individual responsivity to methyphenidate in attention deficit disorder. *Journal of Child Psychology and Psychiatry, 29*, 453–475.

DuPaul, G. J., Power, T. J., Anastopoulos, A. D., & Reid, R. (1998.) *ADHD Rating Scale–IV*. New York, NY: Guilford Press.

Egger, J., Carter, C. M., Graham, P. J., Gumley, D., & Soothill, J. F. (1985). Controlled trial of oligoantigenic treatment in the hyperkinetic syndrome. *Lancet, ii*, 540–545.

Elliott, S., & Gresham, F. (1991). *Social skills intervention guide: Practical strategies for social skill training*. Circle Pines, MN: American Guidance Service.

Feigin, A., Kurlan, R., McDermott, M. P., Beach, J., Dimitsopulos, T., Brower, C. A., et al. (1996). A controlled trial of deprenyl in children with Tourette's syndrome and attention deficit hyperactivity disorder. *Neurology, 46,* 965–968.

Fletcher, J. M., Taylor, H. G., Shaywitz, S. E., Lyon, G. R., Foorman, B. R., Stuebing, K. K., et al. (1998). Intelligence testing and the discrepancy model for children with learning disabilities. *Learning Disabilities Research Practice, 13,* 186–203.

Florida Department of Education. (2001). *Technical assistance paper: Auditory processing disorders. Paper #FY-2001-9.* Tallahassee, FL: Author.

Flowers, D. (1993). Brain basis for dyslexia: A summary of work in progress. *Journal of Learning Disabilities, 26,* 575–582.

Ford, M. J., Poe, V., & Cox, J. (1993). Attending behaviors of ADHD children in math and reading using various types of software. *Journal of Computing in Childhood Education, 4,* 183–196.

Fowler, M. (1992). *Attention deficit disorders* (2nd ed.). Plantation, Florida: Children and Adults with Attention-Deficit/Hyperactivity Disorder.

Frankenberger, W., & Fronzaglio, K. (1991). A review of states' criteria for identifying children with learning disabilities. *Journal of Learning Disabilities, 24,* 495–500.

Gadow, K. D., & Sprafkin, J. (1998). *Child Symptoms Inventory.* Stony Brook, NY: Checkmate Plus.

Gadow, K. D., Sprafkin, J., & Weiss, M. (2004). *Adult Inventories–4.* Stony Brook, NY: Checkmate Plus.

Gadow, K. D., Sverd, J., Sprafkin, J., Nolan, E. E., & Grossman, S. (1999). Long-term methylphenidate therapy in children with comorbid attention-deficit hyperactivity disorder and chronic multiple tic disorder. *Archives of General Psychiatry, 56,* 330–336.

Gagne, J. P. (2001). Audiovisual-FM system is found more beneficial in classroom than auditory only. *The Hearing Journal, 54*(1), 48–51.

Gajewski, N., Hirn, P., & Mayo, P. (1993). *Social star: General interaction skills (Book 1).* Eau Claire, WI: Thinking Publications.

Gajewski, N., Hirn, P., & Mayo, P. (1994). *Social star: Peer interaction skills (Book 2).* Eau Claire, WI: Thinking Publications.

Gajewski, N., Hirn, P., & Mayo, P. (1996). *Social star: Conflict resolution and community interaction skills (Book 3).* Eau Claire, WI: Thinking Publications.

Gajewski, N., Hirn, P., & Mayo, P. (1998a). *Social skill strategies: A social-emotional curriculum for adolescents (Book A; 2nd ed.).* Eau Claire, WI: Thinking Publications.

Gajewski, N., Hirn, P., & Mayo, P. (1998b). *Social skill strategies: A social-emotional curriculum for adolescents (Book B;* 2nd ed.). Eau Claire, WI: Thinking Publications.

Gardner, M. F. (1993). *Test of Auditory Reasoning and Processing Skills.* Wilmington, DE: Wide Range.

Geffner, D. (2005). *Attention-deficit/hyperactivity disorder DVD: The journeys—The people and their stories* (DVD). Eau Claire, WI: Thinking Publications.

German, D. (1989). *Test of Word Finding.* Circle Pines, MN: American Guidance Service.

German, D. (1989). *Test of Adolescent/Adult Word Finding.* Austin, TX: Pro-Ed.

German, D. (1991). *Test of Word Finding in Discourse.* Austin, TX: Pro-Ed.

German, D. (2001). *It's on the tip of my tongue: Word finding strategies for remembering names and words you often forget.* Chicago, IL: Word Finding Materials.

Gillingham, A., & Stillman, B. W. (1997). *Gillingham manual: Remediation training for students with specific training in reading, spelling, and penmanship.* Cambridge, MA: Educators Publishing Service.

Goldenberg, G., Oder, W., Spatt, J., & Podreka, I. (1992). Cerebral correlates of disturbed executive function and memory in survivors of severe closed head injury: A SPECT study. *Journal of Neurology, Neurosurgery and Psychiatry, 55,* 362–368.

Goldman, L. S., Genel, M., Bezman, R. J., & Priscilla, J. S. (1998, April). Diagnostic and treatment of attention deficit hyperactivity disorder in children and adolescents. *Journal of the American Medical Academy, 279,* 1100–1107.

Goldsmith, B. (2002). *Are you an innovator or an implementer?* Retrieved August 2004, from http://www.bartongoldsmith.com/articles/innorimp.html

Goldstein, S., & Goldstein, M. (1990). *Managing attention disorders in children.* New York: John Wiley and Sons.

Goldstein, S., & Ingersoll, B. (2000, March). *Controversial treatments for children with attention-deficit hyperactivity disorder.* SamGoldstein.com Monthly Article, Article 12. Retrieved from http://www.samgoldstein.com/template.php?page=postings&type=articles&id=12

Goldstein, S., & Teeter-Ellison, A. (2002). *Clinician's guide to adult ADHD.* St. Louis, MO: Academic Press.

Gordon, M. (1983). *Gordon Diagnostic System.* DeWitt, NY: Gordon Systems.

Gorman-Gard, K. A. (2002). *Figurative language: A comprehensive program* (2nd ed.). Eau Claire, WI: Thinking Publications.

Gottlieb, D. (2002, February). The overly sensitive child. *Attention!, 8*(4), 37–41.

Greenberg, L. M., Leark, R. A., DuPuy, T. R., Corman, C. L., & Kindschi, C. L. (1994). *Test of Variables of Attention.* Los Alamitos, CA: Universal Attention Disorders.

Greenberg, L. M., & Waldman, I. D. (1993). Developmental normative data on the test of variables of attention (TOVA). *Journal of American Academy of Child and Adolescent Psychiatry, 34,* 1019–1030.

Guinness World Records. (2005). *Guinness world records 2005: Special 50th anniversary edition.* London: Author.

Hagerman, R. J., & Falkenstein, A. R. (1987). An association between recurrent otitis media in infancy and later hyperactivity. *Clinical Pediatrics, 26,* 253–257.

Hallowell, E. M., & Ratey, J. J. (1994). *Driven to distraction.* New York: Pantheon Books.

Hallowell, E. M., & Ratey, J. J. (1996). *Answers to distraction.* New York: Pantheon Books.

Hallowell, E. M., & Ratey, J. J. (2005). *Delivered from distraction.* New York, NY: Ballantine Books.

Hamersky, J. (1995). *Cartoon cut-ups.* Eau Claire, WI: Thinking Publications.

Hammill, D. D. (1998). *Detroit Tests of Learning Aptitude* (4th ed.). Austin, TX: Pro-Ed.

Hammill, D. D., & Larsen, S. C. (1996). *Test of Written Language* (3rd ed.). Circle Pines, MN: American Guidance Service.

Hammill, D. D., Leigh, J. E., McNutt, G., & Larsen, S. C. (1981). A new definition of learning disabilities. *Learning Disability Quarterly, 4*(4), 336–342.

Hart, C. E. (2001, December). Don't lose sleep over it! ADHD and sleep problems. *Attention!, 8*(3), 24–27.

Hart, E. L., Lahey, B. B., Loeber, R., Applegate, B., & Frick, P. J. (1995). Developmental changes in attention deficit hyperactivity disorder in boys: A four-year longitudinal study. *Journal of Abnormal Child Psychology, 23,* 729–749.

Hawkins, J., Martin, S., Blanchard, K., & Brady, M. (1991). Teacher perceptions, beliefs, and interventions regarding children with attention deficit disorders. *Action in Teacher Education, 8*(2), 52–59.

HealthCommunities.com (2005). *ADHD.* Retrieved March 2005, from http://www.neurologychannel.com/adhd/medication.shtml

Hess, L. J. (1993). *FACE to FACE: Facilitating adolescent communication experiences.* Austin, TX: Pro-Ed.

Hesslinger, B., Tebartz van Elst, L., Mochan, F., & Ebert, D. (2003). Attention deficit hyperactivity disorder in adults: Early vs. late onset in a retrospective study. *Psychiatry Research, 119*(3), 217–223.

Holborow, P., & Berry, P. (1986). A multi-modal, cross-cultural perspective on hyperactivity. *American Journal of Orthopsychiatry, 56,* 320–322.

Homework strategies for children with ADHD. (2001, July). *Advance, 11,* 10–11.

Honig, W. K. (1978). Studies of working memory in the pigeon. In S. H. Hulse, H. Fowler, & W. K. Honig (Eds.), *Cognitive processes in animal behavior* (pp. 211–248). Hillsdale, NJ: Erlbaum.

Horan, L. (1999, Summer). ADD coaching: Empowering people to succeed. *Attention!, 6(1),* 12–15.

Howlett, B. (2001). *Sound reading solutions.* Ithaca, NY: Sound Reading Solutions.

Huessy, H. R. (1990, August). *The pharmacotherapy of personality disorders in women.* Paper presented at the annual meeting of the American Psychiatric Association, New York.

Humphries, T., Koltun, H., Malone, M., & Roberts, W. (1994). Teacher-identified oral language difficulties among boys with attention problems. *Developmental and Behavioral Pediatrics, 15,* 92–98.

Hurley, M. (2004, May). I scream you scream: Communication strategies to temper the temperamental child. *ADHD Research Symposium,* p. 6.

Individuals with Disabilities Education Improvement Act of 2004 (IDEA 2004), 20 U.S.C. § 1400 *et seq.* (2004).

Ingram, S., Hechtman, L., & Morgenstern, G. (1999). Outcome issues in ADHD: Adolescent and adult long-term outcome. *Mental Retardation and Developmental Disabilities Research Reviews, 5,* 243–250.

Interactive Metronome. (1993–2004). *Interactive metronome.* Weston, FL: Author.

Iskowitz, M. (1998, July 20). Dyslexia and ADHD. *Advance, 8,* 12–13.

Jensen, P. S., & Cooper, J. R. (2002). *Attention deficit hyperactivity disorder: State of the science. Best practices.* Kingston, NJ: Civic Research Institute.

Jensen, P. W. (2001a, June). ADHD: What's up, what's next? *Attention!, 7*(6), 24–27.

Jensen, P. W. (2001b, December). Reflection on co-occurring conditions. *Attention!, 8*(3), 22–25.

Jensen, P. W. (2004, May). *Long-term effects of ADHD treatment: What we know.* Presentation at the CHADD of Suffolk and Nassau County ADHD Research Symposium, Manhasset, NY.

Jerger, J., & Musiek, F. (2000). Report of the consensus conference on the diagnosis of auditory processing disorders in school-aged children. *Journal of the American Academy of Audiology, 11,* 467–474.

John, E., Corning, W., Easton, E., Brown, D., Ahn, H., John, M., et al. (1977). Neurometrics: Numerical taxonomy identifies different profiles of brain functions within groups of behaviorally similar people. *Science, 196,* 1393–1410.

Johnson, B. D., Altmaier, E. M., & Richman, L. C. (1999). Attention deficits and reading disabilities: Are immediate memory defects additive? *Developmental Neuropsychology, 15*(2), 213–227.

Jones, C. B. (1998a). *Attention deficit disorder: Strategies for school-age children.* San Antonio, TX: Communication Skill Builders.

Jones, C. B. (1998b). *Sourcebook for children with attention deficit disorder: A management guide.* San Antonio, TX: Communication Skill Builders.

Jones, C. B. (1999). Being an advocate for your child in the school system. In C. B. Jones, R. H. Searight, & M. G. Urban. *Parent articles about ADHD.* San Antonio, TX: Communication Skill Builders.

Joseph, J. (2000). Not in their genes: A critical view of the genetics of attention-deficit hyperactivity disorder. *Developmental Review, 20,* 539–567.

Kagan, J., Moss, A. A., & Siegel, J. (1960). Conceptual style and the use of affect labels. *Merrill-Palmer Quarterly,* 261–278.

Katz, J. (1986). *The Staggered Spondaic Word Test.* Vancouver, WA: Precision Acoustics.

Katz, J. (2000). *Phonemic Synthesis Picture Test.* Vancouver, WA: Precision Acoustics.

Katz, J., & Fletcher, C. (1997). *Phonemic Synthesis Picture Test.* Vancouver, WA: Precision Acoustics.

Katz, J., & Fletcher, C. (1998). *Phonemic Synthesis Test.* Vancouver, WA: Precision Acoustics.

Keith, R. (1994). *SCAN–A: A Test for Auditory Processing in Adolescents and Adults.* San Antonio, TX: The Psychological Corporation.

Keith, R. (2000). *SCAN–C: A Test for Auditory Processing in Children.* San Antonio, TX: The Psychological Corporation.

Kelly, K. (2004, April 26). Can the distracted brain be rewired? *U.S. News & World Report,* p. 60.

Kelly, T., Lee, W., Charrette, L., & Musiek, F. (1996, April). *Middle latency evoked response sensitivity and specificity.* Paper presented at the annual meeting of the American Auditory Society, Salt Lake City, UT.

Kleiman, G., Humphrey, M., & Lindsay, P. H. (1981). Microcomputers and hyperactive children. *Creative Computing, 7,* 93–94.

Klein, R. G., Abikoff, H., Klass, E., Ganeles, D., Seese, L. M., & Pollack, S. (1997). Clinical efficacy of methylphenidate in conduct disorder with and without attention deficit hyperactivity disorder. *Archives of General Psychiatry, 54,* 1073–1080.

Korkman, M., Kirk, U., & Kemp, S. (1997). *A Developmental Neuropsychological Assessment.* San Antonio, TX: Harcourt Assessment.

Kovacs, M. (1992). *Children's Depression Inventory.* New York: Multi-Health Systems.

Krassowski, E. B. (2001). *Word joggers: Exercises for semantics and word retrieval.* Eau Claire, WI: Thinking Publications.

Kube, D. A., Peterson, M. C., & Palmer, F. B. (2002, September). Attention deficit hyperactivity disorder. *Clinical Pediatrics, 41*(7), 461–469.

Kurlan, R. (2002). Treatment of ADHD in children with tics. A randomized controlled trial. *Neurology, 58,* 527–536.

Kusmer, K. (2004, December 17). *Lilly warns doctors on Strattera use.* Associated Press Business Writer. Retrieved from http://biz.yahoo.com/ap/041217/strattera_warning_6.html

Lachar, D., Gdowski, C. L., & Snyder, D. K. (1984). External validation of the personality inventory for children (PIC) profile and factor scales: Parent, teacher, and clinician ratings. *Journal of Consulting and Clinical Psychology, 52*(2), 155–164.

Lahey, M. (1988). *Language disorders and language development.* New York: Macmillan.

Lambert, N. M., & Hartsought, C. S. (1999). Prospective study of tobacco smoking and substance dependencies among samples of AD/HD and non-AD/HD participants. *Journal of Learning Disabilities, 31*(6), 533–544.

Larson, V. L., Sterling-Orth, A., & Thurs, S. A. (2002). *Working out with listening.* Eau Claire, WI: Thinking Publications.

Lazzari, A. M., & Peters, P. M. (1995) *HELP for word finding.* East Moline, IL: LinguiSystems.

Learning Fundamentals. (1994–2004). High Level Attention Module (Computer software). San Luis Obispo, CA: Learning Fundamentals.

Lesesne, C. A., Visser, S. N., & White, C. P. (2003). Attention-deficit/hyperactivity disorder in school-aged children: Association with maternal mental health and use of health care resources. *Pediatrics, 111*(5), 1232–1238.

Levin, E. D., Conners, C. K., Silva, D., Hinton, S. C., Meck, W. H., March, J., et al. (1998). Transdermal nicotine effects on attention. *Psychopharmacology, 140,* 135–141.

Lexia Learning Systems. (2000). Lexia Reading System (Computer software). Lincoln, MA: Author.

Lexicor Health Systems. (2001). *Datalex.* Retrieved on June 11, 2002, from http://www.lexicor.com/datalex.asp

Light, J. G., Pennington, B. F., Gilger, J. W., & DeFries, J. C. (1995). Reading disability and hyperactivity disorder: Evidence for a common genetic etiology. *Developmental Neuropsychology, 11,* 323–336.

Lindamood, C. H., & Lindamood, P. C. (1988). *The Lindamood phoneme sequencing program for reading, spelling, and speech.* Austin, TX: Pro-Ed.

Lindamood, C. H., & Lindamood, P. C. (2003). *Lindamood Auditory Conceptualization Test* (3rd ed.). Austin, TX: Pro-Ed.

Lubar, J. F. (1991). Discourse on the development of EEG diagnostics and biofeedback for attention-deficit/hyperactivity disorder. *Biofeedback and Self-Regulation, 16*(3), 201–225.

Lucker, J., Geffner, D., & Koch, W. (1996). Perception of loudness in children with ADD and without ADD. *Child Psychiatry and Human Development, 26*(3), 181–190.

Manuzza, S., Klein, R. G., Bessler, A., Malloy, P., & LaPadula, M. (1993). Adult outcome of hyperactive boys: Educational achievement, occupational rank, and psychiatric status. *Archives of General Psychiatry, 50,* 565–576.

Marasa, G., & Geffner, D. (2003). *Prevalence of otitis media with effusion, reading disorders, and neurological factors associated with central auditory processing disorders in children.* Unpublished master's thesis, St. John's University, Jamaica, NY.

Marks, D. J., Newcorn, J. H., & Halperin J. M. (2001). Comorbidity in adults with adult attention deficit hyperactivity disorder. *Annals of the New York Academy of Sciences, 931,* 216–238.

Marquis, M. A., & Addy-Trout, E. (1992). *Social Communication: Activities for improving peer interactions and self-esteem.* Eau Claire, WI: Thinking Publications.

Martin, N. A., & Brownell, R. (2005). *Test of Auditory Processing Skills* (3rd ed.). Austin, TX: Pro-Ed.

Masters, M., Stecker, N., & Katz, J. (1998). *Central auditory processing disorders: Mostly management.* Boston: Allyn & Bacon.

Mayes, S. D., & Calhoun, S. L. (2000). Prevalence and degree of attention and learning problems in ADHD and LD. *The ASHA Report, 8*(2), 14–16.

Mayes, S. D., Calhoun, S. L., & Crowell, E. W. (2000, September/October). Learning disabilities and ADHD: Overlapping spectrum disorders. *Journal of Learning Disabilities, 33*(5), 417.

Maynard, S. (2004, May). Clutter clean-up. *Additude, 4(3),* 18–21.

Mayo, P., & Waldo, P. (1994). *Scripting: Social communication for adolescents* (2nd ed.). Eau Claire, WI: Thinking Publications.

McCarney, S. B. (1995). *Attention Deficit Disorders Evaluation Scale* (2nd ed.). Columbia, MO: Hawthorne Educational Services.

McGann, W., & Werven, G. (1999). *Social communication skills for children.* Austin, TX: Pro–Ed.

McInnes, A., Humphries, T., Hogg-Johnson, S., & Tannock, R. (2003, August). Listening comprehension and working memory are impaired in attention-deficit hyperactivity disorder irrespective of language impairment. *Journal of Abnormal Child Psychology, 31*(4), 427.

McKinnis, S. (2000a). *The processing program (Level 1).* Eau Claire, WI: Thinking Publications.

McKinnis, S. (2000b). *The processing program (Levels 2 and 3).* Eau Claire, WI: Thinking Publications.

McLean Hospital 2002 Annual Report. (2002). *McLean Motion and Attention Test (M–MAT).* Retrieved on December 22, 2002, from http://www.mclean.harvard.edu/about/annual/2002/newtest.php

McMahon, M. (2002). Designing an on-line environment to scaffold cognitive self-regulation. In quality conversations proceeding of the 2002 annual international conference of the higher education research and development society of Australasia *(HERSDA,* pp. 457–464). Retrieved September 2004, from http://www.ecu.edu.au/conferences/herdsa/main/papers/ref/pdf/McMahon.pdf

McNeil Consumer & Specialty Pharmaceuticals. (n.d.). *Action agreement.* Retrieved August 10, 2004, from www.concerta.net/html/concerta/tools/action_agreement.pdf

Medical Letter, The (2004, August 16). Atomoxetine (Strattera) revisited. *46. The Medical Letter,* Retrieved July 21, 2005, from http:www.medical-letter.org

Mendel, L. L., Danhauer, J. L., & Singh, S. (1999). *Singular's pocket dictionary of audiology.* San Diego, CA: Singular Publishing.

Miller, L. (2004). *Scripting junior: Social skill role-plays.* Eau Claire, WI: Thinking Publications.

Minskoff, E., & Allsopp, D. (2003). *Academic success strategies for adolescents with learning disabilities and ADHD.* Baltimore, MD: Brookes.

Misener, V. L., Luca, P., Azeke, O., Crosbie, J., Waldman, I., Tannock, R., et al. (2004, May). Linkage of the dopamine receptor D1 gene to attention-deficit/hyperactivity disorder. *Molecular Psychiatry, 9,* 500–509.

MTA Cooperative Group. (1999). A 14-month randomized clinical trial of treatment strategies for attention-deficit/hyperactivity disorder: The MTA cooperative group multimodal treatment study of children with ADHD. *Archives of General Psychiatry, 56,* 1073–1086.

MTA Cooperative Group. (2004). National institute of mental health multimodal treatment study of ADHD follow-up: 24-month outcomes of treatment strategies for attention-deficit/hyperactivity disorder. *Pediatrics, 113(4),* 754–760.

Nadeau, K. (2003, December). Neurocognitive psychotherapy for ADHD. *Attention!, 10(2),* 26–29.

Nadeau, K., & Quinn, P. (2002a). *Understanding girls with ADHD.* Longwood, FL: Advantage Books.

Nadeau, K., & Quinn, P. (2002b). *Understanding women with AD/HD.* Silver Spring, MD: Advantage Books.

National Institute of Mental Health. (1993). *Learning disabilities* (NIH publication No. 93-3611). Washington, DC: U.S. Government Printing Office.

National Institute of Mental Health. (2000). *NIMH research on treatment for attention deficit hyperactivity disorder (ADHD): The multimodal treatment study. Questions and answers.* Retrieved September 10, 2003 from www.nimh.nih.gov/events/mtaqa.cfm

Netherton, S. D., Holmes, D., & Walker, C. E. (1999). *Child and adolescent psychological disorders.* New York: Oxford University Press.

New approach to managing autism and ADD. (2002). *Advance, 12,* 11.

New York University School of Medicine Institutional Board of Research Associates. (2003, June). *Adult ADHD often undiagnosed by primary care physicians New York University School of Medicine survey reveals.* Retrieved December 12, 2004, from www.med.nyu.edu/communications/news/pr_21.html

Nickerson, R. S. (1986). *Reflections on reasoning.* Hillsdale, NJ: Erlbaum.

Nicolosi, L., Harryman, E., & Kresheck, J. (2004). *Terminology of communication disorders* (5th ed.). Philadelphia, PA: Lippincott, Williams, and Wilkins.

Novartis Pharmaceuticals. (2002). *Nationwide survey of more than 3,000 people uncovers gender differences in ADHD.* Press Releases. Retrieved January 15, 2005, from www.pharma.us.novartis.com/newsroom/pressReleases/releaseDetail.jsp?PRID=221

Office of Disability Policy, Educational Testing Service. (1999, June). *Policy statement for documentation of attention-deficit/hyperactivity disorders in adolescents and adults.* Retrieved July 2, 2004, from www.ets.org/disability/adhdplcy.html

O'Laughlin, E. M., & Murphy, M. J. (2000). Use of computerized continuous performance tasks for assessment of ADHD: A guide for practitioners. *Independent Practitioner, 20,* 282–287.

Olton, D. S. (1979). Mazes, maps, and memory. *American Psychologist, 34,* 583–596.

Parish, P. (1995). *Come back, Amelia Bedelia.* New York: HarperTrophy.

Parker-Pope, T. (2002). Hyperactive or just a kid? New tests claim to get rid of the guesswork. *Wall Street Journal,* Di.

Phelps-Terasaki, D., & Phelps-Gunn, T. (1992). *Test of Pragmatic Language.* Austin, TX: Pro-Ed.

Pliszka, S. R., Carlson, C. L., & Swanson, J. M. (1999). *ADHD with comorbid disorders.* New York: Guilford Press.

Prutting, C. A., & Kirchner, D. M. (1987). A clinical appraisal of the pragmatic aspects of language. *Journal of Speech and Hearing Disorders, 52,* 105–119.

Psychological Corporation, The. (1970). *Developmental learning materials.* San Antonio, TX: Author.

Pugh, K. R. (2004, March). *Neuroimaging studies of reading development and reading disability.* Paper presented at the annual conference of the International Dyslexia Association, New York.

Pugh, K. R., Mend, W., Jenner, A., Katz, L., Frost, S., Lee, J., et al. (2000). Functional neuroimaging studies of reading and reading disability (developmental dyslexia). *Mental Retardation and Developmental Disabilities Research Reviews, 6,* 207–213.

Purvis, K. L., & Tannock, R. (1997). Language abilities in children with attention deficit hyperactivity disorder; Reading disabilities and normal controls. *Journal of Abnormal Child Psychology, 25*(2), 133–144.

Putnam, G. J. (1998, March 16). ADD in the workplace. *Advance, 8,* 27–29.

Quinn, P. (2002, October). Special issues for women with AD/HD. *Attention!, 9(2),* 39–44.

Quinn, P., & Wigal, S. (2004). Perceptions of girls and ADHD: Results from a national survey. *Medscape General Medicine, 6(2).* Retrieved July 10, 2004, from www.medscape.com/viewarticle/472415_1 (Requires registration.)

Rabiner, D., Palsson, O., & Freer, P. (2003, December). Does neurofeedback help kids with ADHD? *Attention! 10(2),* 30–35.

Ramer, L. (2001, April). *Help! They're driving us crazy: A collaborative approach to working with students with ADHD.* Paper presented at the annual conference of the California Speech-Language-Hearing Association, Monterey, CA.

Ramer, L., & Gordon, D. H. (2001). *How to help students with AD/HD succeed: In school and in life.* Lincoln, NE: Authors Choice Press.

Rapp, D. (1991). *Is this your child?* New York: Morrow.

Rehabilitation Act of 1973, 29 U.S.C. § 794 *et seq.* (1973).

Reynolds, C. R., & Kamphaus, R. W. (2004). *Behavior Assessment System for Children—Parent Rating Scales* (2nd ed.). Circle Pines, MN: American Guidance Service.

Reynolds, C. R., & Richmond, B. O. (1985). *Revised Children's Manifest Anxiety Scale.* Lutz, FL: Psychological Assessment Resource.

Reynolds, W. M. (1989). *Reynolds Child Depression Scale.* Lutz, FL: Psychological Assessment Resource.

Reynolds, W. M. (1989). *Reynolds Adolescent Depression Scale.* Lutz, FL: Psychological Assessment Resource.

Riccio, C., & Jemison, S. J. (1998, January/March). ADHD and emergent literacy. *Reading and Writing Quarterly, 14*(1), 43.

Rief, S. (1998). *The ADD/ADHD checklist: An easy reference for parents and teachers.* New York: John Wiley & Sons.

Rief, S. (2000, September/October). ADHD: Common academic difficulties and strategies that help. *Attention!, 7*(2), 47–51.

Roberts, J., Hennon, E. A., & Anderson, K. (2003, October 21). Fragile X syndrome and speech and language. *The ASHA Leader,* 6–27.

Robertson, C., & Salter, W. (1995). *The phonological awareness kit.* East Moline, IL: LinguiSystems.

Robin, A. L. (1998). *ADHD in adolescents: Diagnosis and treatment.* New York: Guilford Press.

Robin, A. L. (2001, April). Improving time management skills. *Attention!, 7*(5), 7–11.

Robin, A. L., Tzelepis, A., & Bedway, M. (1998). Understanding the personality of adults with ADHD: A pilot study. *Attention!, 5*(4), 49–55.

Rosenberg, G. G. (2005). Sound field amplification: A comprehensive literature review. In C. C. Crandell, J. J. Smaldino, & C. Flexer (Eds.), *Sound field amplification: Applications to speech perception and classroom acoustics* (pp. 72–112). Clifton Park, NY: Thomson Delmar Learning.

Ross-Swain, D., & Long, N. (2004). *Auditory Processing Abilities Test.* Novato, CA: Academic Therapy Publications.

Rosvold, H. E., Mirsky, A. F., Sarason, I., Bransome, E. D., & Beck, L. H. (1956). A continuous performance test of brain damage. *Journal of Constant Psychology, 20,* 343–353.

Roth, N., Beyreiss, J., Schlenzka, K., & Beyer, H. (1991). Coincidence of attention deficit disorder and atopic disorders in children: Empirical findings and hypothetical background. *Journal of Abnormal Child Psychology, 19,* 1–13.

Rowling, J. K. (1998–2005). *Harry Potter* series. New York: Arthur A. Levine Books.

Rucklidge, J., & Kaplan, B. M. (2000). Attributions and perceptions of childhood in women with ADHD symptomatology. *Journal of Clinical Psychology, 56*(6), 711–722.

Safer, D. J., & Allen, R. D. (1976). *Hyperactive children: Diagnosis and management.* Baltimore: University Park Press.

Sandson, T. A., Bachna, K. J., & Morin, M. D. (2000). Right hemisphere dysfunction in ADHD: Visual hemispatial inattention and clinical subtype. *Journal of Learning Disabilities, 33,* 83–90.

Sanford, J. A., & Turner, A. (1995). *Intermediate Visual and Auditory Continuous Performance Test.* Richmond, VA: BrainTrain.

Sattler, J. (2002). *Assessment of children: Behavioral and clinical applications* (4th ed.). LaMesa, CA: Author.

Scarry-Larkin, M. (1994-2001). Attention and Memory (Volume 1) [Computer software]. San Luis Obispo, CA: LocuTour Multimedia.

Schwartz, L. S., & McKinley, N. (1987). Make-it-yourself barrier activities: Barrier activities for speakers & listeners. Eau Claire, WI: Thinking Publications.

Schweitzer, J. B., Faber, T., Grafton, S., Tune, L., Hoffman, J. M., & Kilts, C. D. (2000). Alterations in the functional anatomy of working memory in adult attention deficit hyperactivity disorder. *American Journal of Psychiatry, 157,* 278–280.

Scientific Learning. (2001). Fast ForWord (Computer software). Oakland, CA: Author.

Sea, B. (2001, Spring). 50 (or so) great things about having ADD. *GRADDA Newsletter.*

Searight, R. H. (1999). Marriage and intimacy. In C. B. Jones, R. H. Searight, & M. A. Urban (Eds.), *Parent articles about ADHD* (pp. 185–187). San Antonio, TX: The Psychological Corporation.

Searight H. R., Burke J. M., & Rottnek F. (2000). Adult ADHD: Evaluation and treatment in family medicine. *American Family Physician, 62*(9), 2077–2086.

Seidman, L. J., Biederman, J., Monuteaux, M. C., Doyle, A. E., & Faraone, S. V. (2001). Learning disabilities and executive dysfunction in boys with attention-deficit/hyperactivity disorder. *Neuropsychology, 15,* 544–556.

Semel, E. (1999). Following directions: Left and right (Computer software). Winooski, VT: Laureate Learning System.

Semel, E. (2000). Following directions: One and two level commands (Computer software). Winooski, VT: Laureate Learning System.

Semel, E., Wiig, E. H., & Secord, W. A. (2003). *Clinical Evaluation of Language Fundamentals* (4th ed.). San Antonio, TX: The Psychological Corporation.

Shafritz, K., Marchione, K., Gore, J., & Shaywitz, B. (2004). The effects of methylphenidate on neural systems of attention in attention-deficit hyperactivity disorder. *American Journal of Psychiatry, 161,* 1990–1997.

Shaywitz, B. A., Fletcher, J. M., & Shaywitz, S. E. (1994). A conceptual framework for learning disabilities and attention deficit hyperactivity disorder. *Canadian Journal of Speech, 9,* 1–32.

Shaywitz, S. (2003). *Overcoming dyslexia: A new and complete science-based program for reading problems at any level.* New York: Knopf.

Silver, L. B. (1999). *Attention-deficit/hyperactivity disorder* (2nd ed.). Washington, DC: American Psychiatric Press.

Sims Baran, L. (1996). Sanford's Social Skills (Computer software). Boulder, CO: Attention Getters Publications.

Smalley, S., Kustanovich, V., Minassian, S., Stone, J., Ogdie, M., McGough, J., et al. (2002). Genetic linkage of attention-deficit/hyperactivity disorder on chromosome 16p13, in a region implicated in autism. *American Journal of Human Genetics, 71,* 959–963.

Social Skill Builder. (2004). My Community (Computer software). Leesburg, VA: Author.

Soliloquy Learning. (2003). Soliloquy Reading Assistant (Computer software). Needham Heights, MA: Author.

Sowell, E. R., Thompson, P. M., Welcome, S. E., Henkenius, A. L., Toga, A. W., & Peterson, B. S. (2003). Cortical abnormalities in children and adolescents with attention-deficit hyperactivity disorder. *Lancet, 362,* 1699–1707.

Spector, C. C. (1997). *Saying one thing, meaning another: Activities for clarifying ambiguous language.* Eau Claire, WI: Thinking Publications.

Spencer, T. (2002). *Pharmacologic treatment of attention-deficit hyperactivity disorder in children.* Retrieved December 16, 2002, from www.medscape.com/viewprogram/1927_pnt

Spencer, T. (2003, May). *Group CS: Long-term once daily OROS®️ methylphenidate treatment for ADHD: Evaluating effect on growth.* Paper presented at the annual meeting of the American Psychiatric Association, San Francisco, CA.

Spencer, T., Biederman, J., Coffey, B., Geller, D., Wilens, T., & Faraone, S. (1999). The 4-year course of tic disorders in boys with attention-deficit/hyperactivity disorder. *Archives of General Psychiatry, 56,* 842–847.

Spencer, T. J., Biederman, J., Faraone, S., Mick, E., Coffey, B., Geller, D., et al. (2001). Impact of tic disorder on ADHD outcome across the life span cycle: Findings from a large group of adults with and without ADHD. *American Journal of Psychiatry, 158,* 611–617.

Spencer, T., Biederman, J., Harding, M., O'Donnell, D., Faraone, S., & Wilens, T. (1996). Growth deficits in ADHD children revisited: Evidence for disorder-associated growth delays? *American Academy Child Adolescent Psychiatry, 35,* 1460–1469.

Stern, J., & Ben-Ami, U. (2000). Talking to your children about their attention deficit disorder. In *Information and resource guide to AD/HD.* Landover, MD: CHADD.

Strayhorn, J. M. (2002a). Self-control: Theory and research. *Journal of the American Academy of Child and Adolescent Psychiatry, 41,* 7–16.

Strayhorn, J. M. (2002b). Self-control: Toward systematic training programs. *Journal of the American Academy of Child and Adolescent Psychiatry, 41,* 17–27.

Studies compare ADHD treatments. (2002, April 28). *Advance, 12, 19.*

Stuss, D. T., Binns, M. A., Murphy, K. J., & Alexander, M. P. (2002). Dissociations within the anterior attentional system: Effects of task complexity and irrelevant information on reaction-time speech and accuracy. *Neuropsychology, 16*(4), 500–573.

Sunburst Technology. (1999). Type to Learn Junior: Grades K–2 (Computer software). Elgin, IL: Author.

Sunburst Technology. (2001a). New Keys for Kids: Grades 1–3 (Computer software). Elgin, IL: Author.

Sunburst Technology. (2001b). Type to Learn 3: Grades 3–Adult (Computer software). Elgin, IL: Author.

Swanson, J. M., & Castellanos, F. X. (2002). Biologic bases of ADHD: Neuroanatomy, genetics, and pathophysiology. In P. S. Jensen & J. R. Cooper (Eds.), *Attention deficit hyperactivity disorder: State of the science. Best practices* (pp. 7-1–7-20). Kingston, NJ: Civic Research Institute.

Szegedy-Maszak, M. (2004, April 26). Driven to distraction. *U.S. News & World Report,* pp. 53–60.

Talan, J. (2004, June 1). High-tech tools focus on ADHD: Non-drug approaches to diagnosis and treatment draw new research. *Newsday Health and Science,* B56.

Tannock, R. (1998). Attention deficit hyperactivity disorder: Advances in cognitive, neurobiological, and genetic research. *Journal of Child Psychology and Psychiatry, 39,* 65–99.

Teicher, M. H., Ito, Y., Glod, C. A., & Barber, N. I. (1996). Objective measurement of hyperactivity and attentional problems in ADHD. *Journal of the American Academy of Child and Adolescent Psychiatry, 35,* 334–342.

Temple, E., Deutsch, G. K., Poldrack, R. A., Miller, S. L., Tallal, P., Merzenich, M. M. et al. (2003). Neural deficits in children with dyslexia ameliorated by behavioral remediation: Evidence from functional MRI. *Proceeding of the National Academy of Sciences, 100,* 2860–2865.

Test tracks changes in attention states. (2001, June 18). *Advance, 11,* 5–9.

Thinking Publications. (2001). The Deciders Take On Concepts Mission I. (Computer software). Eau Claire, WI: Author.

Thinking Publications. (2001). The Deciders Take On Concepts Mission II. (Computer software). Eau Claire, WI: Author.

Thinking Publications. (2002). The Deciders Take On Concepts Mission III. (Computer software). Eau Claire, WI: Author.

Thinking Publications. (2003). Nickel Takes On Teasing (Computer software). Eau Claire, WI: Author.

Thinking Publications. (2004a). Nickel Takes On Stealing (Computer software). Eau Claire, WI: Author.

Thinking Publications. (2004b). Nickel Takes On Anger (Computer software). Eau Claire, WI: Author.

Thinking Publications. (2005). Nickel Takes On Disrespect [Computer software]. Eau Claire, WI: Author.

Thomas, C. (2003, June). *123 Altropane SPECT shows potential as diagnostic tool for ADHD.* Paper presented at the annual meeting of the Society of Nuclear Medicine, New Orleans, LA.

Tinius, T. P. (2003). The intermediate visual and auditory continuous performance test as a neuropsychological measure. *Archives of Clinical Neuropsychology, 18,* 199–214.

Torgesen, J. K., & Young, K. (1983). Priorities for the use of microcomputers with learning disabled children. *Journal of Learning Disabilities, 16,* 234–237.

Tourette's Syndrome Study Group, The. (2002). Treatment of ADHD in children with tics: A randomized controlled trial. *Neurology, 58*(4), 527–536.

Tremblay, K., Kraus, N., & McGee, T. (1998). Central auditory system plasticity: Generalization to novel stimuli following listening training. *NeuroReport, 9,* 3557–3560.

Tucker, B. P., & Goldstein, B. A. (1992). *Legal rights of persons with disabilities: An analysis of federal law.* Horsham, PA: LRP Publications.

Ullman, R. K., Sleator, S. K., & Sprague, R. L. (1998). *ADD-H Comprehensive Teacher/Parent Rating Scale (ACTeRS).* Champaign, IL: MeriTech.

United States Census Summary File. (2000). Retrieved January 16, 2003, from www.census.gov

United States Department of Education. (1999). Regulations of the offices of the Department of Education, 34 C.F.R. §3 (1999).

Valente, S. M. (2001, September). Treating deficit hyperactivity disorder. *Nurse Practitioner, 26*(9), 14–29.

Volkow, N. D., Wang, G. J., Fowler, J. S., Logan, J., Gerasimov, M., Maynard, L., et al. (2001, January 15). Therapeutic doses of oral methylphenidate significantly increase extracellular dopamine in the human brain. *Journal of Neuroscience, 21*(2), 121.

Wagner, R. K., Torgesen, J. K., & Rashotte, C. A. (1999). *Comprehensive Test of Phonological Processing.* Austin, TX: Pro-Ed.

Ward, M. F., Wender, P. H., & Reimherr, F. W. (1993). The Wender Utah rating scale: An aid in the retrospective diagnosis of childhood attention deficit hyperactivity disorder. *American Journal of Psychiatry, 150*(6), 885–890.

Wechsler, D. (1991). *Wechsler Intelligence Scale for Children* (3rd ed.). San Antonio, TX: The Psychological Corporation.

Wechsler, D. (2001). *Wechsler Individual Achievement Test* (2nd ed.). San Antonio, TX: The Psychological Corporation.

Wechsler, D. (2002). *Wechsler Preschool and Primary Scale of Intelligence* (3rd ed.). San Antonio, TX: The Psychological Corporation.

Weiss, M., Murray, C., & Weiss, G. (2002). Adults with attention-deficit/hyperactivity disorder: Current concepts. *Journal of Psychiatric Practice, 8,* 99–110.

Westby, C. E., & Cutler, S. K. (1994). Language and ADHD: Understanding the bases and treatment of self-regulatory deficits. *Topics in Language Disorders, 14*(4), 58–76.

Whitman, T. L., Burgio, L., & Johnson, M. B. (1984). Cognitive behavioral interventions with mentally retarded children. In A. Meyers & W. E. Craighead (Eds.), *Cognitive behavior therapy with children* (pp. 193–227). New York: Plenum Press.

Wigal, S. (2004). Mixed amphetamine salts significantly better than atomoxetine in treating children with ADHD. *EurekaAlert!* Retrieved May, 2004, from www.eurekalert.org/pub_releases/2004-05/pn-mas050404.php

Wigal, S., Gupta, S., Guinta, D., Swanson, J. (1998). Reliability and validity of he SKAMP rating scale in a laboratory school setting. *Psychopharmacology Bulletin, 34,* 47–53.

Wiig, E. H., Larson, V. L., & Olson, J. A. (2004). *S-MAPs: Rubrics for curriculum-based assessment and intervention.* Eau Claire, WI: Thinking Publications.

Wiig, E. H., & Secord, W. (1989). *Test of Language Competence.* San Antonio, TX: Psychological Corporation.

Wiig, E. H., & Wilson, C. (2001). *Map it out: Visual tools for thinking, organizing, and communicating.* Eau Claire, WI: Thinking Publications.

Wiig, E. H., & Wilson, C. (2002). *The learning ladder: Assessing and teaching text comprehension.* Eau Claire, WI: Thinking Publications.

Wilens, T. (2001, December). Effect of AD/HD medication on future substance abuse. *Attention!, 8(3),* 40–43.

Wilens, T., Pelham, W., Stein, M., Conners, C. K., Abikoff, H., Atkins, M., et al. (2003, April). ADHD treatment with once-daily OROS methylphenidate: Interim 12-month results from a long-term open label study. *Journal of the American Academy of Child and Adolescent Psychiatry, 42*(4), 424–433.

Wilkinson, G. S. (1993). *Wide Range Achievement Test* (3rd ed.). Wilmington, DE: Wide Range.

Willot, J. F., Hnath, C. T., & Lister, J. J. (2001). Modulation of presbycusis: Current status and future directions. *Audiological Neuro-Otolarygology, 6,* 231–249.

Wilson, B. A. (1988). *Wilson reading system.* Oxford, MA: Wilson Language Training.

Wirt, R. D., Lachar, D., Klinedinst, J. E., Seat, P. D., & Broen, W. E. (2002). *Personality Inventory for Children* (2nd ed.). Los Angeles, CA: Western Psychological Services.

Wodrich, D. L. (2000). *ADHD: What every parent wants to know.* (2nd ed.). Baltimore: Brookes.

Wolraich, M. L., Greenhill, L. L., Pelham, W., Swanson J., Wilens, T., Palumbo, D., et al. (2001). Randomized, controlled trial of OROS methylphenidate once a day in children with attention-deficit/hyperactivity disorder. *Pediatrics, 108,* 883–893

World Health Organization. (2003). *Adult ADHD Self-Report Scale-V1.1 Screener.* Geneva, Switzerland: Author.

Zentall, S. S. (1988). Production deficiencies in elicited language but not in the spontaneous verbalization of hyperactive children. *Journal of Abnormal Child Psychology, 16 ,* 657–673.

Ziegler Dendy, C. (2000). *Teaching teens with ADD and ADHD.* Bethesda, MD: Woodbine House.

Author Index

f = figures   s = sidebars

t = tables   SM = Study Mores on the CD-ROM

Fletcher, J., 29, 30, 46

Flowers, D., 46

Fodor, J., 173

Foorman, B., 29, 46

Ford, M., 196

Fowler, J., 144

Fowler, M., 183s

Frankenberger, W., 29

Frazier, J., 146

Freer, P., 229

Frick, P., 203

Fronzaglio, K., 29

Frost, S., 46

G

Gadow, K., 79, 207

Gagne, J.P., 178

Gajewski, N., 228

Ganeles, D., 161

Gardner, M., 30, 92, 93

Gary, L., 46

Gdowski, C., 78

Geffner, D., 57–58, 64–65, 65t, 66t, 273

Geller, D., 263–64

Genel, M., 9, 141

Gerasimov, M., 144

German, D., 92–93, 165, 166, 167

Giedd, J., 267, 268

Gifford, J., 262–63

Gilger, J., 32

Gillingham, A., 186

Goldenberg, G., 44

Goldman, L., 9, 141

Goldsmith, B., 279–80

Goldstein, B., 254

Goldstein, M., 108

Goldstein, S., 108, 155–56, 157, 237

Gordon, M., 94

Gore, J., 12, 265

Gorman-Gard, K., 175t

Gottesman, R., 268

Grafton, S., 267

Graham, P., 35

Greenberg, L., 95, 96

Greenhill, L., 142, 145

Greenstein, D., 268

Gresham, F., 228

Gumley, D., 35

H

Hagerman, R., 64

Hall, J., 68t

Hallowell, E., 165, 209, 215s, SM9.2

Halperin, J., 206

Hamburger, S., 267

Hamersky, J., 168

Hammill, D., 29, 88, 92, 93, 189

Harding, M., 262

Harryman, E., 48

Hart, C., 33

Hart, E., 203

Hartsought, C., 159

Hawkins, J., 252

Hechtman, L., 265

Henkenius, A., 9, 12, 268

Hennon, E., 39

Hess, L., 195

Hesslinger, B., 209

Hinton, S., 152

Hirn, P., 228

Hnath, C., 201

Hoffman, J., 267

Hogg-Johnson, S., 51–52

Holborow, P., 30

Holmes, D., 23s

Honig, W., 51

Subject Index

f = figures   s = sidebars
t = tables   SM = Study Mores on the CD-ROM

A

AACP. *See* American Academy of Child and Adolescent Psychiatry

AAP. *See* American Academy of Pediatrics

Abilitations, 126–27s, SM6.4

ACTeRS (ADD–H Comprehensive Teacher/Parent Rating Scale), 80

acts, legislative
  Americans with Disabilities Act, 239, 249–50s, 255–59, 292
  Health Insurance Portability and Accountability Act, 259, 292
  Individuals with Disabilities Education Improvement Act, 107s, 239–45, 250–51, 254
  Rehabilitation Act, 239–40, 245–51, 249–50s, 258–59
  See also Public Law 94-142

ADA. *See* Americans with Disabilities Act

ADDA (Attention Deficit Disorder Association), 286

ADDAPPT (Attention Deficit Disorder Association of Parents and Professionals Together), 200

ADD Consults–AD/HD, 200

Adderall, 144, 145–46, 149t, 263

ADDES–2 (Attention Deficit Disorders Evaluation Scale–Second Edition), 79

ADD–H Comprehensive Teacher/Parent Rating Scale (ACTeRS), 80

addictions. *See* substance abuse

ADDW–3 (Copeland Symptom Checklist for Attention Deficit Disorder–Adult), 81

AD/HD Rating Scale, 79

adolescents
  assessment, 250s
  comorbid conditions, 31
  discussing symptoms, 230–31s, SM10.3
  growth deficits and, 262–63
  maturation schedule, 269
  prevalence, 203, 265
  substance abuse, 206
  therapeutic relationships, 229

Adult ADD (website), 200

Adult AD/HD Self-Report Scale (ASRS), 81, 207–8

Adult Inventories–4 (ASRI–4), 207

adults
  assessment, 73–74, 207–9, 250s, SM9.1
  comorbid conditions, 18, 23, 25, 31, 205, 206

347

B

Draft:Builder (Don Johnston), 189, 198

driving habits, 206, 214

drugs. *See* medications; substance abuse

DSM–IV, 4, 73, 76, 103, 208–9, 305, SM1.1

DTLA–4 (Detroit Tests of Learning Aptitude), 85t, 88–89, 93

dyscalculia, 272

dysgraphia, 272

dyslexia, 31–32, 206, 272, 274s, 287, 289

dysphoria, 26, 305

dysthymic disorders, 21, 305

E

Earobics (Cognitive Concepts), 187t, 188, 196–97

earphones, 233

Edison, Thomas, 218

educational psychologists, 110–11, 116t

educators. *See* teachers

EEG, defined, 306

EEG biofeedback, 157, 228–29

EEG studies, 45–46, 84, 98–99, SM1.1

Effexor (venlafaxine), 24, 150

Einstein, Albert, 218

Eli Lilly and Co., 200

emotional disturbance category, 241

Emotion Game (LinguiSystems), 187t

emotions, 55, 60, 187t, 194

employment

    adult difficulties, 204–6

    career choice considerations, 205, 260s, 272, 278–79

    coping strategies, 211–13

    entrepreneurs/innovators, 279–81

    hyper-focus on career, 269, 278–79

    legal rights and provisions, 255–59

    vocational rehabilitation services, 259

    vocational resources, 297

    See also workplace

encopresis, 84

entrepreneurs/innovators, 279–81

enuresis, 34, 84

environmental causes, 11–12

environmental modifications

    assistive listening devices, 125t, 163–64, 178, 233, 299–301

    classroom, 124–25t, 126–27s, 162–64, 233, SM6.4

    fidgets, 127s

    home, 162

    organizational systems, 127s, SM6.4

    physical adaptations, 126s, SM6.4

    room acoustics, 163–64, 176, 178, 178t

    workplace, 164–65, 209, 212–13

escape behavior, 11

estrogen, 14, 15, 271–72

executive function, 12, 44, 48, 168–70, 306

executive function disorder (EFD), 68t, 168–70, 190–91

exercise, 210

expository discourse, 49, 306

expressive language

    assessment, 85t, 88–90, 91s, 92–93

    comorbidity, 111

    deficits, characteristic, 54–56

    intervention, 165–70

    See also written expression

helplessness, 270

HIPAA. *See* Health Insurance Portability and Accountability Act

Home Situation Questionnaire, 80

homework, 131–32, 131t, 133f, SM6.5, SM6.6

hormones, 13–15, 271–72

humor, 53, 174, 174f, 175t, SM8.1

Hyperactive-impulsive subtype, 4, 6s, 7f, 14, 21, SM1.2

hyperactivity, 77s, 100–102, 124t, 307

hyperacusis, 57–58

hypomanic episodes, 22, 307

hypoxia, 84, 268

I

I-123 Altropane, 97–98

ICD (International Classification of Disease) system, 4, 6s, 209, 307

IDA. *See* International Dyslexia Association

IDEA (Individuals with Disabilities Education Improvement Act), 107s, 239–45, 250–51, 254

identification. *See* assessment

IEE (Independent Educational Evaluation), 245

IEP (Individualized Education Program)
  about, 241
  parental involvement, 107s, 252s, 253, SM11.3
  special education criteria and, 244–45
  suspension/expulsion and, 243, 254

IES (Interim Educational Alternative Setting), 254

imipramine (Tofranil), 26, 148

impulsivity, 77s, 100–102, 125t, 268, 307

inattention, 100–101, 100s, 124t, 307

Inattentive subtype
  about, 4, 5–6s
  in adults, 14
  EEG divergences in, 45
  language characteristics, 7f, SM1.2
  learning disabilities and, SM1.1

inclusion, 242

independence, 224

Independent Educational Evaluation. *See* IEE

independent work, 125t

Individualized Education Program. *See* IEP

infrared sound systems, 164

inhibitory control, 26, 307

innovators, 279–81

input disorders, 43, 52–54, 68t

insomnia, 33–34

insurance companies, 115, 153

intake form, diagnostic, 75f, SM4.1

intent, 50, 54

interdisciplinary teams, 105–16

Interim Educational Alternative Setting. *See* IES

Intermediate Visual and Auditory Continuous Performance Test (IVA CPT), 96–97

International Classification of Disease system. *See* ICD

International Dyslexia Association (IDA), 289, 295

Internet resources, 200, 285–92

intervention, direct
  auditory processing deficits, 176, 178, 179s, 180–86, 183s, 187t
  computer-based skills training, 187t, 189, 194–95, 196–200
  deficit-specific, 180–86, 183s

National Institute of Mental Health (NIMH), 288

NCAPD (National Coalition on Auditory Processing Disorders), 290

NCN (National Coaching Network), 138

NDMDA (National Depressive and Manic Depressive Association), 290

Neeleman, David, 218, 275–76

Neo keyboard, 233

nervousness, 26

    See also anxiety entries

neural organization technique, 157–58

neurobiological disorders, 1–2, 65t, 264–68, 309

neurocognitive psychotherapy, 223, 237

neurodevelopmental screening, 83–84

neurofeedback, 229

neuroimaging, defined, 309

neuroinhibitors, 309

NeuroNet Kit (Balametrics), 199–200

neurophysiological neuroimaging, 309

neuroplasticity, 201–2

neuropsychological tests, 82–83, 208, 309

neurotoxins, 11, 84, 267, 271, 309

newsletters, 296

Nickel Takes On Series (Thinking Publications), 195

nicotine, 11, 34, 152, 159, 271

NIMH (National Institute of Mental Health), 288

Nintendo effect, 196

No-Glamour Auditory Processing Cards (LinguiSystems), 187t

noise

    assistive listening devices and, 163–64, 178

    comprehension difficulties in, 53, 58

    desensitization to, 185–86

    room acoustics and, 163–64, 176, 178, 178t

    See also auditory figure-ground

nonliteral meanings, 54, 90, 91s

nonstimulants, 149t, 150–51

nonverbal communication, 49, 49s, 177s, 272, 282

norepinephrine, 144, 149t, 271, 309

Norpramin (desipramine), 26, 148, 149t

nortriptyline (Pamelor), 26

note taking, 182, 191, 193

nurses, 108–9, 115t

nutrition. *See* dietary intervention

O

observations, 76, 77s, 100s

obsessive-compulsive disorder, 18

obstetric complications, 11–12, 84, 209, 267, 268, 271

occupational therapists, 114, 116t, 128

oligoantigenic diet, 35, 309

omega-3 fatty acids, 210

125 Ways to Be a Better Listener (LinguiSystems), 187t

on-task behavior, 124t, 164, 191, 196

oppositional defiant disorder (ODD), 17–20, 309, SM1.1

optometric vision training, 158

Oral and Written Language Scales (OWLS), 85t, 92, 189

organizational difficulties, 118–23, 119–22f, 124–26f, 127s, 190–91, 192f

Orton-Gillingham method (Gillingham & Stillman), 186

otitis media, 64, 65t, 84

output disorders, 43, 52, 54–56, 68t

OWLS (Oral and Written Language Scales), 85t, 92, 189

oxygen insufficiency, 84, 268

P

pagers, 126s

Pamelor (nortriptyline), 26

panic attacks, 25

paraphasic errors, 54

parents

    assessment role, 4

    family therapy and, 224–25, 225s, 226s

    gender differences and, 13

    IEP involvement, 107s, 252s, 253, SM11.3

    Internet resources, 200, 285–92

    interviews, 67, 69–70s

    management tips, 179s, 225s, 226s, SM8.4, SM10.1

    procedural safeguards, SM11.2

    special education services and, 252s, SM11.3

    support groups, 200–201, 211, 293–96

    as team members, 106, 107s, 115t

Password, 166

pediatricians, 115t

peer relationships, 226–28

peer tutor, 234

pemoline (Cylert), 149t, 151

perceptual deficits, 60, 61f, SM3.3

perimenopause, 15, 309

personality clusters, 14, 261

Personality Inventory for Children (PIC), 78

pervasive developmental disorder (PDD), 48

PET (positron emission tomography), 46, 84, 267, 310

phonemic awareness, 171

phonemic synthesis, 59

Phonemic Synthesis Test (PST), 85t, 87–88

phonological awareness, 186, 187t, 310

Phonological Awareness Kit (LinguiSystems), 186, 187t

Phonological Awareness Success (Thinking Publications), 187t

phonological processing, 85t, 87–88, 165

physical examination, 73, 83–84

physicians

    AD/HD perception, 208

    assessment role, 2, 73, 83–84

    as team members, 108, 115t

PIC (Personality Inventory for Children), 78

positron emission tomography. *See* PET

post-traumatic stress disorders, 17–18, 270

pragmatics

    assessment, 85t, 93

    deficits, characteristic, 47–51

    intervention, 175–76, 177s, SM8.2

pregnancy complications, 11–12, 209, 267, 271

prematurity, 267

premenstrual syndrome, 272

primacy effect, 58, 310

problem solving, 169, 222

Processing Auditory Directions (Super Duper), 187t

Processing Program (Thinking Publications), 172, 187t

pronoun identifiers, 55, 168

prosody, 173–74, 174f, 175t, 310

rubrics, 311

rules, following, 125t

S

Sanford's Social Skills (Sims Baran), 194

SCAN–A, 85t, 86

SCAN–C, 85t, 86

Scategories, 166

schizophrenia, 24, 311

school nurses, 108–9, 115t

school records, 83

schools

funding for services, 251–53

suspension/expulsion, 235, 243, 253–54

See also classroom intervention; teachers

seating behavior, 124t, 126s

Section 504. *See* Rehabilitation Act

Seeing Stars (Bell), 171

seizure disorders, 41, 84

selective serotonin reuptake inhibitors. *See* SSRIs

self-advocacy, 173, 178

self-control, 236, 311

self-esteem, 216, 282, 282s

self-monitoring, 169–70, 222, 224

self-regulation, 48, 52, 170, 311

sensory addictions, 11, 311

Sensory Snuggle, 126s

sequencing difficulties, 53, 55

serotonin, 149t, 271

sexual abuse, 18

sexual adjustment, 236

similes, 61

Single Photon Emission Computed Tomography. *See* SPECT

sleep disorders, 18, 33–34

smoking. *See* cigarette smoking

social skills

deficits, characteristic, 44, 49, 60, 226

group therapy, 227

intervention, 193–95, 195s

resources, 227–28

See also antisocial disorders; relationships

socioeconomic status, 206, 271

software programs. *See* computer-based skills training

Soliloquy Reading Assistant (Soliloquy Learning), 198

somatic complaints, 84

sound blending, 58–59

soundfield FM systems, 163–64, 178, 233

Sound Reading Solutions (Howlett), 186

Sounds and Symbols (American Guidance Service), 187t

Sound Smart (BrainTrain), 187t, 197

spatial organization, 128, 199–200, 233

spatial reasoning deficit, 272

spatial span, 52, 60, 226, 312

special education administrators, 113–14, 116t

special education placements, 244, 245

specific learning disability, 240

SPECT (Single Photon Emission Computed Tomography), 84, 97–98, 312

speech-language pathologists, 111–13, 116t, 227

speed of processing, 53, 184

See also response time

SSI (supplemental security income), 257–58

SSRIs (selective serotonin reuptake inhibitors), 148, 272